Programmed Inequality

History of Computing

William Aspray and Thomas J. Misa, editors

Janet Abbate, *Recoding Gender: Women's Changing Participation in Computing*

John Agar, *The Government Machine: A Revolutionary History of the Computer*

William Aspray and Paul E. Ceruzzi, *The Internet and American Business*

William Aspray, *John von Neumann and the Origins of Modern Computing*

Charles J. Bashe, Lyle R. Johnson, John H. Palmer, and Emerson W. Pugh, *IBM's Early Computers: A Technical History*

Martin Campbell-Kelly, *From Airline Reservations to Sonic the Hedgehog: A History of the Software Industry*

Paul E. Ceruzzi, *A History of Modern Computing*, 2nd ed.

I. Bernard Cohen, *Howard Aiken: Portrait of a Computer Pioneer*

I. Bernard Cohen and Gregory W. Welch, editors, *Makin' Numbers: Howard Aiken and the Computer*

Nathan L. Ensmenger, *The Computer Boys Take Over: Computers, Programmers, and the Politics of Technical Expertise*

Thomas Haigh, Mark Priestley, and Crispin Rope, *ENIAC in Action: Making and Remaking the Modern Computer*

John Hendry, *Innovating for Failure: Government Policy and the Early British Computer Industry*

Mar Hicks, *Programmed Inequality: How Britain Discarded Women Technologists and Lost Its Edge in Computing*

Michael Lindgren, *Glory and Failure: The Difference Engines of Johann Müller, Charles Babbage, and Georg and Edvard Scheutz*

David E. Lundstrom, *A Few Good Men from Univac*

René Moreau, *The Computer Comes of Age: The People, the Hardware, and the Software*

Arthur L. Norberg, *Computers and Commerce: A Study of Technology and Management at Eckert-Mauchly Computer Company, Engineering Research Associates, and Remington Rand, 1946–1957*

Emerson W. Pugh, *Building IBM: Shaping an Industry and Its Technology*

Emerson W. Pugh, *Memories that Shaped an Industry*

Emerson W. Pugh, Lyle R. Johnson, and John H. Palmer, *IBM's 360 and Early 370 Systems*

Kent C. Redmond and Thomas M. Smith, *From Whirlwind to MITRE: The R&D Story of the SAGE Air Defense Computer*

Alex Roland with Philip Shiman, *Strategic Computing: DARPA and the Quest for Machine Intelligence, 1983–1993*

Raúl Rojas and Ulf Hashagen, editors, *The First Computers: History and Architectures*

Dinesh C. Sharma, *The Outsourcer: The Story of India's IT Revolution*

Dorothy Stein, *Ada: A Life and a Legacy*

John N. Vardalas, *The Computer Revolution in Canada: Building National Technological Competence*

Maurice V. Wilkes, *Memoirs of a Computer Pioneer*

Programmed Inequality

How Britain Discarded Women Technologists and Lost Its Edge in Computing

Mar Hicks

The MIT Press
Cambridge, Massachusetts
London, England

First MIT Press paperback edition, 2018

This book was set in Sabon by Toppan Best-set Premedia Limited.

Library of Congress Cataloging-in-Publication Data

Names: Hicks, Mar, author.
Title: Programmed inequality : how Britain discarded women technologists and lost its edge in computing / Mar Hicks.
Description: Cambridge, MA : MIT Press, 2017. | Series: History of computing | Includes bibliographical references and index.
Identifiers: LCCN 2016021258 | ISBN 9780262035545 (hardcover : alk. paper) | 9780262535182 (pbk. : alk paper)
Subjects: LCSH: Women--Employment--Great Britain--History--20th century. | Sex discrimination in employment--Great Britain--History--20th century. | Electronic data processing--Great Britain--History. | Technocracy. | MESH: Computers.
Classification: LCC HD6135 .H53 2017 | DDC 331.40941/09045--dc23 LC record available at https://lccn.loc.gov/2016021258

For Britt

However revolutionary the technology, account must always be taken of constraints upon its speed of adoption and diffusion and hence, derived manpower demand. Technological innovation does not exist in a vacuum; it forms but one element of a complex social system.[1]

—UK Computer Sector Working Party, Manpower Subcommittee, 1979

Contents

Acknowledgments

The idea for this book began to take shape when I was working as a UNIX systems administrator in the Electrical Engineering and Computer Science Division at Harvard University. I had graduated from Harvard with a degree in history, but no computer science courses. My boss, Peg Schafer, hired me and many other people without formal computer science training because she felt that a good systems administrator could be made from any reasonably intelligent person. Peg believed that the most important things sysadmins needed to know—like how to handle people coextensively with technical problems—were learned on the job. The odd gender split in that workplace, with my older supervisors being mostly women and my younger peers being mostly men, and the conversations we all had about this, led me to wonder about gendered labor change in computing's past. It eventually resulted in my graduate research and this book.

When I entered the field over a decade ago, the topic of gender in computer history had nowhere near the cultural resonance or acceptance that it has today. When I told people about my project, I often was met with blank stares or occasionally even open hostility. But I never had this problem within the Society for the History of Technology and its Special Interest Group on Computers and Information in Society, whose members were always incredibly kind and welcoming. That these groups made me feel as though I were working on an important topic made a world of difference to my ability to complete this project. In addition, both the National Science Foundation and the Charles Babbage Institute for the History of Computing (particularly the fellowship endowed by the Tomash family) provided support that allowed me to do much of the research for the dissertation upon which this book is based.

I especially would like to convey my gratitude to Cathy Gillespie, Ann Sayce, and Colin Hobson—former computer workers who spoke to me about their time in British computing in the 1960s and beyond and who were extremely generous with their time and stories. In addition to the useful tacit knowledge and background information they shared, their perspectives lent an immediacy and warmth to this history that archives alone could not. My thanks also go to the many dedicated archivists and librarians who guided my inquiries at the UK National Archives, the British Library, the UK National Archive for the History of Computing at the University of Manchester, the Modern Records Center at the University of Warwick, the Women's Library in London, and the Vickers Archive at Cambridge University.

The comments of anonymous reviewers of the manuscript and the many people who read versions of drafts that became the chapters in this book provided invaluable insights. Although space and the vicissitudes of memory limit my ability to thank everyone who made an important contribution to this project, I would like to note the major contributions of my advisor and my dissertation committee members—Alex Roland, Susan Thorne, Ross Bassett, and Robyn Wiegman. Many of my fellow grad students at Duke University supported and encouraged me during our years together in the program and afterward—in particular, Anne-Marie Angelo, Eric Brandom, Andrew Byers, Mitch Fraas, and Jacob Remes. I would also like to thank Katie Helke, Justin Kehoe, and the rest of the editorial team at the MIT Press.

I owe a great debt to all of the colleagues who gave me invaluable advice, help, and intellectual support throughout the process of researching and writing this book, particularly (in alphabetical order) Janet Abbate, Anna Åberg, Bill Aspray, Margy Avery, Martin Campbell-Kelly, Deborah Cohen, Nathan Ensmenger, Maureen Flanagan, Laura Forlano, Barbara Hahn, Katie Hindmarch-Watson, Jennifer Light, Eden Medina, Tom Misa, Andy Russell, Corinna Schlombs, Jeff Schramm, James Sumner, and Jeff Yost. Friends and colleagues outside academia, many of whom are current or former computer professionals and all of whom are ardent feminists, showed interest in my work that was equally important—especially Louise Hicks, Chalam Tubati, Kathryn McCarthy, Janice Dsa, Kristen Brown, Chris Dzoba, Melissa Pierce, and Marian Mangoubi. In addition, an unexpected lifeline during my writing process were my followers on Twitter, who regularly engaged with me on topics related to my work, offered support, and consistently connected me to different perspectives both inside and outside academia.

Finally, I would like to thank my partner, Britt, who read, edited, and commented on more drafts of this work than any person should ever have been asked to, and without whose moral support and unflagging enthusiasm this book would likely not have been possible.

Introduction: Britain's Computer "Revolution"

In 1959, a computer operator embarked on an extremely hectic year, tasked with programming and testing several of the new electronic computers on which the British government was becoming increasingly reliant. In addition, this operator had to train two new hires with no computing experience for a critical long-term project in the government's central computing installation. After being trained, the new hires quickly stepped into management roles, while their trainer, who was described as having "a good brain and a special flair" for computer work, was demoted to an assistantship below them.[1]

This situation seems to make little sense until you learn that the trainer was a woman and the newly hired trainees were men. Yet this is not simply an example of unfair labor practices. It is part of a larger story about attempts to shape the newly developing digital economy. This woman's tale is emblematic of broader changes: In the 1940s, computer operation and programming was viewed as women's work—but by the 1960s, as computing gained prominence and influence, men displaced the thousands of women who had been pioneers in a feminized field of endeavor, and the field acquired a distinctly masculine image. How and why this change happened holds important lessons for contemporary economies and high-tech labor markets, yet the change is still poorly understood.

When the gender makeup of a field flips, the first assumption is usually that the content of the work within the field changed. When a field feminizes, people often assume that the work became simpler. When a field becomes male dominated, the assumption is the reverse: that the work became more difficult or complex. Yet as one can see from this example, that was not the case in early computing.

A second, related assumption might be called the "technological switch." This is the idea that a major technological change inexorably alters the labor composition of a field. Usually, more machinery and automation lead to feminization—a familiar historical pattern seen in everything from textile manufacture to typewriting. Yet the changeover from electromechanical to electronic computers did not result in further feminization, nor did it coincide neatly with computing's masculinization.

A final assumption about gendered labor change is that when women disappear from a field, a lack of interest, a lack of relevant skills, or an inability to get hired plays a major role. This, again, does not account for why women lost out in computing. Like the operator in the earlier example, many women were present in the field, interested in the work, and even had opportunities to prove their proficiency.

A wistful cartoon from the era remarked on this change, noting, "When trains sets become electronic, men are in, and that's ironic."[2] As electronic computing technology improved and became easier to use, women were no longer welcome. Seen from the perspective of the "yearning miss" in

YEARNING MISS

I had a yen to be a boy,
To sit around and play with trains,
Such fun, but not girls' games.
A lady now, but still mechanical
(In Computers and they're satanical)
But when train sets became 'lectronic
Men are in, and that's ironic.

J.C

Figure 0.1
"Yearning Miss." Cartoon from *Tabacus: The Company Magazine of the British Tabulating Machine Company*, May 1957, 4.

the cartoon, the flip was arbitrary, sudden, and unfortunate. It was not a natural evolution, but a noticeably quick change during which men were slotted into previously feminized jobs.

Over a decade later, a 1970 article on computer training entitled "Terminals Beat All the Toy Trains" uncannily echoed this cartoon. It claimed boys had a natural interest in computing that needed to be encouraged. The accompanying photo showed three students from Eton College, an elite all-boys boarding school, clustered around the paper printout terminal of a local university's mainframe. They had been given the opportunity to play games on the mainframe simply to become comfortable with computers.[3]

By the time that article was published, the gender of computing work had changed and its class status had risen dramatically. As the earlier anonymous cartoonist had predicted, the computer became the new train set for a generation of privileged young men—electronic training wheels for youngsters who were expected to grow up to become leaders in government and captains of industry. With the help of computers, young men like these would grow up to be far more powerful than the yearning miss could ever hope to be—but not because they possessed any special or higher level of technical skill.

Gender, Power, and Computers

Once computing started to become a more desirable field for young men, women were largely left out, regardless of what they might have been capable of or what they might have preferred. A gendered history of top-down structural discrimination defines the shape of the modern computing industry in the Anglo-American world. It has been the topic of several histories of US computing and has increasingly been a topic of contemporary news coverage.[4] Yet many persist in believing that lower numbers of women in computing are the result of individual choice or inadequate education. Historical examples from the US context show the existence of anecdotal discrimination, but because they focus primarily on computer history from the perspective of industry and use a varied array of business sources, structural discrimination is hard to prove.

The British case is different: In Britain, gendered labor change was part of a top-down government initiative to computerize. Not only women but also the explicit structural discrimination against them played a crucial, formative role in the uptake of computers and in the ultimate failure of the British computing industry. Computing defined the standard for Britain's postindustrial information economy and powerfully shaped how the nation modernized, all against a highly gender-discriminatory background. It was one of the state's most critical modernization projects, played out in the context of the government's strong control over industry after World War II. Computerization of government and industry was meant to revolutionize how nearly everything within the nation functioned and return Britain to a leading role on the global stage.

In this way, the British case is a parable of how nations can modernize in ways that are not merely uneven but that actively reconstitute categories of social inequality. It shows how new technologies often help certain classes consolidate power while stripping power from others.[5] Perhaps most importantly, the British example elucidates power dynamics that are harder to discern in the US context. It enables us not only to see gender discrimination in action more clearly but also to recognize class as a prime factor motivating change in the history of computing.

During World War II, Britain led the world in cutting-edge computing technology. In the crucible of war, Britain engineered and deployed the world's first digital, electronic, programmable computers. At a time when the ENIAC project in the United States was still not functional, these codebreaking computers actively changed the course of the war, most notably by ensuring the success of the D-Day landings. In the years that followed, British computing paralleled or anticipated many American innovations, and through the 1950s and early 1960s British computers seemed poised to offer strong competition to US offerings by capturing the lucrative British home market along with Commonwealth and postcolonial markets. Yet as the sixties stretched on, Britain's computer industry struggled despite government support. By decade's end, the government was promoting an industry-wide computer company merger in an effort to save the computing industry, to no avail.[6]

Focusing on the case of the British Civil Service and nationalized industries, I will show that gendered labor organization was a key aspect of the nation's drive to computerize. The British example lays bare how computerization molded particular people into a technological underclass to support society's growing technocratic impulse. This history also shows why computerization efforts ultimately ran counter to the modernization projects of the state, hurting industry and the nation at large. As David Edgerton has shown, projecting our obsession with innovation into the past gives a false sense of futurity, obscuring the technological and social continuities that complicate our view of progress.[7] The British case offers a powerful example of how cutting-edge technologies often run counter to social progress and economic justice.

An analysis like this invites a different perspective on computerization and the shift to an "information" economy by explaining the material effects of gendered labor discrimination. Underlying this change were powerful ideas about women's sexuality. Assumptions that women's lives would be defined by heterosexuality in ways that required them to leave the work force made work outside the home secondary to the dictates of marriage, procreation, and family. This study is not only an example of how gender has molded computer technology but also an example of how sexuality plays a silent but critical role in the history of computing. Expectations about women's lives based on a nearly compulsory form of midcentury heteronormativity stranded most women with limited career prospects. Many women worked throughout their lives in addition to raising families, but society organized itself around a male breadwinner wage meant to support a nuclear family. The result was that sexuality, the organization of labor markets, and the functioning of the economy as a whole became inextricably linked.

Although this history has been told from the viewpoint of British computer manufacturers and from the perspective of how American companies influenced the British market, a key missing element in most of these narratives is labor. Specifically, the labor of the everyday people whose work made computer deployment possible and determined what computers could do has received little attention. As important as hardware may be, computing systems functioned due to vast arrays of human workers, expressed through workflow organization, operators' actions, and software. Networks of labor and expertise extend into the systems themselves, constructing the social and technological bedrock on which all computing projects rest.[8] Ultimately, these factors determine which computer projects succeed or fail.[9] These less tangible components of computing systems play a formative role in what paths and priorities gain momentum and what kinds of impacts and accomplishments are possible—both in the immediate sense and for decades afterward.

Feminization, Mechanization, Automation

Because technologies are inseparable from the history of their utilization, the impact of gendered labor change on the history of computing is difficult to overstate.[10] Although a fairly recent topic of interest, studies on gender and computing have begun to proliferate in the past decade.

Jennifer Light reoriented our understanding of programming's origins by applying a gendered analysis to the ENIAC project, and Jean Jennings Bartik's recent memoir has fleshed out the details of Light's account.[11] Nathan Ensmenger has shown how management's understanding of labor is the necessary connective tissue between the political, economic, and technical elements of computing history. "Who has the power to set certain technical and economic priorities," Ensmenger points out, is "fundamentally [a] social consideration that deeply influences the technological development process."[12] In addition, multiple books in sociology, history, and other fields have tried to connect computing's past to the field's current labor problems.[13] Most recently, Janet Abbate wrote back into history many of the highly successful women programmers in the early decades of US and British computing, showing how programming initially was not a male domain.[14]

With this work, scholars have begun to unpack how normative constructions of gender play a key role in computing history. Histories like these allow us to contest the fiction of a neatly binary system of gender that continues to structure economies and political systems today. They also begin to show how computerization is an explicitly hegemonic project built on labor categories designed to perpetuate particular forms of class status. Gender's intersection with multiple other social and economic categories—particularly class, race, nationality, ability, and sexuality—defined the supposedly feminine traits that attached to women operators and programmers and played a major role in the construction of modern computing.

The British case provides an indispensable example for extending the work on women and gender, and on technology and power, by showing how gender changes the core historical narrative of computerization just as it did the history of industrialization.[15] Deskilling, labor rationalization, and feminization have defined work processes throughout the history of automation. The ability of low-level labor—shaped by management—to determine technologies' paths has a prehistory in literature on the industrial revolution and in histories of twentieth-century manufacturing work. Maxine Berg has shown that the conceptual utility of the term "industrial revolution" in fact turns on the existence of feminized and feminizing fields of work.[16] In discussing the British economy in the eighteenth and nineteenth centuries, she points out that industries that posted the most economic gains and seemed the most progressive technologically, like textiles, were those in which mechanization relied on women's labor.

Although lower wages have historically played a role in women's dominance in many industries, other rationales underlay the preference for women (and children) as industrial workers. Feminized labor extended management's power and made the reorganization required for automation easier.[17] As a class of workers in the nineteenth and early twentieth centuries, women had lower rates of trade union participation, less flexibility and control over where and when to work, and less ability to demand higher rates of pay. In certain industries, relatively high wages for women allowed upward mobility, and in others men were increasingly drawn into deskilling processes. Nonetheless, gender-segregated categories of work persisted in defining women's economic position as lower than men's, and in making women's economic lives secondary for most of the twentieth century.

Even though many quintessentially "revolutionary" industries within Britain's long industrial revolution turned on feminization, women's work was not performed by women because it required a particular set of physical or mental aptitudes. Instead, socially and economically constructed characteristics of women workers in the aggregate defined what work they were allowed to do in particular time periods. With the growth of the information economy, gender and class became increasingly important in defining the worth of particular skill sets.[18] Many characteristics of women industrial workers, such as their association with machines, bled into the new types of white- or pink-collar work that came to define the postindustrial economy.

Women's twentieth-century roles outside the workplace also owed a cultural debt to industrialization. In the nineteenth century, British society increasingly codified separate spheres of endeavor for men and women in response to the changes brought about by industrialization. Factory acts began to restrict where and when women could work, ostensibly to preserve their more delicate natures.[19] Middle-class women were corralled in the home so as not to have their femininity tainted by the industrialized city. The "angel in the house" ideal circumscribed middle-class women's lives and strongly discouraged them from seeking paid work in an expanding economy. If required to work, the modesty expected for their future roles as mothers and wives limited middle-class women's options: "They should not flaunt their independence like the mill girls did."[20] In the twentieth century, most women who aspired to middle-class existence therefore found their choice of job dictated not only by gender but by class.

Office Work: The Girls in the Machine

Clerical work, so prevalent in London's concentrated environment of government offices and businesses, became the repository of middle-class Victorian notions about women's proper role within society. As Meta Zimmeck has shown, hiring managers consciously redefined clerical work from a male- to a female-coded occupation in order to slot middle-class women into respectable jobs. During the latter half of the nineteenth century, the number of workers employed as clerks exploded. From 1851 to 1911, their numbers increased ninefold from 95,000 to 843,000, making clerks nearly 5 percent of the total British workforce.[21] Although ideally dependents, growing numbers of single, middle-class women had to, or chose to, maintain themselves and others both before and after marrying, and the growing British economy demanded their labor.

Male clerical workers increased only sevenfold from 1850 to World War I, whereas the number of women increased by eighty-three times, boosting their proportion of the total clerical workforce to 20 percent in 1911.[22] This large pool of female labor did not mesh seamlessly into the modernizing office. Instead, British offices were reorganized to comport with the changing shape of the labor market, carefully segregating women from men. Women took different entrances and stairwells in and out and dined in separate lunchrooms so that they would not encounter male colleagues even in passing. The prospect of men interacting in potentially sexual ways with these young, mostly single women was so unseemly that until 1911 the General Post Office in London forbade its female workers from leaving the premises at lunch.[23] This physical segregation mapped onto the organization of office work, changing work processes. Certain office work became gendered feminine, while other work remained a masculine preserve.

The way work was reorganized by gender in the modernizing office was nothing new. Factories had long divided mixed-gender workforces to better exploit women's labor. For example, in her study of British autoworkers, Laura Downs shows the speciousness of the concept of deskilling, which was used to segregate and devalue women workers.[24] The car manufacturer Rover classified women's work as unskilled despite its skilled nature by dividing work by gender. Rover's efforts to Taylorize its assembly line, and downgrade women's work even more, provoked an equal pay protest that ultimately succeeded, but women could not undo the way their work had been classified as lower skilled than men's.

Management used the gendered organization of the work to construct a hierarchy of labor, with "women's work" at the bottom.

A similar dynamic operated in white collar workplaces. In 1874, the post office received seven hundred applications for only five "woman clerk" posts. This flooded labor market greatly privileged employers and allowed managers to deskill women's office work from the start. Managers quickly developed the idea that competence working with machines was a feminine attribute to differentiate it from the supposedly more intellectual work done by male clerks. Soon, women became synonymous with office machine operators and their work became tied to typewriters, desktop accounting machines, and room-sized punched card equipment installations. Not coincidentally, women's entry into office work in large numbers occurred at the same time as the "industrialization of the office."

Clerical work continued to expand rapidly and by the 1950s women made up a majority—60 percent—of all clerical workers. By the 1970s the figure was over 70 percent.[25] Yet women workers still lacked the right to a wage on which they could live, whereas men were entitled to demand a family wage that could support a wife and children. Even within the nation's premier meritocracy, the Civil Service, white-collar women workers were treated as short-term and unskilled, had lower pay scales, and had few opportunities for promotion or a career.[26] Their alignment with machine work in offices persisted through waves of equipment upgrades and eventually through the changeover from electromechanical to electronic systems.

Office managers did not see anything unusual about the association of women with increasingly complex machines, because the association of women with automation was nearly a century old by this point. As one organizational expert put it while discussing the ever-growing numbers of women "mechanicals" in the 1950s and 1960s, many women who would have gone into factory work in earlier decades now sought work in offices: "Jobs involving the use of office machinery now closely resemble the sort of light production work that these entrants might have done on the factory floor."[27] Positions like these proliferated in the massive bureaucracies of the state: Most people working for the nation's largest employer, the Civil Service, worked in office environments.[28] Yet women's work in government offices was not considered firmly within the realm of the white collar. Instead, it was constructed as almost industrial—and therefore liminal to the "real" work of offices.[29]

Accounting for the Total Labor Force

Even as women's workforce participation continued to rise—it skyrocketed during World War II and grew steadily after the war—women as a class remained the lowest-earning and lowest-achieving participants in the paid workforce. They were generally limited to deskilled (or ostensibly deskilled) work at low rates of pay, hurting their ability to contribute to the nation's economic growth.[30] Legal, economic, political, and social independence from a heteronormative family unit was not feasible for most women in this context. The moral burdens of a particular historical construction of womanhood continued to shape women's lives for much of the twentieth century.

Not only work organization but also technological organization piggybacked on these assumptions. The process of computerization in the public and private sector actively relied on explicitly feminized workforces, constructed under an umbrella of technocratic control. A technocratic heteronormativity relied on the structures of patriarchy and the nuclear family to produce the ideal staff for Britain's modernizing, information-based economy. In a very real sense, this arrangement defined what information technology and office-automating technologies could do.

Computerization and the job categories it created were intentionally and explicitly built around a particular mid-twentieth-century sexual status quo. Computer work grew on top of state measures that strengthened sexist labor patterns predicated on binary gender, compulsory heterosexuality, and the equation of womanhood with motherhood. The provisions of the postwar welfare state, for instance, institutionalized women's benefits based on a model that assumed their dependency on a husband's wage.[31] This contributed to the government deferring equal pay for its many women office workers for decades on the grounds that the women did not "need" it.

Despite economic rationalizations like these, biases that had nothing to do with the bottom line shaped managerial conduct. The practice of firing women immediately upon marriage, for instance, was a cultural dictate with no economic benefit for employers, because it removed trained workers from the labor market. The negative effects of this practice on the GDP show that the government's attachment to labor segregation by gender and marital status often made little economic sense.[32] Still, so important was women's dependent role to the maintenance of British societal norms that economic drawbacks like this were seen simply as an unavoidable cost.

Computing and the State

In addition to its major impact on private industry in Britain, computerization was also deeply enmeshed with the modernization objectives of the mid- to late twentieth-century British state. In her work on computing in Chile, Eden Medina discusses how states try to marshal technologies to reshape national economies in line with their political agendas.[33] In the case of Chile, a socialist government tried to use computing for a radical social justice project that would give greater economic and political power to the working class. In the case of Britain, however, the goal of computerization was the reverse: to consolidate as much power as possible in the hands of a small technocratic elite, removing it from unreliable machine operators as the power of electronic computers became clear. Medina's example shows that Allende's government used computing to intentionally decentralize decision-making and share power by constructing systems that privileged the working classes. However, examples of governments using computing technology to proactively share or decentralize power within a nation are exceptional: For most of the twentieth century, computing functioned as a centralized—and centralizing—technology that lent itself to the further consolidation of power in the hands of a few.

Electronic computing systems that often provided solutions to managerial problems in the private sector were closely linked to top-down governance in the public sector. This period in computing's history prefigures many of the trends toward the manipulation of ever-greater amounts of data for centralized decision-making and control today. Early electronic computing greatly increased governmental power on the national level.[34] This machine-aided revolution in management across the public and private sectors has resulted in histories of computing that often focus more on the mostly male scientists, designers, engineers, and businessmen who created or sold machines than on the mostly female workers responsible for their deployment and successful day-to-day functioning.[35]

In a broader sense, the computing revolution also offered Britain a final chance to reclaim the power of a fading empire and revive the flow of capital from overseas that it had enjoyed in the past. Both Conservative and Labour governments agreed on the need for government intervention in high technology to effect this end. As a result, the British government put a premium on the effective use and production of cutting-edge business computing technology and the organizational models that went along with it throughout the mid- to late twentieth century. The government's keen interest in computing was not an issue of short-term efficiency or labor cost savings, though it was often publicly explained as such. Upgrading the farrago of older data-processing and office-automating machines promised benefits of control rather than price, and supporting the British computing industry offered the possibility of once again raising Britain's global political standing via technological innovation.

Neither the state's project to computerize itself nor its support of the computing industry achieved its intended goals, however. As a result, the British case is both an alternative history to the triumphal story of American technological progress and a cautionary tale for future technological development. In the US context, narratives that include women have enhanced our understanding of diversity but sometimes struggle to show how gender is a formative category for postindustrial labor markets and how gendered analyses alter the main contentions of the historiography of computing. Britain's experience tells us very different things about the relationship between technology and empire and about the essential, hidden role that gender plays in shaping industries and defining economic modernization itself. It forces a radical rethinking of the "revolutionary" narrative of the history of computing, and a reappraisal of the explanatory value of positivist histories of the information age.

Narrative Outline

The chapters that follow chart two related, overlapping changes: The first is the diminution of women's contributions in computing. The second is the increasing inability of the British government—and by extension, Britain itself—to make good on promises of a technological revolution that would help the nation maintain world power status and equalize Britain's highly class-stratified society. The chapters are organized to give a bird's-eye view of the change to a modern information landscape, grounded in specific details of government initiatives to deploy computers and mold workers. The book starts with the promise of a new technological order during World War II, proceeds to the "technological revolution" of the mid-1960s proclaimed by Prime Minister Harold Wilson, and ends in the late 1970s, when the idea of Britain refashioning itself as a technological superpower had largely crumbled. The narrative explains why gendered labor struggles prevented the nation from leveraging the mass of its trained technical workforce and shows how this resulted in negative consequences.

Chapter 1 delves into the origins and consequences of wartime work in computing. The "total war" style of combat included conscription of women's labor, resulting in a wartime intelligence establishment that was overwhelmingly female. The training and use of women workers at Bletchley Park ultimately won what at times seemed like an unwinnable war for the British. Yet, the thousands of women who worked in these skilled roles were erased from the historical record due to British wartime secrecy and postwar paranoia as the Cold War loomed. This chapter shows how the gender integration of Britain's high-tech labor force enabled the nation's wartime successes, and why the women who worked with the world's first digital, electronic, programmable computers had a critical, material impact on the outcome of the war.

After the war, women's technical abilities dropped in value. Instead of helping women prosper in an increasingly machine-dependent and data-driven economy, these skills actually hurt them. Chapter 2 traces the creation and institutionalization of a feminized underclass of women machine workers within the sprawling bureaucracy of the Civil Service and nationalized industries. Many women operated and programmed electromechanical and, later, electronic computers because of the perception that these machines made work rote. Yet this was not a natural progression but an intentionally instituted set of labor practices that defined both the public and private sector. These newly formed "machine grades" were a job classification that ensured computing stayed low paid, feminized, and a dead end careerwise within the Civil Service. "Subclerical" women workers could therefore be kept away from the more important and legitimate work of government offices. Women's proficiency with machines meant they largely lost out on equal pay, and this wage inequality would alter computing for decades to come.

Positioned as deskilled and feminized going into the sixties, electronic computing work seemed low level by its very nature. Chapter 3 shows how British companies used the image of this feminized labor force to market the systems they were trying to sell both at home and abroad, intentionally exporting British gender norms to other nations as they marketed their systems. Computer work occupied the opposite end of the spectrum from nontechnical office work, which was seen as more intellectually demanding. But as computer use expanded, the machines' rising price tags helped alter management's understanding of their power and potential. Suddenly, taking cues from the highest levels of government, leaders within the Civil Service began to regard computers—and therefore the workers associated with them—as more important than previously thought. Those who had the technical proficiency to command computers could, by extension, gain power over vast swathes of information and therefore people.

In 1964, Prime Minister Harold Wilson initiated a "white-hot" technological revolution meant to burn up inequalities within British society as it modernized the country. White Heat raised the profile and importance of computing and provided more encouragement to insert executive-level men into computer work. Yet, the feminization of computing made this nearly impossible. As a result, labor shortages slowed computing's progress and helped give women an early lead as the status of the field rose. While these jobs began to command higher wages, however, a popular discourse emerged that created false messages about women's actual roles. In an era when few understood what computer work was, advertisements showed women's computing work as simplistic in order to better sell machines. This powerfully shaped mainstream ideas about computing and affected how women were hired. By contrasting oral histories and government records with advertisements and computer companies' publications, chapter 3 shows the exciting opportunities available to workers, both men and women, in the era of White Heat—and how these workers were represented in the media.

This period of plenty did not last, however. Chapter 4 discusses why the revolution was doomed to fail. Although the twin forces of luck and labor shortage rapidly propelled many women into higher-level jobs as the field professionalized, there was a catch: Those high-level jobs were thought to be inappropriate for women. Technical workers were still seen as liminal to the white-collar hierarchy of the Civil Service, and women were viewed as unsuitable for management roles, particularly when the staff to be managed included men. As computers became the chosen instrument of government power at home and abroad, government hiring managers redoubled their efforts to create a class of technocratic elites to take over all computer programming and operation. Chapter 4 explains how these new recruitment efforts focused on changing who performed this work and on aligning machine workers with management. When high-level government ministers realized that technical work was more important than previously assumed, they aimed to construct a talent pool of career-minded, management-aspirant young men. These new technically minded managers were supposed to be able to manage machines as easily as people and have the skills to go effortlessly from machine room to boardroom.

This gendered labor shift was not a side effect of computerization but a core goal of the project to computerize the state—and ultimately the nation. Chapter 5 explains why just as efforts to construct a new technocratic class floundered, so too did British computing. In consolidating a male-identified ideal for computer work, the government also whittled down the available labor pool for computer jobs. Most computer work in government was still done by women. By no longer considering this labor pool for computing posts, the government neglected most of its trained technical workforce. The ideal technocrat was extremely hard to find at large in the labor market, and these new hiring standards had the effect of draining training budgets and exacerbating labor shortages.

At the same time, the national government—the largest buyer and most important supporter of British computers—demanded systems that fit its needs. Government support was meant to strengthen the computer industry, but it also put the government in the driver's seat. The government's evolving vision of computing relied on a small cadre of technocratic managers who would orchestrate all computing from a centralized perch and take control out of the hands of a feminized class of workers seen as inherently unreliable and increasingly unruly. This organizational model dictated ever more powerful and centralized mainframe computing solutions. In an effort to ensure that the supply of British-made mainframes met this need, government officials became increasingly involved in the computer industry, eventually orchestrating a merger of the most promising companies into one large corporation that would supply the needed machines in return for full government support.

Although it seemed that such machines would solve the government's computer labor troubles, the focus on expensive, highly centralized computing solutions did not work, and the consolidation of computer companies hurt the industry's ability to compete at home and abroad. The concluding chapter explains why the problems that the government was trying to solve—Britain's "shortage" of skilled technical workers and difficulty competing in the global high-tech marketplace—were worsened by the actions government leaders took to alter their hiring pool and mold computer technology. The restrictions borne of gendered labor shifts imbued organizationally conservative ideals into the new field as Britain moved into the seventies. The promise of meritocracy through technological change had not been fulfilled, and it continued to hinder the modernization of the British economy. With equal pay complaints once again bubbling to the surface and computer workers going on strike, British leaders realized that centralizing computing had been a double-edged sword. With it, they had unwittingly cut the legs out from under the British computer industry and wrought havoc on their own computerization projects.

Government records and the records of the nationalized industries provide the details of this history. They are complemented by the records of British computing companies, staff association and labor union records, and media from both trade and popular publications. Census data and oral interviews provide perspective on the symbiotic relationship between the public sector's labor force and the private sector.

Although women figure prominently in the pages of this book, most of the women were not themselves prominent. Throughout the narrative, the focus shifts from women's work to men's work, and from labor to management, as the gender of the field changes. Fundamentally, this is a history less about women than about how changing constraints of gender, class, and sexuality mold labor forces, industries, and nations. Most women in this study did not make major contributions as individuals, but they were important as a class of workers on whose shoulders was laid incredible technological responsibility with little corresponding economic or social status.

Understanding this labor as a class, rather than through the lens of a few remarkable individuals, sheds light on the importance of gender as a formative category in technological organization and design. It forces us to rethink many of the assumptions of computer history narratives that hold up individuality and innovation as key explanatory elements. It also provokes a reconsideration of how histories of computing sometimes reflexively and unconsciously privilege those with the most power and implicitly endorse an ahistorical fiction of technological meritocracy. That the workers in this field were disproportionately white is no more a coincidence than the fact that they were overwhelmingly women. Throughout history, it has often not been the content of work but the identity of the worker performing it that determined its status, and these workers, while below their male peers, still occupied a position of privilege compared to many other women.

This study attempts to avoid further lionizing computing skill in a way that gives automatic approval to its worth. Instead, it complicates how our impression of the high value of computer programming has been historically constructed by class, gender, nationality, and race, and it is skeptical about the technological boosterism that sometimes attaches to narratives seeking to unearth women's contributions to computing.

The book focuses on workers rather than professionals to highlight the classes of women who often could not, or would not, take on the neat identity of "programmer" but who did the work nonetheless.[36]

This history holds lessons for other postindustrial nations whose economies and societies are becoming ever more reliant on computing and computer workers. The experience of Britain in the twentieth century has many similarities to the US context in the twenty-first century. The problems that ultimately scuttled the British computing industry—and helped exacerbate the nation's slide into second-rate world power status—formed in a sociotechnical context where gender and an assumption of heterosexuality were primary organizational factors that shaped everything from the deployment and usage of electronic computers to their design and provisioning. The British case shows how these social categories played a surprisingly large role in shaping computing technology, right down to the hardware, and how economic modernization turned on enforcing hierarchies of social difference through technology. Contrary to popular belief, high technology is often as socially regressive as it is technically revolutionary or progressive. Histories like this offer examples that help us think about where increased dependence on computerization and digital labor forces may lead in the future. The construction of classes of ostensibly deskilled high-tech workers continues to enable the boom-and-bust cycle of technical advance and shape the social patterns that cohere around these systems.

In the end, the treatment of labor in the British case created severely limited horizons for both those at the top and those at the bottom. Gendered labor's "butterfly effect" began at the lowest levels of British computing and reached all the way up, drastically altering decisions about technology made at the highest levels of government and industry. The failure of Britain's thriving midcentury computer industry serves as an unhappy reminder of the ways in which technologies can rarely fix social or economic problems and how they instead often make real the limited and myopic goals of small but powerful segments of society. Technologically determinist solutions—in which technologies are wielded to determine the course of a nation—always use the raw material of the status quo and therefore often fail to bring about meaningful change. In the case of British computing, the reasons for this failure remained invisible, because critical parts of the system were never considered salient factors in the first place. As the *Times* of London put it in 1970, "computers need people."[37] This is a history of why that need went unmet, and what emerged as a result.

1

War Machines: Women's Computing Work and the Underpinnings of the Data-Driven State, 1930–1946

In recent years, the restoration of Bletchley Park has attracted worldwide attention. The country estate in Milton Keynes, United Kingdom, was the site of the most important codebreaking operations of World War II and home to the first digital, electronic, programmable computer: the Colossus. The British-designed and manufactured Colossus computers, of which there were ten in all by war's end, were critical to the conduct of Allied wartime operations. Unlike their better-known U.S. counterpart, the ENIAC, the Colossus computers were actually deployed during the war, actively changing its outcome. Kept secret for decades, the full import of the developments at Bletchley has only recently become widely known.[1] Yet while popular culture has begun to recognize the importance of Bletchley's wartime operations, misunderstandings persist about the nature of the information work performed there. The 2014 blockbuster *The Imitation Game*, for instance, cleaves the Colossus computers from the narrative entirely in favor of building a "great man" narrative for a single codebreaker.[2]

Hidden within the story of Bletchley is a less popular narrative that cannot leverage the appeal of a lone genius and his accomplishments. Thousands of women worked at Bletchley during the war—most in technical roles.[3] Although it is generally accepted that the striking and wide-ranging roles of the mostly women workers within Bletchley Park give lie to stereotypes about computing as a traditionally masculine field, the contributions of these women have not been analyzed as constitutive of larger trends in the history of computing. Instead, these workers have been positioned as a "reserve" labor force impelled into masculine-coded jobs due to the exigencies of war—and dispensed with immediately thereafter.[4] Looking at the labor of women computer operators during World War II as though they were a temporary and completely exceptional type of workforce, however, hides important historical connections. US-centric narratives of computing and of the war also make it difficult to take the labor performed by these British women seriously; with the US experience as a backdrop, these women simply look like high-tech Rosie the Riveters. When taken on their own merits in the context of Britain's experience of the war and the decades immediately before and after, however, this narrative can reorient our conceptions about computing's development in Britain and internationally.

Women's integration into the earliest computing systems both during and after the war shows their labor as formative to the project of computing and the twentieth-century technological state in a way that remains understudied. As our current understanding of computing technologies has grown to focus on how, why, and who deploys the power of cutting-edge technologies, the history of labor has become integral to the history of computing. With this attention to labor has come a renewed focus on the gendered dimensions of work with technology—a focus that resonates deeply with current concerns about underrepresentation in science, technology, and engineering. The history of women's role in computing helps explain gendered categories that still construct labor forces in the Anglo-American context today.[5] Yet this history is often perceived as a specialized, parallel narrative, rather than a foundational one. When women do not fulfill the role of inventor or entrepreneur in a way comparable to the men who have up until now been the main focus of computing history, their labor is often regarded as not being integral to the main narrative of computing's history.[6]

This chapter analyzes how feminized work—work that was assumed to be rote, deskilled, and best suited to women—was critical in defining early computerization, from the inception of modern, pre-electronic computational methods in the early twentieth century, through the crucible of high-speed wartime codebreaking, to the postwar transition in government and industry that civilianized computing systems and their technological goals. This purportedly feminized work was anything but deskilled, and the needs, power, and money of the British government were instrumental in using it to create modern computing and computer workers before, during, and after World War II. Computing's early beginnings as a feminized field presaged specific gendered labor hierarchies in peacetime—ones that put computing work at the bottom of the white-collar labor pyramid until the rise of technocratic ideals in the 1960s that reshaped the expectations and status of machine workers.[7] Far from merely being artifacts of wartime pressures that appeared suddenly and disappeared with the coming of peace, these labor patterns defined British computing and its possibilities throughout the twentieth century, gendering the edifice of the technological state.

Creating Information Workers

Unlike the heavy manufacturing and munitions work into which women were drafted during World War II, computing held prewar associations with women's labor. As in other industries, feminized "reserves" of labor shaped the viability and success of computing endeavors.[8] Both British and American projects employed women from the outset as human computers—that is, workers who performed manual calculations—and then, very often, as computer operators and programmers. In Britain, women often built the machines as well. The manufacturing workforce at IBM UK was so feminized that management measured its production in "girl hours" rather than "man hours" into the 1960s.[9]

Prior to World War II, most women who worked as human computers did their work using a variety of desktop calculating machines. Working as clerks or scientific assistants, they made tables for civilian and military applications or did accounting tasks. At the same time, more complex machines and systems of calculation were being developed. Trained as an astronomer, the New Zealand–born Leslie John Comrie employed women workers to produce astronomical tables with the aid of general-purpose electromechanical punched card machines.[10] While working at the British Nautical Almanac Office, Comrie earned a reputation as the father of large-scale application of punched card machines to scientific computing. Comrie's major insight was that with effective organization general-purpose office machines could be used for complex scientific calculations—essentially creating an electromechanical supercomputer system from standardized punched-card components and well-trained labor.

Soon after, Comrie deployed his system for military applications, doing contract table-making and statistical work for the British government during World War II. Young women workers were key to his success, and he did not shy away from detailing why they were an ideal fit for his system. In his "Careers for Girls," Comrie notes that women have the capacity to be easily trained to perform this work, along with the secretarial or typing work they might already do in the same office.[11] In addition, their numbers in the labor force were plentiful and, Comrie asserted, they diligently did work that young men saw as boring, dead-end drudgery. Like many other men in charge of computing systems, Comrie saw women's labor not as an add-on but as foundational to his systems' success.

During the early twentieth century, managers had gradually come to see young women as ideal office machine operators and had begun employing and training them to run a variety of machines. The growing popularity of the typewriter in late Victorian offices had helped create an association of automation with feminized labor pools. An emblematic document, prepared by Comrie to help government and business users compare the features of Hollerith and Powers-Samas punched card accounting machinery, described the operators of accounting machines as "girls from fifteen to eighteen or twenty years of age, who receive perhaps thirty or forty schillings a week for their work, *and in some cases much less*" (italics mine).[12] By determining labor costs and hiring patterns, gendered ideals influenced equipment purchasing and created the structure and expectations of modern office work. These women could have short, serviceable careers "before they (or most of them) graduate to married life and become experts with the housekeeping accounts!" Comrie quipped.[13] Turnover through marriage was supposed to ensure women didn't tire of the work or require promotion to better—and better paid—work, as that would throw his system out of alignment.

Yet women workers often did not agree to the limited career paths set out for them, and sometimes young women in these roles pushed back against expectations. In the British Civil Service, Comrie's ideas defined many women's working lives, but these workers did not merely accept their lot. A flustered Treasury official reported in 1941: "Mrs. Arrow and I visited the Admiralty today. They have 180 [machine] operators, some established, but the majority temporary, and these girls are kicking up something of a fuss."[14] His report detailed how low pay and poor promotion prospects were creating an untenable situation and how managers had few outlets to appease the disgruntled workers given how the work was organized. Since the work had been deskilled, there was little room to advance.

Systems like Comrie's did more than just slot people into socially appropriate work roles. They disciplined workers in accordance with certain gendered and classed labor ideals predicated on the heteronormative concept of a male breadwinner wage and unpaid domestic work for women within the nuclear family. These ideals were often not as fitting or practical as they seemed, resulting in more and more young women who had to support themselves and their families on near-poverty wages, particularly as the gendered contours of office labor continued to shift. In 1881, under 3 percent of all clerks were women. By 1921, this figure had rocketed to over 46 percent. By 1940, and continuing after the war, women held a clear and growing majority.[15] In both the private and public sector, women clustered in low-level office jobs. Often, this work was referred to as subclerical—that is, below real clerical work, an idea later echoed by the informal appellation pink-collar labor. Defined by a lack of authority over other workers as much as by an assumption of skilllessness, subclerical work increasingly became seen as ideal for young women in the twentieth century. It was the ultimate holding pattern for

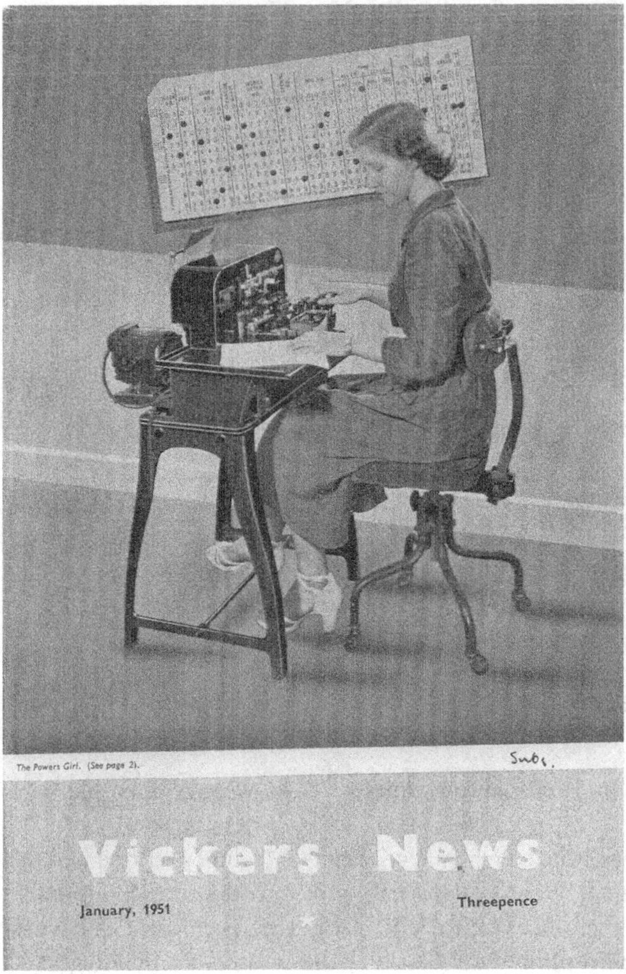

Figure 1.1
The "Powers Girl" was an advertising mascot of Powers-Samas who portrayed women's labor as an integral part of mechanized accounting systems. *Vickers News*, January 1951.

Figure 1.1 (continued)

temporary labor, and only during times of crisis were women likely to break out of it.

Subclerical work utilized machinery heavily. Machines represented the incursion of manual, vaguely industrial work into the supposedly intellectual sphere of the office. As a result, clerks who performed this work suffered from a perception that what they did was not really integral to the real work of offices. Yet offices of the early to mid-twentieth century relied on machine workers in order to meet immediate demands and to define long-term goals. This style of machine-aided work quickly became essential to maintaining and expanding the powerful bureaucracies that constructed both government and industry. Many large institutions could no longer simply add to their number of workers to meet new objectives. Without mechanized systems and the cheap, plentiful labor pool of women who ran them, the reach and structure of these institutions could not scale.

Gendered War Work and High-Stakes Electronic Computing

As firsts in computing go, the Colossus computers stand out as being the first successful application of high-speed computing to accomplish time-sensitive, mission-critical goals. While the ENIAC was still under construction on the other side of the Atlantic, the second Colossus was ensuring the success of the Allies in the D-Day landings. Lone codebreakers, notably Alan Turing, receive much of the credit for British intelligence operations during World War II, but the most important and voluminous intelligence work of the war was machine-aided and feminized. Codebreaking operations employed thousands of women and hundreds of machines in addition to the elite cadre of men who led the work.

Along with the revolutionary codebreaking computers built by London Post Office researchers and operated by the Women's Royal Naval Service (WRNS), work at Bletchley Park—the nerve center of the British intelligence establishment—also relied heavily on systems of punched card machines and women's labor, like those designed by Comrie before the war. When commissioning Hollerith equipment for the park, Ronald Whelan reported that "following the setting up of the initial equipment in Hut 7 the workload increased rapidly." In order to meet labor demands for punch and machine operators, "recruitment was made of local girls" who were trained in-house and worked the machines in shifts around the clock. Later in the war, "a great increase in operating strength came when a large component of WRNS personnel was drafted to us, in addition to a contingent of 20 university graduates."[16] Workers like these, many of whom were university educated or trained to a high standard at the park, would become the sinew in the information arm of the British war machine.

In times of crisis, the association of women with machine work strengthened and extended, opening up opportunities. Although wartime work as a whole upset social and economic hierarchies, the prewar association of women with electromechanical machine work contributed powerfully to wartime labor organization and, later, to the postwar labor landscape. In this context, working with the first digital, electronic, programmable computers the world had seen was not an unlikely role for many of the women workers who volunteered or were conscripted to work for the war effort.

In late 1941—in the same year that the Admiralty machine operators were "kicking up a fuss" about their pay and promotion prospects—the government began conscripting women into war work, registering and then calling up all British women between the ages of eighteen and sixty. Both married and single women were drafted into compulsory service across the home front. Assignments were made irrespective of locale: "You must be prepared to leave home unless this would mean exceptional hardship," warned government announcements.[17] Beginning in 1942, all young women were required to seek jobs only through the government's Women's Employment Exchange, set up to channel prime workers into essential industries.[18]

These women sometimes worked jobs that would have been unavailable to them in peacetime, and they also traveled and lived in ways that ran counter to peacetime social and familial mores. Nonetheless, the expectations and ideals of peacetime society—particularly in regard to a patriarchal, heteronormative family—continued to influence how and where women were deployed and who was called up. Single or childless widowed women between the ages of twenty and thirty were regarded as the most portable and dependable, followed by married women without children. Married women who had children under the age of fourteen escaped conscription or industrial reassignment; their service within the home was seen as more important. They were encouraged to volunteer, however.

Most women who worked for the war effort worked unusual hours or swing shifts, and either commuted far from home alone or relocated to spartan dormitories set up by the Ministry of Labour. Many of the women working at the heart of Britain's intelligence establishment at Bletchley Park were housed in the servants' quarters of a nearby country manor, with four bunks filling each small room beyond their intended capacity.[19] Others streamed in by train each day. Women's labor formed the nucleus of the British wartime information machine. They staffed the majority of posts in the information processing hub at Bletchley and at its related information collection outposts.

By 1942, all job training centers had been filled with women, and government documents noted that the shortage of manpower required a *total* reliance on women trainees from then on.[20] The Ministry of Labour reported that its "broad position" was therefore that women were as of now "eligible equally with men for all the training," and "as regards the actual curriculum of training, the same course is available to men and women." In the midst of crisis, the ministry conceded that "it has been found that women prove to be equally apt pupils," even though in peacetime women would not have been trained for many of these jobs.[21] Women were now allowed into all general engineering courses, including draftsmanship, fitting, inspection, instrument making, panel beating, sheet metal working, welding, electrical installation, and many more. Yet in the same memorandum that stated women were "equally apt" trainees, the Ministry of Labour also noted that *only* women who "show[ed] promise" would be "treated in the same way as men" and retained for longer training courses. The rest were given an abbreviated training period of a few weeks and sent out to work. Only trainees who were seen as having exceptional potential could rise above the social stigma that positioned women's paid labor as simply a temporary stage in their lives.

As Ministry of Labour officials scrambled to keep up with war demands, they tried to make the most of available labor pool by increasingly adapting to the living patterns of married women and women with children. The ministry urged factories to set up training programs for women who could only work part time. Their labor was important enough to the war effort to warrant the waste and logistical inconvenience of rearranging training schedules and configuring shortened shifts. Creative solutions to the manpower shortage had to be sought for munitions production in particular.[22] Much more so than it ever had in peacetime, the government recognized and tried to mitigate the "double shift" effect that accrued for married women who ran their households in addition to working outside the home, in order to keep wartime factories running efficiently and keep factory floor accidents down.[23]

In the first months of 1942, over 150,000 women flowed into industrial placements each month. The Armed Forces survey for the year ending in June projected that over 700,000 men and 350,000 women were needed. In addition, Civil Defense and home front services such as nursing, the Women's Land Army (farming), and the Navy, Army, and Air Force Institutes (NAAFI, which provided cafeterias and laundry services) required another one hundred thousand women. Munitions factories gobbled up over 350,000 men and 650,000 women. Altogether, this meant the armed forces and munitions industries utilized more than 1.1 million men and more than 1.1 million women during 1942.[24] Adjusting for the close to three-quarters of a million men in these statistics who were sent to fight in this time period, one can see that women workers held a sizable majority on the home front by the end of the year. The Ministry of Labour estimated that 80 percent of all single women between fourteen and fifty-nine years of age, 41 percent of wives and widows, and 13 percent of mothers with children under the age of fourteen were at work, or in uniform with the auxiliary forces, by 1942.[25]

From there, their numbers only rose. By 1943, 90 percent of single women and 80 percent of married women between the ages of twenty and thirty-one worked for the war effort.[26] At the same time, any woman who already held a civilian job was legally bound to stay in it unless given explicit government consent to leave it. Two main categories of war work—an assigned job in a war-related industry or conscription into the Women's Auxiliary Services—defined women's experiences. The former could be any civilian job, many of which were in manufacturing. Jobs in the latter category often took the form of information work, from logistics, to data gathering, to military data-processing work.

From Listening to Morse Code to Breaking Enigma: Codebreaking's Layers of Data Processing

In December 1943, a British team at the Post Office Research Station in Dollis Hill, London, finished assembling the world's first digital, programmable, electronic computer under the direction of Tommy Flowers, a Post Office research engineer. After testing, they disassembled it to send it to Bletchley Park, where machine codebreaking operations using hundreds of much slower electromechanical machines—called Bombes—had been successfully underway since March of 1940.[27] In popular narratives of the war, men and machines formed an unstoppable cybernetic system on the battlefield, fed by information unlocked by top cryptanalysts. In reality, this relationship was far less neat and far more mediated by layers of communication and data-processing.

Over ten thousand women and men worked at Bletchley Park during the war and, like most home front industries, the workforce was overwhelmingly women.[28] For decades the substance of the key roles they played was overlooked or misunderstood.[29] Secrecy and national security meant Bletchley workers could not discuss their work either during or after the war: "We would wear no category badges, and if anyone asked us what we did, we were to say that we were secretaries," recalled Eleanor Ireland, one of the hundreds of WRNS members who worked in codebreaking.[30] Today, many of these workers are unknown, having gone to their graves without ever talking about the content of their war work. Many of their identities—and even knowledge of entire categories of jobs they performed—have been lost.[31]

Reconstructing the chain of data-processing labor at Bletchley begins with the intercept stations that gathered encrypted data. The information provided to codebreakers like Turing and his colleagues was intercepted, recorded, read, and punched by hundreds of young women working as wireless operators and wireless transmission "slip readers" at the Knockholt intercept station in Kent before being transferred via teleprinter to Bletchley. The volume of traffic intercepted by Knockholt was so great that less than 10 percent of all intercepted messages were decrypted.[32] This grueling and tedious work required extreme accuracy, and women would listen and transcribe encoded German wireless signals sent out in Morse code for hours on end in real time. "They would be transmitting all over the place and we would really have to cramp our fingers to write it down nonstop, because you only had one chance to get it," recalled Joan Nicholls, who finagled her way into the women's army auxiliary force—the Auxiliary Territorial Service (ATS)—at the age of 15 by claiming she was 17.[33]

Wireless intercept operators had to record signals that seemed entirely random—the encrypted messages they listened to did not form words or sentences. Yet they listened so carefully that they got a feel for the grammar of these unintelligible signals and many intercept workers could recognize each individual German operator simply by the particular way he sent the Morse code—the particular staccato or lilt of the dots and dashes. It was essential to be "absolutely accurate" even to the point of knowing how many blocks of information one had missed if the signal faded. It "didn't matter how tired you were or how sleepy or bored you felt, the minute that station came alive again you would be ... tearing pieces of paper off the pad and scribbling away like mad."[34]

The entire chain of information gathering and processing—from reading the intercepted codes and transferring them to punched tape with exacting accuracy to operating the electromechanical and later electronic computers that helped crack them—fully relied on women's labor. Most of the women working at Bletchley came from the Women's Royal Naval Service (WRNS) and were commonly referred to as *wrens*. The nickname was both a transliteration of the acronym for the Women's Royal Naval Service and a pun on the British slang term *bird*—a slightly condescending term used to refer to women, especially young, single women.[35] Many of the WRNS members fit these categories: "96 percent of those who came were between the ages of seventeen and a half and twenty," noted *The General Report on Tunny*, "though a few of the earlier wrens were rather older and more experienced."[36] The WRNS members were given bunk beds in an old estate house, which Eleanor Ireland—an operator of the second, larger Colossus that broke codes for the D-Day landing—described as "very bleak, and very bare."[37]

Over the course of the war, these workers' numbers rose dramatically. Max Newman's machine codebreaking section, dubbed the Newmanry, was Bletchley's mechanized heart. Here, the WRNS used the most advanced technology at the park. The Newmanry contained only two cryptanalysts and sixteen members of the WRNS in April 1943, but by April 1945, there were a total of 325 workers, including 273 WRNS workers (all women), twenty-eight maintenance and construction engineers (mostly or all men), and twenty-four cryptographers and administrators (mostly men).[38] At any given time, the number of women working far exceeded the number of men at Bletchley—on average, over 80 percent of the workforce was female. They fell into precisely the same demographic as prewar machine operators: young, single, white, and middle class.[39]

The WRNS members used a number of different machines for codebreaking, and methods varied depending on the cypher. Early in the war, electromechanical computers formed the basis for machine codebreaking operations that attacked the Enigma encryption. These machines, known as Bombes, were designed by Alan Turing and Gordon Welchman who reverse engineered a captured Enigma machine. Manufactured for the government by the British Tabulating Machine company in Letchworth, Hertfordshire,[40] Bombes reproduced the action of eight Enigma encryption machines at once, with each rotor spun by an electric motor to quickly step through possible code settings.[41] After setting up and running the machines, WRNS operators searched for combinations that were not logically inconsistent. They would then examine the promising output batches further to see if a longer string of code deciphered with the current setting produced German. By the war's end, the WRNS members were operating two hundred of the huge, noisy Bombes, whose operation sounded like a mixture of loud clunking, thumping, and metallic scratching.[42] Each one stood nearly six feet high and took up roughly thirty-two square feet of floor space.

Because the Bombes were electromechanical, however, their speeds could not match the increasing volume of critical encoded traffic. Encrypted information needed to be unlocked quickly enough for the

Allied armed forces to be able to act on it. In addition, the relatively simpler Enigma code—which the Bombes helped crack—was being eclipsed by more complex encodings. Tunny (the British codename given to the German Lorenz code used between 1941 and the war's end for top-priority messages from the German High Command) had far stronger encryption than Enigma code.[43] The machine used to encode Tunny messages used twelve wheels to set the code, instead of the Enigma machines' three or four. As a result, breaking Tunny was far more difficult, time consuming, and labor intensive. A prevalence of certain letters in certain languages, along with attempts to guess "cribs" of likely text, had guided early breaks, but these methods were too slow and uneven to provide a long-term solution.

A depth, or a pair of messages sent using the same encryption settings, provided Bletchley with many early advantages, but as the war proceeded German forces enhanced security and the depths dried up.[44] As a result, a "statistical method" for brute-forcing analysis of encoded traffic, devised by codebreaker William Tutte, began to emerge as the only sure option. But Tutte's method could take hundreds of years for a *single* message to be decoded by hand. It required more advanced machines, far faster than the Bombes, in order to work. Although Turing has gone down in history as the key hero of British codebreaking owing to his brilliance, his socially provocative and courageous political stances, and his tragic death, the machines and methods designed by Max Newman, Tommy Flowers, and William Tutte were more instrumental to the codebreaking that allowed the British to weather the later, more brutal parts of the war. These methods also ensured the success of the D-Day landings, which turned the war's tide in the Allies' favor.[45]

The first machine effectively applied to Tunny was designed by Max Newman and deployed in June 1943. Partially electronic, but mainly relay based, this machine could compare two high-speed tapes of encoded information using a photoelectric reader. Unfortunately, it was neither fast enough nor reliable enough; the same data fed through twice might produce a different result each time. The WRNS operators who struggled to make it work named it the Heath Robinson after the rickety and comically pointless machinery of the cartoonist Heath Robinson—the British analogue of Rube Goldberg.[46] It was a nickname borne of profound frustration with substandard tools that did not inspire confidence.

If the Heath Robinson could perform its analysis successfully, the resulting data would be run through the Tunny machine, an electromechanical machine that had been created by reverse-engineering the

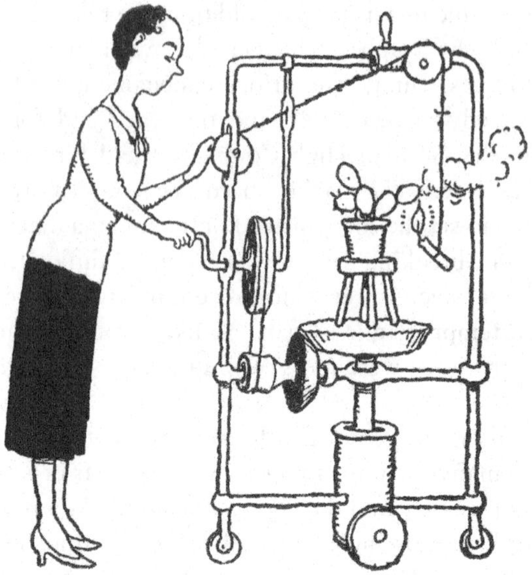

A Handy Device for De-Spiking Cacti

Figure 1.2
A drawing of a fanciful machine (above) for "de-spiking" cacti by cartoonist William Heath Robinson (1872–1944) bears a striking resemblance to the codebreaking machine dubbed the Heath Robinson (facing page) by WRNS operators. Cartoon from Heath Robinson and K. R. G. Browne, *How to Make a Garden Grow* (London: Hutchison, 1938); photo of Super Robinson from I. J. Good, D. Michie, and G. Timms, *General Report on Tunny with Emphasis on Statistical Methods*, 1945, 382, HW 25/5, TNA. Courtesy of the Heath Robinson Museum, UK, and UK National Archives, respectively.

German Lorenz enciphering machine. The WRNS recruits performed this analysis on each encoded message in order to find encryption settings for that day's messages. Working with the machines designed to break Tunny code consisted of trying different wheel settings and repeatedly resetting the plug boards with settings taken from the runs on the Heath Robinson machine.[47] "Tunny was plugged up just like an old fashioned telephone exchange," explained Dorothy Du Boisson, an early Colossus operator. She added, "It used to give me electric shocks as I put in the plugs."[48] Tunny machines also had a paper tape reader to take input from the Robinson machine, but the two Heath Robinson machines perpetually broke down, mangling the tapes that were to be fed into the Tunny in the process.

As a result, operators had to perfect the art of how to keep the tapes intact through the Heath Robinson's high-speed runs, which often

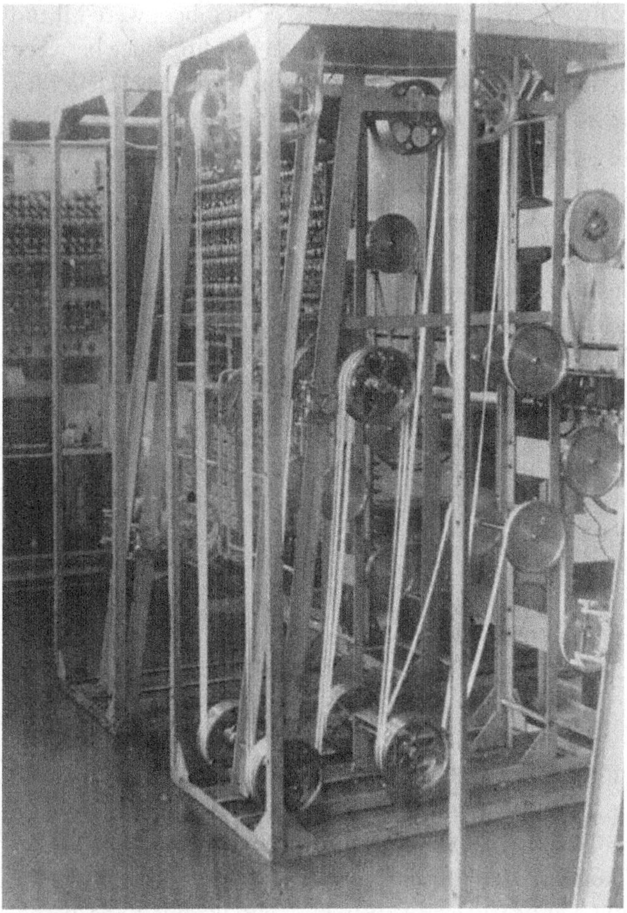

Figure 1.2 (continued)

stressed the paper media to the breaking point. As a last resort, glue was used to repair tapes when they broke, even though pieces of tape sometimes flew all over the room if they had been spinning at a high speed. The WRNS workers would collect the pieces and meticulously put them back together. "We went into a very huge room where they produced the tapes and repaired them. We had Bostick, and we used to Bostick them together," recalled Eleanor Ireland.[49] Even when they did not break, stretching of the tapes could produce erroneous results. Handling the input and output of the machine, in addition to designing their runs and programming them, was a delicate and complicated process requiring both skill and hard-won tacit knowledge. WRNS members were all too aware that the outcome of their work could mean the difference between life and death for British soldiers serving at the front, as well as for the civilians being bombed on the home front. Given that these young women had family and friends in the line of fire, the idiosyncracies of their machines were as frightening as they were frustrating.

Max Newman, who was insulated from the problems of running the machinery that made up his unit, requested more Heath Robinson machines be built in order to speed codebreaking. However, the solution to the problems of these unwieldy and inaccurate machines was not simply more of the same. In the opinion of leading Post Office engineer Tommy Flowers, the only way to speed the pace of codebreaking further—and enhance accuracy—was to use an all-electronic computer. This presented major problems, however, because it had never been done before and there was no time for a proof of concept. In the United States, the ENIAC project was barely off the ground. Indeed, ENIAC would not be functional, nor be public knowledge, until after the war, and its uptime for computing would not be reliable and productive until well after that.[50] In addition, ENIAC was focused on completely different computing objectives: It was designed for mathematical computation for ballistics trajectories, not logical programming required to break codes.

Flowers faced an uphill battle to get approval for his project. Aside from the Heath Robinsons, only electromechanical machines like the Bombes had been used consistently for codebreaking success on both sides of the Atlantic. Newman was sure a machine with thousands of vacuum tubes would not work reliably. Statistically, he reasoned, some of the tubes would be failing at nearly every given moment, leading to perpetual downtime and a machine that was effectively unusable. Plus, owing to wartime shortages, the vacuum tubes and other supplies needed to construct such a machine were scarce—as was money. Although Flowers was eventually given enormous leeway and resources, he later revealed that he also spent significant amounts of his own money in order to complete the project.[51]

Wrens Shoulder a Colossus: Britain's Secret Technological Revolution

In late 1943, Flowers and his team completed a behemoth of his own design that contained well over one thousand vacuum tubes.[52] Dubbed the Colossus, it took Newman and his machine codebreaking section by surprise.[53] It manipulated data electronically, obviating the need to compare two high-speed punched tapes.[54] The data was still fed into the machine using high-speed punched tape, however, contributing to an extremely noisy working environment that was a far cry from later electronic computing installations. By running a lower current than normal through the machine's many vacuum tubes, and never turning the machine off (since most tubes failed during the stresses of warming up or cooling down), Flowers was able to ensure a level of consistent, reliable uptime that would be unheard of in other computer installations until well into the 1950s. With this machine, Tutte's statistical method, which was essentially a way of brute-forcing codebreaking by trying a huge number of possible solutions at extremely high speed, suddenly became a reality. Colossus allowed a method that had been theoretically sound but, up until this point, impossible in practice to become the best tactic available for breaking Lorenz code. Immediately after seeing the first Colossus's capabilities, Newman asked for more. By the war's end, there were ten of the massive, room-sized Colossus computers at Bletchley, operated around the clock by close to three hundred WRNS recruits.

The WRNS programmed Colossus using switches and plug boards in order to electronically emulate the different wheel and pin settings of the encryption machines. When Colossus arrived in January 1944, it took over the role of finding the patterns and wheel settings for the Tunny machine from the Heath Robinson.[55] Able to process twenty-five thousand characters per second, Colossus I and II provided critical, nearly real-time intelligence for the D-Day landings. Colossus II in particular was instrumental in allowing the Allies to get the information they needed to launch a successful offensive: The information it decoded allowed Allied forces to see that the German Army was moving away from the Allies' planned landing site, having been fooled by intentionally leaked information that said Allied armies would be elsewhere. Yet Colossus II was not a smoothly working upgrade that effortlessly expanded the Allies' information arsenal. It was installed less than a week before D-Day, under extreme pressure and suboptimal circumstances. Flowers's team worked nonstop to get it operational. Once it was, the operators had to wear thick rubber boots so as not to be electrocuted by the machine, because the machine room floor had flooded.[56]

Because of the complexity of the encrypted code, the WRNS operators used each Colossus to break a different level of encryption. Operators had to repeatedly set and reset the machines and manage paper tape input and output for each run. The harried pace and makeshift machine rooms contributed to a frenetic environment in which workers had to contend with high levels of noise and improper ventilation even before the installation of the Colossus computers.[57] When Colossus came, these problems were magnified: The computer made a significant amount of noise owing to the high-speed paper tape input. Performing precise work under extreme time pressure was particularly arduous in such surroundings. Since each Colossus had well more than a thousand vacuum tubes, which were never switched off in order to preserve their longevity, they significantly raised temperatures in the non-air-conditioned machine rooms. While cooling off with coworkers outside the boiling hot Colossus room one night, Dorothy Du Boisson (pictured in figure 1.3, on the left) recalled a male coworker suggested she and her fellow operators should go topless. But, she added dryly, "we did not take up the offer."[58] In their off hours, contaminated water, poor heating, and noisy living quarters heightened the stress for WRNS workers. In addition, because WRNS supervisors outside the park were unaware of the skilled, nonphysical nature of the work being done, they demanded mandatory morning drilling, which resulted in exhaustion and illness for many workers until their supervising officers were eventually told to stop the drills.[59]

Figure 1.3
WRNS members working on a Colossus. The workers have been identified as Dorothy Du Boisson (left) and Elsie Booker by historian B. Jack Copeland. I. J. Good, D. Michie, and G. Timms, *General Report on Tunny with Emphasis on Statistical Methods*, 1945. Courtesy of the UK National Archives.

Like many other women in Bletchley's data-processing edifice, Colossus operators worked around the clock, in three eight-hour shifts, alternating shifts on a weekly basis. Each woman was allowed to leave only one weekend a month. Many worked extra hours, to the point of exhaustion, especially during times of exceptional need. These difficulties were shared by all WRNS members and indeed all Bletchley staff, not just those working in the Newmanry. At one point, the entire teleprinter transmission staff worked twenty-four hours straight without any break to keep up with the volume of intercepted messages.[60]

A typical work shift in the codebreaking section utilized seven cryptographers and sixty-seven WRNS workers, with one or two of the men cryptographers supervising. (There was only one cryptographer at Bletchley who was a woman: Joan Clarke. She is perhaps best known, despite her accomplishments, for being Alan Turing's "beard" for a short time.) Most of the WRNS members on a shift would work as Tunny or Colossus operators, about twenty for each type of machine, while two would operate Robinson machines and seven functioned as registrars. Because of the secrecy surrounding British wartime intelligence, the exact number of people involved with the Colossus computers and their precise roles may never be known. In 2014, Joanna Chorley, a former Colossus operator, found perhaps the only remaining photograph of thirty-nine of the operators who were present at Bletchley near the end of the war.[61] Another woman, Margaret Bullen, came forward the same year to talk about how she and other women wired up one of the Colossus machines and soldered together its connections in order to prepare it for the WRNS to use it, showing that despite previous assumptions women did perform computer maintenance and engineering work at the park.[62]

In the machine rooms, the women who worked as registrars were critical to successful, efficient codebreaking. Their job was to record and schedule the computers' work assignments so that the problems to be solved were arranged in order of priority and also would flow onto the machines at a constant rate to maximize the available computer power. The registrars had some of the most important work at the park—they needed to quickly solve ever-changing logistical and operational problems under extreme time pressure. While the "details of Tunny Room and Colossus jobs were left to the operators concerned," the work was orchestrated by the registrars and "returned to them on completion," noted the definitive report on operating procedures.[63] The registrars called the shots, even though the WRNS members who operated the machines had a significant amount of responsibility and autonomy. Everyone at Bletchley felt their responsibility acutely, knowing that work slowdowns translated into more civilian and soldier deaths. Hard-won breakthroughs made a huge difference to morale: "There was a great deal of jubilation when we broke one particularly important link," recalled Du Boisson, adding that "to celebrate, someone decorated the room with daffodils."[64]

Killing the Golden Geese

Churchill famously described Bletchley's workers as the "geese who laid the golden eggs but never cackled."[65] His metaphor contained an implicit reference to the WRNS—the dutiful "birds" in the nest of the nation's codebreaking operations. But narratives of women's heroism nonetheless downplayed or obscured the levels of skill and training required for their work. Far from being deskilled functionaries, the WRNS were essential to the nation's cryptanalysis and codebreaking efforts.

The official report of the work at Bletchley Park, kept secret until 2000, stated that several members of the WRNS "showed ability in cryptographic work."[66] Despite this, none were promoted to cryptanalyst positions.[67] Most possessed what was somewhat condescendingly described as "cheerful common sense," but some were trained to test the machines, inaugurating them into a different level of work responsibility from the role of operator.[68] Prior to testing the Colossus computers, WRNS workers were also responsible for testing the majority of the Bombes.[69]

Indeed, all operators needed to understand the Tunny machine and Colossi well enough to be able to fix minor breakdowns, both for reasons of convenience and because of the shortage of official maintenance engineers, all of whom were men. The male-oriented nature of apprenticeship to engineering maintenance work created a dire shortage of maintenance engineers for Bletchley's machines. As a result, a special nationwide program of recruitment for engineering trainees was established for sixteen- to nineteen-year-old boys. These very young men with no experience were seen as a better investment than women who already worked with the machines because they were expected to have much longer careers, justifying the training involved.[70] Innate ability was not a factor. Throughout the war, supervisors struggled to decide on how much to gender jobs in the midst of crisis; an April 1942 report from Bletchley Park investigated the "number of new posts that can be filled by women" and stated the percentages women should take up for each job class.[71] Hand and machine computing work formed the majority of the posts deemed suitable.

The official report of Bletchley's codebreaking operations stated that "wrens (unlike men) were organized in fixed watches and given fixed jobs in which they could become technically proficient," but the accounts of the WRNS members themselves differed from this characterization.[72] "We had to be versatile," said Du Boisson. Initially operating Colossus under the direction of a cryptographer who told them the settings required for the run, the WRNS members soon took responsibility for finding the settings themselves, "freeing the cryptographer for more important work." Another Colossus operator recalled that she was taught to operate the machine by a fellow WRNS member rather than a supervisor.[73]

Training agendas at Bletchley reflected the fact that the machine work conducted by women was central to codebreaking. Arriving members of the WRNS were given two weeks training in binary math, the teleprinter alphabet, sight-reading punched paper tapes, and the structure and workings of the Tunny and Colossus machines.[74] One Bletchley codebreaker recalled Bletchley as a sort of "high-pressure academy."[75] Chosen for their posts by interview, all WRNS workers had passed secondary school mathematics exams, and 9 percent of them had been to university. Over one-fifth had a Higher Schools Certificate, 22 percent had had some previous training, and 28 percent had previous work experience.[76]

WRNS members were also included in the park-wide program of further education for all workers. Printed and oral lectures were organized by a team of one or two cryptanalysts and several members of the WRNS for both men and women working at Bletchley. "It was the policy of the [machine codebreaking] section that all its members should be encouraged to interest themselves in all its activities and to improve their theoretical knowledge," the official report on Colossus noted, because "in practice it became increasingly hard for wrens to get a complete picture of an organization in which they might only have done one job."[77] By 1945, regular lectures aided WRNS workers in becoming better codebreakers as the war drew into its final, grueling stage. These theoretical, mathematical lectures and seminars were "a complete success" for the Colossus operators. The same training was given to new young men recruited for the ostensibly higher-level codebreaking work that did not involve machines.[78] The mounting exigencies of war increasingly destroyed the logic behind gendered training, especially as women outnumbered men by an ever wider margin.

Interestingly, men who supervised machine work were there less to facilitate the work or give guidance to the operators, and more for their own benefit. Park leaders felt male cryptographers came up with better theoretical insights when they alternated their cryptographic research with practical, applied work.[79] Machine work—and the theory and skills it required—was an integral component both intellectually and functionally of the codebreaking process. It was not, as many assumed due to its feminized nature, deskilled drudge work. Supervisory cryptanalysts worked hard to maintain an atmosphere of egalitarian teamwork. One WRNS member who worked under Max Newman recalled that on arrival he decreed everyone working under him should call each other by their first names.[80]

Intelligence jobs dominated by women that were positioned as peripheral to the main activities of Bletchley—like the high-speed slip readers at other installations who copied enciphered traffic from radio transmissions in real time—were also skilled and, during wartime at least, recognized as "highly trained."[81] In a particularly striking example, the "speed of decoding" in the section headed by Major Twin was more than three times slower simply due to a lack of skilled typists: "A Hut 8 girl can do in 2 hours what Twin can decode in 6–8 hours—on one day traffic took 18 hours."[82] Although women workers like these helped prove the value and ensure the success of the earliest electronic computing systems, secrecy surrounding wartime codebreaking operations often submerged these narratives and hid their importance.[83]

Despite the importance of the work they did, machine codebreakers often did not even know which arm of the German military had produced the codes they broke.[84] Workers at Bletchley could only guess what was going on in other sections of the park since projects were atomized for security. They pieced together a picture of the larger military strategy from odds and ends of gleaned information. Secrecy was taken so seriously that many Bletchley machine operators remained silent for decades. When issued her security pass on arrival, Eleanor Ireland recalled that she was instructed to protect it with her life.[85] "We came out of there fairly traumatized by the whole thing," she recalled.[86] Forbidden to speak about their work or location under penalty of imprisonment, no one at the park was allowed to ask anyone in another Bletchley unit what he or she did.[87] Colossus operator Catherine Caughey lamented, "My great sadness is that my beloved husband died in 1975 without knowing what I did in the war."[88] Even Tommy Flowers could make little use of his wartime electronics experience because of the secrecy surrounding his successes.

These extreme security measures continued to influence the historiography of labor and technology for decades after the war, paradoxically ensuring that British accomplishments went down in history as also-rans in a US-centric story of early electronic computing. One high-speed wireless operator and Morse slip reader in the telecommunications wing of Bletchley worked only "steps" away from the Bombes and Colossi, yet like most of the world she did not know of the machines' existence until bits of information began to trickle into the British press in the late seventies.[89] Conversely, the codebreakers knew nothing about the vital information transmission that allowed them to break codes. Even well into the nineties, the curators of the Bletchley Park museum were unaware of the existence of this wireless operator's telecommunications unit or the critical nature of this data transmission work in the codebreaking information chain.[90]

Notwithstanding their abilities and their experiences as the first electronic computing workforce in the world, most of these workers were made redundant at the war's end. One woman from the wireless transmission section at Bletchley tried to make a career in industry after VE day. Having been given over a year's training as a high-speed wireless operator while in the Women's Auxiliary Air Force, she was well qualified. Yet her plans evaporated when she found, to her surprise, that the main cable company was now only accepting men.[91]

The operators of the Colossus computers likewise dispersed to other jobs for the most part, according to available records. Most operators went on to work in fields that were unrelated or only tangentially related to their pioneering computing work, though not for lack of interest. After being ordered to break up their machines into pieces "no bigger than a man's fist" by Churchill's edict at war's end, the WRNS workers were made to again sign the Official Secrets Act and sternly ordered to remain silent. Refusing to accept the total erasure of their work, some secretly snatched mementos from the wreckage. Eleanor Ireland remembered grabbing and concealing a "little, blue" vacuum tube that she treasured for years afterward.[92] At the same time, two Colossus computers survived and were transferred to GCHQ for top secret use throughout the 1950s and into the 1960s. Although records indicating what personnel may have transferred with them are scarce or in some cases still closed to researchers, it is reasonable to infer that at least some WRNS members helped set up the machines at GCHQ. The tacit knowledge built up by the WRNS during the war had become a necessary component in this computing system—no one else knew the practical ins and outs of programming and operation for the machines as well as they did. Even Tommy Flowers had destroyed his schematics of the machines as ordered, meaning that the secret knowledge contained in workers' heads took on an even greater value.

Questions about Colossus operators' postwar roles aside, however, not all of Bletchley's women information workers were discarded or submerged by government secrecy at the end of the war. The fact that the experiences of women shunted out of the field at war's end have expanded to define the texture of women war workers' treatment obscures the important continuities and connections between wartime and peacetime information technology systems and the workers who ran them. In fact, the focus on the Colossus computers runs the risk of rendering invisible many of the other continuities in computing after the war.

The Girls in the Machine

For the most part, the end of the conflict meant a loss of status and opportunity for the many women who had become a critical component of the nation's information infrastructure. Postwar unemployment for women was worsened by "a recurring demand that such jobs as were available should be reserved for men, and women should go back to the home, whatever that might mean," observed the head of the TUC Women's Conference after the war.[93] The temporary reprieve from many gendered job classifications given to women by the government's conscription program was now over, but this was not a key factor in computing work, which had been gendered feminine even before the war.

As a state-building tool in times of stability and peace, as well as in times of war, computerization's history is largely a narrative of how the data-intensive state expands its reach and power by taking for granted, and rendering invisible, ever-greater numbers of information workers.[94] The work itself was meanwhile constructed as feminized and deskilled despite its apparent complexity. When information about the Colossus computers began to become public in the 1970s after being kept secret for decades, women's work with these computers was assumed to be low level and lacking in any significant skill and responsibility. Conceived of as a passive support role to the "real" work of codebreaking, rather than an integral part of the codebreaking itself, women operators paradoxically found themselves and their work undervalued in histories that were being rewritten to privilege the role of the computers they ran. The lower esteem in which women's labor had long been held resulted not only in unequal opportunities and pay, but also in the perception that the work being done by women was somehow implicitly lower in skill and importance. As Annie Burman has noted in her study of gender segregation in codebreaking work at Bletchley, "the discursive conviction of women's inferiority" and the ways in which women's work was discussed using terms that removed their agency and expertise, even down to the practice of calling them girls instead of women, has made it easy to "fall into the trap of assuming that systems built on degrading jobs given to women" actually made these jobs less important.[95] This remained the case even in situations where the work was materially similar or completely identical to work done by men. The double-edged sword of feminization both helped and hurt the progress of computing early on, as it defined understandings of how to structure and deploy large-scale computational projects.

Before the war, the most complex and important administrative and accounting work of the government was handled by room-sized punched card installations. From payroll and pensions to the compilation of census statistics, punched card systems defined how much data the state could manipulate and how quickly and well it could produce and utilize this new information. These systems—made up not only of machines, but also of workers, expertise, and finely tuned processes—redefined the government's scope, creating the capabilities of the modern state. The expansive, data-reliant economic and social programs that characterized modern British and Western European states grew in tandem with computing capabilities. Nationalized healthcare systems, social welfare systems, and the complicated taxation regimes that supported them—not to mention the collection, storage, and manipulation of census data required to ascertain how to provision these resources—all required steadily increasing data-processing power. During wartime, increasingly automatic, systematized information processing saved the state; during peacetime, it expanded it.

Yet after the war, women's war work was firmly constructed as Taylorized and skill-less—a discourse that began even during the conflict. One letter writer to the *Times* said what most felt when he called women "runs of the industrial commonplace" who were only able to work in war manufacturing because the processes had been broken down into smaller, simpler pieces.[96] For evidence regarding the recent public perception of women's wartime computing work, one need look no further than the London Science Museum's 2012 exhibit on wartime codebreaking. The museum descriptions state that Bletchley's "machines operated around the clock." Rather than saying *who* operated the machines around the clock, the exhibit removed the presence and agency of the operators and made the machines seem far more automatic than they actually were. Another description states that women "tended" the machines, rather than more accurately stating that they operated, troubleshot, tested, programmed, repaired, and even helped build them.[97] In a similar example of erasure, the two WRNS members in the only surviving picture of a Colossus being operated are not named in any of the exhibits at the UK's Bletchley Park Historical Site and National Computing Museum, although their identities are known.[98]

Press accounts of the time made sense of women's wartime accomplishments by using the conceptual umbrella of the "home front," which downplayed the major dangers and privations involved. Over fifty thousand Britons were killed on the home front during aerial bombing raids. For 1940 and 1941, the years of heaviest civilian casualties, civilian deaths accounted for nearly one-third of all wartime deaths, and during the height of the Blitz more casualties were recorded in Britain than for British forces deployed elsewhere.[99] The many women who sustained wartime injuries and disabilities received lower payments from the government than men.[100] Their treatment reflected a long-standing, ostensibly commonsense notion that women needed less and contributed less in work and public life.

At the same time, automating technologies increasingly deployed in offices during the twentieth century were creating a postindustrial labor landscape firmly divided upon gendered lines. As British feminists used the war to advocate for equal pay and equal treatment, the developing technological infrastructure organizing peacetime data processing worked to subtly undercut their efforts. The process of further computerization reflected and helped strengthen patterns and expectations that demanded women's labor be seen as secondary or tertiary within the very technological hierarchies where it was a foundational element.

In 1944, the wartime Womanpower Committee and affiliated groups of women workers mounted a major push for equal pay in the Civil Service as a result of the war.[101] The thin end of the wedge was asking for payment of equal injury claims to women who had sustained war injuries. Because women were paid only a percentage of men's wages, the government likewise only gave them a percentage of the men's payment for wartime injuries. The committee sought to change this, but gendered economic logic of this kind was widespread and ingrained. Indeed, it structured the economy, because government and industry took unequal pay scales as a precedent and guide for other payments—from injury claims to pensions.

Key to attacking unequal pay was changing the terms of women's labor from being temporary and supplementary. The repeal of the marriage bar—the rule banning married women from keeping their jobs in the Civil Service (the nation's largest employer), nationalized industries, and as teachers—was a critical first step. Separate women's pay scales throughout industry and government continued to economically reinforce assumptions about women's dependence. Equal pay campaigners, working since before World War I, were unable to give the government enough compelling reasons to enact a moral abstraction of equality, which many assumed would be economically and culturally disadvantageous in practice. As a result, the war left the economic and legal structures that institutionalized women's dependence and their limited opportunities in the labor market largely intact.

Even in clerical and administrative work, a steadily feminizing category, women workers lost out. A clear example was the fate of women civil servants after the war, because "perhaps as much as 50 percent to 100 percent of the established [permanent] complements" had been replaced by temporary women workers due to emergency hiring during the war and postwar reorganization.[102] Many wartime women temps lost their jobs after the war, because the government would only agree to retain temporary women in 15 percent of all vacancies in the postwar reconstruction of the service. Although the staff negotiated for a general examination to allot the permanent posts—after all, the Civil Service was an exam-based meritocracy—the government refused. Instead, the responsibility of choosing candidates was given to the department heads, a system that powerfully reinstilled cultural biases into the structure of the state's institutions.[103]

As a head of the TUC Women's Conference observed after the war, unemployment for women was worsened by the end of hostilities because "women were regarded as a sort of auxiliary force which, to use a military term, was expendable in time of crisis." This created a topsy-turvy world for women workers.[104] For them, the crisis period in which they became expendable and had to struggle to find work was peacetime. Women trade unionists bristled at the prospect of losing opportunities afforded by World War II, and many other women longed for the opportunities that war brought. Mary Coombs, perhaps the first woman to work in commercial, rather than government, computer programming, recalled that she "half hoped the war would last long enough to join up" when she was in school.[105] Much of women's wartime training became wasted—not because they chose to drop out of the workforce, but because they were no longer considered good candidates to hire when men returned to the labor pool.

Only in certain jobs—ones that both retained a feminized image and suffered labor shortages—did women have a fighting chance. The most important exception to this lack of labor continuity for women as the war ended was within administrative and scientific computing, fields where women still retained their status as the favored labor pool. This exception seems on the surface to be a simple continuity from before the war, but in fact it was an important outlier in a context where most women—even those in feminized jobs like clerical work—found themselves fired or struggling to stay employed at the war's end. The gender continuity in the realm of nonelectronic computing was emblematic of a larger changeover to a postindustrial information economy in the second half of the twentieth century, a time when women's labor would play an ever greater but paradoxically more hidden and devalued role.

Although the Colossus operators dispersed after destroying their machines, the many "local girls" hired to run the Hollerith equipment at Bletchley alongside the WRNS members—the "girls" who not only operated but also programmed the machines using plugboards after writing up the programs by hand—did not disperse and disappear. Instead, they went on to work in jobs of similar complexity and content in the same field: "At the end of the war with the setting up of GCHQ it was proposed that a Hollerith installation should be included in the organization, together with the personnel who had worked under Freeborn at Bletchley, and who might wish to continue in this type of work," wrote Ronald Whelan, the head of the Hollerith installation.[106]

The Government Communications Headquarters (GCHQ), known as the Government Code and Cipher School until the end of the war, had played a critical role in intercepting and collecting enemy military information to create actionable wartime intelligence. Therefore, the invitation extended to the Bletchley Hollerith operators to continue their work after the war, in the context of GCHQ, represented an incredible opportunity. Here, women could do relatively important work even after the cessation of hostilities. However, for this the staff needed to become civil servants, taking the exams for entry into the service's complex, nominally meritocratic hierarchy. The women who had proven their worth doing this work during the war under extreme pressure and hardship still needed to prove their abilities according to the government's peacetime standards. The women could compete for places in the Civil Service's prestigious exam-based meritocracy, with no guarantee they would get the jobs. The dynamics of Civil Service hiring were complex and often used quotas to hold down the number of entrants in a given job class. "Providing those wishing to take this step were judged to be suitable" according to government standards, they would transition into secure, life-long jobs in the government's service. It was with pleasure and relief that Whelan was able to report "that those who wished to do so" had been judged to be up to snuff, and "duly became civil servants."[107]

With that, an influx of several hundred workers transferred from wartime operations to peacetime government administration in one of the largest single blocks of wartime workers—and certainly the largest block of wartime intelligence workers—transitioning en masse into the peacetime economy. Although other women lost their jobs, these women were important enough to keep theirs, because they were harbingers of the shape of things to come. GCHQ's "Hollerith girls" became part of a high-stakes, highly gendered technocracy, forged in the crucible of war, that would continue to define British government and society until the century's end. They became some of the first and highest-level computing workers in a technological hierarchy that would use women exclusively to form the broad base of the information technology pyramid. These war workers, though not privy to the top-secret electronic computing work that had gone on during the war, represented the lion's share of workers in computing at the time: women who worked with electromechanical calculating and data-handling systems.

Electromechanical systems would continue to define the shape of industry and government—and the possibilities of administrative computing for many years to come—even as electronic systems became commercially available. The content of this work was very similar, and the skills required for it virtually identical to what was required for early electronic computer installations in the 1950s. As a result, it was a training ground for early computer workers, and many women in jobs like these went on to operate and program electronic computers. That these computing workers were repositioned in the peacetime context of the state's meritocratic bureaucracy as the war ended, specifically as a result of their war work, makes them a key example of how swords were turned to plowshares in computing. Although the technological disjuncture caused by the destruction of the Colossus computers is well known, the process by which wartime computing labor transitioned into the peacetime context is less well known.

The experiences of these women not only powerfully contradict the general assumption that all women left or were forced to leave their war-related jobs at the end of the war, but they also show how women were able to continue in computing specifically as a result of their war work. Their experiences and their machines—though less glamorous and groundbreaking than the Colossus operators and their faster, state-of-the-art machines—represent a clear continuity between wartime and peacetime computing labor and correct the misperception of electronic computing as somehow a separate class of work from electromechanical computing. In fact, there was significant continuity and convergence when it came to electromechanical and electronic computing labor.

Although women faced a postwar labor market in which employment opportunities were not of a similar level of complexity or responsibility, they did not disappear from computing with the return of men from the front, as is sometimes assumed, or with the destruction of the earliest productive electronic computing system, whose practical success they had helped ensure. The Hollerith operators remained as key participants in the emerging data-driven state. After the war, they became integrated into a system that would be no less complex, and far larger, than all wartime intelligence gathering.

As high-ranking civil servants retooled the technological infrastructure of the state for peacetime, an emerging technological regime based on ever-greater computing power would have a critical impact on women's labor equality. Because peacetime computing in the service of the state would rely on strictly gendered labor categories even more than wartime computing had, women's labor would become configured as supplemental rather than foundational, even as this labor continued to form the backbone of the country's data-processing systems. So taken for granted were these technical women workers that they became seen as part of the computing system itself. As more massive, more complex, and faster data-processing systems took hold in government and industry, these workers were consolidated into an essential underclass of non-working-class, sub-white-collar office labor. This classification would have an impact on the long-term productive capacity of the nation as a whole in significant and unexpected ways.

Nowhere were the fraught gendered dimensions of the transition from a war to a peacetime economy—and the role these dimensions played in women's lives—more apparent than in the Civil Service. The Civil Service would become ground zero for the changes in computing labor that would define women's position in the new technology landscape as not only subordinate but as fundamentally separate from their male peers. Starting in the immediate postwar years, gendered labor reorganization in conjunction with technology defined the government's vast workforce and the fiber of its institutions for decades to come. Yet because of the Civil Service's unique position as a nominally meritocratic sphere under the government's direct control, it was also the most logical place for labor reformers to try to address the pressing gendered labor inequalities that defined these jobs.

Equal Pay, Marriage Bars, and Dead-End Machine Work

Women's growing numbers and their potential power in the white-collar labor market were fast becoming seen as one of the biggest threats to the national order since industrial labor organization. The government particularly feared that long-established labor hierarchies would be upended and that huge costs would ensue if the persistent campaign for equal pay in the public sector could not be squelched. Before equal pay, however, another issue stood in the way of postwar women's worth: the marriage bar. In government as well as industry, women were required to leave their jobs upon marriage. Legally, the practice should have been abolished by the Sex Disqualification Removal Act of 1919, which aimed to eliminate exclusion from jobs on the basis of sex or a woman's marital status.[108] The 1919 act was broad and ambitious, but it was unevenly applied and it contained no enforcement machinery. One of the earliest legal claims brought under the act, against the practice of firing married teachers, was denied outright.[109] Even aristocratic women were unable to use the law to their advantage: In 1922, the daughter of Lord Rhondda tried and failed to get permission take the place in the House of Lords bequeathed to her by her father.[110]

In white-collar professions, women made uneven gains; the legal profession and accountancy opened their doors to women at this point, but the Civil Service, the nation's largest employer, continued to forbid married women from continuing their careers. Even though it had long been described as a "fair field with no favor," the Civil Service required women to resign on marriage, thereby mandating inequality of opportunity.[111] Relaxed during World War II, the rule was swiftly reinstituted at war's end. Baroness Beatrice Nancy Seear, a labor reformer who worked in government and industry, recalled that in the Civil Service at war's end, "those women had to be out of the men's departments at the speed of light," even though there was no danger "that men wouldn't get their jobs back."

The 1919 act, along with the 1918 Representation of the People Act that gave the vote to a limited number of British women for the first time, seemed to come as a reward for women's dedicated war work on the home front during World War I and seemed to be a move to preempt the revival of the violent and disruptive tactics of the prewar suffrage movement. Women labor reformers hoped that the end of hostilities in the most recent war and women's wartime service could similarly work to their political advantage. Reformers like Seear saw "absolutely no excuse" for how women were made to leave their jobs after the war, noting: "It was just sheer status quo. And back these women had to go."[112] Women's paid work remained perceived as largely "incidental" rather than as economically or socially necessary.

This image clashed with the actual shape of the government's work force: Women accounted for over 66 percent of the main Civil Service clerical union after World War II.[113] Many married women did not receive an adequate wage through their husbands, and others were raised in a tradition of working, politically independent women. As the nation returned to prewar norms, the interests of women workers once again became submerged in trade unions and professional organizations dominated by men. Women thus had little power to present pay claims or other complaints to employers through their unions. Rather than continue to fight, observed Seear, many women "accepted a great deal of this. The national agreements had two rates, one for women and one for men ... They took it for granted."[114] In the aftermath of World War II, the government's attitude had changed little from just after World War I, when a War Cabinet report stated: "Girls and women have regarded their work as incidental rather than as a main purpose of their lives."[115]

This idea echoed in the government-commissioned Equal Pay Report of 1946, which stated that women were ancillary to the workings of the labor market: "It seems sensible to assume that virtually all *men* are and always have been and always will be in the market for employment. But experience shows that the proportion of *women* seeking employment is variable within limits in response to the influence of social forces" (italics mine).[116]

The attitudes of the Equal Pay Report and other similar government reports disciplined women into certain roles as much or more than they described women's actual roles. As a young woman, feminist reformer Enid Hutchison was mentored by women who had been allowed to achieve relatively high positions in the Civil Service and in industry owing to the demographic shifts created by World War I. Seeing these possibilities, Hutchison determined not to go into nursing or teaching—the jobs usually "meted out" to educated women in the early twentieth century—after finishing her university degree.[117] Raised in the weaving district of Lancashire, she was accustomed to a labor landscape in which working women only took time off temporarily to have children and did not end their careers upon marriage.

Although many women complied, willingly or not, with the regulation to resign their Civil Service posts upon marriage, a difficult-to-measure minority revolted. Some of these women got around the restriction by not obtaining a formal marriage license. Others used different kinds of subterfuge to try to travel a middle route. In bustling London, whose population peaked at nine million people after World War II, the anonymity of the crowd sometimes meant that women could hide their marriages.[118] Hutchison recalled that "there was always this thing, that if you married, then you had to have babies surreptitiously, as people did, be married surreptitiously as people could do in the London area ... You had to live a life where you couldn't really be known."[119] Women unable or unwilling to live this kind of secretive double life had few options. At age twenty-seven and "getting on in years," Hutchison herself gave in and married her longtime companion, also a government employee, who was unable to hide the engagement due to his relatively high position. Hutchison's supervisor was reluctant to lose a capable, trained employee, but she nonetheless fired Hutchinson in accordance with regulations when Hutchison refused to resign.[120]

Like many other women, however, Hutchison did not stop working after losing her job. She had worked her way up from "the lowest possible job that it *was possible to have* in the Ministry of Labour, a *temporary woman clerk III*" (emphasis in the original) and now restarted the process in industry. When she was able to return to government service due to the labor shortages of World War II, she recalled with exasperation:

> It was back again to the Temporary Woman III grade at the bottom of the heap. Once more you go to the bottom of the heap. ... I went to see the man in charge of the Assistance Board Offices, because I knew I could get a job straightaway there, really. And he said "The trouble is, you're married" ... And I said: "does that still operate? Isn't there a war on?" So he rang up his headquarters and he was told he could employ a married woman. Within a few months, all the staff were married women, and he was lucky to get them. But that was [still] the regulation. The regulation had not been changed![121]

War's end meant the return of the marriage bar. Given the large and growing proportion of civil servants who were women, this variation in treatment according to gender undercut the government service's meritocracy in the broadest sense. Some women were allowed to come back to work in the Civil Service after being forced to resign, but they were only allowed to return as temporary workers, at the lowest pay and skill grade. It was usual for women who had worked their entire adult lives to find themselves downgraded to the lowest rung on the career ladder after marriage, with no pension rights or other benefits, in both the public and private sector. The marriage bar did not so much prevent women from working as it prevented career progression.

Machines as well as people played into the decision to return to the marriage bar after the war. The government feared that removing it would negatively impact large swaths of lower-level workers doing machine work, with harmful overall results: "Staffs in the routine grades will be condemned to longer periods of monotonous work than if the marriage bar had been enforced." This work was thought to be so demoralizing that changing the rules of the Civil Service in a way that could keep workers there indefinitely would injure the very workings of the state itself: "Any general worsening of promotion prospects among the large bodies of staff engaged on routine work would, by its adverse effect on staff morale, be against the interests not only of the staff themselves but of the public service," warned the committee set up to reconsider the bar. Because this class of workers was growing by the year, the potential for it to become unruly and discontented seriously worried Civil Service executives.[122]

Class as well as gender played a role in the marriage bar. An interwar commission that considered the bar from 1929 through 1931 had argued that it should not be removed in the lower job classes—but perhaps in the higher classes.[123] This proposal helped the already privileged and continued to lay a burden on the least powerful. It showed how the government's unwillingness to rethink the valuation of its employees tended to widen divisions and strengthen inequalities even during the passage of reforms designed to lessen inequality. Later, with equal pay, this pattern would be repeated.

As a result, these reforms had disproportionate effects on women who worked with automating equipment in government and industry. Since the very machinery of the government bureaucracy relied on these temporary, low-paid workers, high turnover through forced resignation upon marriage was one way to ensure a constant supply of this indispensable, if undervalued, commodity. The marriage bar created a self-fulfilling prophecy of deskilled and expendable women workers; because women would resign on marrying, they were never given career opportunities that would encourage them to stay. "And as the time and expense spent on the training of those resigning is lost to the service, women as a whole are, for this reason amongst others, less valuable than men as a whole," reported the Whitley Council Committee—the body tasked with protecting workers' rights in the Civil Service.[124] That the body designed to protect worker rights viewed women as less valuable than men highlighted women's precarious position. Little wonder, then, that women were passed over for better training and more responsible work, confined instead to gender-segregated, partially automated work that was held in low esteem regardless of its actual content or complexity.

The 1944 to 1946 committee set up to consider equal pay pointed out that this system of widespread gendered job segregation flew in the face of the ideal of job "aggregation" that was supposed to allow Civil Service employees to navigate the career rungs of the Service's meritocracy. Aggregation was supposed to allow civil servants to move from one post to another across departments, and to be promoted in a consistent fashion even after changing jobs. For women, aggregation barely applied: "While in some Departments women are employed on the same duties and work side by side with the men, in others they are employed in separate branches and have separate avenues of advancement. ... The latter system, if rigidly observed, amounts to the reservation of certain posts to men and women respectively," the Royal Commission on Equal Pay noted.[125]

Immediately after the war's end, the government surveyed a variety of organizations—including city and local government offices, the nationalized industries, and private companies—and ultimately decided to lift the Civil Service marriage bar in 1946, though equal pay remained unaffected. They had failed to remove the bar before World War II, pointing to divided opinion within labor unions, but after the war the main clerical union vociferously supported the measure because its membership was now mostly women.[126] The British Broadcasting Corporation (BBC), London County Council, and Boots Drug Company also removed their marriage bars after the war, stating that no major disadvantage could be found in employing married women. Other national governments like the USA and USSR opposed the concept of a legal marriage bar, though their cultures encouraged it to different extents. Sweden, Denmark, and Finland also stood opposed. Meanwhile, Commonwealth countries like Canada, Australia, and South Africa returned to their prewar ban on married women workers.[127] Many large British employers, like the Bank of England, made a provision for married women whose husbands had

Figure 1.4
Cartoon from Mavis Tate, MP, Equal Pay Campaign Pamphlet, "Equal Work Deserves Equal Pay," 1954.

died during the war but reinstituted their overall policy of not employing married women, as did the four main railway companies, the Cadbury and Rowntree Co., and most local government offices.

The disaster the government feared from the marriage bar's repeal would turn out to be a phantom; a decade after repeal most women still continued to leave upon marrying. A cartoon from the 1950s (figure 1.4) poked fun at the depressing reason. In it a pretty, young woman, chained to her typewriter desk, declared her intention to marry a slovenly ne'er-do-well in order to escape: "You can't be worse than my job," she says, running toward him.[128] Stuck for the most part in positions that had little career potential, most women in government found the prospect of working after marriage understandably unattractive.

The government's expectation that women would resign on marriage aligned with a general perception of women workers as an elastic and incidental labor force who conveniently inhabited a holding pattern doing unpaid work in the home when not needed in the paid labor force. However, the idea that most women only required a wage until marriage masked a more complex situation. Seen as temporary workers, women were usually given less responsible jobs that were not likely to lead to careers. One woman trade unionist groused that "it was not for any high moral principles that [industry] was getting rid of their married women ... they wished to employ cheap labor," and employers often "seized on any opportunity to worsen the conditions of employment" for married women, on the assumption that a married woman already had the needed level of income through her husband.[129] As expendable labor, women's jobs often followed automating tools, and this in turn created organizational methods that kept their wages depressed.

In the context of growing postindustrial workforces, increasingly automated offices, and higher numbers of working women, resistance to removing the marriage bar had as much to do with economics as culture. Government ministers rightly conjectured that agitation for equal pay and promotion would increase once women's working careers were lengthened by the removal of the bar, and feared this would worsen labor problems. The new expenses of maternity leave, and pensions for greater numbers of women working after marriage, might significantly raise labor costs.[130] Lower-order Civil Service executives feared that the lack of turnover and promotion outlets in these feminized job grades could ignite a labor powder keg. It was an untenable situation.

As a result, shortly after the marriage bar's removal and on the recommendation of a government commission, the Treasury department, with its broad oversight over staff, orchestrated a change in the very structure of the Civil Service itself. Less than two years after the death of the marriage bar, the "machine grades" were created, and women's economic dependence on husbands was replaced by their economic dependence on machines. The latter dependence, just like the former, would ensure that women's wages remained depressed. This new class of machine-operating work would interact catastrophically with the campaign for equal pay: It would institutionalize the connection between low-paid women workers and computing for decades to come.

The Expansion of Computerization as a Tool of the State

In 1945, Alan Turing presented a proposal for an "Automatic Computing Engine" to the National Physical Laboratory. His paper outlined a stored-program electronic computer that would revolutionize data processing by vastly increasing the speed at which input and output could be run through the computing unit. Through eliminating "all that is done by the normal human operator" and transferring these functions to the machine, this system could vastly reduce what Turing called "the human brake."[131]

Turing's concept of a human brake on computers' efficiency and his research on how to circumvent it were early steps in the study of human–computer interaction. Through programming that could be stored inside the machine's memory, he reduced the human brake at the level of hardware, but the brake persisted elsewhere. As large computerized systems made up of machines, workers, and organizational entities grew, opportunities for "braking" multiplied—not everything could be subsumed by hardware.[132] The difficulty of dealing with the relationships between machines and humans inherent in computing systems could not be designed away. This would become a major stumbling block as the computer moved out of solely scientific and military operations and into a wide variety of commercial and governmental workplaces, its sphere of influence continually growing. The importance of the human brake would increase as faster digital, programmable computers designed with business and administrative applications in mind began to replace mechanical and electromechanical office-automation machinery.[133]

Defined by its wartime origins, electronic computing was arguably Britain's most critical twentieth-century project. Hidden, wartime computer operators had a growing analogue in peacetime: the "broad base" of the Civil Service's data-processing establishment, which rested on feminized and largely ignored classes of machine workers. As a tool in times of stability and peace, not just in times of war, computerization's history is largely a narrative of the expanding reach and power of the data-intensive state.[134] The peacetime organization and deployment of electronic computers within the government's Civil Service and the nationalized industries would soon become a microcosm of the nation's attempts to grapple with large-scale technological change.[135] Although the groundbreaking deployment of electronic machines by the British government remained secret for decades after the war, the labor patterns that allowed those systems to function persisted. The same gendered labor assumptions that helped Bletchley Park maximize its wartime codebreaking also strongly impacted how the national government organized automation and large-scale information-processing projects after the war. Although the war helped women gain greater opportunities and a springboard to argue for greater work equality, these benefits soon collided with the structural discrimination of the government's large-scale data projects.

As British offices and institutions computerized, the interaction of labor and management with new technology became essential to the maintenance and expansion of the government's power. Successive governments recognized harnessing the power of these early computing systems, which were often untested and unwieldy, as a crucial component of national progress. However, early electronic computers did not naturally lead to a streamlining of public sector bureaucracies. Human interaction with automated systems formed a critical facet of the history of early computing because the British government modeled the organization of new information systems on older office-automating machinery, which was in turn designed around a specific kind of deskilled, feminized labor force. Computer deployment in government would become unhelpfully fixated on the removal of the "human brake." Despite Britain's early lead in the field of computing, this labor landscape undercut the nation's "revolutionary" technological project.

Although women faced a postwar labor market in which higher-level technology jobs were very difficult to get, they also entered a labor landscape where their femininity marked them as machine workers. In this way, neither the war nor its end was a watershed moment for the gendering of computing labor. What the war had done, however, was put a spotlight on the dangers of having a gendered class structure that produced particular kinds of workers for different jobs. This gendered class structure resulted in a scramble to quickly retrain large numbers of women for the war effort. Once the labor shortages of wartime ended, however, these inequalities once again became a secondary concern. Until, that is, operators' labor once again became recognized as a critical part of the computing systems on which the nation relied.

2

Data Processing in Peacetime: Institutionalizing a Feminized Machine Underclass, 1946–1955

After the removal of the marriage bar in 1946, feminist labor activists turned their full attention to the issue of equal pay in the public sector. As women's numbers in the labor force grew, so too did their association with office work and computing in both government and industry. Gaining equal pay for the hundreds of thousands of women who worked for the government would have benefits far beyond those women immediately affected. Reformers knew that getting the government to agree to equal pay in the Civil Service would publicly establish the state's moral commitment to equality, which would put pressure on industry to follow suit.

As the nation tried to return to normality under Prime Minister Clement Attlee, however, the state believed its moral obligations to lay elsewhere. Labour under Atlee embarked on a vast series of reforms that would construct the expansive social safety net known as the welfare state. As part of the program to aid recovery, Atlee also nationalized the fuel, power, and steel industries, the railways, and the Bank of England, which made up over one-fifth of Britain's economy. He presided over a grim period of economic austerity; rationing still operated through the early 1950s, and bread—which was not rationed during the war—became rationed in peacetime. Britons faced significant hardships, from lack of housing to inability to heat their homes. At the same time, the nation lost global influence day by day, with its empire continuing to contract and its power sinking in relationship to the new superpowers of the United States and the Soviet Union. India's independence in 1947 was perhaps the clearest example of Britain's diminishing international reach and the need to reorient its role in the world.

Against this background, the government turned its full attention to the recovering home front with ambitious socialist policies aimed at minimizing want. Although Atlee used his power aggressively to try to equalize society and the economy, equal pay was not a part of Labour's plans to create a more fair and just Britain. Seen as a side issue, women's civil rights would only be addressed through reforms that preserved the status quo of gender inequality. Women now would be positioned as dependents of a paternalistic and patriarchal system of state benefits instead of as dependents on a husband's wage.[1] The government alternately argued that the state could not afford to grant equal pay and that women did not really need equal pay because of the enhancements afforded to citizens under the new social safety net.

At the same time, the period that followed the war saw a backlash toward anyone perceived as stepping outside the bounds of mainstream gender or sexuality. A crackdown on moral "laxity" began as the leniency of the war years evaporated. Police in London and other major cities began to aggressively patrol for prostitution and homosexual sex in public parks, private nightclubs, and elsewhere. Those seen as out of place or nonconforming faced increased scrutiny. Alan Turing, at work on the Manchester Mark I at the time, was perhaps the most famous figure to have been ensnared in this sudden change in standards. His experience powerfully showed the life-and-death nature state power could bring to bear on those who did not fit the normative ideals of gendered citizenship reemerging after the war.

Because the nation needed both to rebuild and to subsidize enormous, ambitious welfare state projects, efficiency became one of the highest concerns of the British state. The government's intense interest in enhanced productivity was reflected in the frenetic production of reports on productivity that it commissioned from the Department of Industrial Research. The Civil Service was also subjected to desperate cost-reduction measures. Despite price increases caused by the significant devaluation of the pound in 1949, the government froze pay for all civil servants in an effort to raise efficiency relative to outlay.[2] However, this action was not enough to make the needed difference, and the drive to reduce costs continued. Two factors came to form the basis of the government's efforts to hold down costs and enhance efficiency: women workers and automation.

When employed in high enough numbers, women's below-market-rate pay stabilized salary outlay at a lower level. At the same time, the government sought new automation solutions to try to stem the need to hire more civil servants. Used together, these tactics were to be a magic bullet for the government's rising labor costs. Institutionalizing the connection between machine work and unequal pay would become the single most important labor strategy in the government's plans to wring maximum efficiency from its workers, but it would also produce unexpected results. The process of turning swords to plowshares in the realm of automated work involved a return to a specific kind of normality: one in which computing was still mainly electromechanical and in which meritocratic ideals ignored gender and class discrimination in the workforce. The late 1940s and early 1950s would set the stage for the "high" technocratic era to follow in the 1960s and 1970s—an era in which the government hoped that computing technology would put the country back on track as a global, imperial power.

The changes in this period provide essential background for how, much later, computer programming aggressively altered from feminized work to a firmly masculine professional endeavor. In order to understand that gendered power shift one needs to understand how feminized machine work was engineered into the technocratic state in specific and discrete ways over a decade before. This chapter provides that background by painting a portrait of the class of machine workers on whose labor these systems were built and institutionalized. Many of these women stayed in their jobs for only a short time, and even those who worked for decades remain relatively faceless due to undervaluation of their work. They appear in the archival record as a group rather than as individuals and therefore must be historically analyzed as a class. This can help reconstruct how institutional strictures combined with cultural norms to shape more than just women's career paths: The entire edifice of the technological state depended on the development of this category of labor.

Ensuring High Turnover for Women Workers

In January 1937, the Civil Service Arbitration Tribunal heard a request brought by the Civil Service Clerical Association on behalf of the all-female typing grades. Since 1929, any civil servant in the typing grades who was required to take on the work of a higher post, due to the absence or overwork of a higher civil servant, would be entitled to extra pay only after performing the job for a period of six months. The official reasoning was that such a timeline provided a "qualifying" period for the temporary post holder, but six months was also the time limit for an absent employee to take paid leave. As a result, low-level women workers often fulfilled the duties of higher civil servants without any extra salary outlay on the Treasury's part. By the time the six-month training period was over, the absentee had usually returned. This created a situation in which women workers at the bottom of the labor pyramid perpetually took on the work of their supervisors without recognition or compensation.

The government balked at shortening the break-in period or paying stand-in employees more to do extra work, because it felt that "double payment ought not to be made for the same post."[3] As long as the former post holder was still drawing a salary, the Treasury resisted paying the current post holder for that work, irrespective of what she might deserve. Most stand-in employees never attained a higher wage or any of the promotion opportunities attached to the higher post.

The arbitration tribunal heard the complaint and quickly ruled in the Treasury's favor, preserving the current mode of operation. This practice exemplified the government's view of labor and pay equity in the mid-twentieth century: What mattered was what was most advantageous to the government as an embodiment of the state and its people, not what was most fair to the worker. In addition, with the marriage bar in place, most jobs that employed women had relied on turnover, rather than promotion, to cycle new workers in and older workers out. The government committee that had cautiously recommended the marriage bar's abolition in 1946 feared the disruptive effect the change would have on standard operating procedure, warning: "A decision to remove the marriage bar would also have complications of the utmost importance as regards the turnover of staff in the large routine grades which are *inevitably required* in the Civil Service. The amount of routine work is so great—and will continue to be so, in spite of increasing mechanization—that the Civil Service staff 'pyramid' is bound to have a very broad base, and *promotion to higher ranks cannot come to all*" (italics mine).[4]

The marriage bar had ensured that "a large number of women civil servants never enter the field of competition for promotion, since they resign on marriage after only a few years' service."[5] The bar had limited the career options available to women and encouraged managers to view them as black holes for career training regardless of how highly they scored on Civil Service exams, and removal of the bar did not automatically result in better prospects. Its removal could not undo ingrained patterns of labor discrimination or change the structure of the Civil Service, which relied heavily on low-level, high-turnover workers, especially to run its increasingly prevalent automated systems.

Without the turnover afforded by the bar, the proportion of available promotions in relation to workers was even further reduced. The government had feared that the effects of removing the marriage bar would be "violently resented" by male staff "whose prospects would thereby be worsened."[6] To prevent this situation, new measures for dealing with the large feminized classes of workers needed to be instituted; an underclass of women workers was in fact a key building block of the Civil Service's supposed meritocracy.

Making matters worse, through the mid-1950s civil servants faced a situation made harsher by government wage restraints designed to bolster the economy and stave off inflation. While rationing and shortages lingered on, the government undertook an "economy campaign," reducing the numbers of civil servants and cutting hundreds of thousands of pounds from government expenditure. The Foreign Office, a typical Civil Service department, saw £200,000 slashed from its spending through a mixture of staff and spending cuts.[7]

During austerity, Britons faced conditions that had not been vastly improved by the coming of peace. Rationing of food, fuel, and consumer goods stretched on, making a return to prewar standards of living impossible. Particularly in London, where the largest numbers of government workers were concentrated, shortages of fuel led to disaster in the winter of 1952. The high sulfur content from nutty slack—the low-quality home heating coal that had just come off ration—combined with stagnant weather conditions to create a deadly week-long smog. The lack of visibility produced by the smog brought all air, river, and ground transport in and out of London to a virtual halt, blackening the air so badly that policemen had to lead buses through the streets with flashlights. The seriousness of the "fog" ultimately led to Britain's first Clean Air Act in 1956, but it also produced thousands of fatalities.[8] The reliance on this low-quality coal was caused by the government selling more expensive, cleaner-burning coal abroad to ease the state's difficult financial position. Government workers mourned for the "many more victims of 'nutty slack,' or whatever it is which is carrying off the over-fifties" in their annual departmental reports that year.[9]

Although the government defended cutbacks as necessary to national recovery, many civil servants saw the conditions as emblematic of a larger devaluation of their work: "It can safely be stated that the government's declared policy of wage restraint finds little sympathetic echo among civil servants, many of whom reflect a trifle bitterly that had they 'listened to their Dads,' they might all have been good little, rich little coal-miners on a five day week."[10] Workers in nationalized industries like coal gained improved hours and wages, whereas government office workers in supposedly "better" jobs were stuck with the same "emergency" work week of 45.5 hours without overtime that had been instituted during the war.[11]

Even in the early 1950s, these workers still had to work a half-day on Saturday, unlike most workers in private industry. "How pitying, too, the remarks of outside employees who regard civil servants as 'the poor souls who traipse up to town every Saturday' and how galling for the poor souls themselves, who often suffer two hours traveling for three hours' work," lamented a staff association.[12] Civil servants had long considered themselves at the top of the labor hierarchy because they were nonmanual, professional workers with prestigious, lifelong government jobs. Now, they found themselves struggling.

For women workers, who made up 48 percent of the service at war's end, these privations were even more acutely felt.[13] The repeated concession of equal pay in theory—but not in fact—deepened their hardship while underscoring the unfairness of government wage controls and inculcating a distrust of the pay-negotiating tribunal, the National Whitley Council. Deprived of the right to strike due to their position as agents of the state, civil servants relied on the National Whitley Council to negotiate their terms of employment. A body created specifically to arbitrate the concerns of government workers, it was supposed to represent both the workers' and the government's sides equally. In truth, the government—and particularly the Treasury—had significant control over the nominally impartial proceedings. For instance, for years the government repeatedly refused to negotiate on equal pay, asserting that it was not a claim for wage increases but rather a matter of national policy and therefore outside the purview of the Whitley Council.[14]

Both equal pay campaigners and the postwar Labour and Conservative governments recognized the need to deal with the ever-growing labor relations problem created by unequal pay.[15] However, although the expansion of a female labor force enhanced pressure for equal pay, this same growth swelled the government's potential expenditure if it conceded. Operating with the aid of American-backed reconstruction loans and stung by the 1949 devaluation of the pound, the government considered the issue extremely reluctantly. Unequal pay was a major boon to the government as it struggled to raise productivity and lower costs.

The estimated outlay for the entire Civil Service itself in 1948 was nearly £2 billion. The maximum cost of equal pay placed it at barely more than 1 percent of the budget.[16] The 1945–1951 Labour government considered itself unable to muster the estimated £13–£25 million for equal pay[17] while spending hundreds of millions of pounds laying the foundations for the creation of new social services[18] and even upward of £40 million on the Tanganyika groundnut scheme, which has gone down in history as a classic example of a boondoggle.[19] That plan to grow nuts for oil in Africa was intended to solve the short-term problem of cooking oil rationing at home, but it was expensive and poorly thought-out. The government chose unsuitable areas of east Africa and sent wave after wave of men, supplies, and construction equipment. Even at the time, it seemed clear that the money hastily earmarked for the plan was little more than an expensive gamble. No nuts were ever grown since the British could not even successfully clear the land for farming. Dense vegetation destroyed the heavy machinery that had been transported to Africa specifically for the purpose. Given the relative costs, the argument that the government could simply not afford equal pay in the short term was disingenuous. Cultural priorities as well as economic factors determined the governmental response to the equal pay campaign.

Computer Labor before "Computers"

Prior to the widespread use of electronic computers, the machines used by the Civil Service were placed into four general categories: desktop accounting machines; punched card collators, tabulators, and punches; typewriters; and printing machines. The higher-volume and more complex recordkeeping required by the welfare state made government data processing ever more important to the national good. These machines were mostly electromechanical (rather than mechanical), and their forms ranged from desktop sized (for typing, punching, and certain accounting machines) to furniture sized (for punched card tabulators, collators, and output or reproduction machines). Most of the data crunched relied on large, room-sized punched card installations where operators moved from machine to machine. Tabulator and collator operators would work standing, sometimes overseen by multiple supervisors who might be women or men. Meanwhile, the women performing data input generally worked seated in large pools, overseen by a woman supervisor.

By the 1950s, when *Office Machinery* magazine declared that the accounting machine represented "the logical progression from the era of the typewriter and adding machine as separate entities," office machine work had become more complex than either typing or accountancy alone.[20] The work was envisioned as being limited and easy to train for, despite the reality that it required better-than-average levels of education.[21] Hiring managers sought women exclusively, and the jobs sustained low wages and limited promotion prospects. "Women operate these machines," assured one Powers-Samas article in a company magazine,

Figure 2.1
Later images of "Powers Girls" showed the advance of electromechanical, and then electronic, computing. *Vickers News*, January 1951.

adding that they handled "payroll and works statistics with great facility."[22] Company literature used both text and photographs to give managers a detailed picture of how women would handle every step in the data-processing chain.

The process of programming the electromechanical computers in punched card installations involved plugging up a board that either was attached to the machine or could be swapped in and out, allowing operators to quickly run programs they had set up on other boards. "Plugging a board is a fairly skilled operation that involves the connection of perhaps scores of leads, all of which must be put in the correct hole," wrote a consultant in a management and methods magazine.[23] In this sense, the plugboard-based programming was similar to the programming work done by WRNS working on the Colossus computers during the war, and the programming done by the ENIAC women.

After the machines were set up, operating staff loaded data on punch cards into a sorter, feeding in a specific series of control cards that contained instructions on how to sort and manipulate the data on the bulk of the cards. Cards were sorted at a rate of hundreds per minute using distractingly noisy machines. Made of a high-quality stock that could make several hundred passes through sorting and tabulating machines, these data cards had to be imported until the 1930s because British manufacturers were unable to produce cards of a sufficient quality.[24] Once the cards were sorted, women fed them in batches into an electromechanical tabulator that stored amounts in counters before recording the output to punched cards, paper tape, or, in some cases, a printer. In most punched card installations, employees rotated between tasks, except for the largest installations, where dedicated data-input staff was kept separate from other workers. Women data librarians kept the cards organized and filed for storage when a data set was not in use for a job, forming a kind of external, card-based computer memory bank.

At the most basic level, the data-processing chain for a punched card installation began with the process of transferring data onto cards from written lists or slips. Accounting information, civil engineering data, and customer profiles were just a few of the types of information sets that might be prepared. Through the use of punch machines with spring-loaded knife mechanisms, plus automatic feed and ejection, punchers could attain incredibly fast speeds of 300–400 forty-five-column cards per hour—or more than six cards per minute. Many workers could punch six holes per second, at an error rate of under 3 percent.[25] Packed into huge, factory-like rooms with dozens of other punchers, these women had to be able to tolerate noise and distraction while performing monotonous work accurately at a consistently high speed; it was crucial to the entire data-processing chain that punchers' work be virtually error-free. A low rate of error was a critical prerequisite to the functioning of massive data-handling systems, and therefore the lowly job of punching actually defined what was possible at the higher levels of automated work systems. Within the government, everything from auditing to the timely production of payroll, and from scientific analysis to economic forecasting relied on punchers' accuracy and speed. Even so, management believed punching did not require much intelligence or intellect and treated punchers accordingly.[26]

The Fiction of Deskilling

A government-wide inquiry found, to its surprise, that better-educated "grammar school girls" made much better punchers, able to produce consistently more characters per hour with higher accuracy.[27] Grammar schools, the more academically rigorous option for students within the state-run school system, generally helped boys move on to professional work or university. One accounting department supervisor wrote of his punchers: "Oddly enough the brightest manually, as well as mentally, came from the Harrowgate and Knaresborough grammar schools whereas girls coming from shop counter experience and from the council schools were less adaptable."[28]

Mounted by the Treasury, this investigation sought to determine whether the lack of manual dexterity tests in the Civil Service exams for young women candidates had caused the government to be "embarrassingly let down by getting girls who were naturally left handed or otherwise not trainable to machine efficiency."[29] It compiled detailed information on machines in use, the average speed of the operators, the average error rates, and the length of training required for maximum efficiency. The focus of the inquiry was on basic tests of dexterity, but the Treasury was surprised to find how much of a difference to punching speed and accuracy a better education made.[30] Although these jobs were seen as manual, the Treasury inquiry found they had an important intellectual component.[31]

Even so, the Treasury continued to see machine work as inferior, despite the fact that its findings showed the work required more than just vocational training.[32] Clerical workers resisted being downgraded to these jobs, particularly disliking the hectic, unforgiving job of punch operator: "There were several cases where Clerical Assistants proved to be definitely allergic to machine duties and it was found almost impossible to turn them into mediocre operators," noted one investigator.[33] Paradoxically, the less competent women civil servants who were unable to perform keypunch work to the high standard required were literally promoted out of it, into clerical jobs that came with higher status, better working conditions, and more opportunities for promotion. "The utterly useless from a machine point of view were not so numerous that they could not be absorbed into general low level clerical duties," wrote an executive in the Post Office Savings Bank's large accounting department.[34]

Training and time to reach maximum efficiency on accounting, punched card, and other machines varied from one month to six weeks, and the operators for each machine were far from interchangeable, due both to training and innate skills. Certain machines required workers with particular aptitudes, often referred to as "temperaments" in government documents discussing the selection of women employees: "Care is and has always been taken in choosing suitable officers to operate overprinting machines," for instance, noted the Post Office, because "the officers selected [are] required not only to be manually dexterous, but to be of a calm, steady nature and ... in fact temperamentally suited to get the best results from the machines."[35] Punchers, meanwhile, had to be able to tolerate noisy, boring, and monotonous work while remaining fast and accurate. When describing women workers, managers cloaked discussion of skill and talent in the language of temperament, subtly downgrading women's abilities by using language that implied emotional rather than intellectual suitability for the job.

Machine operators were largely ineligible for the pension benefits available to civil servants until the mid-1950s.[36] "Establishment" examinations, whose successful passage determined pension eligibility, were only given every five years for machine workers. This led one supervisor in the Stationery Office, which employed a large number of machine operators, to complain that operators were unfairly being treated as de facto temporary workers, warning that this fact could soon "detract from efficiency and output."[37] Positioning these jobs as transient had short-term economic benefits but created long-term problems in the forms of high turnover and constant retraining and reorganization.

By the early 1950s, an estimated one-third of all working Britons—close to 7.5 million people—were women, and many in the middle class and sometimes working class gravitated to higher-status, cleaner, and often better-paid work in offices.[38] Even well into the twentieth century, working as a domestic servant was one of the most likely jobs for a woman.[39] Women could work in factories, but entry into skilled trades was primarily reserved for boys. In 1951, only one in fifteen girls entering the workforce was apprenticed to a trade, whereas one in three boys apprenticed.[40] In this context, clerical work had growing potential as a career path for women, and many sought the higher-paying, more prestigious positions in the government's service.

Within the service, there was a huge range of of work. One could hold nearly any office job available in industry, and then some. Government clerical workers provided labor for the Post Office, which controlled the majority of British telecommunications through 1981 and was a testing site for much of the country's cutting-edge technology. The National Health Service also required ever-increasing numbers of administrative workers. The government employed nearly three quarters of a million workers in the Civil Service, well over double the number employed just two decades earlier and roughly three percent of the entire UK working population.[41] Despite increasing automation, the number of civil servants continued to rise. Long described as "a fair field with no favor," the service was supposed to eschew preference based on social standing by using a skills-based, examination-mediated meritocracy. Yet there were different qualifying examinations and different jobs to be examined for depending on whether the applicant was a man or a woman. Increasingly, the Civil Service began to institute a gendered class system built around computing work.[42]

The Mechanical Ceiling

The fact that machines were used to perform certain office work put that work slightly outside the pale of the supposedly clean and cerebral activities of the office. Women who performed machine work were regarded as more akin to light industrial workers than their clerical peers, alongside whom they worked and whose work responsibilities they often covered. This distinction between clerical and subclerical work was unclear and permeable, but it defined pay and career prospects for the majority of women in government work—most women were concentrated in these lower-level clerical grades.

In early 1948, as agitation for equal pay roiled, the Treasury took broad and drastic steps to reorganize the structure of work in the Civil Service, consolidating a feminized underclass of machine workers and codifying that change in the service's rules and promotion structures. "It has been decided," relayed the first Treasury circular of the year, "to create a specialist class of machine operators within the clerical/subclerical group." The new machine operator class, comprised of several different Civil Service job grades, would be an official women's class employed primarily on so-called subclerical work. "The duties of the class will cover all work on calculating, punch card, and accounting machines and will range from the simplest to the most complex work," announced the memorandum introducing the change.[43]

At first glance, this recategorization might not seem like a drastic or particularly important change. Women were already gathered near the bottom of the labor hierarchy. But in fact the Treasury's decision altered the work that women were allowed to do in the Civil Service and how that work was valued. Anticipating the spiraling costs that equal pay might soon bring, the Treasury saw a need to keep women's wages depressed as the number of women employees grew, buoyed by the growth of automated systems. With its service-wide organizational oversight powers, the Treasury created a broad new work category to consolidate many feminized job classes into one, and formally separate them from the rest of the service's meritocratic, exam-mediated hiring and promotion. This new class would have its own separate pay scales and limited promotion track. The reorganization would also have the effect of pulling women from higher classes of the service into a feminized, subclerical class of machine jobs. Most importantly, it would formalize women's previously informal association with calculation, data processing, and other computing work.

The new class would increase the number of positions for women machine workers so that instead of coming into the Civil Service as temporary clerks or clerical assistants as before, most women would now have one aspect of their work—machine operation—expanded to signify their entire job. Because machine operation was not as respected as clerical work, and often more specialized, the effect was to institutionalize women's isolation from the "real" work of offices in the very structure of how they were hired and trained. Machine work was defined in functional rather than intellectual terms. Women's work in the Civil Service, which varied widely—from accounting to surveying to payroll to scientific calculation—was now defined by the methods used to complete it rather than by its content.

Department heads were invited to apply to the Treasury for permission to use this new job category not only for new hiring but also to "re-grade" their existing staff. Only the lowest, most entry-level rung of the class, however—the machine assistant grade—had been instituted at the time of the announcement. This meant all machine operators would start at the bottom of the new job class, regardless of their level of experience. Only later, when the higher levels within the machine operator class were decided upon, would there be the possibility for workers to apply for a job title and pay that reflected their experience. The tactic set up the machine operator class from the outset as a job category designed to deskill workers and depress wages.

Although government reports referred to the great mass of their women workers as doing the "monotonous routine work" that made up the broad base of the Civil Service "pyramid," inquiries into the exact content and nature of machine operation commissioned by the Treasury itself repeatedly contradicted the characterizations of it as deskilled work.[44] These reports showed how machine workers needed many of the same skill sets as higher clerical workers and how machine operation jobs were best performed by higher-skill, more educated workers. Even machine workers at the lowest levels, who dealt with narrowly specialized calculations, possessed similar skills as clerical workers: "The lower grades of the technical part of the engineering field and the [scientific] Assistants are both fairly close to the Clerical Class in many respects," admitted an internal Treasury memo.[45] Despite this, most women workers were now partitioned off from the higher-status clerical class.[46]

Eventually, the machine operator class would have three levels: The entry-level rung was the position of machine assistant. The middle rung of machine operator, took on more complex work. Women would rise to machine operator in their midtwenties. The top grade was senior machine operator. These women would perform the most complicated work in the class, including programming and systems analysis. The expectation was for women to attain that rank in their later twenties or early thirties, because at that point promotion and pay increases ceased—much earlier than for workers in clerical jobs. The structure of the new class enforced a shortened, dead-end career, partly because of the idea that women should leave by this point to get married and take care of a family, but also as a reflection of the low worth accorded to this work. Many Civil Service leaders in this era could not conceive of technical or machine-aided office work as interesting, as complex, or as providing preparation for higher work. The fact that the association of women with machine work in offices had initially evolved from women's association with typewriters helped reinforce this attitude.[47] Yet the machine class was not simply a reflection of the status quo. It was the Treasury's attempt to deal with rising numbers of women employees by reorganizing the government's postwar workforce.

Machine operators who worked in large data-handling sections of fifty machine operators or more were supposed to form the core of the grade. Initially, the Treasury leaders who designed and instituted it claimed that "the class will be introduced only where large blocks of staff are regularly engaged on machine duties."[48] In practice, however, this guideline soon broke down. Because the Treasury saw this reorganization as a cost-saving measure, machine operator grading was applied wherever women were employed on automated or even partially automated work. As such, the grading could be applied to women workers virtually anywhere. Even the memorandum announcing the change had stated that the number fifty was meant only as a "very rough guide" and that "the fifty need not all be located in one centre."[49] The specialized nature of the grade meant that there was virtually no hope of transferring out of it, especially as machine work grew in relation to clerical work. More machine operators were required every day, and few civil servants preferred this work.

In industry, women tried to escape such strictures through trade union action. Similarly, staff associations in the service attempted to protest these new categories. Within the Civil Service, two women's clerical associations had broken away from the main civil servants' union and amalgamated into the National Association of Women Civil Servants (NAWCS). The NAWCS formed in 1932 in response to a reorganization of the Civil Service that created a separate and unequal selection process for women recruits, and formalized lower pay for women working in the same grades as men. The NAWCS found itself confronting a similar instance of structural discrimination with the machine grades, but the NAWCS did not have enough members to make it a powerful pressure group. Because the group had split off from the main union run by men, new women civil servants could choose to join either group. Many opted for the larger, more powerful union run by men, the Civil Service Clerical Association (CSCA).[50]

The obstruction of the more powerful CSCA proved to be a major stumbling block. The NAWCS had spent the interwar and war years agitating for increases in pay and benefits, for mandatory placement of young men into the lowest all-women's grades, and had fought for pension and other rights for the all-women typing grades. In 1948, the government agreed to open certain all-male grades in the Post Office to women after negotiations with the NAWCS, but the CSCA, which had official negotiating rights for those grades, refused, continuing a pattern of antipathy toward equal pay and equal opportunity reforms.[51] CSCA leaders believed opening these grades to women threatened the status of male workers in those jobs and were apoplectic that the NAWCS continually went against what they felt should be a closed-shop negotiating situation with the government. A similar conflict occurred with the typing grades. In that case, the NAWCS had formal negotiating rights, but when they secured concessions from Civil Service management, the CSCA refused to agree to many of the changes, instead trying to trade the typists' improvements to secure pay raises for other job classes that would benefit more men than women.

This intraworkforce animosity delayed long-awaited pay raises for typists for another several years, and even once the pay raises were gained, the two associations continued to argue over them. The CSCA issued a vituperative pamphlet, reprinted in the office journal sent to all civil servants, that insisted the efforts of the NAWCS on behalf of women in the typing grades had been worthless. Entitled "Who Did the Job? A History of the Recent Typing Structure Negotiations with Documentary Evidence," it was a scathing indictment of the NAWCS, which CSCA leaders alleged had no power as a negotiating body and had willfully misled women workers.[52]

Because the NAWCS focused on fighting for equal treatment for women, it was repeatedly squeezed out of labor negotiations, and the interests of the women's grades were never prioritized within the CSCA. Nonetheless, the NAWCS protected women workers in ways the CSCA never even attempted, in particular by keeping gendered labor-force segregation front and center as an issue. Yet the National Whitley Council refused to arbitrate any complaints about unequal pay throughout this period: "No claim, however based, may be taken to arbitration if it includes a demand for the same rate for men and women," declared the council.[53]

Raising Productivity through Lowering Pay: The Trouble with Gendered Scientific Management

Anne Godwin, a delegate of the national Trades Union Congress, called job segregation tactics like these a "persistent feature" of devaluing women's work. She lambasted "the practice of fixing the rate for a job and applying it to male workers only, as though they alone were the genuine workers on the job," thus depressing women's wages.[54] Although lower pay marked women as second-class workers, it also meant their labor was in high demand when employers tried to raise productivity by cutting labor costs. Women were considered a suitably "less expensive alternative" because they received only 75 percent of the men's rate in central government offices and 63 percent in local government offices.[55] As faster and more complex office automating machinery solidified machine operators' key role within the lower reaches of the government hierarchy, the machine grades helped produce economies that the government was unwilling to give up. Perhaps fittingly, Prime Minister Winston

Churchill—who returned to power in 1951—again presided over a period in which women's labor was deployed as a tool to help the state survive. This time, the organized devaluation of women's work helped the government survive austerity, much as it had helped the government survive the turmoil of war.

However, women were not used for all jobs in which cost savings could accrue—even in machine operation. For example, managers decided to use men for teleprinter jobs in the Admiralty, in part because the technology's newness gave it a higher status, but also because teleprinter transmissions to "highly paid Cable Company male operators at the other end of the circuits" meant that the "work should be regarded as being a much higher standard than that of a typist."[56] Yet teleprinters were simply typewriters that were hooked up to data transmission lines. Even though it was easier to attain the slower standard of speed required for teleprinter operation versus typing and it required less training than shorthand typing, teleprinter operation was nonetheless better paid. During labor shortages, women who were taken from typing duties and put on teleprinter duties were reluctant to return to typing, but were forced to on the basis that it was easier to train new staff for teleprinter operation rather than taking "excellent typists" and "squandering [them] on teleprinting."[57]

In the case of teleprinter operation, the newer technology and the immediacy and expense of the communications transfer contributed to the employer perception that teleprinter jobs required a higher level of responsibility. Whom workers would interact with defined the job as men's work more than its actual content. Teleprinter operation and typing were virtually identical. If anything, typing was more difficult because not only did it need to be performed faster and in higher volume, but typists also usually had to transcribe from dictation or scribbled notes. Women's lower labor cost hurt them in cases like this; it marked them as less valuable workers who could not be used for higher-status work. This, in turn, shaped staffing decisions.

As the machine operator class grew, machine operation jobs replaced most of the women's jobs in partially feminized job categories that had higher responsibility and better pay scales. Some department heads became unwilling to continue to pay and train women as anything other than machine operators: If they wanted to pay more for labor, they could have men instead, they reasoned. As a result, managers often gave women less interesting and responsible work, reflecting their lowered status. Chasing ever-elusive productivity gains through lower labor costs sometimes backfired, however.

When the department that made the nation's official, highly detailed, and technical maps—the Ordnance Survey—Taylorized women's draftsmen and surveyor posts in their spheroidal trigonometry section in order to change them into machine operator jobs, the head of the section recoiled at the results. Although the section head had originally favored the idea as a way to get more staff, after seeing the change in practice he realized that the standards set out for machine operators were not "connected with the work our women do." Women competing for placements in the Civil Service under the examinations for machine operators were required to have different—and fewer—skills. Once he realized this, the section head felt "that the decision to re-grade our women as machine operators was an ill-advised one."

By deskilling women in the department who performed machine-aided calculation, their work actually became *less* efficient, and no money was saved as a result. "We have experienced more and more disadvantages of having these women as machine operators rather than as Surveyors, Draftswomen, or Computers ... Our work is at every stage closely linked with and dependent upon a full understanding of the technical process," the head of the spheroidal trigonometry section wrote. The new machine class workers, with their limited job mandate and lack of training, "could not be expected to participate" fully in the work, he added.[58] He described the new system as like having two men balancing different columns in a ledger: When a mistake arose, no one knew who was accountable or what went wrong. He now argued that all new women employees should "be either draftswomen or surveyors, so that they can undertake any work for which draftsmen and surveyors are normally employed" rather than being limited to machine operating work.[59]

In effect, the jobs for machine class workers had to be cut up into smaller pieces to make them suitable for this feminized grade, even though it was predominantly women who had been performing the work already. This situation shows the difference between labor feminization and work that is simply performed by women: True feminization entails deskilling, or at least the perception thereof. The problems in the spheroidal trigonometry section also highlight the differences among levels and intensities of labor feminization. The earlier surveyor, drafting, and calculating jobs for women had been feminized insofar as that they lacked some of the pay, promotion, and training opportunities men enjoyed in similar jobs, but when replaced with machine operators, the jobs had to be explicitly redesigned to require less skill and autonomy. More intense forms of labor feminization mean not only that women are predominant and less well paid, but that this predominance leads to lower standards, lower prestige, and foreclosing of opportunities. As a historical process, feminization makes work less valuable as women become the majority of those doing it, setting up a vicious cycle in which workers' status drops further as the work becomes devalued, sometimes out of all proportion to the work's actual content.[60] Once this process has occurred, even men who return to these job categories are subject to the effects of labor feminization, meaning that feminization can affect workers of both genders negatively.

In response to the problems outlined by the head of the spheroidal trigonometry section, his superior replied: "I am not absolutely convinced that it is not possible to arrange the work in your Division [so] that there is adequate [work] to keep a staff of Machine Operators employed on duties appropriate to that class and thus enable a great proportion of your male staff to be employed on outside surveying duties."[61] By constructing the problem as one of organization of the department's work rather than a problem with the structure of the machine grades, he was able to throw the problem back to the lower-level manager and demand that intradepartmental reorganization rectify what was in fact a problem created by the organization of work service-wide. The "inflexibility and loss of responsibility" created by regrading the staff, however, was widely acknowledged within the department.[62]

In instituting the machine operator grade, the Ordnance Survey had made a calculated gamble. It had appealed to the Treasury's ongoing drive to hold down costs, suggesting that certain men could be replaced by women in order to gain more staff. If the section head of spheroidal trigonometry recategorized his employees as machine operators, he could immediately employ 35 percent more women and "release technical men for more appropriate survey duties," he argued. In entering into this deal to acquire more staff, he had realized he was taking a risk and had tried to impress upon the Treasury the "special character" of the work his women employees performed: "It includes reductions of theodolite observations, adjustments of triangulations by least square methods and the computation of coordinates from minor trig and traverse observations etc. ... These, I think you will agree are more difficult and call for more training than the use of the punching machines referred to specifically [in the circular]." He had also noted that the only way to get "suitable" women workers would be to offer some kind of career opportunity to them.[63]

The Treasury's opposing agenda to keep down costs, however, won out. Machine operators were placed in the department with little regard for the nature of the work, and soon after that the Treasury came back to inquire about "how many of the male Technical Civil Assistants could be replaced by women," hoping to cut costs further.[64] The Treasury only wished to institute the machine grade and authorize additional posts in a department if it meant a reduction in labor cost relative to output. Although the Ordnance Survey remained convinced that its machine operators needed to be of a higher caliber so that they could interact with and "be put on similar work to the male surveyor computers alongside whom they work," this was impossible under the initial rules of employment and training for the machine operator class. The Treasury had created a top-down structure in order to more easily manage, control, and pay for the growing number of women workers in government offices, and they would not be swayed by examples that seemed to contravene their new system.[65] Machine operation jobs were now explicitly given exclusively to women, usually young and single.[66] A once-informal practice had become formally institutionalized.

Limited opportunities in the expanding class began to have the effect of cutting short women's careers despite the repeal of the marriage bar. This low promotion ceiling caused women who deserved promotion to senior machine operator to be held back because of their young age: "Notwithstanding her outstanding ability, it would be unwise to absorb Miss Crook into the Senior Machine Operator Grade for a year or two," department managers agreed—and Miss Crook was not the only one.[67] One supervisor wrote that several of his senior machine operators had hit their pay and promotion maxima and had nowhere to go: "The four Senior Machine Operators employed in Trig Comps are unsuitable for employment in Level Comps now as their much greater skill would be wasted in Level Comps. Should they ~~marry~~ leave for any reason it would be necessary to replace them by well-qualified male or female surveyors with a good mathematical background who could then become efficient machine trig computers" (strikethrough in original).[68] As a result of the new machine operator class, high-skill women workers already in the service became trapped in a job category meant for low-skill workers. When they left the workforce, they were inevitably replaced by less well-trained workers, and departments were encouraged to Taylorize their work further to accommodate the new system, with little cost benefit. Departments that resisted, and women machine operators who picked up skills on the job that made them more valuable, threw the system into disarray.

The Machine Grades: Grassroots of the Equal Pay Campaign

This reconfiguration of women's work in concert with increasing automation inflamed sentiment in both the women's and men's Civil Service associations, although for different reasons. On the one hand, more women were being confined to low-level jobs. On the other hand, these women could replace men, depending on how departments organized their work. When the high price of the Civil Service pension, something most women did not collect, was factored in, Treasury leaders generally believed the government gained economically by replacing men with women despite the associated drawbacks of deskilling. This heightened the antagonistic relationship between the mixed gender but male-dominated CSCA and the smaller, all-women's NAWCS.

Labor organization along gendered lines was often difficult and inexpedient for women, yet it was sometimes the only way to make their voices heard. Within gender-integrated unions, men held most positions of power. After peaking in 1944, women's membership in the national Trades Union Congress (TUC) declined until 1947—but from 1951 to 1952, over ninety-eight thousand women joined the TUC in response to women trade unionists' massive recruiting campaign designed to appeal to women workers on the basis of issues specific to them.[69] In the Civil Service, however, the women's association increasingly struggled to attract enough new members to bolster its negotiating power.[70]

Meanwhile, the CSCA levied repeated complaints against the Ordnance Survey Department for a variety of issues related to machine operators' work. The CSCA, however, did not advocate on behalf of machine operators. Instead, it demanded that machine operators be given even less responsibility. Most offensive to the CSCA was the use of a limited number of senior machine operators as supervisory staff, particularly when the staff under their supervision included, or could potentially include, male workers. In a heated exchange, CSCA leaders complained that "clerical and technical employees using machines appear to be clashing badly," and that "definite lines of demarcation [are] needed to avoid serious repercussions."[71]

The CSCA believed it had been assured that the women of the machine operator grades would include no supervisor posts, even at the highest rank of senior machine operator. In order to placate the CSCA, the government acquiesced to these demands—and in fact went a step beyond, also preventing the few women executive officers in the managerial classes of the service from leading sections when men resented their supervision.

In some cases, "if it is proposed to put a female Executive Officer in charge I think it may cause trouble," wrote a Treasury official in reference to the skirmish with the CSCA, noting that due to an exception "under paragraph 14 a man may be in charge."[72]

Downgrading women so as not to anger men also applied to pay scales. Although men in the machine grades were nonexistent, the CSCA nonetheless negotiated a men's pay scale for the grade to protect their interests. The senior machine operator scale for men in 1953 started at £460, rising to £570, whereas women's pay started at £385 and grew by smaller, less frequent increments to £460.[73] The fact that women's pay maximum was the lowest salary point for men was not a coincidence, but rather an attempt to preserve clear gendered hierarchies, even in a class in which these hierarchies were only theoretical because there were no men, nor any structures in place to hire them. Senior machine operators' promotions were also held back on the grounds that it would be improper for a woman to attain such a post before she was twenty-eight to thirty years of age; otherwise, her pay might rise above a clerical officer of the same age. Because the latter job grade had a higher status, department heads worried that comparable pay would engender resentment and provoke requests for a clerical officer pay raise.[74] At the same time, the Treasury also wanted to delay machine operators' promotions in order to lower long-term outlay. Many machine operators would resign to marry before reaching maximum pay at age thirty.

Unfortunately, these tactics to restrain operators' promotion worked all too well. They meant that machine operators had to be willing to move wherever a vacancy was available in order to get promoted, and their current department had to agree to the loss of a now valuable, trained staff member. Making promotions more available became crucial for departments to be able to keep their skilled staff. Department heads were joined by the staff associations in pressing the Treasury to create more senior machine operator posts where they were needed. However, the Treasury was reluctant to do so. In long back-and-forth sessions, it haggled with departments that were straining to enact their own management vision in the face of the Treasury's strong top-down control.[75]

At the other end of the spectrum, some departments found themselves with machine operator redundancies and had to put their operators on nonmachine clerical tasks. The opposite situation also occurred, and higher-level women civil servants were sometimes demoted onto machine work simply because the amount of machine work in their departments increased. One complaint from the Institute of Professional Civil Servants sought redress for the fact that several women who had been at a much higher rank in a different job class had been made to do machine work for over a year.[76]

Not surprisingly, the NAWCS had opposed the institution of the new machine operator grades, foreseeing that this categorization would condemn all women clerical workers to poorer career prospects. At their annual conference the year that the change was introduced, members expressed concern and sent a contingent to the Treasury to argue against the plan. They noted with alarm that the Treasury's plan contained another barb: Although men were not to be employed in this women's grade, the pay scales for theoretical male workers were only at the level of machine operator and senior machine operator, but not at the lowest grade of machine assistant. That grade was to be exclusively female, even in theory. This meant it had no possible comparison to a male wage and therefore could never attain equal pay, even if the government eventually agreed to raise women's pay up to the level of men who were doing the same job.[77] Machine assistants, at the lowest end of the scale, earned as little as £80 per year in the early 1950s, a salary that made dependence on family or a husband a necessity.[78] During her early twenties, by contrast, a machine operator would usually earn about £300 per year, making it a relatively high-paying position for young women before they hit the maximum pay, which was not much higher, a few years later. This was not unusual in jobs designed to attract young women workers who were expected to leave the workforce within a few years.[79]

As soon as the machine class was created, the NAWCS attempted to rally machine operators to "protect and promote their grade interests." Key to improving women's conditions in the Civil Service was being able to recruit women who were isolated from the channels of power in the service and were often temporary workers. A NAWCS pamphlet from the early 1950s pitched at machine workers proposed complete interchangeability between the machine grades and the more highly regarded clerical grades, asked for pay equality and equality of opportunity between men and women, and demanded that no subclerical grade be solely women. "You are a women's grade" and "We are a women's association with your interests at heart," declared the pamphlet, trying to rouse the machine grades to political action.[80]

As women flooded into more Civil Service jobs, the CSCA realized how dangerous the NAWCS could be if it successfully convinced more women civil servants to join together in pay negotiations separately from men. Arguing that the NAWCS was guilty of "misrepresentation added to

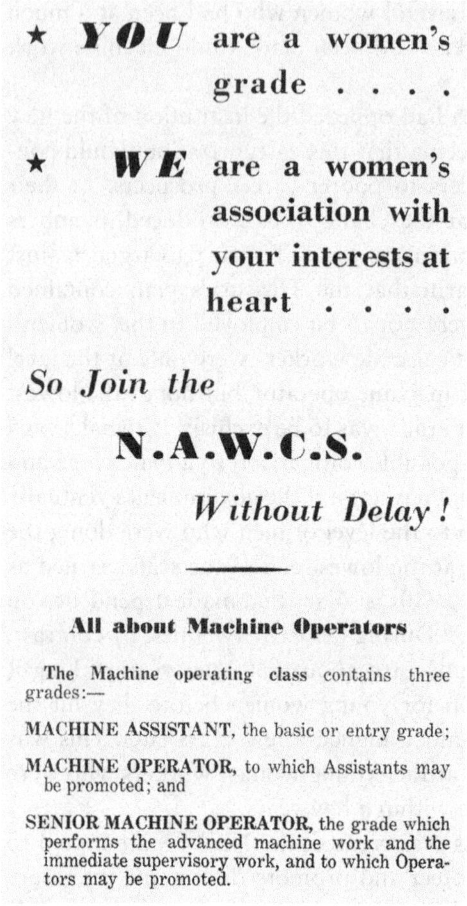

★ ***YOU*** **are a women's grade . . . .**

★ ***WE*** **are a women's association with your interests at heart . . . .**

So Join the

N.A.W.C.S.

Without Delay!

All about Machine Operators

The Machine operating class contains three grades:—

MACHINE ASSISTANT, the basic or entry grade;

MACHINE OPERATOR, to which Assistants may be promoted; and

SENIOR MACHINE OPERATOR, the grade which performs the advanced machine work and the immediate supervisory work, and to which Operators may be promoted.

Figure 2.2
Recruiting pamphlet from the National Association of Women Civil Servants targeting the machine grades, 1950.

incompetence," the CSCA inaccurately claimed it had negotiation rights for typists and attempted to convince the Treasury to negotiate only with them. To the CSCA's disappointment, the Treasury insisted on informing the NAWCS of the proposals under consideration.[81] Aside from this vocal in-fighting, the long-overdue and unusually large £40 raise granted to the typing grades in 1950 was perhaps the clearest signal that something was very wrong with the way feminized work was valued and remunerated in government. The 10 percent raise in a year during a period of austerity, when normally pay raises were on the level of 2–6 percent, hinted at how depressed typists' wages had become and also how women's access to the negotiating process was increasing.

After the issue with the Ordnance Survey, the CSCA continued to police other departments' uses of senior machine operators. While the NAWCS argued for opening more opportunities for supervisory work to machine grade workers in the early 1950s, the CSCA sought the enforcement of job descriptions for women senior machine operators that expressly forbade such employees from supervising workers in nonfeminized grades.[82] The protection of higher-paying men's jobs influenced this complaint, but the anger seething through CSCA discussions on this topic reflected the idea that women supervising men was socially taboo. The fact that these women were lowly machine workers heightened the humiliation. Senior machine operators should not have even been allowed to supervise other women, the CSCA felt, since this would take a supervisory position away from a man.

The rising numbers of women machine workers, however, had already begun to transform the structure of the entire Civil Service. The NAWCS followed developments in government automation, fastidiously recording the numbers and types of computers on order and in use in government in their association's slim annual reports.[83] Although electronic computers had not yet replaced the electromechanical tabulating machines used for most government administration, the NAWCS recognized that electronics would soon take over, and strategized about how this change might be leveraged to improve women's opportunities. However, electromechanical installations shared many similarities with early electronic ones, making the changeover more evolutionary than revolutionary. Because punched card equipment formed the backbone of data handling within the Civil Service before the advent of electronic computing, it also defined the workflow and labor organization of later systems. As electronic systems began to replace electromechanical ones in the mid- to late 1950s, many women saw their computing jobs change very little, if at all. The same labor forces, with the same labor problems, carried over from electromechanical to electronic computing work.

As office-automation jobs became ever more numerous, raising the status of the office machine operator became the key to raising women workers' status overall. In 1957, the NAWCS-allied International Federation of Business and Professional Women devoted its annual conference to the topic of "Automation and the Individual" in an attempt to figure out what was to come and how women workers could best navigate the changing technological landscape.[84] Women labor leaders mounted campaigns to try to situate machine operators firmly within the bounds of white-collar clerical work in order to support the idea that they deserved more respect. Yet although women computer operators were often portrayed as white collar in advertisements, in practice they resided slightly outside the world of the white-collar office worker. In fact, many operators covered their attire with coveralls while on the job, much like working-class laborers in more physically strenuous or dirty jobs might. Indeed, office automators explicitly took cues from earlier forms of industrial mechanization that had Taylorized jobs to utilize women's labor: "When we consider," one business computing specialist said, "the extent of automation in the factory, it seems that management has a right to expect the same degree of automation in the office."[85]

In figure 2.3, two women operate the same computer, the Power-Samas Electronic Multiplying Punch (EMP). The advertising image on the left shows a woman in crisp office attire operating a computer in a neatly closed case in a "push button" fashion, but the photo of an actual operator using the same machine shows the operator wearing coveralls and working with the machine's internals to set up the program. The advertising image shows the "black box" of computing technology closed

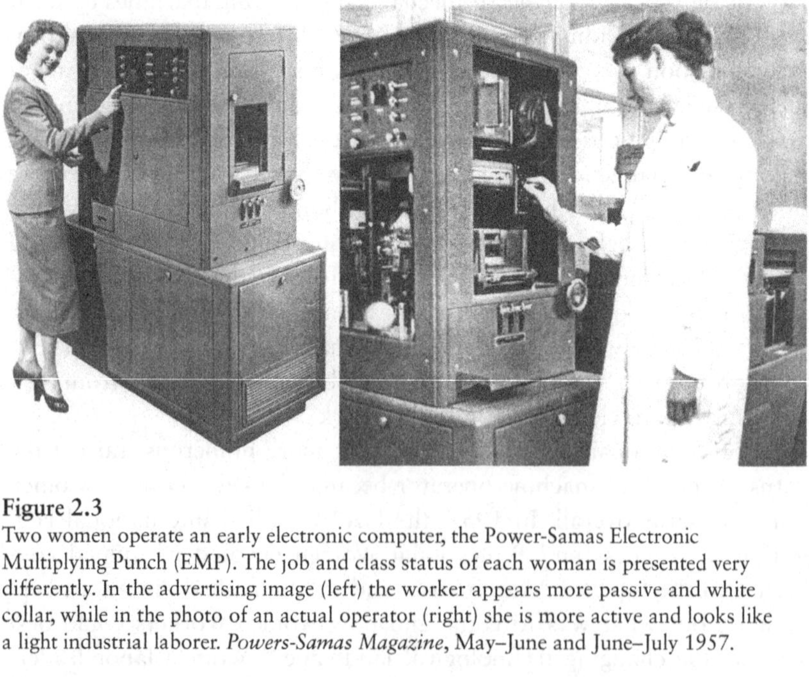

Figure 2.3
Two women operate an early electronic computer, the Power-Samas Electronic Multiplying Punch (EMP). The job and class status of each woman is presented very differently. In the advertising image (left) the worker appears more passive and white collar, while in the photo of an actual operator (right) she is more active and looks like a light industrial laborer. *Powers-Samas Magazine*, May–June and June–July 1957.

and positions the worker as a mere accessory, whereas the photo of a real computer worker shows that she must literally open the black box in order to perform her job, making her labor seem far more integral than peripheral.

Another computer company's staff magazine from the same year had a more comical take on women operators opening the black box. In a cartoon (figure 2.4), two operators dive in to fix their malfunctioning computer (note the prominently drawn vacuum tubes), while the maintenance engineer, just arrived on the scene, looks on in shock and dismay.[86] The cartoon plays on the complicated gendered expectations of computer work: Women could operate, manufacture, and test machines—all of that was firmly feminized labor—but they were not supposed to alter or fix their machines. These fine-grained job distinctions showed that the ways in which gendered work divisions were enforced had little to do with the work itself. In reality, these divisions were enforced by the different types of job training available for boys and girls. At their 1960 annual meeting, the Women's Trades Union Congress argued that "more trained

HOLLERITH
" Another bobby-pin, Jean, and away we go ".

Figure 2.4
"Another Bobby Pin." Cartoon from *Tabacus: The Company Magazine of the British Tabulating Machine Company*, 1957.

technicians and technologists are required in this country and many girls are capable of qualifying for work of a technical character if given suitable opportunity," noting that women high school graduates were not needed as untrained, "cheap labor but as qualified technicians."[87] As the leaders of the TUC pointed out in a confidential internal memorandum: "The use of computers and other electronic devices has increased in large engineering companies and nationalized industries since 1958. ... Experience has shown that most work fed into these machines is prepared by female labor. This may be due to their manipulative skills but it is suspected that it is because it is a cheaper form of labor as 'equal pay *for work of equal value*' has not yet been established" (italics mine).[88]

From 1954 to 1958, the government installed eight electronic computers, mainly for scientific purposes.[89] In 1958, the Post Office installed its first electronic computer specifically for administrative purposes, and five other administrative computers were installed in other parts of the Civil Service that same year. All together, they cost close to £150,000.[90] Already hundreds of thousands of pounds had been spent on scientific and technical computers, but these dedicated administrative computers changed the focus of computing in government, turning the computer from a specialized scientific tool to a general-purpose information processing necessity.[91] By the end of the decade, there would be over a million pounds worth of computers in the central government; in the next decade, that figure would be multiplied nearly thirty-four times.[92] Yet these machines heralded the start of a new era in government mechanization in a technical sense only. They were not so much a break with the past as the continuation of plans to automate administrative work that had long been underway. For years, the leading business periodicals on office automation referred to "data processing—with or without computers" in talking about the patterns of office work that had paved the way for the introduction of electronic computing.[93]

Deserving and Undeserving Workers

While the proportion of women machine workers became ever greater, questions about their worth—and the worth of all women workers—began to take center stage. A section in the government's postwar report on equal pay had explained away the divisions between men and women in the Civil Service's "fair field with no favor" on the grounds of women's needs rather than the needs of their employers. Most women, the commission wrote, could not argue that they needed equal pay, whereas most men had a valid claim to a higher wage because they shouldered a "moral responsibility ... backed by the sanction of law" for "founding and maintaining a family group."[94]

The government noted that the social effects of a widespread rise in women's wages "would be to improve the position of women in relation to men throughout employment generally."[95] This was not seen as a good thing. If women's position relative to men's rose, then it would put "a married man with a family in a relatively worse economic position than any other section of the community."[96] Treasury officials contended that their research showed single women already had a relatively higher standard of living on their lower government paycheck than single men had on their higher wage: "You would find that with a woman civil servant and a man civil servant on the same level, the woman can afford to take more expensive holidays than the man. She can go abroad. The man has to go and dig in his garden or perhaps snatch a week at Southend," a Treasury official claimed.[97] So persistent were these assertions that the Communist Party of Britain released an equal pay pamphlet, illustrated with cartoons of a large, imposing woman and a small, bookish man, that pointed out that women consumed goods in similar proportion to men and paid all the same prices for consumer goods and services, all on lower wages.[98]

The Equal Pay Commission—composed of four women and five men and chaired by Sir Cyril Asquith—had taken seriously the problem that equal pay could "create a sense of injustice in the men."[99] In their view, the typical working woman was a "spinster."[100] The image of the spinster was often a mirage, however. As the Industrial Health Research Board noted, many "spinsters" were women who might lose their jobs if their marriages were known. Married women were known to "conceal their marriages from their employers while others remained single in a legal sense only."[101] Many single women also had dependents. Mary Coombs, one of the earliest commercial computer programmers, recalled how her low salary meant severe hardship for her since she had to use a portion of her wages to support her mother.[102] By and large, the category of single women who had dependent children or other family members to support was not considered a valid group for inclusion in wage discussions, if they were even acknowledged to exist at all.

Arguing that work compensation for women should be seen in the light of need and social welfare, the government remained highly reluctant to accede to the idea of a "rate for the job" that would be paid to all holders of a given post irrespective of their social roles *outside* work. On

Beveridge's recommendations, the government took for granted a nuclear family supported by a male breadwinner wage, with women playing dependent roles both at home and in the labor market.[103] The findings of the Beveridge Report, which were to be the model for a progressive, postwar society, strengthened the long-standing connections between gendered wage policies and social services.[104]

Among temporary workers in government offices, 57 percent were women. In the lowest clerical category, clerical assistants, 55 percent were women. Only a handful of women worked in the higher grades of the Civil Service. The vast majority were confined to lower clerical posts, temporary positions, and machine operator jobs with little room to advance.[105] The clerical officer grade was only one-third women, whereas the next grade up, higher clerical officer, had just slightly more women members—an anomaly due to the large numbers of women who entered the workforce during and directly after World War I and never married due to the war's toll on their generation's men. Continuing up the job pyramid, the number of women declined to one-fifth of the executive class, and then to less than one-tenth of the administrative class.[106]

Arguments against equal pay often vacillated between saying women did not need higher pay and saying that they did not deserve it given their track record. Another reason women were ostensibly denied equal pay was because they were perceived as being less valuable and productive workers. Statistics suggested they were more likely to take sick days. Interestingly, the statistics gathered also showed that in the Civil Service, the higher the ranking and salary of a job, the lower women's average rate of absence was. In primarily women's professions, such as teaching, single women had an absence rate almost the same as men.[107] Women who did not work in male-dominated environments or at the lowest levels of the labor pyramid consistently took fewer sick days. The stressful nature of the jobs in the all-female machine grades may indeed have contributed to higher rates of illness—or at least a greater willingness to miss work whenever possible.[108]

In addition, the long-held management folk wisdom that women were effectively a waste of training because they would leave to have children played a major role in how the government regarded women workers: "It is evident to common sense that women workers do not regard their career as offering an alternative career to marriage and motherhood," stated a Department of Science and Industry report as late as 1961.[109] One woman applicant for a Post Office computing job in the 1960s recalled that she would not have gotten the job if she had not convinced the hiring managers that she did not intend to have children, even though at the time she applied she was divorced.[110] Assumptions about women's ideal life patterns, as much or more than perceptions of their potential acumen, ensured that most women never joined the ranks of management or more skilled workers.

The flip side of this attitude was the conscious effort on the part of Civil Service officials to remove men from the lower grades through sometimes arbitrary promotion. "Male subclericals are a nuisance in several ways," noted one supervisor, expressing a representative opinion: The Treasury urged departments to hire men only as clerical officers. On the other hand, "for women, there might well be a separate selection and a separate quota," and it would be advisable "to fix either a maximum proportion for women or a minimum proportion for men in the Clerical Officer Selection," advised the Treasury.[111] Allowing men into feminized job categories would upset the balance of low pay and poor promotion prospects designed into those job classes. As a result, men were not only expected but also encouraged, through formal recruitment processes, to take the majority of higher, permanent posts in the service, and women were kept out.

Women assistant draftsmen, for example, "relieve skilled draftsman of routine work which does not require the full qualification of the grade of architectural and engineering draftsman." Men might filter through that job category, but only women were allowed to become permanent staff there. "Establishment in the grade of drawing office assistant is confined to women," the Equal Pay Commission explained, adding that "men are employed only as temporaries and only if the employing department is satisfied that there is scope for them to acquire the qualifications for entry to the draftsman grade."[112] Certain job grades positioned as only training for young men were set up to be permanent jobs for women.

Far from being a simple breakdown of meritocracy, this system was a major goal of effective industrial and governmental organization. It ensured that the people viewed as the most promising candidates, who were nearly always men, were given opportunities to succeed, on the assumption that reproducing the current hierarchy would keep the metaphorical machine of government running.[113] Stephanie Shirley, who worked for the government in this period as a scientific officer performing calculations, recalled how multiple men resigned their posts on the promotions board rather than have to deliberate on women's promotion applications because they "disapproved on principle of women holding managerial posts" regardless of qualifications. "What shocked me,"

Shirley stated, "was the more I became recognized as a serious young woman whose long-term aspirations went beyond a mere subservient role, the more violently I was resented and the more implacably I was kept in my place."[114]

Equal Pay versus Equal Value

As the fight for equal pay ramped up in the 1950s, labor activists had to contend with the difficult problem of how to define the concept itself. At the most basic level, equal pay could be defined as the practice of equalizing the wages earned by men and women in jobs with identical titles, but this definition left out a great many women workers, because gendered hiring practices and job categories segregated most women from men even within the same workplace. Equal opportunity in training and hiring became a major part of the campaign. In 1950, the NAWCS teamed with the National Union of Women Teachers (NUWT) to commission a short film on equal opportunity. Directed by feminist Jill Craigie, the film was rented to equal pay campaigners for public screenings, and it played along with newsreels in some London cinemas.[115] It attempted to show the problems inherent with the "same rate for the same job" model of equal pay and how the influx of women into the workplace in low-level jobs had stunted equality of opportunity. It dwelled on the hidden distinctions between people in the same workplace by contrasting the elevated status of certain white-collar jobs with the relative drudgery engaged in by many women office workers.

In an attempt to garner men's support, it also pointed out how various industrial processes had led to lower-paid women workers taking men's jobs: "In the old days, glass was mostly hand-blown, glassmaking was a man's world. Today it's manufactured, and the glass industry is largely a women's world. For women are cheap labor."[116] Using the example of feminization through industrial mechanization as a harbinger of things to come in white-collar professions, the film argued that equal pay and opportunity concerned every worker trying to protect his or her job. It culminated with the specter of international opprobrium: Britain had signed the UN charter on human rights that had guaranteed equal pay for equal work in the nations of signatories yet had failed to institute equal pay.[117]

By the late 1940s the British government had publicly and repeatedly affirmed their commitment to equality of pay in theory, even while declining to enact the principle. "As a broad affirmation of a general principle, the government accept, as regards their own employees, the justice of the claim that there should be no difference in payment for the same work in respect of sex," stated the Chancellor of the Exchequer in 1947, adding nonetheless that "the government are definitely of the opinion that this principle cannot be applied at present time."[118] The assertion that Britain could not afford equal pay was not particular to austerity. Earlier, the same argument had been given for refusing equal pay in the decades after World War I. Such economic arguments were always enmeshed in a larger discourse of women's dependence within society.[119]

Seen as a "reserve" labor force whose low cost and elasticity in times of economic contraction benefited the state, women were one of the government's most effective tools for keeping the cost of their burgeoning public sector under control. From 1931 to 1955, the Civil Service had grown from 340,000 workers to 720,000, not counting the nationalized industries or the NHS.[120] Equal pay promised serious repercussions for the massive bureaucracies of the state, given the growing feminized labor forces on which they ran. As a result, the economic argument against equal pay continued to be put forward in the House of Commons right up until the passage of the Equal Pay Act. Even in the years after, economic hardship was given as the reason equal pay could not be granted all at once but instead needed to be phased in over several years. Both Labour and Conservative governments maintained this view of financial impossibility, despite adding more than the amount needed for equal pay to the wages of the Civil Service as a whole and presiding over an economic recovery from 1952 onward.[121]

Once again refusing to implement equal pay in early 1954, even while agreeing to it in principle, the Chancellor of the Exchequer quipped, "Like a good many things to do with women, this is entirely illogical."[122] If equal pay continued not to make financial sense to the government, however, it had begun to make more sense to trade unions. Trade unions began to foreground the need for equal pay in the mid-1950s, and the clerical associations in the Civil Service followed suit. Women's growing numbers had also shifted the labor dynamics of the public sector. This impressed upon staff association leaders the necessity of gaining equal pay so that men's salaries would not be undercut by the continued expansion of women's paid labor. If pay scales were not equalized before women workers gained a majority, CSCA leaders realized they would face an uphill battle in all future wage claims.

Once unions had made equal pay a priority in their wage claims, the campaigns orchestrated by national and local women's associations

Figure 2.5
Presenting the equal pay petition to Parliament, 1954. Courtesy of the Women's Library, London.

achieved a critical mass.[123] Petitions presented to the House of Commons in 1954, with over 1.3 million signatures, reflected the changing tide. After again delaying a vote on equal pay in the House of Commons in early 1954, the government finally entered into talks with staff through the National Whitley Council and quickly hammered out a plan for equal pay by early 1955. Under Atlee's Labour government, equal pay had been successfully held off. Ironically, it was under the Conservatives, during Churchill's second term as prime minister, that workers finally succeeded in gaining it.[124]

There was still far to go, however. The plan was for equal pay to be gradually implemented over the course of more than six years to protect the government from financial distress. By 1956, for instance, some women would gain as little as £5 toward their new pay rate, a tiny fraction of the total difference in pay.[125] Ultimately, though, the pay raises were phased in more quickly than laid out in the initial plans. Equal pay had not been so enormous a financial burden as the Treasury claimed after all. This was because the equal pay provisions paradoxically left untouched the vast majority of women who worked in the Civil Service.

The Excluded Grades and the Formation of a Machine Work Underclass

Most women in the Civil Service did not, in fact, gain equal pay in 1955, because the government had assented to the principle of the "rate for the job" only in those jobs in which men and women were employed in exactly the same job categories and, furthermore, in which the rate of pay for men was considered the "market rate" for the job. This meant that for job classes in which men formed the majority or a critical mass of those employed in a grade, the government raised women's pay up to the men's rate. However, because jobs in the Civil Service had for decades been divided by gender and many categories explicitly feminized, only a minority of women were employed in the same job classes as men. Fewer still had exactly the same job titles as men. The financial difference between interpreting equal pay as raising women's pay to the corresponding men's rate and raising women's pay to the corresponding men's rate only in cases where women were not the overwhelming majority of a job class was considerable. A whopping 54 percent of women civil servants would be left unaided by equal pay, because these women were employed in "grades confined to women."[126]

The Treasury argued that in job classes in which women made up most of the employees, they should not have their pay adjusted upward to the men's rates of pay, because in these situations women's pay was the market rate for the job. The machine operator class, which the Treasury had set up only six years earlier as an explicitly feminized grade, was by far the largest and fastest growing of these job classes. Even though the machine operator class had wage scales for men, they were not considered the market rate. Women had been doing the work long enough and in such huge majority that their lower value in the economy had transferred onto the work. The government argued that, for example, "in a situation where over 98 percent of our typists are female, the assessing of pay by reference to a male rate is highly artificial, and indeed, runs counter to the principle of fair comparisons [with industry]."[127] Because the market rate for this labor was depressed, the Treasury argued, it would not make sense to give women typists and machine operators equal pay.

In making this argument, however, the Treasury sidestepped the government's role as an economic and ethical bellwether: Equal pay in the public sector had not been meant to reflect private industry's practices but rather to help correct them. In the years following, the Treasury would dispense with the notion of "fair comparisons" as soon as labor shortages in these ever-expanding, automation-adjacent job classes made it difficult to compete for workers.

Prior to the Equal Pay Act, these feminized job classes had been called "women's grades." However, the absurdity of the notion that the women's grades would not get any benefit from legislation designed specifically to help women seemed lost on the Treasury. After the passage of the act, the Treasury officially changed the name of the women's grades to the "excluded grades" to make clear, in the long term, their exclusion from equal pay provisions. As if by economic sleight of hand, the job classes in which women had been intentionally corralled and subjected to lower wages and poorer prospects had now become the ones in which women were seen to be receiving fair remuneration. This both reflected the rationale for government automation and encouraged its further extension. Women continued to flood into machine grade jobs, increasing the number of low-wage workers each year.

Some members of the machine classes, recently transferred from desk work to punching, verifying, and tabulating work, expressed great anger that they would not receive equal pay in their new positions. There was "a good deal of discontent among the machine operators," wrote one supervisor in the Transport Commission, "a number of whom have been specially selected for the work, having previously been on desk work, and had they remained on that work they would have automatically qualified for equal pay." He brought a complaint against the new wage structure on behalf of his employees, but his arguments were in vain.[128]

Now nominally gender neutral, the excluded grades were not simply a disappointment to women civil servants, but also a danger to men. The staff negotiating bodies quickly recognized that if in the future these job classes became gender integrated, it would result in depressed wages for men. The effect on wages would not only be felt by those within the excluded grades but also by those outside them, because salaries in the Civil Service operated on a strict system of "internal relativities," whereby remuneration in each job class was tied to all the others. In this way, the strong precedent equal pay set for the continued devaluation of women's work also set a precedent for devaluing men's work.

Machine grade jobs maintained complementary men's pay scales for many years afterward.[129] Although rarely if ever used, clerical associations had fought for men's scales in pay negotiations precisely for the purpose of trying to prevent the eventual depression of men's wages in feminized grades down to the rate for women. After equal pay, staff repeatedly brought pay complaints that argued for using the men's scales in the machine grades as the true standard, trying to use these largely unused pay scales to raise women's pay. Clerical bodies persisted in shoehorning a few men civil servants into the excluded grades as test cases, each time rearguing the principle of equal pay. The government quickly rejected such claims, reiterating that "one of the arguments for paying lower scales of pay for the 'Excluded Grades' was that they were confined to women and that the work they performed was 'women's work.'" In fact, the staff association's complaints backfired because they caused the Treasury to officially state that the market rate for excluded grade jobs now applied to men as well. As a result, in any rare future case in which a man might work as a machine operator, he would no longer get the higher men's rate of pay. Making its position perfectly clear, the Treasury warned that it was "important that there should be an understanding that any man selected for an 'Excluded Grade' post should be paid no more than the 'Woman's' rate." Even though "both men and women do the jobs this will not be used in the future as ground for raising the scales of pay for 'Excluded Grades' up to those for 'equal pay' grades," the Treasury confirmed in a memorandum.[130]

Nevertheless, wage claims for machine work intensified, with staff representatives arguing that this work would "with the extension of mechanized accountancy and the development of electronics ... occupy an increasingly vital position in the general scheme of things." Dealing unfairly with machine workers threatened to become the next major point of contention within the Civil Service. Managers began to realize that "any difficulty which might arise in recruiting or retaining such staff could have serious repercussions on the whole scheme of mechanized accountancy."[131] Work that was barely white collar and viewed as rote and requiring little skill and ability now threatened to make up the most widespread and thereby most important job class in government. The respectability and importance of this work sat in constant tension with its devaluation—a situation that could not remain tenable for long.

The Aeronautical Research Council, considering the problems of making a long-term career path in computing for workers after equal pay, noted that "a high proportion of the [Scientific] Assistants are girls; this appears to be because they like the routine work." The council added that "the resignation of a large proportion on marriage certainly eases the problem of careers in computing." Nonetheless, it was starting to become an issue that machine-aided calculation work was a growing class of jobs from which men were cut off. The presence of a career trajectory could undo this feminization, reasoned managers. "Boys generally prefer laboratory work to computing," the document continued, but "this might be due in part to the absence of any recognized career in computing and of any suitable specialist courses or qualifications." If a career path could be provided, the council wrote, then "it may be possible to make computing into an attractive career for some boys."[132] These efforts to broaden the labor pool would quickly run into problems, however, because of the jobs' feminized past. Even as the reach and importance of machine work in the office continued to grow, the labor force associated with it had become poorly paid and perceived as low skill and unprofessional, tanking the status of the jobs.

Toward the Electronic Office

The year that limited equal pay was granted, the government had only one electronic computer—but as the fifties drew to a close, there were over twenty, at a total cost of over a million pounds. In the next ten years, their cumulative cost would rise to over £36 million.[133] Foreseeing these spiraling costs, the Treasury worked to keep labor costs low by ensuring women's wages stayed depressed as their numbers, buoyed by the growth of automated systems, grew. By codifying the difference between machine workers and other office workers with the creation of the machine grades, the government formalized women's previously informal association with calculation, data processing, and other technical work. These changes in the Civil Service labor force would form the basis for the state's electronic computerization projects going forward.

In the same year equal pay was approved by the government, the ubiquitous nationwide bakery chain Lyons Teashops incorporated the division of its business that had three years earlier produced the world's first business computer: the Lyons Electronic Office, or LEO.[134] In 1951, Britain had gained the distinction of having invented the first electronic computer designed for business rather than scientific computing.[135] The LEO I provided a proof of concept for computers designed and built specifically for administrative use, and LEO Computers quickly became an early leader in British business computing. Computers like these would increasingly transform the national discourse on work productivity from the late 1950s onward.[136] Competing products evolved from Turing's ACE project, which formed the basis for English Electric's Deuce line of business computers, and computing research at Manchester University led to Ferranti's line of business and scientific computers. The LEO itself was created from the EDSAC computer developed at Cambridge.

Executives inside and outside the Civil Service saw that the government would soon be beholden to electronic computers for administrative tasks simply to keep pace with the ever-growing volume of data that government departments needed to handle. As early as 1956, when the government mounted fact-finding missions to the major corporations in the American electronic computing industry, government organizational experts came to believe that computers and the workers who operated them would become an exponentially greater part of a successful state bureaucracy, even to the point of affecting political governance.[137] "The Civil Service is likely to be affected far more than commercial concerns," noted *Office Magazine*, the main industry source for information on automation. "Indeed it probably has a greater need for commercial computers."[138]

This put the nation on track for a labor nightmare as machines were upgraded from electromechanical to electronic and began to play an ever-greater role within governance. The Treasury had reorganized the Civil Service to construct a class of low-cost machine workers divided from the rest of the service along gendered lines. This was a critical step in the process of government computerization, a way to heterogeneously engineer the labor force of the state to better accept the increasing automation of government. However, using equal pay legislation in the public sector to divide the workforce into clerical workers who deserved equal pay, and machine operators who did not, created a formal division between the feminized classes of workers that performed the critical calculation and tabulation work of the government's bureaucracies and the higher classes of workers in the government's bureaucracy that ostensibly oversaw this machine-aided work.

Far from being ancillary to questions of productivity and national progress in postwar Britain, equality of pay and opportunity for women were constituent issues in Britain's attempts to automate. Civil servants were part of a larger "government machine" in which they became components of a system of mechanized labor that ultimately sought to dispense with them altogether through ever-greater automation.[139] Women were the key, vital components of this machine because of how their socioeconomic position shaped their working lives in a way beneficial to employers. The Treasury recognized that because they could "no longer cut rates of pay ... one should think increasingly in terms of cutting down the number of workers by mechanization."[140] By this logic, the feminized machine classes were simply a step on the way to full automation—a human brake that would soon disappear. As the Treasury turned its attention to electronic computers as a tool for cost reduction, believing that they were "likely to be the most important development in the field of government," they ignored the role that labor would have to play.[141] The intertwined nature of the history of equal pay and computerization made computer work low status going into the 1960s and had the added effect of creating computer labor shortages down the line.

In 1955, Anne Godwin, the head of the National Trades Union Congress for Women Workers, devoted her address at the annual meeting of all women trade unionists nationwide to the issue of office automation:

> It is generally thought that women replaced men in offices. They did not. They entered offices at a time when clerical employment was expanding through the speeding up of industrial processes and they took over the new machines, the typewriter and the telephone—and have developed their spheres of employment as machine operations in offices have expanded. Now a new development—the automatic electronic calculating machine—is emerging and threatens to open up a whole range of problems affecting not only the future employment of women in offices but men also.[142]

Godwin's words would prove prophetic. Even though the creation of a deskilled, feminized class of machine workers seemed to make sense from a short-term financial standpoint, greater automation would in fact require more workers—and more skilled workers—than the government expected. The labor model for data processing engineered by the state in this period presaged a postindustrial order in which gender and automation were interdependent categories. This structuring of automation around a feminized technical workforce would soon become a major stumbling block.

As the government expanded and upgraded the data-processing systems on which the public sector relied, its actions in the 1940s and 1950s created a situation in which a great mass of skilled workers had no recognition, authority, or avenues for promotion. The Treasury had brought into being an underclass of information workers who were functionaries of the state without having full civil rights, and a sphere of work whose importance was rapidly increasing out of all proportion with the value accorded to the workers who performed it. This prestige gap would shape not only computing labor within the public sector but also the government's computing projects themselves, and would ultimately affect the fortunes of the British computing industry. The institutionalization of this workforce as the template for modern, machine-dependent intellectual work became a foundational, and ultimately counterproductive, part of the coming computer "revolution."

3

Luck and Labor Shortage: Gender Flux, Professionalization, and Growing Opportunities for Computer Workers, 1955–1967

Against this backdrop of the struggle for women's rights, Labour would retake control of the country on a platform that promised technological revolution. In 1963, Harold Wilson, soon to be prime minister, gave a rousing speech on technology's power to transform society that would become known as his "White Heat" speech. At the annual Labour Party conference, Wilson posited a new British social order rising from the ashes of a white-hot technological revolution that would burn away the nation's class-bound, antimeritocratic tendencies. "The Britain which is going to be forged in the white heat of the revolution will be no place for restrictive practices or for outdated methods," Wilson declared, positioning high technology—and computers in particular—as the last, best hope for Britain to regain global superpower standing. Wilson warned that "Britain cannot opt out of the automative revolution. If we do we shall be left behind and this country will become a center of industrial stagnation. We have to get in the race, get ahead, and stay ahead."[1]

Computers would play the most important role in Labour's vision for the future. While christening a new computer center at the English Electric factory, Wilson positioned the electronic computer as critical to national growth, likening its role to that of the steam engine in the industrial revolution.[2] That the industrial revolution had enabled British imperial endeavors was no coincidence: Skillful use, design, and sale of British computers, Wilson hoped, would turn the tide of Britain's imperial contraction.[3] Labour's rhetoric implied that technological might would stand in for military might; after the dismantling of the British Empire under the previous two administrations, computers might be the tool to return Britain to the top of the global heap. Technology would once again function as a tool for colonization—in this case, a softer sort of economic and political colonization. Under Wilson, the Labour Party scored points by reviving the idea of British exceptionalism and appealing to national pride. If British computing could succeed at home and abroad, the country stood a good chance of riding the electronic paradigm shift back to superpower status, many believed.

However, even though the public image of computing heading into the 1960s presented it as a powerful tool, the reality was quite different. Most computers in the late 1950s and early 1960s were little more than faster, electronic versions of punched card systems. Even as late as 1965, for instance, the popular ICT 1901 mainframe—perhaps Britain's closest comparator to the IBM System/360—was described as being "especially designed for former punched card applications."[4] This evolution rather than revolution in hardware was mirrored in the labor for the systems. The machine grade workers who had run the government's pre-electronic computing carried over into electronic systems. Computers and computer workers existed on two planes: first as cultural ideals that represented a new, modern, technological society, and second as actual artifacts and actors within a world that was changing less quickly than rhetoric might make it seem. The image and the reality of computing coexisted uneasily into the sixties, often coming into direct conflict with each other.

The existing drive for government efficiency through automation continued to gain steam, but the platform of technological revolution proclaimed as part of Labour's effort to win power in 1964 was meant to be as much a social revolution as a narrowly technical one.[5] "In science and industry we are content to remain a nation of Gentlemen in a world of Players," Wilson scoffed.[6] A working-class success story, and firm believer in meritocracy, Wilson insisted that amateurish men catapulted to positions of high power owing to their class connections were crippling the nation's ability to effectively modernize and compete. Computer technology, he felt, could become a new engine of meritocracy: It would undo these social patterns because only the most talented would be able to master it. Wilson believed that technology, carefully guided by government, would save the modern proletariat by creating a skill-based meritocracy: "Since technological progress left to the mechanism of private industry and private purpose can only mean high profits for a few, a high rate of employment for a few, and mass redundancy for many, if there had never been a case for socialism before, automation would have created it," he reasoned.

Soon after becoming prime minister, Wilson set up a new Ministry of Technology to enact this vision of technosocial change. Dubbed MinTech for short, it was briefly headed by Frank Cousins, but the second minister of technology, Tony Benn, became its most memorable and dynamic leader. A true believer in Labour's technosocial project, the young and dynamic Benn pursued Labour's dream of national salvation through technological advance with mixed results.[7] Wilson's government institutionalized the concept of strong, centralized, top-down guidance for technology in industry through MinTech, which tried to control the shape and growth of all British computing. MinTech brokered computing company mergers and orchestrated large government loans and investments for the industry. It also attempted to direct computer purchasing, use, and labor policy in both private industry and the massive public sector, which included the national government, the nationalized industries, and the National Health Service.

By directing computing policy and leading by example through large installations of British computers, the government injected much-needed capital into British computing. It did so for the sake of a technological future in which British tools, machines, and techniques would hopefully once again have world-changing influence. Labour's belief in the transformative power of computing would prove misplaced, however. Labour's technological revolution was a bundle of contradictions, promising equality at home and hegemonic power abroad. These contradictions were mirrored in computer work in the 1960s. Computing was quickly becoming an exciting field and labor shortages were pulling both women and men into it, but it also was defined by the older models of office automation on which it was based and it was still shaped by the staffing and labor expectations for those jobs.

Britain's technological revolution would be halting and ultimately unsucessful because it became a reconsolidation of traditional hierarchies—not a revolution at all. Complicated by faulty systems, labor shortages, and organizational growing pains, the era of White Heat extended British cultural and economic mores into a new high-technology future rather than breaking with the past. Labour's utopian, socialist visions fell short, even by the party's own standards, and Wilson's government continued to shape computing policy around fundamentally old-fashioned social ideals. Under him the Civil Service continued to build its computing edifice around computer workers who embodied the government's antimeritocratic hierarchies.

This chapter discusses these contradictions by comparing the perspectives of actual workers with the advertising discourses that determined how computing appeared to the government, the public, and managers in private industry. Although advertising and the popular press made computing look seamless and automatic, in reality the labor of many women, and soon men, impelled into early computing jobs was critical to the success of computer installations because they were not, in fact, automatic or well-functioning. As the sixties wore on, not only did these workers' skills begin to be recognized, but they also stopped being low-cost labor. In an era when electronic machines still regularly "broke down," most computers offered more speed but less stability than established electromechanical systems. Operators continued to be a critical human link in the data-processing chain—facilitators more than "human brakes"—and their labor allowed government and industry to take on ever more data-intensive projects. Although machines were still sold with the image of a low-skill, feminized staff, operator work was starting to become recognized as skilled. In the flux of the mid-1960s, actual and perceived computer labor shortages first helped women stay in the field, then eventually removed them from it, by inflating the status and pay for computer work out of the realm of "women's work." By juxtaposing the conflicting popular discourses of computing with the personal accounts of men and women who worked in early computing installations, it is possible to gain some sense of how the computing revolution simultaneously meant many different things to different people, and how the trajectory of the field tended toward reinstating older forms of labor hierarchy rather than upending them.

The Fiction of Full Automation

A survey by the London *Times* of computers installed in the United Kingdom between 1953 and 1960 discovered over £16.3 million worth of computer purchases, not including peripherals.[8] At an average cost of just over £100,000 per computer, this put the number of new computer installations at more than one hundred for these years, or about ten new computing installations on average per year before the start of the 1960s. Computers were still being deployed only in small numbers heading into the heyday of the mainframe. By 1960, the government only had twenty-two electronic computers, but these numbers would pick up quickly. By 1963, computers in government numbered sixty-three and all together had cost close to £7 million, and by the end of the decade there would be well over two hundred mainframes in the central government, totaling over £36 million.[9]

These numbers, and a focus on hardware, obscure the nature of computer use during this period. Brought in to replace time-tested electromechanical systems, early business computers had little field testing. Throughout the 1950s, and even into the 1960s, systems were prone to failure. Presented to consumers and the public as "electronic brains" that worked with minimal human intervention, early computers were anything but self-actuating or fully automatic. Nevertheless, they were increasingly put to ever-greater use in offices to solve workflow problems in businesses and government. From the mid-1950s on, computers were purchased and installed for a variety of business uses rather than for the mathematical and scientific uses to which they had previously been put.[10] The fault-riddled state of these systems helps reconstruct an image of the low-level, day-to-day, human control required for early computers to function, and it humanizes a labor force often taken for granted as a mass of interchangeable workers.

J. Lyons & Co., the British teashop and bakery conglomerate, was an unlikely but very successful computer pioneer, creating an in-house computing division first to solve its own nationwide inventory problems and later to market its machines and expertise throughout Britain, Britain's former colonies, and Commonwealth countries.[11] Lyons was first in the field of applying electronic computing to business endeavors—not just in Britain, but globally—and was arguably the most successful company to use the new technology early on. Ironically, Lyons initially had to look to America after World War II for ideas on electronic computing. A fact-finding mission to the United States by several Lyons managers in 1947—several years after the secret destruction of most of the Colossus machines—sparked the project that would become LEO. However, it was ultimately the EDSAC project at Cambridge University that enabled LEO: Lyons bought and successfully adapted the plans for the EDSAC to its needs.[12]

Initially, Lyons applied electronic computing to the problem of a large, complex, nightly production and inventory cycle. The speed of an electronic machine was the only way to complete the daily task in the time allotted, especially as the company grew. After setting up a pool of "girls" at their London headquarters who telephoned shop manageresses throughout the nation at the end of each day, Lyons collected inventory data to feed to the LEO I so that each teashop could be shipped neither too much nor too little of its perishable bakery products each morning. Soon, Lyons also transferred seven thousand of its employee payroll accounts onto the new computer. This change, made in 1954, eliminated twenty-three clerical and accounting staff members who previously did the payroll with conventional accounting machines.

In the following months, thousands more Lyons employees had their pay transferred to the computerized system as it proved its reliability.[13] However, even the apparently seamless work of the original LEO machine, engineered specifically for Lyons's needs, belied an enormous amount of behind-the-scenes troubleshooting and maintenance. Operators worked literally around the clock to ensure that the inventory and payroll systems continued to function, with little chance for system downtime and maintenance. Stress levels ran high while operators tried to perform precise work with imperfect tools. Lucy Slater, an operator and programmer of the EDSAC computer upon which the LEO was based, remembered the recalcitrant machine overheating and catching on fire. Slater recalled that sometimes she would give the machine "a hearty kick" to get it working again—or at least to vent frustration.[14] In addition to standard problems caused by programming or punching errors, there were often phantom errors that had to do with the machine's robustness. Mary Coombs, an early LEO programmer, recalled one particularly maddening program fault that turned out not to be a program error at all: The machine was malfunctioning due to the proximity of an elevator whose workings interfered with the hardware's state.[15] Colin Hobson, a Lyons computer operator, likewise recalled that "the earliest machines were very temperamental ... Some of the early applications needed a lot of nursing."[16]

Large retailers like the grocery chain Sainsbury's and the pharmacy Boots, along with large banks and many insurance companies, also made efforts to computerize early on. Nationalized industries like British Rail, the dockyards, and numerous national and local government departments similarly led the way in installing business computers ranging in price from roughly £50,000 to £350,000 between 1955 and 1960.[17] By comparison, the annual salary for an office employee in this period ranged from £300 to £1,500. Advantages of cost were by no means guaranteed. The first dedicated administrative computer for central government, an ICT 1201, was purchased for the Post Office in 1957 and installed in the fall of 1958.[18] From this point on, more computers were installed rapidly within the government.

It was still usually an open question whether or not electronic machines would work as reliably as the electromechanical systems they replaced, much less result in dramatic increases in work speed or gains in productivity. Administrative systems had not yet reached a point of maturity and stability, and carefully engineered solutions to specific problems of workflow, like the LEO I, were the exceptions rather than the rule. In 1959, well into the era of computerized payroll, thousands of men went unpaid at the Rosyth dockyards due to a computer failure in which not one but two payroll computers "broke down" simultaneously.[19] With no manual fallback system, the men paid for their trips home by drawing IOUs for train tickets. Many received meal vouchers to tide them over or received an advance on their next day's pay in a haphazard fashion, being overpaid by as much as £10 as the payroll office struggled to portion out money until the machines could be brought online again. At a time when a normal yearly salary was between £500 and £1,000, being overpaid by £10 for one day's work represented an enormous error.

Computer hardware itself was not solely to blame for all computing failures. Poor systems analysis and implementation often hindered effective use. In 1960, the large chain of pharmacies, Boots, installed an Emidec 1100 computer at its headquarters in Nottingham to handle inventory for over sixty thousand different products stocked by the company. In order to arrive at the "the transfer of orders from the shops to computor [sic]," the company undertook a pilot study lasting more than two years' time. In part, this was because input needed to go through several steps in order to become part of the database. Instead of simply inputting the data directly, items had to be transferred by hand onto a special card using mark-sense lead, in a piecemeal fashion by nondedicated staff. The card was "then converted to a punch card by a mark-sensing punch and ... passed to the card reader."[20] The enormous advance offered by the machine was hobbled by an uneconomic and poorly thought out implementation system. In the end, it was only utilized for the more common products stocked by the pharmacy. The outlay for the machine and its associated start-up costs were never recouped.

The physical infrastructure of midcentury office environments also added to the creakiness of the endeavor to modernize. Old buildings lacking air conditioning or even sufficient power made British industry almost inimical to computerization on a physical level. Vacuum tubes often broke in environments without temperature control. Punched card entry could fail due to moisture-warped cards or for other reasons. A spectacular failure at LEO during this period occurred "one very hot summer" when Colin Hobson and his staff of young men were working "stripped to the waist, with all the windows open." At that point, "a plague of newly hatched black flies came in from the playing field opposite." The flies "got everywhere and caused data failures when the card readers tried to read them," recalled Hobson.[21] More commonly, however, open windows were used to bring the computers themselves in. Many photos from the era show mainframes being brought in through upper-story windows by means of cranes in order to bypass the tight stairwells and hallways characteristic of many older buildings.

Proper electrical systems also could not be taken for granted, even in the offices of a business computing pioneer like Lyons. This created dangerous situations for both machines and staff. "Our chief operator was paralyzed from the waist down" and got around in a wheelchair, remembered Hobson. "He used to help himself along by grabbing the card punches on one side of the aisle and the card sorters on the other." One day, he stood up, "for the first time in years." Unfortunately, "it turned out that the punches and sorters were on different power supplies and the earth [ground] on one was faulty, catapulting him into the air."[22] Even though computing advertisements showed an idealized tableau in which computers were arranged in clean and spacious machine rooms, this sort of immaculate modern office was still very much in the minority. Internal computer company magazines talked about the spectacular lengths to which companies often went to shoehorn new computing systems into old and unsuitable buildings via added floor reinforcement and other tactics.[23]

A government inquiry from 1946 to 1949—which resulted in the Gowers Committee Report on Health, Welfare, and Safety in Non-Industrial Employment—recognized these problems and extended the health and safety benefits of the Factory Acts to those in white-collar employment. In an increasingly postindustrial setting, labor laws had to struggle to keep up with the changes wrought by modernization.[24] Calling for sweeping updates in British office infrastructure, the Gowers Report resulted in the passage of bills throughout the 1950s that created higher standards of health and safety for office workplaces and mandated the creation of modern offices.[25] These advances, however, were slow in coming. Throughout the 1960s, a majority of employees and employers contended with far less than ideal building infrastructure. Even the health of office workers was not as robust as their industrial counterparts. Rates of illness and infection—particularly tuberculosis—were much higher in the crowded and often poorly heated and maintained buildings that populated highly polluted city centers.[26]

During this period, the British computing industry's public relations machine presented a very different image of the state of computing. Computer companies presented a sleek, automatic vision of the future designed to make labor recede into the background. A widely run advertisement for the Electronic Computer Exhibition and Business Computer Symposium of 1958 proclaimed that "management will be able to see the advanced stage reached in the application of electronic computers as a means of achieving greater productivity in office and factory."[27] Throughout the late 1950s and well into the 1960s, the publicity and the reality of British business computing sharply diverged, but the industry sold machines on their ideal potential rather than their record of use.

Figure 3.1
An ICT 1301 mainframe is delivered to a local government office by means of a crane (left) showing the difficulty of setting up suitable machine rooms in existing offices. *ICT House Magazine*, no. 71, February 1965. By contrast, advertising images of the same machine showed spacious, futuristic settings (right). *ICT Magazine*, no. 9, September–October 1961.

Leading and Stumbling: Computers, Staff, and Government Bureaucracy

As the largest early adopter of computing technology in Britain, the government and nationalized industries played a major part in shaping the role of the administrative computer and its operators. The provisions put in place by the Beveridge Report for the expansion of government health and welfare services, in addition to the continually growing national bureaucracy, created ever more daunting data-processing tasks and a need for faster and more powerful electronic computers. The computers that businesses and government took advantage of fell into two general categories: either smaller or larger multipurpose mainframes. Between the two categories there was a major jump in price, with even "midrange" offerings falling into a much higher price range than small systems. Whereas smaller computers like the English Electric Deuce sold for around £50,000, midrange computer systems installed by the government and larger banks or insurance companies began pricing at triple that amount and could invoice for much more depending on their configuration and peripherals.[28] The Air Ministry, for instance, installed a £190,000 computer from EMI Electronics for its eighty thousand–employee payroll in 1959, and Lloyds Bank installed three IBMs in 1960 for around £350,000 to handle hundreds of thousands of customer account entries each week.[29]

Even well into the 1960s, the government found that its systems often did not live up to the promises of manufacturers. A 1965 memo from the Treasury to the Central Computer Bureau (CCB) noted that "more than a year ago we replaced our troublesome ICT 1201 computer by a well-recommended second-hand 1202 machine but, regrettably, this has also turned out to give us an unacceptable performance." Even though International Computers and Tabulators (ICT) "threw in clearly uneconomic [for ICT] maintenance resources to keep [the bureau] going," the Central Computer Bureau, one of the largest government computing installations, could not get its ICT computers to work reliably and consistently. The solution to this problem, Treasury officials felt, was to purchase yet another ICT machine, at a discount—despite the company's fairly damning "unsolicited admission of inability to satisfy."[30] Even when the machines failed to work as expected, the government continually increased spending on computing, because its data processing was becoming ever more reliant on the speed offered by electronic systems. In addition, many top ministers favored ICT over other companies, hoping that it would grow into a British equivalent of IBM. The government's purchasing was a way of investing in both the company's future and the future of British computing while at the same time buying needed equipment.

Buying was not the only option, however. As a result of the high costs of ownership, many businesses and government agencies took advantage of so-called computer center or computer bureau services, like the ones run by LEO and Hollerith in London. These centers processed large datasets to help customers facing higher-than-average workloads that stretched beyond their own systems' capabilities, and they sold time on computers operated and maintained within the computer manufacturer's own offices for customers who did not have their own computers.[31] Using a computer center's services might allow a smaller business to escape having to purchase a mainframe, but for larger users computer centers served as a place to have overflow work performed and also often as training grounds for their own computer operators.

In 1966, the central government followed the model of these computer centers when setting up the Central Computer Bureau. Based in London's Bunhill Row, the bureau reflected the computer center ideal of a central computing installation that ran jobs for many different users. The

Central Computer Bureau took over from the earlier Combined Tabulating Installation, which had provided similar services using electromechanical machines. Nonetheless, consolidating government computing in one location and thereby lessening the need to rely on outside agencies or individual departmental computers never achieved as much success as the government hoped.[32] Complete centralization of government computing, meant to save money and standardize procedures, could not keep up with the diverse needs of many different departments and users—much like computer bureau use could never be as flexible or responsive as having an in-house computing staff.

Prior to going electronic, the central government had employed a variety of electromechanical tabulating, sorting, and printing machines. The speeds attainable by these older systems, however, were expected to be inadequate for the needs of the growing national bureaucracy and its many centrally administered social services. The government now needed to keep track of the many different accounts and systems of payment required by the pay-as-you-earn (PAYE) system of employee taxation and government pension contribution instituted in 1948. In addition, other government-run systems of benefit payments—such as welfare, war injury, and disability payments—all but required the speed of new electronic systems. The modern welfare state was created by policy in an abstract sense and by technology in a literal sense.

The massive record keeping required by the Ministry of Pensions and National Insurance, the source of the largest computing installation in the country, handled the millions of entries for the recently instituted PAYE contribution system and for old age, welfare, disability, and war injury benefits. The ministry utilized a LEO II system for its own administration, but by 1960 it employed a more specialized Emidec 2400 for pension payment processing. The Emidec was capable of reading more than twenty thousand characters per second from magnetic tape, and it printed out over twenty million annual statements, reportedly working at the rate of nine hundred statements per minute.[33] For its first year of operation alone, it required an estimated 1,200 miles of magnetic tape—more than double the length of England—with two hundred characters recorded on every inch.[34]

Emphasis on these figures and statistics, however, obscures the fact that for every few thousand characters, or every few feet of tape, there was an entire chain of labor that included programmers, operators, data input workers, and systems analysts. Added to that were the computer manufacturers and their staff, who provided the machines and trained government employees on the use of the new systems. Of these groups, operators and data input staff were the largest. Their numbers represented an overall increase of staff in many cases, rather than a reduction, when compared with the workers they replaced. But because the amount of work had increased, more work was being performed by fewer workers.

The 1960 yearly report from the Ministry of Pensions laid out the staff training underway to bring the Emidec 2400 system online. In its first year of operation, executive and clerical staff underwent close to 43,000 man-days of training (over one hundred man-years). The following year they spent 8,500 man-days more on training (or more than twenty man-years) over the previous year to become technically proficient with the new system. The 16 percent increase in staff training for the first year alone added to the significant outlay for the machine. Close to a thousand new clerical staff were recruited, seven hundred of whom were in the central office performing the start-up work and data input required to prepare the new system for use. These new recruits brought the total number of workers in the ministry to just over thirty-seven thousand people. Data input staff had the daunting inaugural task of preparing a master punched card for every one of the country's millions of workers, pensioners, and welfare benefit recipients. Within the first year of the undertaking, only 5.5 million cards had been completed. In the pensioners category alone there were more than 5.5 million accounts.[35]

The original electronic computing system employed to run the twenty-five thousand–member payroll for the Ministry's own workers, a LEO II, had resulted in a net decrease in staff. It replaced a largely manual system in which about one hundred workers dealt with variations in data by hand before machine operating staff fed the material through conventional punched card machinery.[36] The LEO II removed the need for the hundred workers who computed variable factors like overtime, and it required fewer operators because it eliminated the need to pass punched cards through several machines several times during each run in order to arrive at the desired output.

The larger Emidec system, on the other hand, created an increase in staff. Rather than automating an older system already in place, it enabled the construction of a new system of payments and records. The Emidec computer, by virtue of its speed and versatility, helped to create a new set of tasks within the Ministry of Pensions that could not have been completed with older, slower technology. It was purchased with the express intention of defining a new system for doing work that had not previously existed. As a result, it brought new workers into the Ministry, workers whose jobs relied on electronic computing. A similar process was taking place throughout the government as other departments found they needed to turn to computing to redefine, rather than simply speed up, their short- and long-term operations. By the middle of the decade, computer staff in government was growing at a rate of 30 percent each year and this showed no signs of slowing. A significant number of computing projects were delayed or left incomplete due to the government being unable to recruit computing staff in large enough numbers.[37]

In 1965, six hundred computers operated throughout the country, with four hundred more on order from computer manufacturers. Nearly every British citizen now relied on computers and computer workers to provide some crucial service or state benefit. The national government led the way in computer purchasing, spending £14.1 million just on computing hardware for sixty-two installations from 1958 through early 1965, and more than half a million additional pounds were spent buying time on other computing installations each year.[38] In 1965 alone, Western Europe as a whole spent £250 million on computers.[39] British government studies projected that the need for over three hundred thousand office jobs, or roughly 9 percent of the clerical workforce, would be obviated by computer installations before 1975.[40] At the same time, computer labor was in high demand, and computing staff were being hired in ever-greater numbers. That computing would increasingly define the future of labor was becoming clear—but what that labor would look like was obscured by layers of media representation.

Envisioning a Future of Low Labor Costs

A poem reprinted in a 1960 issue of an office machinery and management magazine conveyed the faith most computer purchasers placed in their new mainframes:

In the spring, young men (grown vague and lazy)
And girls (grown starry-eyed and hazy)
Being human
Lack acumen
How undistracted, single-minded,
Never mooning, never blinded,
The computer,
Being neuter.[41]

The "neuter computer" contrasted sharply with the gendered bodies of workers—particularly women workers. The clerical workforce of both the public and private sectors was heavily feminized by the 1960s and was becoming more so. Of the almost 7.8 million working women in Britain in 1961, nearly 2.7 million were clerical workers. This number did not even include office machine operators, who were often counted under a separate census designation; adding them in raised the number of clerical workers by close to a million.[42] For the most part, early computer operators were drawn from this pool of pseudoclerical labor.

However, highlighting workers' gender could be a potent selling point. Powers-Samas, which combined with British Tabulating Machines in 1959 to create ICT, consolidated the trope of the "Powers Girl" early on, a figure who demonstrated their electromechanical machines in advertisements and brochures. When the machines became electronic, the Powers Girls remained and served much the same function as before. Dressed in ladies' business attire, the Powers Girls showed how it might look to use a computer, humanizing opaque, intimidating, and potentially confusing machines. They also served a didactic function by showing the kind of worker that should operate Powers machines once a company purchased them. Finally, they showed purchasers that computers would not require a huge outlay for labor in addition to the hardware: "The conventional method is to hire women trained to operate any of the many machines available on the market," wrote one author when discussing the economics of purchasing a new electronic Powers machine.[43]

"Most 'operative' jobs," wrote *Office Methods and Machines* magazine, "are performed by female staff, and this group is absorbing the majority of the present 40 percent of girl school-leavers entering office work."[44] In other words, close to half of all young women leaving school went to work in offices by 1967, and of these, most went into computer operation work. This was key to selling machines, because from 1950 to 1966 wages and salaries in the aggregate had nearly tripled, but gross trading profits of companies had little more than doubled.[45] Women continued to be seen as the best financial bet for much computing work.

In industry, untouched by any equal pay legislation until 1975, the discussion of the benefits that discriminatory wages produced was often quite candid. In 1965, the chief accountant of Bibby and Baron Ltd., the largest paper bag manufacturer in England, wrote a series of articles on how office managers could wring the greatest efficiency from their workers at the lowest cost. He urged employers to hire women, saying: "Equal pay for male and female workers is unlikely to be accepted by industrial concerns ... [and] because female clerks can be obtained at a cheaper price than males, and may be just as good if given the same opportunities and training, it should be your policy to employ them wherever possible."[46]

Throughout the 1960s, British computing companies' advertisements were dominated by figures similar to the Powers Girls, who became the object of a specific kind of managerial "male gaze." Nearly all photographs used to sell and showcase computers in the early 1960s pictured a conservatively dressed, plain-looking female workforce standing or sitting while working at machines.[47] As most machines became electronic, however, subtle changes in advertising style crept in. In earlier ads, Powers Girls smiled and engaged the viewer. By the late 1950s and early 1960s, often the Powers Girls only presented their backs to the viewer. Workers became increasingly faceless and expressionless as companies marketed more expensive machines. In the advertisement shown in figure 3.2, the woman's figure does not even have a face drawn on it.

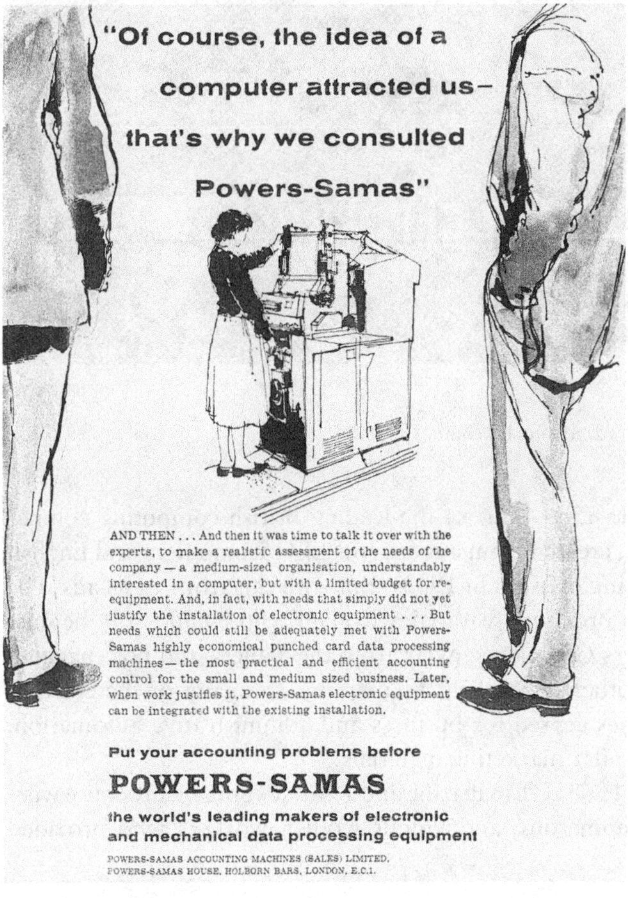

"Of course, the idea of a
computer attracted us–
that's why we consulted
Powers-Samas"
AND THEN . . . And then it was time to talk it over with the experts, to make a realistic assessment of the needs of the company — a medium-sized organisation, understandably interested in a computer, but with a limited budget for re-equipment. And, in fact, with needs that simply did not yet justify the installation of electronic equipment . . . But needs which could still be adequately met with Powers-Samas highly economical punched card data processing machines — the most practical and efficient accounting control for the small and medium sized business. Later, when work justifies it, Powers-Samas electronic equipment can be integrated with the existing installation.
Put your accounting problems before
POWERS-SAMAS
the world's leading makers of electronic
and mechanical data processing equipment
POWERS-SAMAS ACCOUNTING MACHINES (SALES) LIMITED,
POWERS-SAMAS HOUSE, HOLBORN BARS, LONDON, E.C.1.

Figure 3.2
The attraction of a computer meant the continued promise of low-cost, interchangeable labor. Powers-Samas advertisement in *Office Magazine*, May 1958.

Figure 3.3
English Electric–LEO advertising brochure, 1963.

English Electric–LEO—one of the leading British computing companies of the sixties, created from a merger of LEO Computers and English Electric's computing division in 1963—ran with this trope in its ads. The cover of its 1963 brochure featured a woman who could easily be mistaken for a Powers Girl, facing away from the camera and not engaging the viewer. The other major British computer company of the era that produced machines geared for business and administrative automation, ICT, produced similar marketing materials.

Images from a 1963 ICT magazine and 1962 advertising brochure were populated with numerous, anonymous women workers who provided

Figure 3.4
ICT Magazine photograph, 1963.

Figure 3.5
ICT advertising brochure photo, 1962.

little visual interest and failed to engage the viewer.[48] Far from being positioned as "cheesecake" to help attract attention to the machines, the women workers were used simply as placeholders for the company's own staff. ICT's advertising brochure has page after page of photographs of workers' backs, taken in the machine rooms of companies that had already "signed on to progress" and installed ICT computers.[49] As the electronic age wore on, gendered bodies were sometimes used less to humanize computers than to show how people should accommodate themselves to machines.

Despite the orderly machine rooms, the effect of viewing an entire brochure containing page after page of similar photographs of silent, oblivious, women workers did not make computing seem like it would alleviate drudgery, as promised by advertising rhetoric. Through these photographs, drudgery became emphasized, taken for granted as part of a high-performance system engineered to maximize throughput. Human labor was positioned as a temporary inconvenience within systems that anticipated a more fully automated future. If labor could not be made fully invisible, at least it could be made less obtrusive by using temporary, high-turnover women workers with no claim to equal wages, job training, or promotion opportunities. The need for more specialized computer staff required a concomitant increase in training, but "in practice this really means training for male office staff only," noted *Office Methods and Machines*. That group would soon comprise a new and growing "administrative" class of computing professionals, requiring "education in complex techniques and business practices as well as a wide knowledge of the overall activities of the employing company." By contrast, the "operative" group within office staffs generally only received "training mainly in the manual skills needed to work individual office machines" plus whatever on-the-job skills they could pick up.[50]

Powers-Samas, and later ICT, marketed its computing solutions worldwide, focusing especially on Commonwealth and former colonial markets. Just as the machines in the company's advertisements had impact beyond the British context, so too did the images of workers in these ads. As British companies raced to export computers to compete with IBM, overseas markets for British computers were also targeted with information about who should fill computing jobs. Cultural and economic ideals exported along with machines meant that technological transfer was as much about the transfer of labor patterns as it was about the transfer of specific technologies. As early as 1955, Powers-Samas opened a service bureau in Delhi filled with its machines and staff. Powers trained local workers as part of a plan coordinated with the Indian government and the Indian Statistical Institute to promote "economic uplift and industrialization."[51] Powers-Samas dispatches back to its headquarters in Britain discussed the "clean symmetry of Western-influenced architecture" replacing older buildings and touted the company canteen with ice water and refrigeration. Pictures showed a building filled with young Indian women in training to become machine operators and punch operators. Efficient, well-trained, and "proud to be associated with a great venture," the young women mirrored their British counterparts hired to work on Powers-Samas machines at home.[52]

These labor choices were no accident, nor were they the most likely labor patterns in context. Just as "no effort [had] been spared in the planning of this service bureau to conform to modern trends and to show it off as a model," neither was any effort spared to engineer the most effective workforce for the bureau in accordance with British standards and experience. From the ice water in the canteen to the special cooling and lighting in the building, everything about the installation was meant to mirror British ideals of "civilization" and technological modernity. Part and parcel of that modernity was the employment of young women as an easily trained, affordably priced, and ideally highly interchangeable technological labor force.

"The noise of steel against steel in battles fought over this ancient city, gives way to the busy chatter of Power-Samas machines engaged in a combat of a different kind," boasted an article in the company magazine, without irony. With Powers machines fighting "the battle against hunger, poverty, and underproduction," their advertising and business practices were also battling for a share of a lucrative new market. Showing Indian users how best to staff their new installations was one part of the marketing strategy—and it was a marketing strategy used wherever British computing companies tried to sell their machines, including Africa, Asia, and the Middle East.[53] "Language, dress, customs may differ from country to country, but Powers Samas punched card methods are international," proclaimed one ad. "Witness this group of operators in Khartoum and this picture of the operator's training school in Bombay" it continued. Powers conflated technical needs with the effects of the company's heterogeneous engineering of foreign labor forces.[54]

ICT also became a major player in the global computing market, wooing Indian buyers throughout the 1960s. Prime Minister Nehru viewed

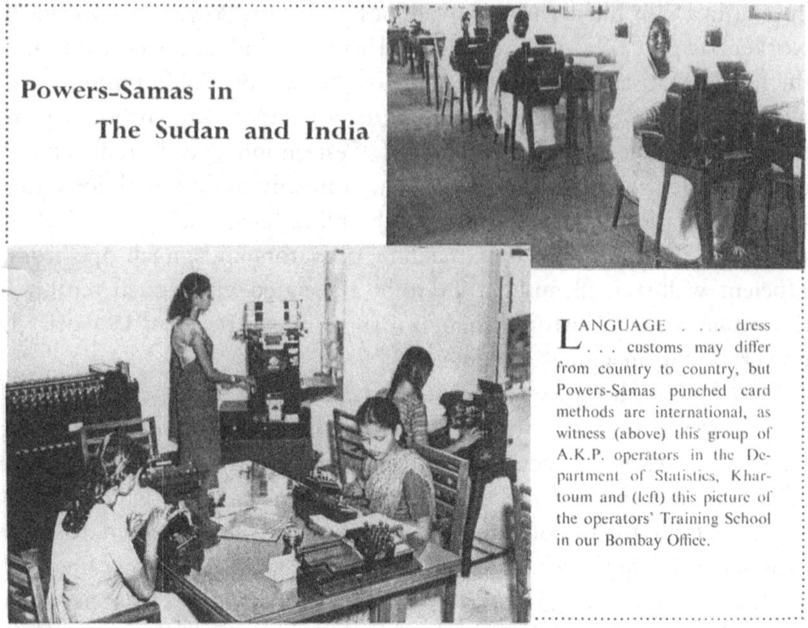

Powers-Samas in The Sudan and India

LANGUAGE . . . dress . . . customs may differ from country to country, but Powers-Samas punched card methods are international, as witness (above) this group of A.K.P. operators in the Department of Statistics, Khartoum and (left) this picture of the operators' Training School in our Bombay Office.

Figure 3.6
The Powers Magazine, March 1954.

ICT equipment at the Indian Industries Fair in 1962, and President Khan of Pakistan was photographed inspecting new ICT equipment at a ceremony at the State Bank of Pakistan in 1961.[55] British computer companies tried to market British technology as the saving grace of less industrialized nations, despite the fact that their toehold in most of these markets came as a result of colonial influence that had been brutal and debilitating. Spurred on by government support in the form of contracts and loans, British computing companies did not simply act on their own as free agents in a fictional, idealized, global free market. The state's support of ICT in particular would grow over the course of the 1960s, until the company was essentially tethered to the government's computing needs. Even in the early sixties, however, most British computer companies took their cues for how to interact with foreign markets from the government's past and present foreign policy. In turn, successive governments relied on those computer companies to extend the reach of British economic and political hegemony abroad.

Figure 3.7
A young woman demonstrates ICT equipment at the Indian Industries Fair in 1962 as the permanent undersecretary of the Commonwealth Relations Office, Sir Savile Garner, and another man look on. *ICT Magazine*, August 1962.

ICT's marketing presented computing as a modernizing force to bring former colonial holdings into an ostensibly clean, orderly, productive future. In this vision of the future, modeled on British culture and experience, women held particular roles within the economy relative to men and machines—technical roles that were nonetheless tacitly conveyed as being peripheral to the true work of technological modernization. Photographs of ICT equipment in Indian and Pakistani installations followed the particular gendered contours of the British labor model. Although British companies tried to position these work organization methods as natural outgrowths of the technology, they were in fact didactic. Marketing images showing women exclusively performing data-input and low-level-operation work both reflected the way British companies staffed their overseas installations and how they taught foreign buyers to use the equipment.

Even though imagery produced by British computer companies presented young women in India operating punch machines and computers, and demonstrating equipment at exhibitions and trade shows, India's punch operator labor force was not as feminized as Britain's. Sometimes, punching jobs were reserved for men only—as in the case of the Tata Iron and Steel Corporation, whose class of punch trainees, all of whom volunteered for the work, were exclusively male.[56] Sometimes, men and women worked side by side: The punch room at Air India in 1961 contained both men and women punchers in roughly equal proportions.[57] When Indian companies set up their own computing installations, the gendered mores of British computing usually did not attach. For this reason, even lower-level jobs in computing were often considered men's jobs in India. As Ross Bassett and Ramesh Subramanian have shown in their respective studies of technological transfer and Indian computing, Indian users, programmers, and engineers were far from passive recipients of foreign high technology, molding foreign machines to the Indian context and soon developing computer software and hardware solutions specific to their needs via their own national computer industry.[58] This history has long been overshadowed because of the powerful marketing attempts of Western powers.

Between 1960 and 1967, the percentage of the Indian computing market held by British companies more than doubled. Still, it remained barely more than a tenth of the market overall, with IBM dominating.[59] British companies reported on each computer sold in their company magazines, and sometimes especially large sales were reported in the national press. Images of foreign machine installations performed a dual function. First, they were meant to show the global advance of British technology. Second, they participated in constructing a type of cultural hegemony through which readers could assess the progress of other nations according to British standards.[60]

In an era when Prime Minister Harold Macmillan was shaking the British Conservative establishment by proclaiming that a "wind of change" was sweeping through Africa, arguing that the growing desire for independence there would soon require a loosening of Britain's imperial grip, British computer companies—with the aid of the press—were repurposing imperial rhetoric to consolidate their own power and importance. Images of British computing abroad presented unsubtle messages of triumph and control that presented women's bodies as trophies. Pictures of women considered "exotic" by British standards often accompanied articles that tried to show British ingenuity structuring economies, bureaucracies, and women's and men's lives abroad. A computer operator in a shiny, form-fitting dress, pictured working on a British computer at Ashanti Goldfields in Ghana, was one of many images that perpetuated a gendered imperial gaze. Linked to a column describing British success selling computers overseas, particularly in former colonial and Dominion countries, the image was captioned "HOT stuff." Below the image, the front page article on ICL's successes in overseas markets proclaimed that in 1970 ICL had won 36 percent of the market for computers in India, close to 50 percent in the "Far East," and more than 80 percent in East Africa.[61] These economic victories were presented as symbolic of British cultural power in a broader sense.

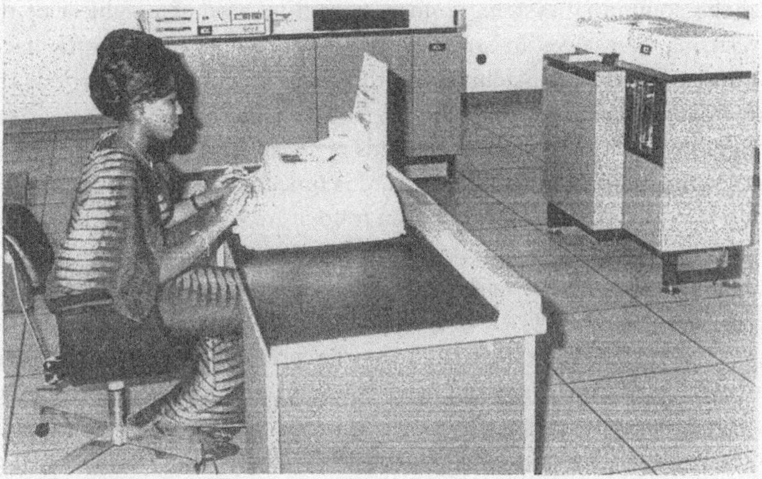

An Ashanti Goldfields operator with the 1901A installed at Obuasi, Ghana.

HOT stuff in GOSO

Figure 3.8
ICL Marketing, February 1970.

At home, computing's progress was also aligned with a distinctly British style of postindustrial civilization and order. Pictures of the Royal Family inspecting or inaugurating computer installations were perennial press favorites. The Queen Mother, the Queen, and the Duke of Edinburgh could all be found sitting at an operator's console or inspecting a new machine whenever a major computing installation was inaugurated or when a new plant was built by a British computer manufacturer.[62] In addition to being publicity events, these photo opportunities not-so-subtly put the mark of the Empire on British computing.

From Low Cost to Best Bet: Women Operators as the Apotheosis of the Machine

As the 1960s wore on, images of women interacting with machines became less literal and, in the process, more freighted with additional meaning. Instead of focusing on a relatively plain-looking feminized workforce, whose presence was simultaneously meant to stand in for low-cost labor and to recede into the background as the viewer considered the computing system, women started to become a subject of the advertising themselves. In earlier advertisements, women were often faceless accessories to the machine, but this trope began to lose favor as the sixties progressed.

In many later images, the formula is reversed: The machines recede or disappear while the woman remains, this time facing the viewer. At a certain point, advertising imagery began to focus more on the fact that managers were buying a system for managing and maximizing labor rather than just a machine. Although this had been implicit in earlier advertisements, in the later sixties it became explicit. Women pictured in the ads retained their importance as a shorthand representation of workers who conveyed all the benefits, and few of the downsides, of modern office labor, but now that message became even more critical to the sales pitch. Women's labor itself was being marketed explicitly as an essential part of the computing system.

The advertisements in figure 3.9 portray workers as nearly superhuman when combined with their trusty computers, which barely appear in the ads at all. In the case of ICL's BARIC ad, a "girl operator" interacts with computer bureau services through her office terminal link. "The implications are obvious to every businessman," says the ad copy. Managers could gain all the benefits of a powerful mainframe with none of the hardware costs and little labor overhead.[63] In another advertisement

This is all the staff you need to process orders, produce invoices, check credit, check and analyse sales, check stocks, produce despatch notes and operate a computer.
INTERACT 75 makes it possible.
The Baric INTERACT 75 service gives you direct access to a major computer system from your own office.
Easily. Quickly. And economically.
But the real advantage of INTERACT 75 is the fact that the computer you plug into is already programmed to carry out the day-to-day commercial processes involved in running your business.
Like recording invoices. Issuing orders. Updating stock records. Checking customer credit limits. And calculating discounts.
In the opening phase of INTERACT 75 we are offering this Commercial Management Service to a limited number of customers.
These will probably be companies with about 200-2,000 personnel; selling from stock; and coping with an invoicing problem.
Briefly, this is how it works.
All your orders, from whatever source, are passed to the girl operator at your INTERACT 75 terminal. She transfers the order data to the computer, via the terminal. The computer immediately checks all the data against permanent file information.
If something is amiss, such as an item being out of stock, it advises her immediately.
If not, her single entry starts a number of balls rolling.
The computer records all the information on the user's private file: quantity, ledger entry, customer's name and address and so on, allowing for later detailed analysis for management reports, stock control, etc.
The computer then scans the file to prepare the invoice, noting any discount arrangements and adjusting the account.
Within seconds it passes the information back to the user's office where it prints out the completed invoice automatically.
The implications are obvious to every businessman.
Unfortunately we can only serve a few. So we would urge you to be quick about writing for details to
Baric Computing Services Limited, 68 Newman Street, London W1P 4EH.
An ICL/Barclays Company.
BARIC
INTERACT 75 Europe's first commercial time-sharing system.

Figure 3.9
Machines begin to disappear, and computer labor becomes the object of marketing. Advertisement for ICL Baric Remote Computing Service in *ICL News*, 1970 (above). Advertisement in *Office Methods and Machines Magazine*, 1967 (next page).

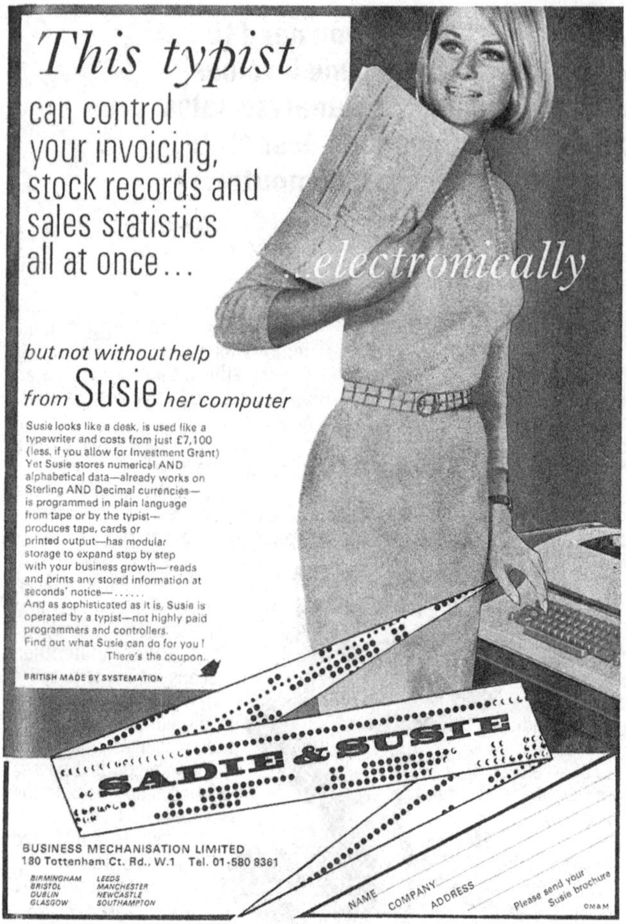

Figure 3.9 (continued)

for a different type of technology, from the smaller company Business Mechanisation Limited, the technique is similar. Selling a minicomputer instead, the advertisement again focuses on the operator. With the help of her small office computer named SUSIE—short for Stock Updating and Sales Invoicing Electronically—the lone "girl operator" fulfilled functions like payroll, invoicing, stock control, and accounting which previously would have required a larger staff.[64] Women's labor was no longer simply the best fit for the system, it was a necessary element in order to get the benefits of cost and control computers promised.

In addition, young, smartly dressed operators increasingly became objects of a heteronormative male gaze. Although previous advertisements used women to showcase machines, there had been little sexual subtext; women in earlier advertisements were shown less as "pretty faces" than as working hands. In the late sixties, computer marketing added sexuality to the pitch by differentiating one operator from the masses and foregrounding her, even to the exclusion of the machine.[65] Using sex appeal strengthened the shift already underway in advertising from focusing on machines and workers to focusing primarily on workers. It was also nothing new in the sense that men's ideas about women's sexuality had been used to structure jobs in computing for decades. After all, compulsory heterosexuality's effect on women's working lives was the main reason women had ended up in low-level machine work in the first place.

The primary purpose of these ads, however, was to assure managers that they could get away with using generic office staff when buying a computer. The ads asserted that operators did not require special training or expertise. The SUSIE computer "is operated by a typist—not highly paid programmers and controllers," says the ad copy. Even though it states that the computer "is programmed in plain language from tape or by the typist," the operator remains just a *typist*, not a "highly paid programmer." Yet the fact that SUSIE came with a 130-page programming manual gives some indication of how inaccurate it was to refer to the operator as a typist.[66] Several of the other computers produced by the group of companies known as Business Mechanisation Limited, later Business Computers Limited, had women's names that alluded to the computer's functions. In addition to SUSIE, there was BETSIE (a betting and bookmaking computer) and SADIE (which stood for Sterling and Decimal Invoicing Electronically). Women's labor had become so closely allied with computers that some machines actually took on their identities.

Another selling technique evolved simultaneously over the course of the 1960s. Some companies, including ICT (later International Computers Limited, or ICL), employed all-women computer demonstration teams who worked on-site at the company operating the demonstration machines for potential customers and also went to trade shows. These teams ensured that business consumers saw computers as easy to staff and not overly complex to run. The young women presented a vision of effortless perfection and conveyed none of the gravitas male staff might have. For similar reasons women operators and programmers at IBM's

Figure 3.10
ICT Demonstration Team photo from *ICT Magazine*, September 1964. From left to right: Carole Tucker, Carol Philbrick, Carol Jordan, and Dorine Conway.

world headquarters on Madison Avenue in New York City were told to work on the computers in the window, in view of the sidewalk, to make the machines look easy to use.[67]

In 1964, the ICT demonstration team traveled to trade shows and customer sites. A photograph shows the team playing with output paper from a machine console at a trade show exhibit.[68] Attired in matching uniforms consisting of a dark business suit with a knee-length skirt and an ICT pin on the lapel, the women's clothes did not aim to draw attention to their youth and gender in trade show settings that would be filled mostly with older men. For the photo of the 1964 team, the individual names of all the "girls" were recorded in the caption, a relatively rare sign of respect for workers who were often seen as interchangeable or ancillary.

By contrast, the 1970 ICL demonstration team aimed to capitalize on the youth and sex appeal of the women operators.[69] In a trade show setting, the impact of the 1970 demonstration team would have

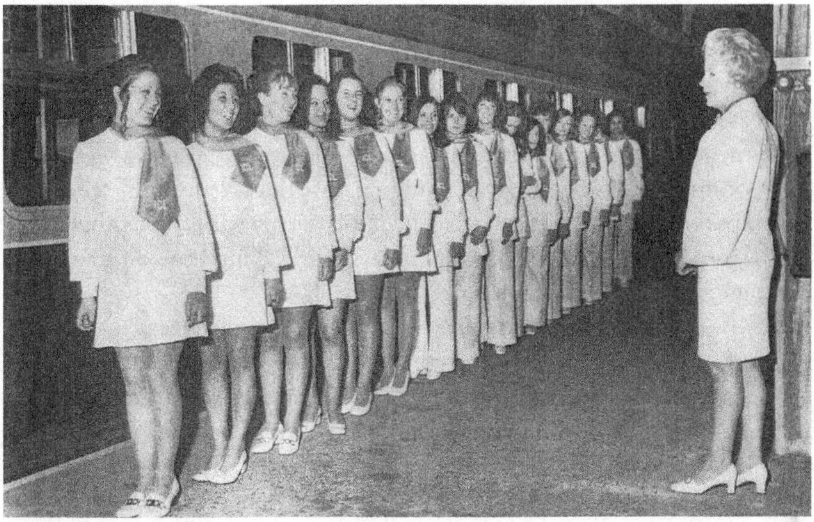

Figure 3.11
ICL Demonstration Team pictured in *ICL News*, 1970.

been quite different from that of earlier teams. White linen outfits and contrasting bright orange ICL scarves visually screamed their presence. Although only a minority of the team members were attired in company-issued minidress uniforms in the image shown in figure 3.11, those young women were deliberately placed in the photo's foreground, whereas the larger number of team members who opted for the pantsuit uniform were placed at the back of the line. As social mores relaxed in the "swinging sixties," the categories that defined women outside the workplace became increasingly visible within it.

ICL's all-male upper management was not solely responsible for injecting sex appeal into the mission of the demonstration team. The head of the department (the older woman pictured on the right in figure 3.11) was credited with choosing the uniforms. Publicity photographs played up the changes. Unlike earlier teams, the women in the 1970 photo were not referred to by name, but only as a group.

Looking at Machines through Workers' Eyes

Although the identities and stories of the women on ICL's 1970 demonstration team may be lost, stories of certain operators can be recovered and the realities of operators' work can be compared with the images used to represent it. In September 1961, four days before his nineteenth birthday, Colin Hobson started work as an operator at the LEO computer company.[70] Still based out of the J. Lyons & Co. bakery and teashops headquarters in Cadby Hall, and then later in Queensway, London, LEO Computers had gone from handling only the inventory of the Lyons teashops to handling payroll and inventory for a variety of other businesses, providing custom-built computers, and selling time on their own computers.

Hobson became interested in computing precisely because the field was new and enigmatic. When a computer company representative came to his school to speak to the students "about these wondrous science fiction things called computers," his interest was piqued: "At the time everybody else called them electronic brains!" he recalled. As a young man recruited straight out of school to work on computers, Hobson was slightly unusual. LEO and other computing companies had different standards for hiring operators than government and industry in general. Unlike the lion's share of operators working at the time, Hobson and his team were all men.

Yet in terms of background, Hobson epitomized the early wave of "computer professionals" who found work in computing installations before the existence of such jobs was widely known and before the field professionalized. Knowing little about computing, other than the fact that he wanted to know more, Hobson trained on the job to become a computer professional long before experience in the field was required or even expected to get such a job. No special educational qualifications as yet served a gatekeeping function. Hobson nixed the idea of going to work for ICT because, he recalled, he "was not impressed by the ICT idea of a computer, which seemed to need a lot of bicycle chains."[71] Conceptions of the futuristic nature of computers figured heavily into his decision of where to work, showing the powerful effects that popular discourses of technology often had on people. Hobson wanted to work with machines that matched the idealized image of computing presented in the press. He quickly found out, however, that the reality and the ideal were quite far apart.

Early on, the role of a computer operator was far from straightforward. When working on the LEO I, II, and III models between 1961 and 1967, breakdowns were frequent, particularly on the machines that relied on vacuum tubes like the LEO I and II, Hobson remembered.[72] In this context, operators needed to be able to handle both hardware and software problems to shepherd programs through a successful run. When he started at LEO he was given hands-on training and also sent on several two-week programming courses to learn both machine code and higher-level languages like Intercode.[73] Because it was important for operators to know enough code to be able to debug programs during runs, most operators knew how to read code and write simple computer programs. As systems got upgraded, operators were sent on more training courses—but Hobson stressed that the most useful training was the hands-on work.

Both performing operating work and training others to be operators was part of Hobson's job. As a LEO computer bureau operator, he operated computers for his company's own use and also ran programs for other companies that bought time on LEO machines. Timesharing was an important part of LEO's business model during an era when purchasing a mainframe was largely out of reach for all but the biggest companies and government organizations. Hobson and other LEO bureau staff were responsible for ensuring programs ran successfully and for delivering output. Later, he worked as a trainer, going to customer sites to train staff who would operate new computers purchased by businesses and government departments. As a result, Hobson provided labor for a wide variety of consumers in the private and public sector. He also witnessed and helped shape the emerging role of the electronic computer operator in industry and government through his training work.

Simply finding enough computer time was a big part of an early operator's job. Computing power was still in short enough supply during the early 1960s that the LEO bureau staff often had to "beg, borrow, or steal" time on LEO machines installed at other companies, and in government offices, to be able to complete all of the bureau's contract work. This borrowed, or more likely bought, computer time filled an important niche in the computing ecosystem, maximizing the use of expensive machines and helping to reduce the cost of owning a machine for some customers. Working overnight on a large government machine in the Post Office, Hobson recalled, "We had very little contact with the staff on these machines because they would hand over and go home. The Post Office machine was particularly impressive because they had a habit of loading it up with four massive programs and then their entire shift (of what seemed like twelve people) would go, leaving one or two LEO operators to finish off the Post Office work and run the bureau work."[74] The operators who "handed off" this work, unlike Hobson's team, were predominantly women. Because operator work was often performed overnight and at other sites, the prevailing view at LEO was that bureau operators needed to be men. Hobson recalled that the company worried that extra supervision, in the form of a women's officer for female employees, would be needed if even one woman were employed—and so none were. Several LEO employees of this era recall the company as being very paternalistic.

Working closely with LEO's engineers and designers on cutting-edge computing applications, LEO operators also felt they were a cut above others. Government installations, like the "particularly impressive" one at the Post Office, seemed overstaffed and undermotivated from Hobson's perspective. From the perspective of the Civil Service computer operators, however, the LEO bureau and other computer companies were no paragons. Ann Sayce, whose career as a computer operator at the Post Office overlapped with Hobson's time at LEO, remembered that "the worst places [to apply for a job] were the computer firms. They didn't want women because they thought they couldn't work at night."[75] The stigma against women working at night differed widely by organization however. Civil servants would often work late shifts, regardless of gender, even though at LEO night shifts and offsite work effectively destroyed women's chances of employment.

LEO's culture, which explicitly barred women but styled itself as a labor meritocracy, presaged things to come as computing became a more desirable field. Lower-level men employees, like paper fetchers, could be trained for operator positions if they showed interest, underscoring the point that technical experience and aptitude were not the barriers keeping women out.[76] In contrast to the operators who formed the demonstration teams at ICL, at LEO a culture of masculine bravado meant that the complicated relationship between men and machines was becoming normalized as a natural partnership. One LEO employee recollected that "the operators were always male, and one of the rumored reasons for this was that the spools on the tape decks were so high that if a female operator tried to load tape, her bra straps were likely to snap!"[77] The iteration of such jokes provided a glimpse into the company's machine room culture, an environment that, intentionally or not, made it difficult for women to be included as equals—or even to be included at all.

Even though his regular shift was all men, Hobson did train women workers from other companies. Trainees came to LEO's offices to help run jobs on computers their employers had ordered, but which were still being tested prior to being installed. The women trainees were no different from the men trainees in terms of skill and aptitude, Hobson remembered, remarking that their relative scarcity at some companies probably had to do with the politics of office supervision or shift scheduling rather than an expectation that women would not perform the work as well as men.[78] Yet while women operators were not welcome, Hobson noted an "odd thing" about the position of other women at LEO: Some of the programmers were women, and "there seemed to be no problems about them hanging around at night in a partially deserted building with a bunch of young men!"[79] Women programmers, like Mary Coombs, could escape some of the strictures placed on women operators because of their elevated professional identity, which was implicitly linked to class distinctions that implied a different set of social behaviors. Coombs was a management trainee at a time when it was rare for women to be trained for management. But Coombs's father, a Lyons employee, had gotten her the job. She jumped at the chance to move to LEO when it was a new division still within Lyons because of the dullness of the hand-calculating job she had been given doing ice cream cost analysis at Lyons. Although women operators might do programming, women like Coombs started at a different level: Their higher class status meant their skill level was automatically imagined to be higher, and their job identity was firmly white collar even though they worked with machines.

Class identity could trump gender to a certain extent, but the intersection of class and gender made gender itself a fundamentally classed category. This meant that women would not be treated the same as men of similar social standing. Mary Lee Berners-Lee, the mother of Tim Berners-Lee, worked at Ferranti in the 1950s. She recalled that women programmers performing the same work as men were paid less because "Ferranti was a paternal firm" that believed "men would have to support a wife and children so they needed more money." Upset by this unfair situation, Ferranti's women programmers eventually presented a case to management for truly meritocratic ranking and remuneration—and won.[80]

Throughout industry and government, an idealized view of the nuclear family and an expectation of heterosexuality continued to powerfully shape women's pay and promotion prospects and determine what jobs they could hold. Exceptions to this rule occurred only in times of labor shortage. When computer labor was in highest demand, women's pay, career prospects, and their ability to get hired at all soared. Although a change was under way in the 1960s to hire "bright young men" for computing jobs instead of continuing to rely on women, as will be discussed in the next chapter, computer labor shortages in the sixties meant that women still got and kept many computing jobs.

Women in the Government Machine: Personal Experiences of Operators

Both Ann Sayce and her friend Cathy Gillespie, who worked at the government's Post Office computing center, benefited from this sweet spot in the early computing labor market—a period during which the field's feminization was beginning to be undone with rising wages and status, but before it had fully professionalized and erected barriers to women's entry. The job advertisement that got Gillespie and Sayce into computing made no secret of the fact that the government was desperate for more computer workers. "Know Nothing about Computers? Then We'll Teach You (and pay you while doing so)," read the job advertisement, which took up a quarter page in the newspaper and ran several times during the summer of 1965. It was designed with a clean, modern look and decorated with numbers evocative of computerized output. Embodying the spirit of Wilson's White Heat, it promised that "here at the GPO London Computer Center you can take your first steps into the fascinating world of computers—and into a fascinating future as well!"[81] The ad attempted to sell promising young applicants on a job in the wondrous new world of computers while asking little in return in terms of skills or qualifications.

Hiring managers for these posts, like most managers, felt that operator work, with the meticulous program reading, writing, and debugging skills it required, was a young person's field. They recruited accordingly, focusing on youth and potential more than qualifications or experience.[82] Operator jobs, which also required some programming, were seen as suitable for applicants with a solid, though not necessarily stellar, secondary school record, and they were not yet considered jobs for college graduates. Academic accomplishments or work background counted only slightly in determining an applicant's suitability. Instead, an ability to learn quickly and an enthusiasm for the work, factors often deemed necessary in ill-defined or new fields of endeavor, were key to being hired.

Youth and gender were all the more important to defining this labor force because on-the-job training had little relationship to subjects of study in secondary school and employers lacked any accurate metrics for identifying innately talented candidates. Although he studied for A levels (advanced subjects) at school, Colin Hobson received only several O-level (ordinary-level) qualifications. This in no way hurt his career at LEO, however.[83] Cathy Gillespie, who did not have money for A-level study, also received O levels. This likewise did not hurt her career in computing, first in the Civil Service and later in the private sector. Indeed,

Gillespie was surprised to have been among the forty people hired to work on the Post Office's LEO III/26 installation, since she imagined she would need O-level qualifications in math and science but lacked them. Ann Sayce, who worked with her, came from a different background. Sayce had attended an academically oriented grammar school rather than a more general, trade-oriented comprehensive secondary school and had also earned her accountancy qualifications. However, this experience hindered her instead of counting in her favor. Her longer work record meant that, at age twenty-four, she was nearly too old to be considered for the job. Applicants for the job needed to be younger than twenty-five years of age.

Much like Hobson, Gillespie and Sayce were each attracted to the job because computers seemed like a fascinating new field. Both women recalled that this job seemed like it would be a cut above dull office work or the service industry jobs that most young women were hired to do, and the reality of the job did not disappoint. Sayce recalled that "operating a computer at that time was quite interesting and exciting," a sentiment echoed by Gillespie: "The atmosphere was fantastic and the best bit was that no one knew what I did as it was so new."[84] Like Hobson, they reveled in the cachet and prestige associated with working with cutting edge-technology. Even though employers had a difficult time attracting more established workers to computing work (for reasons that will be discussed in the next chapter), thousands of younger Britons aspired to make a career out of it, captivated by the futurism and optimism invoked by popular representations of computing.

The job ad that Gillespie and Sayce answered was unusual for its time: It explicitly asked for "male or female" candidates. Job ads for computer workers, and most other workers, broke down along gendered lines. Often, jobs that were presented as career opportunities confined their applications to men, whereas routine office jobs, with potentially high starting pay but little upward mobility, sought only women applicants. Many advertisements that pitched a job to one gender or the other did so explicitly, simply asking for men or for women. Even greater numbers of advertisements, however, employed subtler language or fine print. Some asked applicants to direct inquiries to the company's "women's officer" while others warned that night work would be required, intimating that men were preferred. A variety of code words about career opportunity, pension plans, and the possibility for advancement to salaries over £1,500 were used to convey that young men rather than young women were the target demographic for a staff wanted advertisement.[85] Women were rarely included in job ads when employers were aiming to invest training in entry-level employees for long-term career development. Instead, women were targeted with promises of part-time work, flexible hours, marriage bonuses, sociable outlets at the workplace, and workplaces in districts of London that were described as exciting, fun, and fashionable, such as the shopping area of Kensington or the West End theater district.

The Post Office computer operator advertisement uniquely combined elements that were meant to appeal equally to young men and young women, promising not only careers and good pay, but also marriage bonuses, a stylish location in London, and flexible hours. Equally unusual was the fact that this job ad presented relatively low-level computing jobs as stepping stones to long-term career opportunity. These jobs were not very far removed from punched card machine operation jobs; they were quite similar functionally. Starting at £9 a week and rising as high as £15 by age twenty-one, the already above-average wages were enhanced by a pension that did not require employee contribution, and salaries of £1,000 and above were promised as attainable with time. This sort of salary, in the £1,000 to £2,000 range, was "what all the guys wanted" at the time, noted Sayce.[86] Further education opportunities were mentioned in the ad, along with three weeks' paid vacation. The Post Office advertisement asked specifically for young applicants and promised to train them. This, along with the job's location in the permanent Civil Service, indicated a high-status career opportunity rather than merely a temporary job.

Everything about the ad appealed to Gillespie, who was working in a shoe shop when she applied for the job, after quitting secretarial college because of the dead-end nature of the work. Sayce, who came to the position from within the Civil Service, already had secure job prospects, but was intrigued by computers. Even though she was already employed by the Civil Service, Sayce had to compete against the outside job candidates. She recalled that in addition to passing the required math and writing tests for the Post Office job, she also had to convince the hiring officers that she would not have children in the near future: "You would never get the job until you swore up and down that you wouldn't have children."[87]

Only a few years before, a job advertisement like this would have looked quite different. It would have been pitched to women, rather than men and women, and it would have offered different enticements to potential applicants, along with lower salaries. Training and further educational opportunities for career development would not have been part of the equation. A few years later, the job ad would also have looked quite different: No longer would candidates with no experience whatsoever be given such enticement to apply, and no longer would the advertisement explicitly seek out women as well as men for a position intended to be the start of a career in a high-prestige field. The computing positions Sayce and Gillespie had applied for existed at the perfect juncture of labor shortage and computing's rising prestige. These factors combined to create extremely favorable conditions for those lucky or clear-sighted enough to find work in the field. Computer work was rising in status and offering enhanced opportunities, but its prestige had not yet risen enough to make it attractive to higher-status, career-oriented men.

In the fall of 1965, Gillespie and Sayce started work at the Post Office's LEO III/26 installation. They were age eighteen and twenty-four, respectively, and joined roughly sixty other operators spread across three shifts. They became part of the "massive" operation that Colin Hobson saw when he came to the Post Office to try to eke out extra computer time overnight for LEO bureau work. Both women received a dedicated two weeks of paid training before they began work and learned the machine code in the thick LEO operator's manual. While on the job, they learned how to program in binary and to read hexadecimal, parity, nonparity, and mBIC machine codes. The operators, of whom at least half were women, were overseen by primarily male supervisors and initially worked on feeding cards into the reader and loading the appropriate tapes and paper. Gillespie performed some last-minute punching when needed and later specialized in organizing the batches of cards that would be run on the machine to maximize throughput. In many ways, operator work was akin to what systems administrators would do much later. Early operators were responsible for ensuring the systems stayed in good order and ran programs successfully, just as systems administrators would later be responsible for keeping computing environments stable for users. Gillespie also processed the printed paper output, right down to physically chopping it up and bringing it to the relevant departmental destinations.

Gillespie and Sayce's Post Office jobs were an ideal beginning to a career in computing. Anthony Benn, the minister of technology, had been postmaster general before moving to MinTech, and it was Post Office engineer Tommy Flowers and his team that had created Colossus. For most of the twentieth century, the Post Office controlled and maintained all of Britain's telecommunications infrastructure. A center for technological leadership in Britain well into the latter half of the century, the Post Office researched and implemented projects that found new applications for electronics and telecommunications technology throughout the twentieth century. The research arm of the Post Office was akin to the prestigious Bell Laboratories in the United States. Although LEO employees may have considered themselves "a cut above," the Post Office's large computing projects were on the leading edge of business and administrative computing. Their programs ranged from standard applications like payroll and telephone billing (the Post Office was also in charge of telephone service) to much more complex software that interpreted diverse datasets and dealt with numerous intertwined variables. Sayce recalled running civil engineering programs, for instance, that coordinated all of London's road work with maintenance on underground utility lines so that the same busy streets would not have to be closed and dug up multiple times. Even with standard applications, the scale at which the Post Office computer center worked—for example, managing the billing for every telephone customer in the nation—meant that it pushed the boundaries of administrative computing at the time.

The atmosphere in the computing installations, quite different from the run-of-the-mill Civil Service office spaces, was youthful and gregarious. Gillespie recalled the young, mixed-gender environment of the job fondly, noting that "it was fun to work there and the atmosphere was great. The majority of us were about the same age so it felt like going to a party every day, not work." She worked the early shift from seven-thirty in the morning to roughly two-thirty in the afternoon, and she remembered fondly how someone had programmed the noisy machine to play an approximation of Bob Dylan's "Rainy Day Women" at the start of the day by orchestrating the machine's various whirrs and clatters. "It was like one big party," Gillespie emphasized.[88] In contrast to prevailing norms in computer companies like LEO, the gender of the operator labor force skewed more toward women in the public sector. Gillespie and Sayce worked in an environment in which women operators made up half or more of the operating shifts at the Post Office and, later, at the Central Electricity Board. Overall, "it was a great first job, you were not trapped in an office, you were working fantastic hours, which gave you a lot of freedom, and no one had any idea what you did," recalled Gillespie.[89]

Although there was no overnight shift, there was a shift that worked into the night. Gillespie and Sayce recalled that the married, male engineers who were on site to fix the computers thought women operators were "a bit dodgy" and shied away from them, viewing them as "man eaters." Working with men at night was looked upon in a suspicious light,

Gillespie remembered: "'What sort of a woman would want to do that?' was the idea." Simply working at night could put the stain of sexual promiscuity on women, and the effect was intensified if men worked alongside the women. Gillespie added that "there was also this idea that you didn't indulge in sexual things before marriage." But Sayce disagreed, asking incredulously: "What sixties were *you* in?" The swinging sixties in London were a bundle of contradictions for women. Hemlines were rising, and women were wearing more and more revealing fashions to work. At the same time, trousers were still not allowed for women machine operators despite the physicality of the job, even though protective attire, like a long "overall" coat, was sometimes supplied to operators.

Both Gillespie and Sayce walked a fine line to maintain a respectable image in the midst of this, remembering—only half in jest—that the all-female punching and verifying pool was regarded as "a sexual wolf pack." Described as loud and aggressive as a group, individual punchers were known to stake claims to male coworkers they liked and then sexually harass them as they walked through the punch room. This trope of a predatory, single, working woman was exactly the image Gillespie and Sayce did not want; the engineers' and operators' impressions of the largely working-class young women in the punching pool underscored the fact that performing sexuality in a particular way was an important component of the kind of middle-class respectability that attached to, and was required of, more prestigious jobs in computing.[90]

In addition to being exciting, computer jobs also often came with above-average salaries. Sayce, who supplemented her hours as an operator with a part-time job doing accounting and another job dealing antiques in her spare time, described herself as very "cash rich" at the time. However, even with her high wages she could not buy a home. Sayce attempted to get a mortgage but was turned away despite meeting the financial qualifications, because she did not have a male relative to cosign. "Men earning eight to twelve pounds a week could get a 90 percent mortgage at the time," she recalled ruefully, yet her request for a modest loan prompted "a spotty eighteen-year-old" bank employee to "laugh in [her] face." With money to spare but unable to finance a home, one lunch hour she instead decided to splurge on a car: "I told the salesman that I wanted a car with a radio, and he sold me the longest car that they had at the time!"[91]

Despite the many advantages Gillespie and Sayce enjoyed, the diffuse effects of discrimination shaped their lives and careers in ways that are difficult to quantify. The range of opportunities foreclosed to them simply because they were women, even in a period of better-than-average prospects, can be discerned by comparing their experiences with those of Colin Hobson at LEO. Even though Hobson left school at the earliest allowed age, whereas Gillespie and Sayce stayed in school past the required age of sixteen, Hobson had stepped into one of the most elite positions in the field of computer operation at the time—that of a LEO bureau operator. Gillespie and Sayce, as women, could not even compete for that job, because LEO hired only men. Instead, they entered an open competition for a good government computing job and were extremely fortunate to be hired from a very large applicant pool. In addition, they were particularly lucky to be competing for computing jobs at a time when computer labor shortages worked to their advantage, with the government struggling to fill the ranks of its growing computer installations.

Those conditions would not last. As women coworkers left to have children, the gender balance of operators shifted, and new women hires did not replace the old. Both Gillespie and Sayce saw married colleagues come back to work after having children, only to fill different, less desirable jobs at lower pay. During the 1960s, and well beyond, popular opinion dictated that white-collar women were only supposed to seriously pursue either a career or marriage. Indeed, after taking another computing job a few years later, Sayce left to have children and was never able to return to computing work, despite maintaining her interest in the field. As late as 1975, a survey of school-age girls' career aspirations noted that "the simple and obvious escape route to marriage and motherhood was not merely socially acceptable for girls, but almost obligatory."[92] Even though Sayce was divorced at the time she was employed by the Post Office, she was disqualified from getting a Civil Service pension because she had been married at one time. Marriage, either the future inclination toward, or the remnants thereof, enormously complicated women's career aspirations, even as it offered the most socially acceptable and economically viable way for most British women to live.

Moving Up, Moving On

In 1967, only two years after arriving at the Post Office, both Gillespie and Sayce left the security of their positions for the large, new IBM installation at the Central Electricity Generating Board (CEGB). In addition to leaving behind guaranteed jobs for life in the Civil Service, Gillespie and Sayce also relinquished their excellent working hours. Their new jobs required work on both day and overnight shifts, but leaving the Civil Service was a necessity in order to have opportunities to advance to higher computer operation jobs. The organization of the Civil Service meant there was no guarantee one could gain promotion if one wished to continue to work in computing. Civil servants could be required to work in a totally different office doing completely different work after each promotion, and the limited number of vacancies in the Senior Machine Operator grade in the Post Office meant that, if individuals wished to continue working with computers, they might wait many years until even one senior machine operator post became vacant. Yet leaving the Post Office had downsides as well: In contrast to the relaxed atmosphere there, "at the CEGB things were slightly more serious," said Gillespie.[93]

Representing the early curve of a shift already underway in favor of IBM at the expense of British computers, the CEGB ran IBM 360s. Gillespie's rationale for applying for the job was due as much to her desire for promotion as to her recognition that she would need experience on IBMs in order to advance further. The computer operation staff at CEGB consisted of only about twenty-four operators for three machines, in contrast to the more than sixty at the Post Office's installation, reflecting how systems were maturing to require fewer operators. An IBM 360/30, a 360/50, and a 360/75 occupied two different London offices of the CEGB, the first used mainly for administrative tasks, with the latter two forming part of a new system called Attached Support Processor (ASP). While the 360/50 handled input and output, the 360/75 ran the programs. In order to wring maximum efficiency from the machines, they were used in tandem and their interaction was automated to perform different tasks in the processing chain for the purpose of speeding up programming runs beyond what a human controlling the input, processing, and output functions nonprogrammatically could achieve.[94] Sayce proudly recalled that she once held a speed record for processing data on these IBMs.

In the machine room at the CEGB, Gillespie's job again included organizing input, this time received from a remote location where the cards had been copied to magnetic tape. The tapes were sent to her with a job sheet indicating their contents, along with any paper tapes needed to input the program. In addition to feeding in these programs, scheduling the work, and processing and debugging the jobs, she performed the initial program load (IPL) to bring the system up after crashes and logged hardware faults and other problems to pass along to the engineers who performed overnight maintenance. Engineers were on staff during the day as well to correct insurmountable operating problems and machinery breakdowns. Even into the early 1970s, Gillespie recalled, these problems tended to occur regularly—two or three times each day.

In addition to machine faults, operator faults could wreak havoc. Opening a door to one of the magnetic tape reels too early one day earned Gillespie a broken foot when the still-spinning reel shot out of the case. The scratch tapes, forming the short-term writes that would not comprise the final output, could cause chaos when they were occasionally confused with an output tape. "Imagine how popular you were if you picked the wrong one," Gillespie said with chagrin. In fact, management greatly feared the ease with which scratch tapes could be switched with other tapes, because of how this could be used by disgruntled workers in the context of a labor dispute. Even a small number of tape swaps could throw important work in the government—or industry—into disarray.[95]

While Gillespie was at work one day in 1970, a publicity photograph was taken of her and her machine (figure 3.12). She and her IBM 360 were to be the public face of the CEGB's new IBM 360/85 installation. In the photo, Gillespie sits at the console, typing and answering commands.[96] The machine's dials are set to the initial program load from the

Figure 3.12
Cathy Gillespie performs the initial program load on the CEGB's new IBM 360.

card reader on address 00C, which read the initiation deck containing the information needed to boot up—to bring the computer to the point at which it would be ready to run a program loaded via the read-only input tapes on the units in the background. Acting in place of the modern equivalent of a screen, the paper from the console comprised a hard copy of the daily log, which Gillespie could refer back to in the event of an error. System tapes, to bring the machine up at the beginning of the day and after crashes, are visible in the glass cases behind the console. The scratch tapes, used to record incremental output throughout the day, are shown stored on the rack in front of the tape unit in the photo's background. Dedicated magnetic tapes—or sometimes paper tapes or cards, depending on the application—collected the final output.

Because of the way the publicity photo is staged, Gillespie sits in a seemingly passive role, rather than being shown in a way that telegraphs action. Photographs of men from this era often showed them confidently striding around the machine room, or inspecting output with a sense of gravitas that seemed to heighten their importance. By positioning Gillespie in a way similar to a secretary at a keyboard, a position that she would not have occupied for much of her workday, the publicity photo subtly—and perhaps subconsciously—packaged her role in a way that the public would understand. Viewers might be forgiven for assuming that women in these images were not doing the real, important work of computing, given how they were posed in ways that triggered associations with secretarial work or typing. The image comported with stereotypical expectations of women's work even while showing off a "revolutionary" technology.

At the console, Gillespie performs her duties, but the way the image is arranged freezes her in time, obfuscating the actions and skills required for her job. If looking at the photo without knowing her background, it might be difficult to discern whether Gillespie was a worker or a model brought in specifically for the photograph. Although some advertising used models, many computing company advertisements and most publicity photos from this era did not. Yet, as many of these photos have filtered into the popular imagination, and been stripped of context on the Internet, a widespread contemporary assumption has taken hold that these images portray either low-level workers or not-real workers—simply women brought in for aesthetic value. Small hints in the photo imply that Gillespie is really on the job: On close inspection, the image's sleek veneer is slightly eroded by the clenched look on her face. A tooth extraction the previous day had left her face swollen and numb, and its effects disrupted the utopian image of effortless automation the photo sought to portray. Gillespie's very embodiment as a worker, reporting for duty despite a physical setback, undermined the presentation of a stylized, hyperreal image of computing's future.

In the imaginary void surrounding the field at this time, images like these possessed the ability to become powerful ambassadors for the current state of affairs in computing. They repeated similar tropes—not simply reflecting reality, but reflecting a particular version of reality and shaping the public's image of what computing was and what it should be. Computing imagery participated in defining, rather than just reflecting, what computing was. The positioning of women operators as passive or the confusion of workers with models made—and continues to make—a material difference in how we understand computing's past and write computer history.

Young and Single at Computer Companies

The polished images presented to the press and the public were echoed by ones intended to be consumed only by computer company employees in magazines circulated within each company. Within major computer companies, women employees were often in the minority and never held positions of power in great numbers. Company magazines served to keep employees up-to-date and played an important role in fostering company culture and workplace cohesion. Because content within their covers was mostly freed from the constraints of presenting a tightly controlled public image, they show computer professionals less as flawless exemplars of a futuristic field and more as ordinary workers and people. They often gave expression to less polite behavior, mocking competitors' lines and occasionally even their own company's products. The antithesis of carefully orchestrated publicity, they showed a side of the field that few could see, a view that constructed the experiences of those within the field. The images within them showed the overt sexism women in the computing industry had to deal with on a daily basis. In the pages of these company magazines, young women employees appear first as women and only secondarily as workers. One risqué cover of the ICT in-house magazine in 1964 set a template for the "model" woman employee, wearing only the bottom half of a bikini while holding a strategically placed copy of the company magazine.[97]

Pictures of soon-to-be-married punchers decked out in punched tape for their "retirement parties" adorned the marriage announcements pages,

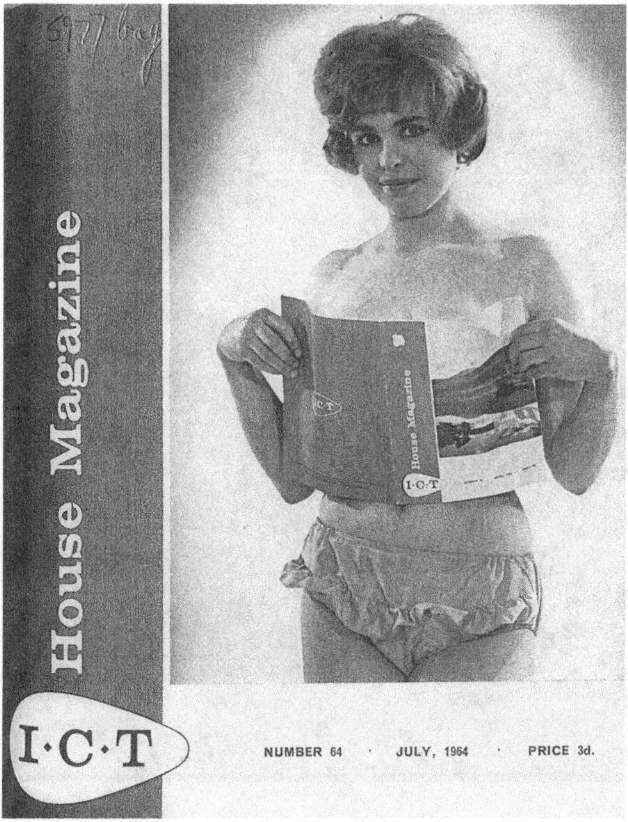

Figure 3.13
ICT House Magazine cover, July 1964.

providing a rare glimpse into the lives of young computer workers just as they decided to leave the field, perhaps permanently.[98] Few marriage announcements related that the new bride would remain at work in the company. At the opposite end of workers' lives, the retirement and obituary columns showed that most unmarried company women remained in lower-level, dead-end jobs. Leaving the company while young and single was still culturally and economically preferable, in most cases, to staying at the company until one was old and single.

Popular culture mirrored these de facto sexual hierarchies in the workplace and reinforced the idea that marriage was the only way women could escape from them. A supposedly empowering 1960s novel for young women, called *Anne in Electronics*, shows the capable main

Figure 3.14
A young woman named Anne Davis wears a punch tape dress at her retirement party. The photo ran in a "women's section" of the company newsletter that was labeled "Strictly for the Birds." *ICL News*, August 1970.

character navigating a male-dominated field by repeatedly asserting her incompetence in comparison to her male peers, while graciously allowing them to take credit for her work. When she makes a major breakthrough on a problem that had held up the production of a state of the art jet, she is delighted to let a man in whom she is romantically interested take credit for her work.[99] The novel's message that being a successful working woman in a male-dominated profession depended on working hard while playing a submissive role was not unusual. The book ends with the protagonist marrying an engineer but, in a twist, keeping her job. On the eve of her wedding, the protagonist complains to her minister about the difficulty of attempting to support her husband's career while taking on more domestic responsibilities and keeping her own career, but is simply told, "That's as it must be."[100]

The Cooling of White Heat

Thinking of her work in computing in the 1960s, Cathy Gillespie recalled that it was "great to be young in a new industry, earning good money and being on a par with the men regarding wages and opportunities." Gillespie entered the field at an ideal time. Throughout the mid-1960s, the shortage of computer labor—or at least the perception thereof—meant the practice of hiring women continued even as the status of computing work began to rise. By later in the decade this perception of labor crisis had diminished somewhat, and as a result many employers—especially the largest employer of computer labor, the Civil Service—began to change whom they hired.

A 1967 Air Force report discussed how the Air Force's mostly female workforce had served it well during periods when careers for computer operators and programmers were not easily found in the Civil Service. At this point in time, however, the Air Force felt that a change was necessary to bring it into line with new ideas about computing within the Civil Service: "The majority of other organizations considered during this investigation recruit young men as machine operators," its report noted, and in order to groom computing professionals, "they offer a complete career to such people." The report states that this trend is due to a widespread presumption that "the computer field generally is a young man's domain" and concludes that "the young man seems to represent the 'best bet' if career opportunities and financial rewards are satisfactory." However, it then points out that "if, on the other hand ... machine operators are required who have no career ambitions and simply want to earn a bit of money, then the best bet is the middle-aged married woman."[101]

In any case, the Air Force report summed up, it had "become quite clear during the course of this investigation that unless some considerable improvements are made to both career prospects and salary levels of the machine operator ... then the recruiting and retention situations which exist at the centre at the present time are unlikely to improve."[102] The situation in the Air Force computing section showed why women continued to be the best bet for much computing labor throughout the public and private sectors in the 1960s. Women were favored precisely because computer work lacked a career ladder. Several women civil servants complained that workers were not allowed to accrue seniority in the same fashion when they were in the excluded grades, as there were two different seniority scales kept for the excluded grades and the clerical grades, and most of the promotional outlets were available in the latter category.

They wished to integrate the two job categories, have a common seniority list, and, critically, allow men to take up excluded grade posts and promotions as well as women. Although women had attained equal pay in the clerical grades of the Civil Service by the late 1950s, the persistent division of "machine" and "clerical" work perpetuated unequal pay and opportunities, and industry was untouched by sex discrimination legislation until the 1970s.[103]

During the 1960s, however, computer jobs began to undergo a metamorphosis. Early on, computers only promised enhanced efficiency, but by this point they were becoming important symbols of industrial and social modernity. As the vanguard technology in Britain's white hot technological revolution in the sixties, meant to lead Britain back to the heights of power on the world stage, computers enjoyed a high public profile and rising status. No longer could they simply be staffed by the lowest workers in the labor pyramid since this would not square with their seeming importance. As a result, Wilson's call for technological meritocracy backfired: By emphasizing the critically important role that technology workers would play in the coming decades, his rhetoric sowed the seeds of technocratic hierarchy. As much as Labour sought a new style of meritocracy to define modern Britain, accidents of birth, in the form of age, class, race, and gender, weighed heavily on who would become part of the technological elite. The supposedly revolutionary technological vision of white heat could not undo—or even see—how gendered hierarchies constructed computer-age Britain.

The rising numbers of punch operators in government and industry were perhaps the best indication that society did not emerge from White Heat on the path to a technological future in which the need for drudgery would disappear. By 1971, punchers and "support staff" formed by far the largest category of computer labor in government.[104] The equalizing effects of technological progress were largely lost on the lowest echelons of workers that should have been helped by them, like those engaged in high-stress, boring, repetitive work. The rapidly modernizing society that Labour envisioned reforming all work along egalitarian lines never materialized, because it implicitly required the continuation of ingrained, antimeritocratic hierarchies to function. Because of this, computer operator labor became increasingly restive beginning in the mid-1960s. An agglomeration of computer operator strikes, union renegotiations, and labor meetings tasked specifically with solving the problem of growing inequality in the technology workforce muddied the image of a technological revolution that had promised meritocracy and egalitarianism.

The effects that computer publicity had in helping to create this context cannot be underestimated. In order for the technological future to materialize, people first needed to be able to envision it. The pictures presented to the public, to hiring managers, and to potential job seekers helped the nation make sense of a new field and powerfully defined what that field looked like in both image and reality. An important element of this visual project was to represent electronic computing as within the reach of any business. That resulted in advertisements portraying the computer workforce as relatively inexpensive, low skill, and feminized. So symbolically and economically potent was the young, female operator that computer companies deployed her outside Britain's borders, exporting British labor patterns to postcolonial and former Dominion markets even though those countries often earmarked such jobs as suitable for men. Advertising created a division between the actual work and how the work was viewed by hiring managers because it made computer work seem low skill and low status when women performed it.

Meanwhile, computing's rising status began to pull more women *and* men into jobs that had previously been considered suitable only for women. In this context of labor shortage, coming hard on the heels of the field's prior feminization, many women succeeded, but the gains made by women operators as a class would begin to disappear in the late 1960s as employers and policymakers placed more hope in the young men who were expected to become experts in the application of computer technology in order to save the British economy. A potent new role for computer workers—that of the technocratic expert—was emerging in society and government, and structural changes made in the public sector would begin to solidify this new identity. This role was not for women, however, and only women who had entered the field before this point in time and remained in it without interruption, like Cathy Gillespie, had a leg up. When high-tech labor crises eased, women were no longer seen as ideal candidates.

On the ground, White Heat left untouched many inequalities, functioning less as a sociotechnical revolution and more as a force that consolidated older forms of hierarchy. The educational and employment practices that made it difficult for men of lower classes and income levels to become highly paid, high-skill technologists, like programmers and systems analysts, doubly affected women of the same class and generation. The computer labor shortages of the mid-1960s slightly delayed the coming of this new technocratic order, but soon management potential, rather than computing experience, would become key to computer workers' success. As will be discussed in the next chapter, this was not a natural evolution but a highly structured process—one that paradoxically unmoored computer work from technical skill.

4

The Rise of the Technocrat: How State Attempts to Centralize Power through Computing Went Astray, 1965–1969

Although growing computerization created an exciting and lucrative environment from the perspective of computer workers in the 1960s, the view from above was different. The fruits of Labour's white hot technological revolution remained economically uncertain and difficult to quantify. First, vastly increased efficiency was not indicated by the government's manpower studies on its own computing systems, but vast outlays on computing hardware and software continued apace.[1] Second, growing labor problems plagued the government. Its installations required an ever-increasing number of skilled computer workers, but in a field with hazy qualifications and no set career path, hiring and retention on the scale needed was becoming difficult. Third, the British computing industry required ever-increasing injections of government funding to stay competitive, in the form of grants, loans, and preferential government purchasing policies for computers used in Civil Service offices and the nationalized industries.

This trifecta of computing problems played out against the backdrop of a protracted economic crisis during the mid- to late 1960s. Britain's gross national product had increased only slowly from the 1950s on, far outpaced by the growth of the economies of its continental rivals. As former colonies and Commonwealth trading partners increasingly turned to the United States, Britain's balance of payments suffered. Attempts to reverse the poor trading situation through technological modernization geared to increase production for both domestic and export markets could not produce a quick or dramatic enough change in Britain's economic outlook, and by the summer of 1965 the economic crisis had sharpened enough to require a government pay freeze and an expenditure reduction policy that necessitated, among other measures, deferring computer purchases—unless they effected major reductions in Civil Service labor costs.[2]

In November 1967, the pound had to be devalued against the dollar for the second time in under two decades, a move that failed to quell inflation or give British exports the necessary boost.[3] The next year, in a scathing report on government inadequacies, the Fulton Committee took the Civil Service's sprawling bureaucracy to task for amateurism, secrecy, classism, poor management, and wrongheaded organizational practices. In the midst of a nationwide modernization drive, the committee condemned the government's own infrastructure for being mired in the past, emphasizing the need for more technically minded governance.[4]

An increasingly dissatisfied British labor force, stung by the economic situation, remained unconvinced by Wilson's reassurances that the "pound in their pockets" remained sound. In addition, the Britain of the "swinging sixties" and early seventies was rife with sexual and racial discrimination, exacerbating the difficulties many workers faced as the nation was buffeted by economic problems.[5] Workers took both official and unofficial measures to try to secure the ever-improving standards of living promised by Labour's modernization program, and industrial action became increasingly common. Computer workers, despite being the vanguard of Britain's new high-technology economy, were no exception. International Computers and Tabulators (ICT), the company heavily favored for government data-processing installations (the majority of government computers were ICT) struck fear into government users when its maintenance engineers went on strike for higher pay in 1965, leaving government and industry scrambling to cope.[6]

The response of ICT's management to the strike was telling. It reflected a shift already underway toward making computer workers an integral, and ideally interchangeable, subsection of middle management. Rather than giving in to the maintenance engineers' demands, ICT used professional workers from their management and supervisory staffs to take the place of the striking workers. Later that same year, the Civil Service Clerical Association (CSCA) considered taking industrial action to protest the fact that such nonunionized ICT workers were being brought in to run several government computing installations.[7]

The prospect that better jobs might be outsourced to computing companies prompted civil servants in the clerical grades to push for better training and demand that government employees be given full responsibility for the new machines, from operating and programming to maintenance and repair. But "trimming" redundant staff was already underway, built in to the high turnover and slow promotion processes of the feminized machine grades.[8] Staff cuts became largely invisible when cloaked by women's turnover, and they were also far smaller than projected.

Ultimately, however, the government would circumvent the clerical unions in a different way. Over the course of the "computer revolution," high-level administrators in the Treasury, Her Majesty's Stationery Office (HMSO), and the Civil Service Department (a department within the Civil Service that oversaw the organization of the service more generally) began to plan broad changes in the public sector's use of computers in order to bring them into line with a new vision of technocratic management and labor control.[9] They endeavored to migrate computing posts from being liminally white-collar, subclerical jobs stuck at the bottom of the Civil Service professional framework to being administrative and executive positions at the top of the service.

The rationale for this shift centered on a new understanding of computer systems as management tools. Such tools required a "high caliber of systems man," government ministers believed, one who could combine his technical knowledge with management expertise and operate in a different milieu than current computer workers.[10] Yet the government faced an uphill battle; such professionals would be hard to find and keep in the Civil Service due to the dead-end nature of computing work there. The public sector served as a major training ground for computer workers, and the Civil Service was by far the nation's largest employer.[11] Despite the job security offered by government posts, computer workers flowed outward: "Those who have a real flair for it ... see their opportunity outside rather than inside the Civil Service," one minister remarked in a report on the government's poor computer labor outlook.[12]

In response to these recruitment problems, the Treasury and HMSO devised plans to create a cadre of high-level technocrats whose small numbers would be mitigated by the use of centralized computing solutions. Workers like these would not be drawn from existing computer jobs but would be moved into the new field from executive positions. Rather than promoting from within the ranks of workers already performing operating and programming work, management-level workers with no technical experience would be brought in to be practitioners and supervisors. A transition away from understanding computing in a primarily technical sense was underway: Now computers were understood as tools that fundamentally shaped the government's ability to wield and maintain power. In the context of a nation in which women still held far fewer positions of authority at all levels of government and industry, these changes were inherently gendered.

By focusing on creating an all-management computer operator and programmer class the government exacerbated labor shortages. Ignoring the women already working in the jobs meant that the single biggest reserve of computer experience and talent went to waste. These labor problems would affect more than just work organization, because placing the responsibility for computing within the hands of an elite group of high-level "computer men" both took for granted and required particular kinds of centralized computing solutions. As the Treasury, HMSO, and MinTech struggled to change how the service's computing systems were staffed, they also tried to remodel the hardware side of the system, injecting government control more deeply into the affairs of the British computing industry.

In the late 1960s, administrators in the Treasury, joined by the Ministry of Technology, encouraged a merger of the last large British computing companies into one new company, International Computers Limited. Not coincidentally, this government-backed computer merger produced a company that could provide highly centralized computer technologies for government installations. It mirrored the efforts, often of the very same ministers, to create a technocratic elite within the Civil Service and tried to counterbalance the effects of computer labor shortages by joining a small cadre of computer "experts" with the most powerful, centralized computing solutions. These changes would have impact far beyond the technological infrastructure of the Civil Service, rippling outward to affect the computing industry and the nation as a whole.

Technological Growing Pains and Reluctant Professionalization

Although the Treasury initially sought computer systems that would reduce the number of staff needed, or create long-term cost savings, departments quickly found that computers were becoming necessary not simply to perform work more efficiently but even to be able to perform the needed work at all. As the volume and nature of the work changed in concert with new tools, those tools became integral to the functioning of the state. "The number of cases in which expenditure on a computer can be regarded as an alternative to expenditure on staff does not now seem to be great," wrote one high-level executive in the Treasury, discussing a study on computers' ability to effect savings on staffing costs.[13]

In 1965, the government undertook a survey of all of its computer installations. The survey found that the central government's forty-five administrative (as opposed to scientific) computers had an estimated capital cost of £8.5 million, including equipment rentals, with an additional seventeen computers on order for installation within the next two years, at a cost of £5.66 million. These numbers did not include computers in the sprawling National Health Service, in local government, in the nationalized industries, or in the university system.

To bolster the UK technology industry, the vast majority of this money was to be spent on British machines, mostly purchased from ICT, which was becoming the government's favored supplier.[14] Long-term plans called for an additional sixty computers to be installed by the early seventies. These estimates, however, turned out to be laughably low. By 1968, there were already close to a hundred administrative computers in government, with nearly that number again for scientific computing, and dozens more on order.[15] Over 75 percent of these computers were ICT machines.[16] By 1970, more than a hundred computers over the number originally estimated had been ordered, and the hardware of government systems was valued at more than £41 million.[17] After realizing how far under the mark earlier projections had been, government forecasters in 1970 projected computers to more than double in the next five years.

The Civil Service, by far the largest computer user in the country, used 5 percent of all of the nation's computers while struggling to meet the staffing needs of all of these systems.[18] For much of the 1960s, the career ladder and composition of the government's data-processing workforce remained relatively constant. The introduction of large numbers of electronic computing installations in place of older electromechanical tabulating and calculating machines, a dramatic technical change, did little to alter the workforce currently in place or the hiring patterns that sustained it. Young, female, and often part-time machine operation staff, who also did programming, continued to be employed. This situation was due in part to financial concerns, a history of feminization in office machine work, and computer labor shortages. But it was also due to the fact that computing jobs lacked any outlet into a career structure within the Civil Service.

When Cathy Gillespie started working as a computer operator in 1965, she recalled: "I could not believe my luck as now I had a job in the government, the Civil Service, with brilliant prospects and it was a job for life."[19] Yet within a few years of receiving government training, she would take her skills to the private sector. Promotion outlets within the service were too few and far between. Given the rigid hierarchies of the machine grades, few senior machine operator posts opened up each year.

This was because a growing movement to tamp down on promotions and remove machine grade workers from high-level computing posts was underway. "The pay scale of the Senior Machine Operator is increasingly causing us unease," wrote an executive officer at the government's Central Computer Bureau in 1969. "Politically, we are sitting on a powder keg and something must be done as a matter of urgency," he continued. "It is out of proportion that these girls, academically unqualified compared with clerical staff, should so quickly be able to reach salary levels above those of Clerical Officers and even Executive Officers," he argued.[20]

Despite the government's great need for computer workers, managers chafed at paying women, and non-white-collar ones at that, the new market rate for computer work. Nonetheless, well into the mid-1960s, many departments regarded programming as appropriate work for higher machine operator posts, a logical progression from lower-level machine operator work, even as the status of programming increased.[21] ICT advertised that its Nineteen Hundred Commercial Language (NICOL) programming language could be learned in only about four days by an operator familiar with punched card systems.[22] Aptitude testing for programming posts proved an unreliable measure of recruits' future success, whereas familiarity with the departmental installations tended to produce programming trainees more easily.[23] For this reason, in the mid-1960s, seventy percent of the workers in the machine grades worked in electronic computer installations and very few members of the clerical or managerial classes did.[24]

Yet administrators at the highest levels of the Civil Service now saw computing in the light of Wilson's White Heat—as a field of critical importance to the national good and a tool that would help them wield greater power. The Treasury's Organization and Methods division and HMSO held the most power in shaping the Civil Service. Both wanted to change the composition of the intentionally deskilled machine grades to bring computer workers into line with the heightened status of electronic computing. The desire to do so intensified during the computer labor shortages of the mid-1960s, when a situation of relative scarcity inflated the cost—and therefore the perceived value—of computer labor. In those years, the service had to scramble to hire more women computer operators, many of whom also programmed machines, but many managers were not keen on this. The sentiment of the head of the CCB that "something must be done as a matter of urgency" about "these girls" echoed throughout internal government correspondence about computer workers.

The Treasury's labor forecasts for the early 1970s showed that the computing workforce would continue to grow as "projects not yet approved and not yet identified" were developed and "technical developments ... widen[ed] the range of applications" for computers.[25] In these conditions, efforts to reshape the current labor structure had difficulty getting off the ground. Plans to install new data-processing systems and then trim less desirable staff in order to bring in higher-level computer workers did not square with reality. Back when the first administrative electronic computers were installed in government in 1958 for "processing large blocks of what had been clerical work," staff were chagrined by estimates that between five thousand and ten thousand people would be made redundant in the next five to ten years. They observed the growing computerization of work processes "with not a small amount of trepidation."[26] Yet throughout the 1960s, new installations required many more staff rather than fewer.

Rise of the "Computer Men"

Specialists in the Treasury's Organization and Methods division had begun to sketch out changes in the service's computer labor force by the early 1960s, discussing in detail how to reprofessionalize certain computing jobs and in the process elevate "computer men" into the executive structure.[27] As early as 1959, HMSO floated the idea of hiring men as computer operators for the Treasury in order to "build up a more reliable core of expertise" for computer work.[28] "Our accounting installations are operated by female staff, and with the continued development of ADP [automatic data processing] we are not at all happy about future staffing prospects," complained an HMSO official.[29] Since the Treasury had the most power to change job classifications, pay, and recruitment, changes to the government's labor force rested squarely in its hands.

While the machine grades had served the Treasury's interests well for over a decade, the high turnover in those grades that helped "hide" staff cuts also presented problems in tight labor markets when the government was scrambling to hold onto staff. In addition, women operators were not seen as an ideal workforce to be relied upon long term, even if they were actively recruited in times of scarcity. The key words "reliable" and "expertise" echoed throughout hiring memoranda during the 1960s as code for hiring young men whose training would not be "wasted" due to their leaving the workforce upon marriage. The gendered dimensions of career development also meant that women were unlikely to accrue "expert" status or be seen as "reliable" workers even if they stayed in the workforce long term. Decades of intentional deskilling made women appear to be unsuitable even when they were already successfully performing the work computer jobs entailed. From the early 1960s on, the Civil Service began to use specially designed computer aptitude tests for machine operator hiring, aiming to find not only good operators but potentially good programmers as well.

Even before White Heat raised the profile of computing, a 1962 overview of government computing policy reported that the government hoped to recruit most programmers from the ranks of the seventy thousand workers in the executive class—the management class of workers with A-level secondary school training, but without the university training of the higher administrative class or any particular skill set commonly associated with early programming expertise.[30] Executive class officers dealt with long-term departmental goals and developed processes for greater efficiency. They were also overwhelmingly men. Paradoxically, these new recruits were thought to be more qualified for the technical aspects of computer jobs even though they lacked any machine experience. The tacit expectation was that higher-level civil servants would be more intelligent overall and therefore would have no trouble picking up supposedly lowly technical skills. A widespread belief persisted in government that work involving machines did not require much intellect. Yet the Treasury's initial feelings that "the operation of computers was expected to be similar to that of punched card equipment and thus proper to SMOs [senior machine operators]" was giving way to the idea that computing jobs were actually too complex and required too much training to continue using feminized labor.[31] "Although a number of staff currently graded in the MO (Machine Operator) class are demonstrably suited to be computer operators," opined one 1966 report, "it must not be assumed that all machine operators capable of traditional responsibilities for that class have in fact 'operating' ability."[32]

This shift in attitude reflected the rigidity of the class hierarchies of the Civil Service. Even though government workers were supposed to be able to rise through the ranks meritocratically, by means of examinations, those in the lower classes of the service were often seen as fundamentally inferior to those at higher levels. As a result, there was little focus on grooming workers already in computer posts for higher positions. Instead, "better" workers would be brought in from the executive class and trained to do those jobs. Whether the nation was headed by Labour or the Conservatives, the highest administrators within the service remained relatively constant in their opinions about modernization within government. "It was early on decided that for most programming of clerical operations one did not need graduates in mathematics or other knowledge of professional standard, but a reasonable level of intelligence and certain aptitudes," explained an organization specialist in the Treasury who authored a 1962 report titled "Electronic Computers Oil the Wheels of Government."[33] Management potential and a broad understanding of the workings of government agencies were the key qualities the Treasury now sought in computer workers.

The growing effort in the late 1960s to carve out a system of careers in computing reflected and was bolstered by universities and other credentialed training courses. In 1966, the British Computer Society, in cooperation with City University, set up a group to study the qualifications of the operating staff sought by manufacturers, businesses, and scientific installations. It would then make recommendations about how to formalize and institutionalize training. Aiming to "establish requirements that borrow from both arts and sciences" in order to legitimize computing expertise, such training signified computer operation's change from an occupation to a vocation, and from a job to a career. Computer operators now needed not only practical, technical knowledge but also needed to be versed in the "big picture"—the management objectives constructing the larger workflow systems of which computers were an important part.[34]

Finding and Wasting Computing Talent

Nowhere were the growing pains of the state's modernization more apparent than in the Central Computer Bureau, a centralized data-processing department for payroll, statistics, and other administrative work. Set up as a subsection of HMSO, the CCB covered all of the Stationery Office's needs. In addition, it ran and wrote programs for other government departments that either did not have their own computers or that had overflow work. The CCB also provided software development help to departments installing new computers. The CCB moved gradually to electronic computers in the late 1950s and early 1960s, changing its name from the Combined Tabulating Installation (CTI) in 1965 to reflect its changing technology.

Early on, a series of staffing problems there illustrated the problems with this new management-only hiring model. The CTI began to reevaluate its staffing methods in conjunction with the installation of a new electronic computer at the beginning of the decade. Even though senior machine operators had previously handled all programming work successfully, the more expensive and seemingly more complex machines engendered an expectation of higher wages and more responsibility. As the computer took over progressively more work, the directors of the CTI endeavored to bring in executive officers for programming instead of continuing to have senior machine operators do it.

The problem, however, was that no executive officers in the Civil Service, at least among those available to transfer to CTI, had any of the necessary experience. The executive officer that the CTI had put in charge of the new electronic computer was "new and inexperienced." His supervisors related that "for the next six months we must regard him as under training." The second executive officer management planned to add to help supervise the new computer section was no better: "He too will require a long period of training and 'running in.'" While these new executive officers were under training in their new posts, all of the programming and testing work would continue to be performed by a senior machine operator already in the job, who was described as having "a good brain and a special flair for this type of work." The new executive officers would "need assistance from the SMO on programming" for some time, the departmental minutes related, adding that "she will be responsible for setting up and testing programs on the electronic calculators" for the foreseeable future.[35]

Given the work that this SMO was doing, there was some discussion of whether or not she should get a promotion. But CTI managers decided against "upgrading her post" to executive officer level because the hierarchies of the service made the jump from machine class to executive class nearly unheard of. Instead, she was temporarily given a bonus plus "the normal allowance for more difficult SMO work." She would spend close to a year handling all of the programming while also helping to train her executive-level replacements. Afterward, she would be demoted to an assistantship position under her former trainees until she could be replaced altogether with another executive officer hire: "We can leave the SMO on programming until the supervisory EO [executive officer] recommended for [programming] in our report is fully trained, say nine months, and then replace her with an EO," related the department minutes. Alternatively, she might be allowed to remain in her position until she left, presumably to get married, and then she could be replaced with a newly hired executive officer. Either way, "the SMO [would] eventually become an assistant to the EO on programming work" until she could be replaced by a management level worker.[36]

As this example shows, the rationale for changing the composition of the computer workforce had little to do with talent and everything to do with prestige. In the effort to make computer work comport with the importance now being accorded it, the talents and experience of many women computer operators were squandered. Their isolation in the machine grades meant that despite their greater technical skills they were seen as worse candidates, even for jobs they were already successfully performing. A key part of computer posts becoming professional and firmly white collar was their being elevated into the power structures of the state and of industry. Now that the jobs were more technocratic than technical, workers with actual computing experience lost out to ones who were seen as having management potential.

Perhaps the most surprising part of this situation was that the senior machine operator under discussion was herself a former executive officer whose job title and career prospects had been downgraded when she decided to go to work as a programmer instead. Stepping down into the machine grades offered her opportunities in the exciting new field of computing, but it was also a one-way ticket to lower status. Although her programming skills were in high demand, she was perceived as having "no special aptitude for supervising staff"—a subtle irony given that she would train and supervise her replacements for close to a year. As a machine grade worker, and a woman, she did not fit the government's new model of management-level, implicitly male programmers.[37] Her worth as a technician became devalued by the new economics of computer labor, which no longer favored recruiting the least expensive workers but rather the most valuable.

Workers like this SMO remain faceless and are usually lost in the official narratives of computerization owing not simply to oversight but to an intentional avoidance of giving them credit for the work they did. In contrast to the candid and specific handwritten minutes, the CTI's formal report on new training and staffing practices for electronic computing stated unequivocally—and erroneously—that none of their current machine operators or senior machine operators were of a high enough "caliber" to be programmers for the new machines. Although the report toyed with trying to recruit women who might be more suitable for the newly upgraded jobs, such as "intelligent grammar school girl[s]," the idea was nixed on the grounds that those applicants would undoubtedly not be happy with the dullness of lower-level machine work—like punching—that the jobs would require of new women recruits, but not of new men recruits.[38]

The Central Computer Bureau: A Microcosm of the State's Computing

Throughout the 1960s, computer workers were hired at a faster pace than any other category of staff. Dozens of "girls" started work each month at the renamed CTI—the CCB—for both punching and computer operation to fill growing staff needs and replace losses from turnover.[39] Even though women machine operators had begun to fall out of favor, the government's computing operations still largely ran on their labor. As the pressing need to hire and train large numbers of computer workers collided with shortages in the nascent field, a beneficial situation for the feminized machine grades emerged.

In 1962, when the movement to replace machine operators with higher-level executive staff was only a few years old, the Treasury suggested a surprising about-face. In response to lobbying from the CSCA, the Treasury considered creating—or rather formalizing—a promotion structure that would effectively give workers in the machine grades greater chances for promotion than ever before. In essence, the Treasury plan would allow women who had hit the ceiling of the machine operator grade to break through into the clerical or executive class, essentially becoming the higher-level, management-aspirant class of technocrats that the service had sought to hire in from elsewhere. Although most computer operators and programmers were drawn from the feminized machine grades the Treasury had created back in 1948, in theory a senior machine operator could be promoted into the clerical class or the executive class, becoming a higher clerical officer or an executive officer. In practice, such promotions were "virtually theoretical," because the number of officers in line for promotion was already far larger than the number of available jobs, and clerical or executive officers were favored over members of the machine grades.[40]

As soon as Treasury officials suggested this, however, vociferous opposition materialized from HMSO. Because HMSO was largely responsible for provisioning computer equipment, administrators there had strong opinions on computer staffing procedures. The Treasury and HMSO often sparred over the minutiae of organization and methods, usually only uniting when criticizing MinTech, a newcomer they both disdained. How government computers were staffed and deployed affected thousands of workers directly and close to a million civil servants through indirect means—to say nothing of the many millions of citizens who relied on government services. HMSO felt that this fact made these jobs critically important. Almost immediately, the Treasury began to backpedal, stating that "in practice the Senior Machine Operators are rarely found to be suitable for this kind of promotion"—a coded way of saying that posts with greater responsibilities and management duties would require women to supervise men.[41] In the context of the time, this was an unsavory proposition.

One high ranking Treasury official in charge of computing policy was Douglas Wass, who went on to become permanent secretary of the Treasury in 1974 (the second most influential post in the Civil Service after cabinet secretary). Wass had perfected bureaucratic doublespeak, admitting that "no one would deny that machines have developed and become susceptible of being used in increasingly complex processes," but hedging that "it is questionable whether these changes themselves necessarily enhance the quality of the Senior Machine Operator job." At the same time, however, he agreed to proficiency allowances for increased output and bonuses for senior machine operators who were in charge of supervising other staff. Tellingly, Wass also bemoaned the fact that losing senior machine operators to the clerical class through "promotion out of the machine grades would represent a loss of a particular talent" that was desperately needed in computing installations.[42] This was another example of how computer workers' high value, at least in the case of women, could work against them. In industry, talented women sometimes found themselves held in computing jobs for the same reason. At LEO, Mary Coombs saw her progress as a management trainee stall once she went to work with computers, recalling she was "too useful" as a programmer "to be promoted to management."[43]

Unable to rebut implicit sexism or classism, the clerical workers' alliance attempted to focus on skills, arguing that "the SMOs' duties have become of higher quality generally." Pointing out that the senior machine operator grade was more broadly used now than originally envisioned at its creation in 1948, the CSCA showed that many senior machine operators already had supervisory responsibilities and performed work similar to clerical officers. As the proportion of women in the clerical classes had grown during the 1950s and 1960s, so too had the CSCA's ranks of women members. As a result, the CSCA had become more concerned about the fact that machine operators were still consigned to a lower pay scale than clerical officers as a result of the unequal Equal Pay Bill put into practice in 1955.

As the haggling continued, the Treasury's Organization and Methods division, supported by several other departments, conceded "that machine grades on ADP work should have better career prospects than the present structure afforded," but almost no department heads believed that enhanced career prospects should take workers out of the machine grades by elevating them to the clerical or executive class.[44] As a result, a compromise of adding a higher chief machine operator grade, one step above senior machine operator, was floated in 1964. In practice, several departments already had chief machine operators, but these promotions were few and ad hoc. It was not an official Civil Service-wide grade, which meant that workers who had achieved it could not step into other positions of equal status elsewhere in the service. Chief machine operators earned the same pay as higher clerical officers, a supervisory grade that required management and organization skills. Making the grade official and more widespread meant that machine grade workers would become management. A chief machine operator grade would have meant a huge rise in status for machine workers; the posts were nearly on par with executive class posts in terms of pay, responsibility, and power.

Because of that, the Treasury decided that the new chief machine operator grade under discussion should not be paid as much as the current ad hoc chief machine operator positions. The Treasury's rationale that "it might be appropriate to fix the [potential new] Chief Machine Operator scale a level rather lower than the present one" nominally turned on the idea that the quality of entrants into the new grade might not be as high as the few ad hoc chief machine operators currently employed, but it was also another way of making sure that machine grade workers would still not be able to easily transition out of their class and into the executive class.[45] After all, the main point of adding a standardized, service-wide chief machine operator grade was to keep valuable staff from leaving computer work.

The Treasury therefore made an offer to the CSCA that aimed to enhance the divisions between the machine operator class and other classes, rather than lessen them. The Treasury rejected the idea that there should be an educational standard for recruitment into the machine grades, effectively short-circuiting attempts to reskill the class. In addition, the Treasury stipulated that if the chief machine operator grade were created, workers in that grade could not be promoted to clerical officer positions without a long trial period on clerical work, effectively destroying their chances to compete for promotions. Several departments dissented because their senior machine operators and ad hoc chief machine operators were already doing some clerical work and being paid and promoted accordingly. Under the new requirements, they would have to be demoted. Under the new plan there would also be machine operators who would be taken back down to the machine assistant grade.

The new proposal called "for the making of two 'streams of staff' ... one in the punch rooms and the other in the machine rooms, with one stream not necessarily inferior to the other."[46] Even as departments employed more aptitude tests to figure out which workers would make good programmers and computer operators, they also needed to find workers "likely to be more suitable to punch operating." Many punchers did not last long: "Besides manual dexterity there was a necessary aptitude required to be content to sit at a desk and do a boring job," wrote the head of the computing division of HMSO.[47] Women who would tolerate punching work were at such a premium that some departments refused to allow their best punchers to be promoted to other jobs. The CCB continued to advertise for "women punchers" throughout the 1960s, intentionally continuing the feminization of data input. To say that the punching stream would "not necessarily" be below the machine room workers could hardly hide the reality. The staff, through the CSCA, had asked for more interchangeability between the technical and clerical grades, but the plan proposed by the government offered only further deskilling and more of the job segregation that the CSCA was seeking to undo. It redoubled the types of divisions caused by the original creation of the machine operator class in 1948. The CSCA angrily rejected the package out of hand and aired its displeasure in the press.[48]

The growing staff anger about promotion for machine grade workers showed how their concerns were about prestige and career opportunity more than merely pay. Many machine operators were well paid, through an assortment of special bonuses given for particular skills and work on certain machines. The staff association's problem with the situation was part of a broader dissatisfaction with the Civil Service's fictive meritocracy. Seeing it as just another example of the classism and educational divisions that organized the service, the president of the CSCA told the press: "By all means encourage young people to start with the best possible education, but do not let these qualifications be used to create watertight divisions and class barriers throughout the organization ... The time has come to abolish the antiquated caste system of the British Civil Service."[49] Increasingly, the service was becoming a microcosm for the larger class antagonisms and gender inequalities that were being laid bare in British society during the social changes of the 1960s. As more women stayed in the workforce longer, feminist agitation became increasingly important to the politics of office labor.[50]

In 1966, in an attempt to align with new staffing models, CCB managers conducted more aggressive searches for executive officer programmers, operators, and systems analysts, even though they were "pleased to see that the quality" of their "girl trainees" was "still very high."[51] While attempting to bring in more executive-level recruits, they also sent larger and larger complements of operators from the machine grades for programming training in NICOL. NICOL, a subset of PL/1, was an imperative computer-programming language designed by ICT for business, scientific, and engineering applications. It was used for programming ICT's 1900 series of mainframes, which provided most of the government's administrative computing power. Learning NICOL made women valuable workers because people trained to program in high-level computer languages had skills that were transferrable to many other computing jobs. CCB management also sent several executive officers for COBOL training.[52] The CCB could only hope that both groups of trainees would stay long enough to provide a return on its investment.

Close to one hundred women worked at the CCB in 1966.[53] Less than a year later, their number had almost doubled.[54] In 1968, bloated with new workload, the CCB relocated to a significantly larger location outside central London. By then, its computing staff had increased more than fourfold, and still more operators, programmers, and data-input staff were needed.[55] In addition to a British-made ICT 1904 computer, staff operated a Univac (Sperry-Rand) 1004 Data Processor. Those in charge of service-wide purchasing in the Treasury and HMSO favored ICT computers, not because they were clearly superior but because buying ICT exclusively solved compatibility issues. In addition, the government saw support of ICT as the best way to support the British computing industry.

The ICT 1904 represented a middle-of-the-line mainframe for administrative and business computing at the time, with 16 kilobytes of memory standard and four to eight megabytes of removable disk memory.[56] It used twenty-four-bit words made up of six-bit bytes that could be represented in octal notation, as opposed to the IBM System/360 that used eight-bit bytes represented in hexadecimal, which was quickly becoming the standard. Input and output were performed on eighty-column cards, paper tape, and line printers, and these peripherals could be just as important as the mainframe itself when it came to speed. Unfortunately, ICT's peripherals often underperformed, creating frustration in government departments that had been strongly encouraged to buy ICT by the Treasury.

In 1972, when the CCB again changed its name—this time to the Central Computer Agency (CCA)—staff had doubled again from the 1968 numbers, soon stretching toward one thousand strong. As one of the government's main centralized computing installations, the CCB's importance both organizationally and functionally had grown quickly. It served as a microcosm of the changes in the Civil Service, and modeled the ideal of highly centralized computing toward which the government was moving. In many ways, it was like an internal computer bureau service for the government.

The total budget for the CCA's two computing centers was £42.5 million per year in the early seventies, but less than a quarter of that was spent on staff. By contrast, in the Civil Service as a whole, staff costs were the largest expenditure.[57] In 1969, when the government was no longer constrained by the lean computing labor market of the middle part of the decade, acrimony over machine operator computer jobs bubbled to the surface again. This time, however, the complaints originated from within the ranks of management, not staff. Despite poor career prospects, the pay for computer operators—especially at the senior machine operator level—had grown quite high in relation to other women's jobs and even many jobs for men at similar ages. Extra allowances for speed, certain skills, shift work, and overtime—common for most computing jobs—greatly enhanced salaries.

By the end of the decade, many career machine operators simmered with resentment at the fact that they quickly reached their maximum pay scale after being in their jobs for only a few years. However, HMSO believed that its pay and promotion structure was not "markedly out of line with work requirements" and that because "the final promotion of most in the class occurred around the age of thirty," it was "adequate to the interests of the [women] workers."[58] The CCB trundled along, with many SMOs being paid high salaries in an ad hoc fashion while still being kept from the emerging avenues of promotion for executive-level computer recruits. Even though reaching final promotion at thirty was unheard of for most Civil Service jobs, the impression that machine grade workers should leave the workforce around that age meant that the situation could be spun as "adequate to their interests."

Once out of danger of the pressing labor shortages of the mid-1960s, CCB management decided these "girls" were getting too much money for their jobs and wanted to stem, rather than encourage, the flow of machine operators into higher positions. Some senior machine operators could make as much or more than workers on the clerical and executive officer scales. The operators at the CCB from 1966 to 1970 made around £800 per year, at a time when £1,000 per year was a good salary for young men in white-collar work. Even so, the government pay scales attached to these jobs were admittedly at or below fair market rate when compared with the private sector and at times too low to even effectively compete with industry in retaining these desirable workers. Workers on the clerical officer and executive officer pay scales who happened to perform computing work received much more than workers on the machine operator scale. In the process of expanding the CCB, HMSO had moved it outside central London to Norwich, and because many workers left for other jobs in central London rather than move or commute to Norwich, the relocation ballooned the number of new hires required. While rapidly hiring over 150 computer operators local to the new location, managers found that "the best of the recruits coming forward in Norwich have tended to be very young" and, as a result, were promoted at younger ages than usual. In early 1969, there were thirty-two full-time senior machine operators with pension rights at Norwich below the age of twenty-five, with more on the horizon. A few made over £1,000 a year—an unusually high salary for women, and nearly unheard of for *young* women. Just under half were married. The majority were single.[59]

The head of the CCB complained to the Civil Service Department—a new department that had been specially set up in 1968 to consider questions of staffing and organization. Although he was "quite satisfied that the MOs being promoted are fully capable of doing SMO work, we are not happy with the size of the group we are building up receiving pay on a scale starting at £814 per annum." Money was not the main issue; the CCB was not being asked to economize. Rather, the problem was the fact that these young women, or "girls," as he called them, were attaining salaries as high as clerical staff and even lower-level executive officers, throwing into disarray the hierarchies of the Civil Service that had for so long placed machine work at the very bottom.[60] Class and gender, rather than money, formed the main sticking point. Instead of rejoicing in their good fortune at finding suitable workers so quickly, CCB managers chafed at the fact that these young, technical, women workers—having no further promotion outlets in the machine operator grade—could theoretically take examinations to move into the clerical or executive classes. That machine operators might be promoted into these jobs and progress to higher management and supervision duties could not be allowed: In his opinion, the situation was a "powder keg" waiting to go off.

The CCB's head suggested that "a fundamental and searching examination of the grading and pay of the machine class [was] badly needed" if such young recruits were rising so quickly through the ranks and earning so much.[61] He pushed the Civil Service Department and the Treasury to negotiate a new, reduced pay scale for all SMOs in the service in response to this temporary situation facing the new CCB. The precedent these workers set threatened to throw into question the "internal relativities" of Civil Service pay, which was in essence an elaborate class system of age, gender, education, and social status represented through wages. At a time when male clerical officers wrote angry letters to Civil Service union newsletters complaining that their salaries meant they could not "afford to keep a wife" or support a family, these young women were dangerously out of their place.[62]

In response to these "undeserving" machine operators, Treasury officials decided that all new hires, irrespective of merit, should be subject to new decremented pay scales with a slower promotion track and lower top-level earnings. This unprecedented action went against decades of government agreements with Civil Service clerical associations; posts were never downgraded once a pay scale had been agreed upon. Many SMO promotions were also intentionally deferred as a result of informal attempts to throttle back the flow of young women into high computing positions: "Where it is not absolutely essential that we fill posts now, we will defer appointments," wrote the CCB manager.[63]

Yet at nearly the same time, the government's Select Committee on Science and Technology was reporting that finding and keeping computer workers was one of the most pressing issues facing the government: "There is an insatiable demand for computer experts at all levels and the most rapidly rising element in capital investment is for computers."[64] The gendered labor hierarchies the Treasury had engineered into Civil Service computing undercut its own efforts to create computer experts and exacerbated the shortage of computer labor.

Divisions between Scientific and Administrative Computing Labor: The Example of the Atomic Energy Authority

The path forward was similarly fraught for other heavy users of computers within the government. As the service slowly revamped hiring patterns and struggled with retention in the mid- to late 1960s, labor shortages and economic crises resulted in a fallback to traditionally feminized machine workforces in certain situations.[65] The Atomic Energy Authority (AEA), the largest scientific computing user within the government, paralleled the CCB's staffing trends in this period, although the AEA also diverged in certain ways that showed the influence of career-track availability on government computing staff.

In contrast to the CCB and other administrative computer installations that used mostly ICT machines, the AEA favored English Electric KDF 9 computers programmed in assembly, ALGOL, or FORTRAN. The most popular system used by the AEA in the mid-1960s, however, was the IBM 1401, usually programmed in FORTRAN. Like other departments with a large amount of computing work, the AEA considered setting up a specialized career path for computing workers in 1965 in order to hold onto staff.[66] Pressure from staff unions brought the issue to the fore, and all the letters of complaint on the topic of poor promotion outlets were lodged by women computer workers, undercutting the idea that career advancement was not a pressing concern for women at this time. As a result, the AEA argued for the abolition of the machine operator class and for its replacement by a new data-processing class that would "include all people whose livelihood depends on the handling of punched cards" and give "the good computer operators" a "career avenue to the top of the class."[67]

Operators in the AEA, as at the CCB, were paid relatively well: The 1966 pay scales ranged from £292 at the lowest end of the machine assistant scale, which was primarily a trainee grade, to £1,040 at the highest senior machine operator post. While relatively good salaries, they were not unduly high in relationship to the cost of living: In the mid- to late 1960s, flat rentals in central London cost between £400 and £700 per year.[68] Executive officers with operating and programming experience earned as much as £1,569.[69]

In AEA computing installations concerned with scientific operations, a larger percentage of workers tended to be men, as opposed to AEA computing installations designated for commercial and administrative work, in which larger proportions of workers tended to be women. For example, in the scientific computing installations in the reactor subsection at Risley—the site of a prototype gas-cooled fast reactor that came online in 1959—62.5 percent of the operators were men. At Winfrith, a prototype gas-cooled reactor in operation from 1962, all were men.[70] The commercial operations groups at Risley and Winfrith, however, were both 100 percent women, as were commercial operations at Dounreay. This gendered distinction between scientific and commercial computing was not hard and fast; both the scientific and commercial operators in the weapons subsection at Aldermaston were mostly women, and the scientific operators at Culham Research Station, which still exists today as a fusion research center, were 75 percent women.[71] At Capenhurst, a gaseous diffusion plant for enriching uranium for other reactors, the scientific production section was 100 percent women. The scientific group at Windscale, the site of Britain's first major nuclear reactor for military purposes, were also all women.[72]

The higher percentages of men in some scientific computer operations in the AEA, compared with the near-domination of commercial and administrative operations by women, shows the way in which similar computing work was divided according to gender. Because men dominated in scientific fields, they also represented a higher-than-usual number of computer operators in scientific installations. Because women formed the vast majority in clerical and administrative work, they tended to be favored for nonscientific computing. Yet women operators and programmers did work in scientific computing in the AEA, sometimes forming the majority at a site.

The case of Windscale hints at one reason for the differing percentages of men and women among scientific installations. The scientific operations with the highest percentages of men were both prototype reactors that were still online in the late 1960s. Capenhurst, which had a scientific computing group that was all women, was not set up for new research but to enrich uranium for other reactors, whereas Windscale, whose scientific group was also all women, had been taken offline years earlier. Built in the far north of England to secretly produce nuclear weapons, Windscale had been a gigantic black eye for the British scientific establishment when the innovative reactor unexpectedly caught fire in October 1957, burned out of control for three days, and spread radioactive material over the surrounding area, all the while threatening to explode. Today, Windscale is known as the UK's worst nuclear disaster, with a severity rating of five on the seven-point international nuclear event scale, but at the time Prime Minister Harold Macmillan covered it up.[73] Computing jobs at Windscale in the wake of the disaster were undesirable jobs focused on cleanup, decommissioning, and monitoring, with little potential for advancement. A bird's-eye view of how the gender makeup differed from plant to plant shows that men were funneled into jobs with the most career potential.

Detailed turnover statistics show that trends in the AEA's computing labor force mirrored the CCB. In several computer installations men were hired to replace operator losses in the late 1960s, rather than continuing the pattern of hiring young women. More computer operation in the AEA was performed by higher-level workers as the decade came to a close. By the 1970s, the AEA, like all other departments, was "exhorted to make specially adapted career development and staff management plans for computer staff" in order to create an elite core of professionals who would be rewarded for going into and staying in computing work.[74]

Lowering Standards to Create an Elite

For much of the 1960s the decision to recruit and train programmers only from the higher-powered and more prestigious executive officer grade was a near disaster. Implementing the policy was difficult, because it required devoting significant time and money to training people with no experience. On the ground, senior machine operators and machine operators had the operating and programming experience for these posts—not executive officers. Throughout the service, men who could combine machine skills with management skills were in high demand but very hard to find. The Treasury's Technical Support Unit, eventually handed over to the Ministry of Technology, provided high-level support for all of the government's computing centers—but in 1965 this unit only consisted of thirty professional engineers, many of whom came from the Post Office and had no prior experience in computing. "On the face of it this looks like a staggering underestimate of the importance of the highly specialized and complex software side of things," sneered the press, later conceding that "it may, however, simply reflect the difficulty of finding experts in this field."[75]

One executive officer in charge of finding programmers pointed out that suitable programmers were not likely to be forthcoming, because volunteering for such work would stall their careers. Unknowingly but uncannily echoing the experience of the EO-turned-SMO at the CTI, he wrote: "There is a fear among staff ... of getting in a 'backwater'" that would limit promotion. He added that assurances should be offered to potential applicants that this would not happen. "Could we say that once on programming an officer is not likely to remain in this work for the rest of his career?" he asked.[76] A report from the Air Force noted another problem: The requirement of performing shift work scared away the workers the government wished to hire, because "shift work may also be seen... as being associated with the 'working class' employee."[77] The gender and class intimations of machine work, a fear of the unknown, and the uncertain career prospects of the jobs combined to frighten higher-level workers away.[78] Worse still, the pay scales offered for computer jobs were hindered by the government's pay freezes and were not competitive with industry. Under such circumstances, moving to a new office location to undertake training for a strange new field was an unattractive option for higher civil servants, who stood to gain little and had much to lose.

In 1964 and 1965, the programmer shortage became so acute that the government made some concessions in hiring, but it still confined internal calls for programming trainees to the higher grades of the service.[79] After the first call for applications met with little success, the Treasury reissued it, adding assurances that applicants who "did not make the grade as programmers" would be allowed to return to their previous posts. This was a procedural nightmare and a plan that would potentially waste thousands of pounds on training unsuitable candidates, but it was a necessity in coaxing men to apply. The Treasury also decided to add a paragraph describing the work a programmer actually did.[80] In addition, the Treasury lowered the minimum age for promotion to the executive class from twenty-eight to twenty-five years of age.[81]

Still, candidates were not forthcoming. Within a few months, the Civil Service changed recruitment literature and job postings to explicitly say that programmer positions were "suitable for women" as well as for men.[82] Opening the jobs to women in the executive officer class, however, helped little. The lack of a clear career ladder for computer workers tended to scare women away from the jobs just as effectively as it had scared men. Women in the executive class were deeply reluctant to be put on machine work, with its reputation for being deskilled, feminized work. In addition, fewer than one in twelve executive class workers were women. Their numbers were so low that inviting them to apply did virtually nothing to enhance the pool of potential recruits.[83]

Ann Sayce, who moved to a computing job in the Post Office from another job within the Civil Service right around this time, was a rare example of someone who decided to make the leap into computing at a time when safer career options lay elsewhere. Fed up with the boring nature of the work in the more established areas of the Civil Service, she felt she had little to lose. She recalled with exasperation how early on in her first government position her supervisor had shown her, in excruciating detail, how to place sticky labels onto envelopes. For some, the leap to computing was worth the risk—but usually only if they were dissatisfied with their current positions.

As the computer labor shortage became acute in 1965, the Treasury once again considered the bureaucratic dodge of trying to regrade machine operators as executive officers so that they could be recruited back into the jobs they were already performing. Their proposal offered "to widen the eligibility of Senior Machine Operators for promotion to the Executive Class, and hence for ADP [programming and systems analyst] work," while still steadfastly refusing to recruit and train members of the machine grades for computer programming in their current positions.[84] The wrangling involved in trying to get the right class of workers into computer jobs showed the government's newfound understanding that computer work could no longer be considered a deskilled, dead-end specialization if state modernization projects were going to succeed.

The Air Ministry put forward another fairly desperate proposal that suggested the creation of "an ADP career grade within the Civil Service" into which "individuals could be recruited initially as machine operators" and then "be provided with a full career within this field." Taking a heavier-handed approach, the Air Ministry's plan required all clerical workers to engage in a two-year "tour of duty" at a government computing installation in order to find recruits for the new computer worker grade. As "probably the largest single user of computing resources in the country," this course of action was critical not just for ending the Civil Service's computer labor problems but also for easing computer labor shortages nationwide, Air Ministry officials believed.[85] But requiring a tour of duty of everyone in the clerical classes, which were now majority female, would have produced the same problems.

Neither of these plans made it off the drawing board; both were too radical. Each one would have required a rethinking of the definition of authority itself by unsettling the gender and class implications baked into the hierarchy of the government service. Opening the competition to the feminized machine grades would have encouraged many more women into positions of authority and elevated them to the status of computer experts. Through the 1970s, it was rare—and generally seen as abnormal—for women to have authority over men in the workplace. As a result, neither plan was ever attempted. Instead, efforts to recruit executive class programmers redoubled.

Struggling to Modernize

In 1968, the Fulton Report on the Civil Service, charged with offering solutions to the perennial problems of staffing and organization in government, handed down findings that supported the idea of building a corps of technocratic elites to handle the state's computing needs.

Recognizing that the Civil Service badly needed modernization, the report laid out a series of measures designed to shift more responsibility for high-level policy decisions to scientists, engineers, and other technical specialists. There should be less reliance on "amateurs and generalists" in the ranks of management, it warned, calling for a new focus on training skilled managers drawn from men who had technical backgrounds. The recommendations from the Fulton report mirrored changes that were already underway, giving them more weight. Its recommendations put technocratic management front and center, betting on it as the best way to improve the workings of the state.[86]

The Fulton report's recommendations also set up the Civil Service Department, which would be in charge of staff oversight at the broadest level. Headed by the Prime Minister and run by the Lord Privy Seal, it was a powerful body tasked with fixing the most pressing problems of national administration. Yet the shortage of executive-level computer staff was so acute that the very department created to raise standards for staff instead lowered them. Having an A-level qualification in mathematics was no longer a requirement for programmers by the mid-1960s.[87] By 1970, the Civil Service Department decreed that the ADP aptitude tests the service had implemented were too difficult. Worried that they were "wasting talent" by turning away men unable to pass the tests, the Civil Service Department suggested ignoring the test results.[88]

Even though the Fulton report had lambasted amateurism and low standards, expectations for computer staff continued to be revised downward. On the ground, individual departments adopted a "train-and-see" attitude to try to find executives who might be good at computing. These measures wasted resources on training unsuitable candidates, but they did slowly increase the number of higher-level civil servants in operating positions: By 1968, roughly a third of all operators came from the executive and clerical classes, instead of being drawn mostly from the machine grades.[89] By 1971, the number of executive-level computer workers was more than 4.5 times greater than it had been in 1964.[90]

Although recruitment was improving, the government lost computer workers at progressively higher rates. By 1971, the rate of loss for management-level computer staff had more than tripled from the figure in 1964.[91] In earlier times, the Civil Service had asked women employees, particularly shorthand typists, to repay their training costs if they left their jobs before a certain period had elapsed—usually one year. Now, the exact behavior the government had for so long feared from women employees—job hopping after getting training in marketable skills—became an even greater problem in the competitive and, by the 1970s, increasingly male-dominated classes of systems analysts and programmers. Programmer trainees often looked for better jobs in industry after as little three to six months. From 1968 to 1969, executive-level computer workers left at a rate of 9 percent, whereas the general turnover rate of men in the executive ranks was only around 1 percent.[92] By the early seventies, this behavior was rampant. Although senior programmers did not have an unduly high turnover rate, junior programmers and systems analysts resigned at a rate of nearly 40 percent in 1970, finding better-paid jobs in industry after taking advantage of Civil Service training programs.[93] One department was reported to have had all of its executive officer trainees leave immediately after completing superficial training in a high-level programming language.[94]

Even lower-level civil servants began jumping ship when their skills allowed. In 1971, computer worker losses from the machine grades reached 17 percent in the Central Computing Agency.[95] Among programmers, only a tiny minority of the total resignations for 1971 (5 percent) were from women leaving to marry.[96] Most workers left either to take another computing position in the private sector or to transfer to clerical work, which had a better career structure and pay scales with higher end points.

This dynamic upset all of the government's projections about training, promotion, and staff retention. "The rate of wastage of ADP (automatic data processing) staff has been disturbingly high at the lower levels," reported the Select Committee on Science and Technology, searching in vain for ways to retain these valuable workers.[97] The Select Committee on Science and Technology warned Parliament that labor was a critically important force in technological change, noting that "the pace of [computing's] development is likely to be determined largely by the availability of ... experienced and high calibre staff."[98] Already "shortages of staff ... had caused delay in starting and completing some projects," warned the committee. Officials in the Treasury and the Civil Service Department knew that the government's computing projects would be injured if suitable staff could not be found and kept in high enough numbers. If the state could not build up "a reliable core of expertise," then the benefits of the computer revolution would remain out of reach.

By decade's end, the government finally did set up a new automatic data-processing grade to cater to the pay and career needs of programmers, operators, and systems analysts. The new grade would reskill and legitimize previously deskilled work. When the Civil Service Department took over the Central Computer Agency, its leaders made the decision to exclude machine operators from the list of classes that would be reviewed and upgraded as part of the process of organizing the new ADP work grade. The rules for the new grade also forbade workers from the machine operator class from applying for jobs, ensuring that no programmers or operators from the machine grades could benefit from the professionalizing effects of the change. Although these decisions drew objections from the Civil and Public Services Association (CPSA)—the new name for the CSCA as of 1969—the plans moved ahead unchanged.[99]

As the government made computer work a field of endeavor in its own right, certain machine-inflected jobs were no longer perceived as ranking below genuinely white-collar, skilled work. By providing formal courses in systems analysis, programming, and "ADP appreciation" for executives, the government hoped to not only shore up the number of trainees but also change where they came from.[100] Only a decade and a half earlier, women "stuck" processing data in the machine operator class were denied the equal pay granted to other civil servants, because their work was seen as requiring less intelligence and skill. By the late 1960s, this tarnish had all but disappeared, with operation, programming, and systems analyst careers positioned as highly desirable. The number of computer workers in the central government grew to over twelve thousand by 1972.[101] Yet with fully half of the jobs concentrated in data preparation and input and a large proportion of the remaining jobs cut out of the new, professionalized ADP grade, most computer workers' prospects worsened.[102]

From 1969 to 1971, losses of mostly male executive-level computer staff to other computing jobs in the private sector leveled off, owing to a system of lucrative bonuses instituted in 1970 for executives doing computer work. These same men did continue to leave, however—and in fact left in higher numbers than in the prior three years—for *noncomputing* jobs. Even with paid training and a generous system of bonuses in place as enticement, many could not be convinced to make a career out of computing.[103] Meanwhile, the Civil Service Department estimated that the central government would need more than ten times as many executive-level computer workers in 1970 as in 1960 and close to twenty times as many by 1975.[104] After studying all departments, the CSD estimated the number of these executives would only grow to 3,500 by the end of 1970 and 4,500 by 1975—far short of the numbers needed. This perception of rapid growth paired with severe labor scarcity inextricably bound the organization of government computing to the struggle to find, train, and retain computer staff. Planning for new computer systems became strongly informed by the specter of continuing labor shortages, affecting the kind of hardware the state sought.

Creating the Government's Ideal Computer

By the mid-1960s, the departments in charge of purchasing and organizing computing hardware—the Civil Service Department, HMSO, the Treasury, and the Ministry of Technology—had all come to perceive electronic computing as quite different from previous forms of data processing. No longer were computers perceived as simply an upgrade from earlier machines. Rather, they were seen as a crucial management tool that could change the very nature of what the government could accomplish. Through allowing enhanced record-keeping and more complicated data collection and manipulation, computing technology encouraged the government to embark on previously unimaginable projects. By the late 1960s, computers were an integral part of national policy because they allowed government ministries to collect, categorize, and wield information in new ways, from the PAYE tax system to the NHS. The Ministry of Pensions and National Insurance database alone held detailed records for more than thirty-five million people.[105] Computing began to reshape the objectives of the state itself: Advancing techniques made possible ever more ambitious projects of data gathering and top-down control.

Despite the large number of government computer purchases, the buying process was incredibly inefficient, unwieldy, and confusing. Determining which departments needed computers, how much should be spent on each, what sort of system should be purchased, and how it should be organized and staffed had become a labyrinthine process. Born out of procedures established over a decade earlier when government mechanization was vastly different and machines had more similarity to each other and much longer life spans, these methods had all but lost any coherent rationale. The higher price of electronic systems led to longer negotiations, and the process of choosing and buying computer systems was a nightmare of red tape and committees.

By the late 1960s, purchasing processes were so cumbersome that just the contract bidding stage alone could take a year or more. Because the decision making encompassed multiple departments, anywhere from three to six years could elapse between a department's signaling intent to buy a computer and the machine's eventual purchase and installation. Added to this were several more months for staff training and bringing the system fully online. Departments often found themselves at cross-purposes, fighting for the power to determine the shape of the Civil Service as expressed through its bedrock: its data-processing structure.

The Treasury, HMSO, the Civil Service Department, and the Ministry of Technology all involved themselves in this process, in addition to the departments in which the computers would be installed. Each would go over the same ground, clouding the process with different recommendations—"plowing the same furrow" and yet never planting seeds, as one official in the Civil Service Department put it.[106] Internal squabbles and the attempts of different departments to seize control over the process made slowness and confusion the norm.[107]

Enormous manpower and management resources got sucked into not only the decision-making process, but also, ironically, attempts to overhaul and fix it. Since 1949, the government-supported National Research Development Corporation (NRDC) had played an important mediating role between government and industry in the effort to support and monetize computing research. After the creation of the Ministry of Technology, the NRDC fell under its auspices.[108] At this point, the focus on fostering innovation in order help the computing industry fell by the wayside. MinTech began to formulate plans that prioritized the government's own immediate computing needs over research that might eventually produce profitable technologies.

Until the creation of the Ministry of Technology, the Treasury's Organization and Methods division controlled the approval and procurement of new computer installations government-wide and advised the NHS, the nationalized industries, and local governments on computer purchases. The Treasury's subdepartmental Technical Support Unit told other central government departments which computers would be suitable for their needs—whether or not those departments wanted the advice. Initially, this guidance dealt with administrative and business computing applications, but by 1964 both administrative and scientific users had to consult with the Treasury and HMSO for all purchases. Soon, HMSO began making all scientific computer purchases on behalf of other departments, even those that could easily have made their own computing decisions, like the Computer Board of the Department of Education and Science for the Universities.

When the Ministry of Technology created its own Computer Division Advisory Service in 1965, it tried to take over the responsibilities of the Treasury's Technical Support Unit. Its mission was to give systems advice both before and after purchases in order to supplement the information given by computer manufacturers. However, the Ministry of Technology's Computer Advisory Board could not wrest control away from the Treasury, which refused to cede authority over these expensive and important decisions.

Computer purchasing became more centralized in line with the government's attempts to create a cadre of technocrats. Increasingly understood as policy decisions and freighted with responsibility for determining, perhaps irrevocably, the future shape of government, computer decisions seemed too important to be left to individual departments. As the idea of the computer changed from a mere "electronic calculating machine" that was "entrusted only with laborious arithmetic and data registration functions" to "an integral part of the activities of government," the government tried to engineer the hardware side of the system to conform to its needs just as it had done with the labor side of the system.[109] Computer purchasing "should be a matter of deep pre-occupation not only to the British government but to all the governments of Western Europe," wrote the Select Committee on Science and Technology in 1971, crystallizing what had by then become the common understanding of computers' importance to government.[110] Because "the computer and its ancillaries [would] continue to penetrate both wide and deep into the nation's activities," many government ministers saw computerization as the most important problem of governance before them.[111]

The growing computer might of the United States was one of the biggest perceived threats, with IBM gobbling up market share globally.[112] Even with a strong indigenous industry, a third of all computers sold in the UK were IBMs during 1962, and the government estimated that worldwide IBM market share was as high as 65 or 75 percent. The threat of US power leaking into the sovereign control of other nations through technology was a pressing concern.[113] "The use of computers and computer technology is so fundamental," claimed MinTech, "that we cannot afford to depend wholly upon US subsidiaries."[114] In computers, "we are confronted with a powerful and pervasive technology which will rapidly become decisive in most of the nation's activities—but with the danger of its being entirely under the control of American-owned companies," wrote the government's Select Committee on Science and Technology. The committee warned that "to fail to produce an indigenous industry would expose the country to the possibilities that industry, commercial, strategic, or political decisions made in America could heavily influence our ability to manufacture, to trade, to govern, or to defend."[115]

Cold War tensions pervaded the relationship of technological exchange between the two allies. At the highest levels, this meant that US nuclear weapons research was not shared as freely as the British felt necessary for their national security, and at lower levels, it meant that the British government had little faith that IBM's computing solutions would be adequate for the work of its massive public sector or trustworthy enough to be given such deep and irrevocable control over state processes. By providing the machines on which the state would run, any computer company favored by the government would have a hand in how the British State functioned. In the atmosphere of secrecy and fear that echoed throughout the Cold War, the Ministry of Technology hearkened back to World War II when homegrown technological innovation had been necessary to British survival. The same mindset that made the government keep the Colossus project secret until it was leaked in the mid-1970s influenced decisions about computing throughout this period. A fear of being beholden to foreign technologies—particularly in times of international crisis during which Britain might have to fend for itself—led to a belief that the United Kingdom needed to produce its own computers, on par with the best that American companies produced but specifically suited to British needs.

However, Britain could not muster enough technical talent, research money, or customer base to support multiple British computer companies, the government felt. Anthony Benn wanted to rationalize the computing industry because he thought consolidating research and design would save British computing. The Treasury sought to tame the confusing and excessively long process of computer purchasing by focusing on one supplier. It relished the idea of gaining greater control over the computers used in government by gaining greater control over the industry. Both departments agreed that more strongly centralized control was a necessity if government computing was going to flourish with the labor resources available to it. To run these computers, the government would need to draw on the small core of executive-level computer staff it had been cultivating. Only these workers could be trusted with the technical roles that would undergird the state's ability to function. This "particularly important" task required a "highly competent, well technically trained group of people," wrote the CSD, people who would fix "the really practical engineering problems" and have an "appreciation of likely developments" in the field.[116]

Since these workers were small in number, the Civil Service needed large centralized systems to achieve these aims. The design of computers themselves would be key to the state's survival, and the government wanted a hand in the process. "The Government is the largest single user of computers in the country" said the CSD, "and its technical requirements can best be represented both to the [computer] manufacturers and to other organizations ... by its own experts." The shape of the "technical element" of the government "will clearly have to be determined by the number of specialists who can be found and, given other demands, can legitimately and efficiently be deployed on this sort of work." These specialists could then oversee and operate systems on behalf of other departments.[117] In this way, the context of persistent computer labor shortage and a lack of enough computer "experts" powerfully influenced discussions about government consolidation of the computing industry.

The field of computer companies capable of producing the large, powerful machines desired for public sector administration had already significantly winnowed by the mid-1960s. ICT, the most successful British company in the international market as well as at home, had been constructed through a 1959 government-encouraged merger of British Tabulating Machines and the wholly British-owned subsidiary of Powers-Samas. Later, in the early 1960s, it had absorbed, again with government encouragement, EMI, GEC, and Ferranti's data-processing divisions. The acquisition of Ferranti's computing interests in 1963 was important to the government's interest: Ferranti's involvement in the Atlas supercomputer project with Manchester University meant that its ensuing product line had come to represent the highest level of commercial computing power available.

The other principal player in British computing by the late 1960s was English Electric, itself a merged company comprised of the former LEO Computers and the original English Electric, with Marconi and Elliott Automation's data-processing interests absorbed along the way. These mergers effectively made the field of high-end British computing a duopoly by 1965.[118] The merger of ICT with English Electric would complete the process of centralization and align the structure of the computing industry with the needs of government.

Wilson had envisioned "a New Britain—mobilizing the resources of technology under a national plan; harnessing our national wealth in brains, our genius for scientific invention ... affording a new opportunity to equal, and if possible surpass, the roaring progress of other western powers."[119] The prospect of losing the incredible power of such a tool through the British computing industry's inability to produce the right sort of machines for the home market—in which the government was the largest customer—was unthinkable, particularly during a period when Britain's slide into second-class world power status was ever more acutely felt by those in power. Although this narrative of decline has been retroactively contested, at the time it was regularly bemoaned in the press and part of the cultural imaginary of late twentieth-century Britons, who saw British might slipping away and their nation becoming a supporting player in the story of American conflict with the Soviet Union, rather than a protagonist in its own right.[120]

In a letter sent to the prime minister, Anthony Benn pleaded for approval of the merger plan: "We are the only European country which has a vigorous computer industry of its own and we have been able to supply up to 50% of our home market. This has been a valuable import saving operation, quite apart from the export earnings that have been gained by ICT and English Electric." Britain was "the only country outside the United States which has a significant indigenous computing industry, capable of development into a world-class international enterprise," he stated.[121] In 1968, after prolonged wrangling with English Electric and ICT, arguments with the Treasury over startup money for the new company, and fending off outside takeover bids, the Ministry of Technology announced the finalized merger.[122] The new company would be known as International Computers Limited (ICL).

As presented to the public, the main intent was to create a large British company with the resources to compete with IBM at home and abroad, but this obscured the government's multiple motivations. The consolidation would greatly simplify purchasing and provisioning of computer systems, because the resultant merged company would be favored with government contracts, doing away with the incredibly unwieldy process of buying machines through a multiple tender process designed to encourage all British computing companies equally. It would also allow for government support in the form of preferential purchasing and loans. For agreeing to the government-backed merger, ICT and English Electric were favored with all available government loans and grants for private sector computing research. Each one of the government's reasons for the computer merger was at base motivated by a shortage of technical staff and skill.

In creating ICL, the government had built a computer industry vertically integrated with its needs and labor force. The merger would ensure the government could provision the specific kind of powerful, centralized mainframes it desired and have more influence over the design and production process than would be possible with foreign companies or with

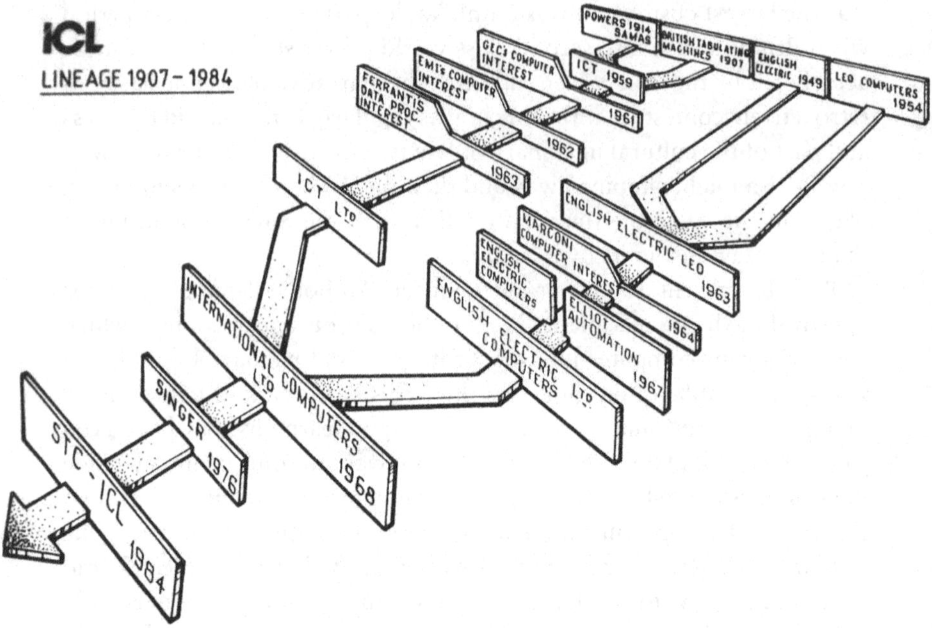

Figure 4.1
Chart of the multiple mergers and takeovers that created ICL. ICL was eventually bought by Fujitsu. National Archive for the History of Computing, Manchester, United Kingdom.

a diverse, competing field of British companies. For three years prior, the Ministry of Technology had been trying to "work out the specifications of a new generation computer system that would be both compatible with the existing systems and compatible with the systems adopted by IBM and hence the world standard." Merging the British computing industry into one company would help MinTech fit it to the exact needs of the government's huge computing edifice. The mainframe successor to the ICL 1900 series, the 2900 series, would come as a direct result of this government intervention and the government's perception of its own technical needs.

In discussing the merger, Benn noted that "computers are, of course, total systems, and have to be seen and sold as systems," from software and hardware to maintenance and labor. He argued for the heterogenous engineering of the computer industry in order to fit the government's needs, rather than the reverse.[123] In engaging in this type of heterogeneous engineering, however, Benn ignored one of the most important facets of robust technological systems: redundancy. He backed this "radical restructuring" and "large-scale rationalization" of the computing industry so that government investment could flow to one company rather potentially go to waste by supporting many different companies.[124] In return, ICL would provide a set of hardware solutions for government computerization. In doing this, Benn positioned himself as the preeminent systems analyst for the entire nation. His experience dealing with large and unwieldy technological systems in the Post Office might have made him ideal for this role, but he took an extremely heavy-handed approach. The best systems analysts know that there is always a delicate balance to be struck between existing and new models of organization.

Fortune Favors the Least Bold

Confidential documents outlined that the government would buy the products of the new, merged company whenever an administrative computer was required. Even scientific government computing installations could not buy from other companies unless they could show that ICL's machines could not perform "similarly" to a foreign machine for a price equal to or 25 percent greater than the cost of the foreign competitor's machine. The policies to favor ICL were not detailed publicly, in an attempt to keep government favoritism secret from IBM UK. In exchange for preferential treatment, the Treasury demanded a level of general control over, and debriefing on, ICL's future projects, primarily to ensure that ICL would produce machines well-suited to the government's applications. "The government will place its expertise at the disposal of ICL and will expect its views to be given due weight in the framing of the research and development program," wrote the Treasury.[125]

For years, the government had taken a keen interest in controlling computer design. For instance, the Select Committee on Science and Technology reported that "ICT started in 1967 to develop a large multiprocessing computer at the top end of the 1900 range, with a claimed maximum power of 10 times Atlas, which was aimed specifically at meeting the future needs of central government and other large users in the public sector." The government supported its development by placing enough orders to ensure its success.[126] The links between the computing industry and the Civil Service had long been strong: In 1961, ICT appointed Sir Edward Playfair as its chairman. Playfair had been a career civil servant who had risen to permanent secretary in the Ministry of Defense—a major computer-using department.[127] Computers continued to be powerful weapons. By 1970, the Ministry of Defense used close to one-third of all government computers.[128]

The same year that ICL was created, the Treasury lost its power over service-wide computer purchasing. As a result of the Fulton report's critique of the government's organization of resources, the new Civil Service Department took over advising on computing purchases, determining staffing policy and standardizing data-processing systems throughout the Civil Service. But the merger ensured that in matters of computer purchasing there was no choice, given the government's objective to "buy British" at all costs. MinTech was also forced to take a back seat. "As a department using computers," the Ministry of Technology "ranks in exactly the same way as other departments" said the CSD, stripping MinTech of its power over government computing.[129] MinTech chafed at being regarded "as merely another central government department to which normal procedures apply," given that its mission was to advise the nation on technology.[130] Now it had to take direction from another department regarding computers because of how the government was rigidly centralizing computing policy. MinTech had shaped the entire nation's computer choices through the merger, yet it was no longer allowed to even buy its own computers.

As short-term technocratic pragmatists, the CSD exuded a thinly veiled hostility toward MinTech. "We ... deal with a project as a whole and not just from the hardware and software angle," intoned one CSD official. Although MinTech might have had "knowledge of ADP from which [the CSD] should benefit, they are completely lacking in the other aspects of advice which we give in respect of say, staffing, recruitment, grading of posts, and many other matters."[131] Hardware could not function without labor and expertise, and the CSD claimed control over these aspects. Another CSD document put it far more bluntly: "In practice, the contribution [of the Ministry of Technology] has not gone beyond pointing to 'blue sky' computer possibilities of the future." MinTech's high-level interventions to try to improve computing processes in government over the last several years, the document stated, had "merely turned out to be irritants rather than valuable contributions."[132]

As in the case of the machine grades, technical knowledge was valued far less than the traditional patterns of organizational hierarchy that confirmed and consolidated centralized power. Even though a disregard for the views of scientific experts had been a key criticism leveled by Fulton, the new department set up to enact the Fulton report's recommendations continued to ignore the government's own technical experts. Undeterred, the Ministry of Technology devoted a large share of its resources to trying to establish computer planning policies, but its suggestions were deflected. MinTech's efforts to streamline the computer selection and purchasing process and to create a central software resource were met with disapproval. Computing in government was "a major machinery of government problem and not a computer problem," claimed the CSD, dismissing MinTech's technical expertise.[133]

Ending Manpower Problems, Creating Hardware Ones

Professor Stanley Gill of Imperial College, a coinventor of the subroutine and a member of the Pilot ACE project, wrote a position paper that resonated with officials in the Treasury and the CSD. Gill believed that the problems facing government computing "stem[med] from a too-complete separation of policymaking from the implementation of ADP systems" and that in order to rectify this in the future the government had to include "ADP planning in policymaking at a high level." This was exactly the view held by the CSD and the Treasury, and they relished an outside expert's confirmation.

Gill took their penchant for centralized control even further. Citing shortsighted decisions "confined to immediate objectives only, leaving the system designers to decide where to leave room for future changes," Gill painted a grim portrait of the government sabotaging the very systems it intended to build. While systems analysts designed government computer systems to the "best of their ability," Gill believed they worked "in ignorance of policy motives" and that in doing so "they unwittingly [laid] traps and obstacles in the way of the administrators, who then [found] themselves in a straitjacket which they took no part in designing."

Gill's warnings that the government's actions might produce the opposite of their desired effects were correct, but for the wrong reasons. Where he saw too little high-level control, there was actually too much. Gill warned that government leaders "must face the fact that [they were] in the process of developing a monumental machine for handling the detailed affairs of government, and that the design of this machine is one of the most crucial matters of policy in hand. It could either benefit, or cripple, the government for years to come."[134]

In a few short years, Gill would be proven correct. The limitations Gill saw in government computer planning stretched far beyond the government's own systems. Through the merger to create ICL, and multiple computer mergers before that, government ministers had taken the "virtue of planning for strictly limited objectives" well outside the operation of their own bureaucracy.[135] Only a year after the merger, a MinTech brief candidly discussed the government's myopia in trying to find a computer company that would function as its "chosen instrument" for control of both government and industry. "These judgments of management strength and capability are very difficult for outsiders to make; and selection of a company as a 'chosen instrument' is a very dangerous thing for a government Department to do ... In light of one year's post-merger experience, it is easy to point to things that would have been done differently if we were doing it all over again," wrote Sir Richard Clarke, who worked in the Treasury and then later in the Ministry of Technology.[136]

Although the merger that created ICL was counted as a success in saving the British computing industry from failure or American takeover in the short term, the merger concentrated power for the industry's success—or failure—into one company, and tied the computer industry to government computing needs. The merger was an attempt to change the very fiber of the computing industry, and it had the effect of pushing companies to act against their own best interests in order to fall in line with the interests of the government.[137] As Jon Agar notes in his history of automation experts in the British government, "Treasury O&M (Organization and Methods) was always constrained by what was made available by British manufacturers, and therefore indirectly by the success of government policy."[138] The Treasury's attempts to upskill computer work had created a vicious cycle in which too few experts led to ever more centralized and vertically integrated solutions to maintain control.

By 1970, the "the manpower-hunger of computers" as they became "more and more sophisticated" meant that staff for government computing installations grew by at least 30 percent each year.[139] Investment in hardware also grew tremendously, with costs expected to stretch toward £100 million by 1975.[140] The idea that computer expenditure could be viewed as a replacement for staff expenditure had all but evaporated.[141] From 1965 to 1975, executive class programmers and systems analysts increased fivefold, and executive class operators increased by almost fourteenfold, although they were still a minority of all operators.[142] Still, the government needed more, reporting close to four hundred vacancies for higher-level computer workers alone in early 1971.[143] This was a massive shortfall, given that the current number of systems analysts and programmers was just over two thousand. The government needed almost 20 percent more computer professionals than they could find, even as labor shortages eased back from their peak in the mid-1960s.[144]

A Backwater Becomes Mainstream

In the early 1960s, careers in computing were barely on the radar for most civil servants. Even in 1965, potential recruits from the professional classes of the Civil Service worried that computing work would shunt them into a "backwater" and remove them from more lucrative and interesting career paths. By the early 1970s, the position had nearly reversed, with workers in higher grades of the service clamoring to get into automatic data-processing jobs and the government sending out hiring calls only to higher-level civil servants.[145] "I know several of my brightest SEOs [Senior Executive Officers] and HEOs [Higher Executive Officers] would like to spend the rest of their working lives in programming, and would willingly exchange whatever prospects they have of rapid advancement in other departmental jobs for a more modest progression in a broader ADP field, coupled with the certainty of staying in it," reported one department head.[146]

Computing jobs' metamorphosis from backwater to the center stage required specific and intentional organizational changes, showing that cultural factors trumped technical ones. Executive-level civil servants had no qualifications for computing, and few were university graduates.[147] Almost all training for computing work occurred either on the job or at the computing company from which the government had bought the machine. The Wales Dock Board, for instance, successfully trained all of its new programmers and operators at the ICL Customer Center in under three months as late as 1970. None of their trainees had any prior experience.[148]

In addition to still dominating the machine grades, women formed close to 44 percent of the clerical classes by this point. But they still only held a small minority—8 percent—of executive class positions.[149] As a female member of the Society of Technical Civil Servants pointed out, the situation regarding women workers in computing in government and industry made little sense: "Although there is a constant shortage of people with the necessary technical background to keep pace with the increasing technological demands of industry, here is a source of supply that has been virtually completely neglected."[150] As computing positions rose in status, hiring procedures intentionally turned away from the largest pool of technically talented workers in the Civil Service and neglected the members of the growing clerical class as potential trainees.

The mismatch between continually rising expectations for computers and the labor force available for the government's computerization projects produced just the kind of unintended consequence that Stanley Gill had predicted. As a Civil Service Department brief succinctly stated, because adequate staff "did not currently exist," the systems favored by the government centralized and winnowed computer labor as much as possible.[151] Even though the story of the computer merger is often discussed with reference to external stimuli—primarily the threat of IBM—in fact its rationale was deeply embedded in the mores of the British class system. Control over the computer industry was not just about bolstering it against foreign competition but about making it into an industry that could serve the government's specific needs, constructed by its particular view on computer labor. ICL was meant to ensure the British State had firm control over the kinds of highly centralized systems—made up of ever more powerful mainframes—that it needed. In essence, the computer merger looked backward rather than forward: Its purpose was to reconsolidate traditional hierarchies through the design of cutting-edge technologies.

Engineering the nation's technological systems on this scale created a host of problems that the government soon decided would be better forgotten than solved. While ICL was held captive by government demands for ever more powerful mainframes, computer technology was starting to move toward smaller, less centralized systems. The government's ossified image of computerization mired ICL in the past, negatively impacting not only the new company's operations, but also the entire British computing industry.

5

The End of White Heat and the Failure of British Technocracy, 1969–1979

By the 1970s, executive officer–level computing work was a "functional specialization" service-wide.[1] Now viewed as some of the most important jobs within the apparatus of the state, transfers to computer posts from high-level executive positions became possible. The Treasury, CSD, and HMSO set up an ADP subspecialty for management-level workers who had chosen to dedicate their careers to the burgeoning but still understaffed field. Efforts to make more attractive career ladders for programmers by offering them promotion prospects in the executive class, rather than sealing them into the limited promotion structure of the machine operator class, came as a direct result of a change in how computer technology was understood at the highest levels of government.[2] The creation of new standards for how to choose both computing staff and computing hardware gradually ushered in a different data-processing environment—one that would be integrated into the management chain more than ever before.

After the 1968 merger, the state poured grant and loan money into ICL, though not enough to ensure the company's success.[3] Instead of having the intended positive effects, the merger saddled successive administrations with a slow-moving behemoth whose needs would soon diverge from the needs of an ever more computerized state. Rather than continuing to try to support the entrepreneurship of the computing industry and monetize its output as the NRDC had in earlier decades, the government focused on immediate, pragmatic results, making ICL a captive supplier for the government's computer needs.[4] By 1971, the vast majority of the government's computers, an estimated 71 percent, were from ICL, and the hope was that soon all government computers would be.[5] Departments were all but required to buy ICL, and the company was shielded from its biggest competitor, IBM UK, by means of secret price protections. Nearly 90 percent of the computers installed in the two years following the merger were from ICL.[6]

Meanwhile, the labor problems that had made increased centralization seem to be a solution to the country's computing woes continued to worsen, and new kinds of labor problems threatened to undo the benefits of centralized systems. Britain endeavored to strengthen its economy, looking abroad to membership in the European Economic Community (EEC), or Common Market, for its economic survival. The nation struggled with inflation, a faltering economy, and labor unions unwilling to accept the state's austerity measures. As the contraction of its computing industry shut down dreams of a return to superpower status through technology, EEC membership offered reduced trade barriers, which would lead to a larger market for British goods and other economic benefits, such as development loans for depressed industrial areas.

Yet inclusion in the EEC required a kind of socioeconomic modernization that, despite decades of technological "revolution," Britain still lacked. Rejected from entry twice in 1963 and 1967, Britain was only able to gain acceptance in 1973. An important requirement of EEC membership was sex discrimination legislation. EEC leadership considered equal opportunity and equal pay to be characteristics of well-functioning, modern economies. This requirement threatened to undo the gender stratification of the British labor force and the economic savings that came with it—but other Western nations were beginning to realize that sexist practices had detrimental effects on their economies, rather than seeing sexist labor practices as simply the *result* of poor economic conditions.[7] As feminist historian Sheila Rowbotham observed, class and gender were so thoroughly intertwined that women's oppression was nearly synonymous with labor exploitation.[8]

Because women's low-cost labor had become ingrained in the economic and technological infrastructure of the state, changing these labor practices required a sea change that the government had successfully held off since the end of World War II. Gendered and classed technocratic ideals had been carefully designed into the public sector, deeply influencing the private sector as well. As Britain struggled to join the EEC, these labor practices would throw into sharp relief the country's failures to truly modernize despite decades of trying, showing how technological change had functioned as a conservative force rather than a progressive one. Although seemingly two very different issues, the failure of ICL and the continued failure to equalize women's place in the labor market both had their roots in the same soil: attempts to engineer a computerized state that gave government more top-down control and strengthened existing hierarchies of gender and class.

Redefining "British" Computing

Wilson's socialist technological utopia had failed to live up to its promise, giving way to less altruistic and less protectionist technology policies under Edward Heath. By 1975, the same year Britain was censured by the EEC for failing to enact meaningful equal pay legislation, the handwriting was on the wall for the British computer industry. One Conservative member of parliament bluntly expressed the widespread and growing dissatisfaction with ICL: "The sooner the British computer industry sinks beneath the waves and allows the Americans to get on with the job, the better."[9]

Yet the changes brought by Heath's Conservative government in 1970 were restrained by the fact that those in control of the bureaucratic machinery of government wielded as much or more power over government computing as elected officials. With control of over ten thousand computer workers and an expectation that outlay for hardware would more than double by 1975 to reach close to £100 million, those in charge of government computer purchasing affected British computing as a whole. Heath's pullback from Labour's nationalization projects could not significantly alter the computer industry's direction at this point.[10] Technological and policy decisions made before his arrival meant that the centralizing processes begun by Labour had significant momentum.

ICL was supposed to hold its own with IBM in the international market while dominating the British and Commonwealth markets.[11] However, at the same time, the company was also tasked with focusing on the needs of British public sector administration—designing the ultimate mainframes for the state's vast data-processing projects. After the merger, ICL became a way for the government to institutionalize computer technology as a concern of the state, but these efforts were short-lived. The problems that had provoked the merger worsened afterward. Just two years later, the head of government computer provisioning wrote: "Besides personnel needs and difficulties of organization, there are two other major constraints on the future development of Automatic Data Processing—the cumbersomeness of government procedure and the often disappointing performance of the British computer industry."[12]

All of these problems had their roots in state initiatives. Personnel needs went unmet due to attempts to reengineer the composition of the computer labor force, whereas procedures to centralize computing further had created more, rather than fewer, organizational hurdles. The disappointing performance of the British computer industry also owed a great debt to the government-backed computer merger. Although the creation of ICL had been intended to strengthen the industry and help the government, tying ICL to government computing paradoxically injured both. Because ICL was encouraged to manufacture very large, expensive mainframes for government use as the trend toward smaller, more quickly obsoleted, and decentralized systems picked up speed, the company lost market share. Also, government departments were forced to buy ICL products that increasingly failed to meet their needs.

To sponsor the computing industry, the government enacted a secret 25 percent price protection policy for British computing companies in 1965, in addition to the close to 14 percent import tariffs added to the cost of foreign computers.[13] The computer merger made the government's favoritism for ICT official, with the promise of millions in loans and grant money and the threat of withheld support had the company refused the merger. The government maintained a 10 percent shareholding in ICL, which was headed in name and spirit by ICT. ICT's 1900 mainframe series became ICL's flagship machine, supplemented by the System 4 range from English Electric. The 1900 range were the government's preferred mainframes, and as such government officials felt that they needed to be protected and that similar, compatible machines needed to be developed in anticipation of the 1900's obsolescence.

Labour earmarked millions of pounds in loans for ICL's research and development to produce a successor to the 1900 series that would "be fully competitive in world markets" and "meet the expected demand for such a system at home" from the public sector.[14] These loans and preferential purchasing measures were meant to ensure a new, powerful computer line specifically designed for government use. However, focusing on R & D meant that many other factors were neglected. The importance of robust manufacturing practices to meet timetables for installation, and the importance of cultivating a market through marketing, software, and customer service fell by the wayside as ICL focused on designing the new 2900 series.

The government kept the details of its "buy British" policy secret to avoid a confrontation with IBM, although IBM UK and Honeywell suspected the source of their disadvantage.[15] As the costs for government computing installations ballooned, protectionist measures became harder to defend. Cost–benefit analyses showed no proof that computer outlays would save money in the long run. From 1965 to 1969, 215 computers costing £41.2 million were ordered for the central government, although only £27.5 million worth had been delivered and installed as of 1969.[16] Most of these computers were British designed and made, the products of preferential government purchasing.[17] The Ministry of Health, for instance, used twelve computers, seven of which were from the ICT 1900 mainframe range. Two more were IBMs, and the remaining machines came from other British companies.[18]

Assessing the "Britishness" of companies and their output was not as simple as first envisioned. A report setting out guidelines for computer procurement in 1965 listed six different "Degrees of 'Britishness' in Computer Suppliers," ranging from British-controlled manufacturers that designed their own equipment to foreign-controlled manufacturers. There were several degrees in between, such as foreign-controlled companies that manufactured or designed equipment in Britain and British-controlled companies that manufactured equipment of British or foreign design abroad. ICT, the government's perennial favorite, topped the list throughout the 1960s, even though several other companies—such as English Electric Leo Marconi (EELM), Elliott, and Ferranti—were equally British. IBM earned points for having manufacturing plants and design offices within the United Kingdom.[19]

The Britishness of public sector computers became an increasingly important but also increasingly fraught issue. In the mid-1960s the Central Computer Agency convened a study group that produced a list of every single computer available on the UK market and specified whether each one was British or not. Most IBM computers were not British according to the criteria laid out by the study, except for the model 1130, which was produced in part in the United Kingdom.[20] These charts and lists painstakingly showed which companies had a more "British" business model than others and why. Yet this only underlined, in the words of one Treasury administrator, "what a jungle this business [of determining Britishness] is."[21]

Paradoxically, these reports laid the groundwork for backing away from supporting ICL later. By showing how Britishness could be a fluid category, open to interpretation, the reports questioned what a British computer really was. In the early 1970s, Honeywell and IBM representatives lobbied the government, trying to spin their machines as British to win government contracts away from ICL.[22] IBM UK pointed to the many British workers they employed and the fact that they performed some research and development work in the United Kingdom. Both of these elements upgraded the company in the government's estimation, but the other main concern was export potential. "Unless we can design, develop, and manufacture ever more sophisticated products, particularly in engineering and electronics, the import/export balance will certainly get worse," MinTech stated.[23] By the early seventies, however, the promise of greater technological choice at a lower price began to undo ICL's British edge.

The Swift Failure of Government Consolidation

By 1970, the missteps of the computer merger had become obvious. ICL was clearly losing further ground to IBM globally. Increasingly desperate to salvage what was left of the British computer industry, the government encouraged ICL to pursue sales to the Soviet Union and China, because IBM was not allowed to sell in those markets. Given that the wartime Colossus computers were still being scrupulously kept secret at this point in time, these actions seemed uncharacteristically incautious. They showed the urgency of Britain's attempts to renew their global standing through high technology exports.[24] Despite the fact that the US government attempted to block the sales, British computing companies sold computers to both China and the Soviet Union with little hesitation and with the active help of the British government.[25]

From the perspective of ICL's government backers, such trading relationships "represent[ed] a major breakthrough in technological exports and potential for some years ahead as well as showing very considerable prospects for business for ICL."[26] Heath continued the political sacrifices begun by Wilson's government in an effort to save the British computing industry. Wilson had been pleased to allow British computers to be exported to China and encouraged ICL to aggressively pursue a close trading relationship with the Soviet Union, because he believed that bolstering computing exports outweighed "the possible risk that the computer would be put to improper uses." Both governments made a significant gamble that granting export licenses for these machines against the wishes of the US government would not significantly impair Anglo-American relations.[27]

Stopgap measures like these could only help in the short term. By 1971, just three years after the consolidation of the computer industry, Heath's government presumed ICL a near-total failure of technology policy. That year, the Treasury floated the idea of "cutting ICL loose" to an American company, if one could be found that wanted to buy it.[28] Extra outlay for

ICL systems, which were usually more expensive than comparable IBM ones, was beginning to seem less defensible. Many ministers still perceived computing as a potentially money-saving technology and chafed at ICL's uncompetitive pricing.

In one cost–benefit analysis, the Central Computer Agency found that one of the state's largest computer installations had a net savings of only about £420,000 over a ten-year period.[29] In fact, these "savings" were not even real. These figures did not account for the tendencies of computer installation operating costs to inflate over time. After adjusting for that factor, the project represented a net loss of £2.5 to £3 million over the same period. Unwilling to give up the fiction of cost cutting by computer, many within the ranks of the government's computer specialists argued for a wait-and-see approach, planning a repeat study to see if the savings laid out in costing forecasts somehow materialized in several more years' time.[30] They never did.

The new ICL 2900 range of computers, which contained some of the most advanced technology in business computers at the time, was meant to correct all the existing problems of government computing, but research and design success could not make the 2900 range an IBM killer. By 1971, IBM sales in the United Kingdom accounted for 38 percent of all systems sold, whereas ICL sales accounted for 32 percent. Worldwide, IBM supplied more than 70 percent of all computing systems by value.[31] In many cases, IBM provided machines that were less advanced, but also less expensive. IBM bolstered the value of its machines with extensive service contracts.

The government found "no good economic/technological/strategic case for continuing to support ICL" but simultaneously fretted that it was "in no easy position to abandon" ICL, given its own role in shaping the company and its previous rhetoric concerning the importance of a native British computer industry. These views were confined to a confidential economic policy report, however.[32] In the early seventies, ICL—which was now effectively the entire British computing industry—enjoyed continued if grudging support, estimated to cost the government £100 to £150 million over the course of the next decade.

Ministers at the highest levels felt it was "inconceivable politically that government, having hooked its own systems heavily on ICL, having encouraged other domestic users to do likewise, and with an eye to the European market, should decide now to abandon them."[33] Having built its systems around ICL, the government now needed to prop it up. ICL was still important for British business and government users that had invested heavily in its equipment. ICL's failure would result in a lack of maintenance, services, and new products for existing installations.

Although ICL had been Labour's creation, both major parties shared similar technocratic ideals. This meant that the impulse to centralize computing flourished under the Conservative party as well because of the party's desire for stronger control over recalcitrant workers. Even though financial outlay to support ICL was increasingly viewed with wariness and suspicion by Conservatives, the centralized control afforded by ICL's creation was welcomed by those increasingly frightened by labor's power to disrupt the essential systems that the nation required to function. Unruly and untrustworthy women workers, perceived as having power disproportionate to their low-level skills, terrified government ministers. In the same way that coal miners had disrupted the nation's power supply with their wage demands, these women computer workers threatened to disrupt the nation's information infrastructure. In 1974, Heath had struggled to use the might of the central government to defeat striking coal miners, rearranging the very work of the nation and its use of technological systems—in this case, the power grid—to try to bring the miners into line. Cutting down the nation's use of electricity to a "three-day week," Heath showed the Conservatives' willingness to use their control of powerful technological systems as a bludgeon, even if it resulted in near disaster.

Nonetheless, Heath's administration decided to quietly reverse course on computing. Instead of a formal policy change, his committee on economic policy suggested "leaving the decision open to Ministers" about whether to continue to buy ICL products or not. This change began to undo the trend of centralized control of computerization so doggedly pursued by the Treasury, Civil Service Department, and the Central Computing Agency. Still, Treasury officials realized that "in any realistic terms, there is a five to ten year stint to get off the hook." Secretly, Treasury officials hoped that technical developments in high-level programming languages, emulators, and other tools might soon strand ICL in a position where it could not reasonably ask for continued government support. Once ICL's operating environment could be easily and cheaply emulated on, say, an IBM computer, or once higher-level programming languages made migration between systems easier, ICL hardware would no longer be so important to government computing.[34]

In the space of less than four years, the government had gone from being the biggest booster of the British computer industry to secretly hoping for its speedy demise. Partly, this was due to the changeover from

Wilson's administration to Heath's—but increasingly those in charge of computer procurement in government had also begun to realize that the single-bid purchasing preference for ICL was "weakening the company's fiber," losing it credibility in the marketplace, and allowing it to cut corners and give poorer service to its largest customer.[35] "It is no secret," wrote one mid-level civil servant, with typical British restraint, "that operators are not always satisfied that British computers are the best for the job."[36]

By the mid-1970s, the government had all but discarded its directive to buy British, its single-tender system for supporting ICL, and its price protection for British computers. The rationale for these changes was alternately given as a tactic to help ICL stand on its own, as a way to allow British industry to gain the benefit of American know-how through the importation of more American computers, and as a simple capitulation to departmental demands to buy IBM's cheaper and more flexible—though usually less powerful—systems. Each of these factors played a part, but the largest concern was rapidly becoming availability and reliability: IBM could supply the same or superior machines more quickly and stand behind them with a more robust service package.[37]

Final Attempts to Centralize Control Over Computing

Although it was becoming clear that the consolidation of the computer industry had been misguided, the government again made the mistake of overcentralizing its own computing. In April 1972, the Civil Service Department, with the aid of the Treasury, had created the Central Computer Agency (CCA).[38] Because the CCA was tasked with overseeing the use of all computers in government, its new computing center was put in the middle of London, close to Whitehall, "in a good modern building to show the right image."[39]

The mission of the CCA was to centralize government computing organization and procedure as much as possible, but the massive responsibility accorded to it exacerbated older problems of procedure and control. The CCA attempted to supersede the Civil Service Department's Management Services Computers Division, which had only recently taken over financial control of computing from the unwieldy alliance of the Treasury, the Computer Procurement Division and Central Computer Bureau of the Stationery Office, and the Technical Support Unit of the Department of Trade and Industry. (Wilson's Ministry of Technology had been dissolved in 1970 when the Conservative Party under Heath came into power.) The year after the CCA's creation, the responsibility for telecommunication in government was also added to its sprawling mandate.

The Civil Service Department now consolidated all authority for computer procurement in the CCA in order to decrease "the independent computer strength of the big departments ... at a time when the development of computers was likely to have implications for the Machinery of Government."[40] The CCA was tasked with reviving the program of centralized, technocratic control that had failed under both the Treasury and its own parent department. The constraints of computer procurement placed on departments by the CCA were inefficient and "by no means always palatable to major users," complained HMSO, adding that CCA rules also led to "the loss of technical 'edge'" in departments performing advanced computing due to the slowness and the strictures that "central policies imposed."[41]

To avoid lower-level workers gaining power over, and through, new technology, successive governments positioned computers as tools for those high up in the administrative hierarchy: men who could be trusted to represent the interests of the state and preserve its status quo. As labor became increasingly restive in the 1970s, the government clung to policies that centralized power and kept technology out of workers' hands. As miners' strikes disrupted the electricity supply, it became ever more clear that health of the economy relied on the control of technological systems. Trying to maintain control through consolidating powerful technology in the hands of a few was a doubled-edged sword, however.

Securing the Machinery of Government against Computer Workers

In the early 1970s, the CCA reported: "So far industrial action by civil servants has only had limited impact upon the government's computer-based operations." Yet it also warned that the government could not "assume that the consequences of any future disputes will be so easily overcome. The Staff Associations have had an opportunity to gauge the strength of the weapon in their hands ... and will undoubtedly have learned something from recent experience about how most effectively and quickly they can disrupt departmental data processing at minimum cost to themselves by determined action on the part of a few key staff inside or outside the computer installation."[42]

The Labour party's inability to gain control over organized labor and reduce the growing number of strikes had helped destroy Wilson's chances in the 1970 general election. His secretary of employment and productivity, Barbara Castle, responded to the labor union crisis with an exceedingly unpopular government white paper called *In Place of Strife*, which proposed curbing the right of unions to strike.[43] Under Heath, Wilson's utopian vision of technology as a power for social equality all but evaporated. Heath's less than four years as prime minister were wracked by major dockworkers' and miners' strikes. He declared states of emergency every year he was in power.[44] By this point, computing had matured into an important tool for control, and a system just as essential to the working of the state as electricity or transport. During this time, concerns about controlling potentially restive labor redefined the way the government used technology. Ensuring that nonmanagement computer operators and programmers—many of whom were women with little reason *not* to engage in labor action—could not wreak havoc became another compelling rationale for centralization that afforded tighter control by management.

This change, long in coming, was now the government's single focus when it came to computer organization. Throughout the 1960s, the Treasury had kept an eye on every computer installed in government and their application to various projects. By the early 1970s, it had ceased keeping track of each machine, focusing instead on the sixty most important data-processing installations. As the CCA took over this role, the nature of oversight changed, and concern about the security of computer systems reached a fever pitch.

In a secret document, a multidepartment study group headed by the CCA outlined how these systems that were handling the "work most vital to government administration" had to be protected against any potential threats posed by dissatisfied workers. The CCA's safety measures called for further centralization of government computing and its management, uncannily echoing a version of an Orwellian state.[45] Its aims were overly ambitious: The CCA aimed to create a centrally organized state computing apparatus that would allow, "in the future, the government as a major computer user [to] be able to speak more clearly with a single central voice."[46] Because "administrators [had] come to depend on computers not only as permanent replacements for large numbers of clerks, but as tools ... to improve the foundations of policy decisions," the CCA created a government-wide subcategory for "highly professional" computer workers within the executive class.[47] This was a last-ditch effort to bring into being the specialized cadre of technocrats upon whom government computing projects could rely.[48]

Even while the CCA continued the process already underway of trying to get management into computer jobs, it turned to a more explicit program of grooming this cadre of ultra-high-level technocrats. As "major government functions become more dependent in ADP, the importance of this small proportion of staff will increase," CCA management reasoned.[49] The days when it was possible for computing staff to simply be workers with technical skills were coming to an end. This program of action continued down the path of masculinizing computing work, fully institutionalized a predominantly male programmer–manager class, and paved a rocky path with organized labor. Government administrators' fears of labor disruptions and their pessimistic view of rank-and-file computer workers further limited training and promotion opportunities for nonexecutive computer workers through the 1970s. With usually no more than A-level qualifications, these budding technocrats were trained to work with computers on the assumption that they would eventually rise to the highest levels of administration in government or industry. These young men "who should be candidates for the highest posts in the Service" were meant to construct a new era of scientific management and technocracy, helping govern the nation by gaining control of the increasingly data-drowned British state.[50]

The head of the CCA outlined to Parliament how his plan would succeed where the Treasury's previous regime of centralized control had failed, focusing on how his agency would "offer greater scope for increased professionalism and for computer careers in government" while sweeping away older models of organization.[51] The CCA's plan would further professionalize computing out of organized labor's reach. However, the desire for strict central control offered great danger as well as great power. Key computing installations in the Civil Service, Post Office, and nationalized industries became ideal targets for the increasingly disgruntled British labor force precisely because they were so centralized.

As nationwide labor unrest in response to wage restraints threatened the government's control over the economy, maintaining the security of computing systems became a pressing concern. Pay freezes for public sector workers added to the burden caused by other austerity measures. In 1973, machine operators and data-preparation staff at several government computer installations went on strike several times, for up to two weeks at a time, to maximize disruption. This prompted a major reevaluation of the security of the government's computing installations.[52] In a secret, numbered-copy report whose circulation was tightly controlled, the CCA drew up a master list of the most vital computer centers in government and compiled a file of industrial actions in computing installations and their effects. The report offered an exhaustive list of proposed solutions to head off future disruptions and carefully evaluated the pros and cons of each.[53]

On the list of the most critical computing installations, surprisingly few were in the realm of defense. Defense applications were of little immediate worry for the CCA, because it concerned itself almost exclusively with the government's huge administrative computing systems. Payroll, social security, and the payment of pension or unemployment benefits formed the most important work of the state's large computing installations, followed closely by stock control, savings bank accounts, VAT and PAYE calculations, tax collection, and driver licensing. In all of these cases, no manual fallback was possible. So-called pink-collar women's labor determined the functioning of large parts of the British public sector and economy, directly impacting national stability.

It would be easy, the CCA noted, to sabotage a full day's work by "switching labels" on output disks and scratch disks, or to cause "damage to sensitive magnetic components and to easily accessible parts of the central processing unit or ancillary equipment." Although this behavior was not expected of executive-level civil servants, they were not yet the majority of computer workers. In some cases, even a simple "disregard of operating instructions" could be enough to severely disrupt work while remaining under the radar as a deliberate action.[54]

Keeping these informational systems running was so important that the CCA explicitly stated security concerns were now "an important factor in determining the appropriate form of computing for particular operations." The use of "cheap, small computers and intelligent terminals," they reasoned, "could make it possible to process information" without resorting to using a large, central computer installation. "This has obvious advantages," CCA officials reported, "in that it disperses and reduces the target for many forms of physical attack." In addition, "it would also help to reduce the impact of industrial action—which would have to be mounted and sustained on a much larger scale than would be necessary to achieve maximum disruption at a central installation."[55]

The ease with which systems could be sabotaged without unions even taking official strike action alarmed the CCA so much that it considered laying off government computer staff and replacing them with contract workers from computer companies. Had this work been privatized, ICL may have gotten a significant share, but a more likely beneficiary at this point in time would have been IBM UK. By 1973, IBM's larger

It's a waste of money paying people like this.

Figure 5.1
ICL advertising played on fears about unruly staff and work slowdowns, offering more automated services as a technological fix for these problems. It is little coincidence that two women are in the foreground; women increasingly represented a threat to employers as their labor force participation and union strength grew. *ICL News*, February 1970.

staff was better equipped to deal with such an influx of work. Of equal importance was the fact that no part of IBM's staff was unionized or likely to unionize. IBM UK's leaders were proudly antiunion and took aggressive measures to ensure that their offices did not unionize, despite significant employee pressure. From 1975 through 1977, both professional and manual employees at IBM UK tried to use the 1975 Employee Protection Act to organize, but IBM UK fought their attempts bitterly, spending thousands of pounds on internal and external public relations campaigns that painted trade unionists as outsiders and troublemakers. Unions, IBM management warned, would ruin the current system of corporate paternalism and merit pay. Internal memoranda warned managers and workers alike about its dangers, intimating that the company would take a highly adversarial stance if workers organized. In 1977, faced with a ballot on unionization, IBM UK workers voted down the measure by an overwhelming margin.[56]

Because IBM workers were encouraged to see themselves as part of a professional class more aligned with management than organized labor, they fit perfectly into the government's technocratic vision. Even IBM's lower-level workers were more like the government's ideal technologists than midlevel civil servants engaged in computer work. IBM employees were safer and easier to control from the government's perspective. Even those who did not identify as "professional" often shared the ideals of management, as in the case of one self-described "working-class, non-management" IBM staff member who wrote a letter to the editor of the local newspaper proclaiming his distaste for unions. In a testament to the reach of IBM's union disinformation campaign, the letter writer felt the need to assert that he was not a "paid, professional letter-writer" writing on behalf of the company.[57]

Although privatization of government computing might have offered more security, the government did not outsource its computing to IBM UK or ICL in any large measure in the mid-1970s. The Treasury and Civil Service Department needed to keep computing in house for maximal control. Treasury leaders recognized the need to carefully maintain good relations with the government's increasingly important technical staff, "but [they had] to find more of the *right people* to meet immediate needs and those who, in a decade or so ahead, [would] be the senior administrators in a highly technological environment" (italics mine).[58] Dealing with the demands of nonmanagement computer workers was a temporary stopgap measure on the way to an all-managerial class of computer professionals.[59] The CCA kept a service-wide register of management-level ADP staff and encouraged them to take time off for more computer training courses, fully paid for by the government.[60]

Nonetheless, the danger of potential strike action encouraged several government departments to consider changing the centralized nature of their computing systems. The Department of National Savings, for instance, feared the effects of even a limited puncher or operator strike, because if its main accounting computer were taken down for any period, it would "bring the business of the National Savings Bank virtually to a complete standstill," during which "updating of all computerized accounts and manual accounts would be impossible."[61] Customer inconvenience would be only a small part of the problem. A failure like this would also hugely increase the risk of fraud and overdrafts. The bank's other, smaller computer installation processed fortnightly dividends for British savings bonds and so could not take on the work of the main computer. There was no redundancy in the system. A strike at either of the bank's two computer installations would have had the effect of halting business and potentially losing the public's trust. Even a relatively minor strike action involving no more than one hundred unionized computer staff at the bank "would be little short of disastrous."[62] No longer was a centralized system a virtue.

These fears were well-founded: Computer strikes became a significant problem in the 1970s—and a powerful weapon for organized labor. In March 1973, a series of selective one-day strikes by the Civil and Public Services Association (CPSA) and Society of Civil Servants closed down a whopping twenty-six computer centers, including several listed as highest priority, and significantly disrupted nine others.[63] Many of these striking computer workers were women—and their proximity to complex machinery gave them power disproportionate to their status. Of several thousand striking workers in the Department of Health and Social Security and the Employment Department, a small cohort of computer workers like these was described by the *Times* as causing the worst trouble: "The union's most damaging strike is that of 25 computer operators at Southend who are working on registration for value-added tax. This strike is in its second week and the work is much behind schedule."[64]

Even worse than the initial, brief strikes were the labor slowdowns and instances of passive resistance that followed. Computer workers at several dozen installations refused to perform mandatory overtime and other work that was not explicitly spelled out in their job responsibilities, adopting a "work to rule" approach in the absence of an official strike. Both mandatory overtime and the removal of overtime opportunities were major points of contention for computer workers, highlighting the fact that they were still largely wage earners rather than professionals.[65] The shift labor patterns of computer operation in fact made it more attractive for women workers with family responsibilities, so attempts to undo this were especially resented.

Slowdowns significantly hindered throughput at each computing installation, causing several projects to miss their target dates, and created a snowball effect that made new projects impossible. Secondary and tertiary projects that relied on these targets were slowed or scrapped, and new top-priority projects that required these bottlenecked computer installations were forced to be rescheduled. Most seriously, the CPSA organized strikes of feminized punching staff for periods of seven days or more. The skills of the lowest-level workers in the data-processing chain appeared formidably important once removed. Ten installations were inconvenienced by a delay of their work, among them the Department of National Savings. But the VAT computer center was critically affected, and the implementation of the new VAT system was not completed on time as a result, impeding the government's ability to collect a major tax revenue.

In some cases, departments were able to use the extended downtime to perform essential systems maintenance. Still, prolonged walkouts heightened fear of what was to come in an era in which low-level, feminized workers like punchers could alter the course of the highest-level government projects and programs.[66] Every hour that computing power was not maximized, the nation lost money. The changes to shift work and overtime schedules that had in part provoked this industrial action were themselves an attempt to keep expensive machines running constantly. Even just worker slowdowns at these sites cost the Treasury tens of thousands of pounds each day. From computers to industrial sewing machines, women trade unionists struggled to change the perception of their work with machines industry-wide, trying to convince management their roles were skilled and important by asserting their power through strike action.

The effectiveness with which workers shut down so many computing installations by withdrawing relatively small numbers of staff spooked government officials and pointed to potentially dire problems going forward if huge centralized systems remained the organizational model. Worrisome too was the fact that a clerical union, the CPSA, was cooperating with unionized workers in higher levels of the service. As workers in different levels of the service joined together to make their displeasure felt, the CCA's agenda to install technocrats in place of all technicians became ever more urgent.

Gender as Class

In computer worker strikes, the delineation of a large proportion of workers from managers was one of both class and gender.[67] In this context, gender becomes illegible in the archives—and women literally disappear from the historical record—without an understanding of the class system that defined women's and men's work. Gender, after all, is a classed category as much as class is a gendered category: Women occupy fundamentally different social levels than even their nearest male peers simply by virtue of being women. As the Conservatives tried to corral labor into compliance with wage and price controls to dampen inflation, the rift between the state and the women workers who made it run grew larger.

The perpetual underpayment of women employees added fuel to the fire of labor unrest as these workers were once again asked to comply with strict monetarist economic solutions at the expense of their standard of living.

In July 1970, newly agreed-upon pay scales for machine operators had raised wages by roughly 12 percent above 1969 rates. This was the largest rate change in several years: Wages had only risen by 3 percent in 1968 and by roughly 6 percent in 1967.[68] Yet this was not wholly positive; a large pay raise was required because machine operator jobs in government were significantly underpaid when compared with similar jobs in industry. Although bonuses for computer work were added to executive-level workers' salaries, machine operator pay scales still topped out when workers reached roughly twenty-five years of age on the assumption that they would, or should, leave to marry. Previously, operators had reached their maximum pay around the age of thirty, but their promotion scales had to be sped up in order to allow the government's wages for computer operators to be at all competitive with private industry. Even so, lower- and midlevel computer staff left at higher rates than all other computer workers in the Civil Service to take other computing jobs, with a turnover rate of over 5 percent in 1971.[69]

Because the government was unable to pay the fair market rate for this scarce labor commodity, computer installations continued to incur the wrath of Civil Service unions. There was no longer any possibility of a temporary manual fallback in most cases, and the fact that these computer workers possessed competencies their managers often lacked made it difficult or impossible to temporarily substitute nonunionized higher executive officers for striking computer staff as had been done in past years. The Civil Service Department and Treasury once again considered contracting out to computing companies in order to solve this problem, but in addition to angering the Civil Service unions, this solution would not get to the root of the problem.[70] They were still convinced that the success of all future projects turned on creating their own "very high caliber" specialists to "specify, monitor, and control" the computers that implemented the objectives of the government.

With women's collective voice growing louder, Treasury and Civil Service Department officials had inspected over twenty-eight departments in the late 1960s to respond to workers' repeated claims that a new, higher promotional outlet was needed for workers in the machine operating grade. Computing (or ADP) staff increased by 25 percent or more each year in the decade between 1960 and 1970, and thousands worked on running, programming, and preparing data for computer installations. Yet instead of accommodating this growth by adding another rung to machine operators' career ladders, more and more effort was made to bring management-level workers into the better automation jobs that machine operators could have been promoted into.

These high-level computing posts continued to be plagued by vacancies and high turnover.[71] On average, over 6 percent of the posts were vacant, primarily in programming and the executive trainee grades. Shortages of executives for advanced computer projects, though smaller, were more critical—and recruiting for these posts was even more difficult. So desperately short-handed were many installations that the required training for computing employees was neglected or postponed indefinitely just to keep the machines running, creating a cycle of perpetual shortage and amateurism.

The most valued ADP staff—the executive class operators, programmers, systems analysts, and computer center managers that collectively made up roughly 32 percent of the whole Civil Service computing workforce by 1972—were now the fastest growing cohort of technologists, slated to increase by 30 percent within the next year and by more than that each following year.[72] Far fewer now left these jobs to pursue other computer work outside the Civil Service due to the bonuses instituted to stem turnover.

The caveat was that many more of these mostly male executives still left to pursue other, noncomputing job opportunities. By the early seventies, men left computing for noncomputing jobs in ever-higher numbers. Even with paid training, a generous system of bonuses, and promotion enticements, few executives wanted to spend their careers in computing.[73] Consequently, the government continued to lose high numbers of computer workers and struggled to integrate individuals with these critical skills into the government's executive structure.[74] The "increasing dependence on computers is an essential part of the administrative system in which [ministers] operate," wrote a high-level CCA administrator, and even though "technical problems were gradually being surmounted" with each passing year, "the managerial and social" issues remained "difficult."[75]

With little incentive to stay in government, many women moved to computing work in the private sector. These were largely lateral moves—women hit similar barriers to promotion in industry even if they gained better pay. The few women who made it to the top, like the talented and creative Stephanie "Steve" Shirley, were the ones who were able to break away from the patterns in place to structure women's careers. After leaving her government post, Shirley created her own software services company that focused on employing skilled women discarded from the workforce because they needed to stay home with young children. Her company reaped the benefits of these programmers' experience by giving them the opportunity to work from home when more traditional employers would not. Yet, even Shirley found herself having to conform to masculine stereotypes in order to succeed: She used the name Steve on her correspondence and adopted it as her nickname when she found that using her real name shut her out of opportunities to bid for contracts.[76]

Similarly, Cathy Gillespie—who had a long and successful career in computing after moving to the private sector—never took a break from the workforce. Her coworker Ann Sayce followed the more usual path of leaving to have children and did not return, despite greatly enjoying the work. Women's paths in computing were not simply a matter of individual choice but rather relied on constraints engineered into the fabric of their lives by the institutions that employed them. Women like Shirley and Gillespie, though admirably successful, were exceptions that proved the rule rather than examples of how women as a group might succeed in the field in numbers equal to men. Shirley's business in fact leveraged women's marginalization in order to succeed, and Gillespie's career path was one that many women could not adopt.

The continued neglect of women's labor was perhaps the single biggest reason for the government's continued computer labor problems. In surveying their own operations, Civil Service departments nearly uniformly said that the supply of suitably experienced staff for computing, or ADP, as it had come to be called by the early 1970s, was "wholly inadequate" and that both current and planned data-processing projects had suffered greatly as a result.[77] Yet turning attention away from the great mass of workers who had the relevant experience for computer work was rarely seen as a cause for concern. Most employers tacitly or even explicitly endorsed structural discrimination that kept women from taking higher-level jobs and preserved them as a low-cost labor force.

By 1971, the Society of Civil Servants, a union covering the middle grades of the Civil Service, was complaining bitterly to the computers division of the Civil Service Department that firms in private industry were being given the responsibility of writing government software instead of civil servants. Seeing their opportunities for advancement and training slipping away as the government gave ICL more contracts to provide software for government computers, the Society of Civil Servants moved to censure the government for "the apathetic manner in which they have dealt with the complex and increasing problems in the ADP field."[78] Doris Lancaster, a leader of the Society of Civil Servants, noted that civil servants were gradually being cut out of the most lucrative computing work in favor of outsourcing software writing, systems analysis, and even sometimes computer operation. The result was that relatively deskilled data input and data processing was all that was left to them. The setup of the PAYE tax system gives some indication of the scale of this drudge work. More than one thousand man-years—or more accurately, woman-years—were required just to input the initial data.[79]

The women at the lowest end of the data-processing chain who performed this work were integral to these massive data projects, but they gained little benefit from their association with high technology. Punchers, who were still exclusively women, were treated as though their work was completely unskilled.[80] Not surprisingly, they had extremely high turnover. By the late 1960s, opportunities to move from punch rooms to higher-level machine work had effectively been walled off.

In 1969, the Central Computer Agency performed research in punch rooms to try to ameliorate worker dissatisfaction. Punching "has clerical content but is also mechanical, repetitive and soon becomes boring," and therefore it was not a field into which management felt "better" workers could be enticed, and so it remained firmly feminized. The CCA report therefore focused on the role of physical plant problems: Up to this point, most punch rooms were treated as though they were outside the realm of white-collar work. The "rigid layout, high noise levels, and lack of amenities gave the impression of a factory rather than an office environment," the CCA noted. Noise levels hovered near eighty-four decibels—high enough to cause hearing loss.[81] Acceptable levels of office noise were nearly half that; they ranged between forty-five and fifty decibels.[82] Even the Post Office, with its many machinery-based jobs, considered seventy-seven decibels the absolute maximum.[83] Civil Service punch rooms could contain several hundred workers and often doubled as a pathway to the machine room, wreaking havoc on the "high degree of concentration [that] is necessary to work with speed and accuracy."[84]

Initiatives to lower the noise levels in punching rooms and add simple amenities like carpet not only produced more accurate work but also lowered the illness rate by 37.5 percent and the turnover rate by as much as 47 percent.[85] Making nurseries and childcare available further reduced turnover. Meanwhile, attempts to enhance efficiency without regard for workers, such as moving punching staff around to different computing installations depending on fluctuating workload, not only increased turnover but greatly diminished efficiency. Treating these workers like cogs within the data-processing machine of government was becoming less and less feasible: "If all punch operators in the UK went on strike for better working conditions and more pay, the data processing business would be in a sorry state," the CCA warned. Yet even as the report paid lip service to the importance of the lowest staff in the data-input chain, the government still did not implement changes that would elevate their status or provide promotion outlets. Instead, it simply focused on making the work more tolerable.[86]

Feminization and the White-Collar Labor Market

By the 1970s, the decades-long process of feminization of clerical labor forces had begun to take a significant toll on the Civil Service. The government's systematic attempts to keep women in lower-level positions, justified from the perspective of what it believed to be sound management practice, were summarized well by the House of Common's study on women and work equality: "The restricted nature of the opportunities open to young women to train for skilled work reinforces the tendency for women to fill the lowest paid, least satisfying jobs. ... They are less likely to be promoted than men and are generally treated as unsuitable to be in authority over men."[87] This style of gendered hierarchy, based on the dictates of a patriarchal nuclear family, became less and less defensible as the numbers of women working grew and their living patterns changed.

In an article entitled "To Train or Not to Train?," *Office Methods and Machines* pointed out that the "balance of the sexes" had become reconfigured in the field of office work in general and the Civil Service in particular. In the past fifteen years, the proportion of young men entering offices had fallen, whereas the proportion of young women had risen dramatically, to 40 percent. Fewer than 10 percent of men worked in offices.[88] By contrast, over two million women—a full quarter of the total female labor force—were concentrated in clerical work. The growing number of women office workers was not being absorbed primarily into typing or data-entry work. From 1961 to 1971, census figures show that the number of women entering clerical work *excluding* typing and data entry rose by almost 26 percent.[89] Women were increasingly forming the middle ranks of the clerical workforce.

Government administrators studied and saved articles like these as they tried to figure out how to reskill their labor force. Treasury officials clipped and shared this article, which reported that few of the 25 percent of young school-leavers who went into office work were given anything more than rudimentary training. Considering clerical work "an unavoidable but increasingly costly evil," managers had ignored the importance of these workers as they rose in number and gained more importance in the labor market.[90] Even though the need for more skilled office staff was rising, women were not groomed for these better jobs. Meanwhile, "boys [were] taking advantage of the opportunities for further education and of entry to jobs in the new technologies," the article warned, meaning that they were "lost to office work forever."[91] The result was a growing overproduction of the wrong kind of worker for the modern office—women who were expected to be skill-less drones—and a situation that all but compelled computer technologies that encouraged further deskilling.

From the perspective of a government experiencing increasing difficulty controlling lower-level workers, this shift was terrifying. If their entry into the higher echelons of the Civil Service were not restrained, these workers might upend the system itself. On the other hand, maintaining a mass of low-paid women workers at the bottom of Civil Service had the effect of dragging down the entire system as the proportion of women civil servants rose. As feminization became the defining feature of white-collar office work, it lowered salaries and benefits across the board. It created a self-fulfilling prophecy of lower-value workers and a bureaucracy that could do less and less with higher numbers of staff. Even so, these dramatic labor market changes did little to alter the practice of training only young men for careers—that is, until UK employers were confronted with the illegality of maintaining these gendered labor patterns.

Gaining Equal Pay, Again

Because Heath had made entry into the Common Market a key part of his platform in the June 1970 general election, mainly for currency stabilization and the short-term economic benefits it would bring, national legislation against sex discrimination became a necessity.[92] Despite applying—and being rejected—for EEC membership twice in the 1960s, Britain had made no significant moves toward equal pay.

At roughly eight million in 1965, the number of women in the British workforce was roughly half of the number of working men. By 1971, 41 percent of all women worked, and the number of working women had grown to more than 8.7 million, boosting women to 36 percent of the total workforce.[93] More than 80 percent of the roughly 10.5 million single women worked, and just under 45 percent of the roughly 13 million married women had paying jobs. Almost half of the married women in the workforce worked full time. London, the seat of national government, had the highest workforce participation rates: Over 60 percent of women in London worked outside the home. Over 75 percent of all working women were also responsible for running a household, meaning the majority played the dual role of paid worker and unpaid caretaker.[94]

Even with their representation in the labor market growing, only one in every twenty women earned more than £20 per week.[95] A yearly salary above £1,000, often achieved by men, was a relative rarity for women. The salaried women in job categories in the administrative, professional, and clerical grades of the service that had roughly equal numbers of men had kept pace with men's wages, owing to the 1955 equal pay provisions for government workers, but this excluded most computer workers.[96] The largest category of women computer workers was still punchers.

During the same span of time, women's trade union participation leapt, bringing women trade unionists from a quarter of all union members nationwide up to a third.[97] Women workers were becoming more dangerous due to their rising strength in unions. It was no coincidence that the most damaging labor action against government computing installations came from the all-female punching grades and the marginally gender-integrated operator grades.[98] Indeed, it was a tumultuous 1968 strike of women machine operators of a different kind that had been the public relations lynchpin that eventually led to a national Equal Pay Act.[99] When women sewing machine operators at two Ford UK manufacturing plants had been recategorized as unskilled workers, despite performing work identical to men classed as semiskilled, the outrage this action sparked, and the resulting strike, helped Labour MPs like Barbara Castle bring equal pay legislation into the national consciousness. Castle, who moved the Equal Pay Act of 1970, had previously attempted unsuccessfully to integrate equal pay for women into the prices and incomes policies of the mid-1960s.[100]

Although 1970 saw the passage of a national Equal Pay Act, it did not come into effect until December 29, 1975. Britain's acceptance into the EEC in 1973 made this legislation a pressing requirement, but the law was delayed in coming into effect ostensibly so government and industry could have time to bring themselves into compliance. In truth, the delay reflected the low priority placed on equal pay and the unfounded fear that equal pay would increase inflation. This five-year delay had the effect of allowing employers time to change the organization of work in ways that would make jobs performed by most women incomparable with jobs performed by men. In this way, companies could skirt the legal mandate to raise pay for most of their women employees.[101]

Yet such dodges were hardly necessary, because the law was seriously flawed. In order to gain equal pay, women had to compare their work and wages with those of a man working within the same organization at the same time. In feminized fields in which there were no suitable or immediate male comparators, equal pay remained impossible. Industry-wide, nearly nine times as many men as women held jobs that were classed as professional. In a largely gender-segregated workforce, in which millions of women were concentrated in under a quarter of all industries and clustered only in certain jobs, most women could not benefit from the provisions of the new law.[102]

The law's limitations meant that employers had to do relatively little in order to be in compliance. Widespread existing segregation of men's and women's jobs made it much less far-reaching than the backers of the original bill had intended. In an effort to secure its passage, no provision was made for equal opportunity in employment, only equal pay in cases in which men and women were already performing the same work or "work rated as equivalent" or "of equal value."[103] This diluted the impact of the act, ensuring it would pass.

Fewer than a third of women in industry were performing the same work as men, and in cases in which a woman argued that her work was the same or broadly similar to work performed by a man for higher pay, her claims were subject to a high level of scrutiny. Class action complaints were not allowed, and so the onus and expense of bringing a claim to the industrial tribunal for arbitration rested with the individual employee.[104] The tribunal could decide to hear only her employer's arguments before ruling on whether to hear her case.[105] Even if the worker won, the maximum she could be granted in remuneration was the wage difference for the two years prior to the date of the complaint, regardless of how long she had illegally received lower pay.[106]

The most effective measure instituted by the Equal Pay Act of 1970 was the elimination of separate wages for men and women in collective bargaining agreements, which resulted in a jump in earnings for women in 1975 when the act came into effect.[107] In 1970, women industry-wide earned only sixty-three pence on the pound compared to men. In 1975, following the enactment of Equal Pay, this shot up to seventy pence, and then seventy-four pence in the two years afterward. By the late 1970s, however, it had begun to creep downward again.[108] Economists have argued, in fact, that the more important factor for women's pay in these years was the effect of incomes policy, which increased wages by a flat rate rather than a percentage.[109] As a result, incomes policy helped the lowest-paid workers, of whom there were more women than men.[110] The government had carefully orchestrated equal pay to make sure that it did not undo its strict control of wages and lead to inflation.[111]

Redefining Women's Work

The Ford sewing machinist conflict was indicative of the limited successes of the equal pay "victories" in this era: In negotiations, women won 92 percent of the men's rate, but their work classification was not upgraded to semiskilled, undercutting the principle behind their protest and ensuring that further pay equalization would be impossible. The Ford case showed how the principle of equal pay could hardly undo decades of labor feminization and job segregation.

By 1971, the number of divorced women had increased by more than 60 percent, peaking in the 35- to 49-year-old age group, and rising divorce rates threatened to upend the patterns of women's lives.[112] Mixed messages about equal pay abounded. Although women were paid less for identical work, the male breadwinner wage was no longer something women were necessarily entitled access to through marriage. As one columnist writing in the *Times* put it, "We're in a no man's land between emancipation and equality."[113]

The Department of Employment highlighted this theme with an animated public service film that implored young women and their parents to take careers for women seriously.[114] It depicts a young woman's rise and fall, beginning with her taking a lucrative job in a factory as a young person, then leaving to marry and raise children. When her husband leaves her, she must return to the same unskilled factory work she was performing all those years before. Government propaganda aside, there was little reason to believe that individual women had the power to change persistent patterns of discriminatory labor organization simply through making different career choices. As the British economy struggled, women's employment options worsened.

After Heath's nearly disastrous four years in power, Harold Wilson returned to the office of prime minister in 1974. His government published a white paper, *Equality for Women*, that reviewed the shortcomings of the nation's equal pay legislation on the eve of its accession into law. As a result of the paper's critique, a separate Sex Discrimination Act introduced additional legislation and enforcement machinery in 1975. Nonetheless, the laws on sex discrimination remained weak and did not go far enough to satisfy the EEC, which brought infringement proceedings against the United Kingdom.[115] The EEC argued that Britain had not made a good faith effort to equalize women's economic position, because it refused to account for institutionalized job segregation, and it failed to comply with the Treaty of Rome by not including provisions for equal pay for work of equal value.[116]

Despite attempts to upgrade women workers to equal status in the 1970s, the feminization of certain jobs and industries and widespread job segregation throughout the economy continued. It was in this context that women computer workers continued to lose ground. Women's changing position in computing was a microcosm of the labor market dynamics that held women workers down even while their fight for equal rights seemed to be progressing. Men's employment expanded most in areas that were generally higher paid, higher status, and full time, whereas women's employment continued to expand in lower-paid and part-time employment. Over three times as many men held executive positions in the Civil Service as women, and in industry men in managerial positions in offices outnumbered women by almost six to one. At the same time, the 1970s saw a decline in full-time jobs, and a rising proportion of part-time workers became a major feature of the British economy.[117] The level of women's employment in the United Kingdom on the basis of hours worked was below the EEC average. By the mid-1980s, 45 percent of all employed women were engaged in only part-time work.[118]

These changes affected more than just women: They contributed to an overall feminization of the labor market. Workers of all genders had to contend with a labor market increasingly defined by women's work patterns and their lower pay. As the seventies stretched into the eighties, several occupational categories underwent major gender shifts. Clerical occupations continued to feminize, with women's participation jumping by another 11.5 percent and men's participation falling by close to 20 percent. The numbers of women in health and welfare jobs skyrocketed, going up by 46.8 percent, whereas men's numbers rose the quickest in engineering and scientific jobs (28 percent) and in management and administration jobs (21.5 percent).[119]

The Civil Service's computing workforce continued to bifurcate along both gendered and class lines, even though among machine operators in industry and government there were still more than 6.5 times as many women as men in 1971.[120] A review of the machine operator grade in the Civil Service conducted from 1961 to 1970 showed pervasive institutional reluctance to admit women to roles other than "operative" ones—or indeed to admit that women were already performing work that could be categorized as more than mere operation.[121] By the 1970s, recruitment practices that targeted only executive officers meant that no clerical or machine workers could move up to higher-level computing jobs.[122]

According to a 1980 government-backed study, nearly a third of women who were employed as computer operators, data processors, and punch card operators worked only part time.[123] The hierarchies of computer workers demonstrated why equal pay legislation could not help most women and these divisions also had a negative effect on productivity within a relatively small but increasingly important segment of the workforce. As the information technology sector of the economy expanded, such inequalities continued to worsen and damage the industry at large. Even the government's own report on equal pay and equal opportunity stated that the "unequal status of women is wasteful of the potential talents of half our population in a society which, more than ever before, needs to mobilize the skill and ability of all its citizens."[124]

After White Heat

By the time Wilson returned to power in 1974, computers were no longer a symbol of a sleek, promising technological future. They no longer seemed to have revolutionary potential, but had instead become tools for enhancing top-down control and strengthening existing hierarchies. On the whole, workers remained dissatisfied with the nation's economic situation. Labour had failed to deliver on promises of technological modernization that would result in a more prosperous and egalitarian Britain. Following Wilson's resignation for health reasons in 1976, James Callaghan's Labour government once again struggled with restive unions. The promise of White Heat was officially dead.

Worse yet, British leaders began to realize that the types of machines they had thought necessary for government work had completely changed. The 2900 mainframe series, the product of years of government-shaped and government-financed research and development initiatives, became available just as the Civil Service began to turn away from large, centralized computing installations.[125] In this context, ICL's much awaited new range became an albatross. When the line ended up being significantly delayed, the Civil Service Department had to restrain several departments from canceling their orders and defecting to IBM. The fact that the 2900 line was not yet tested and stable, and the fact that software houses specializing in new software for the 2900 were rapidly going out of business as production delays lengthened, spooked even the few remaining supporters of ICL. In a rare move, several companies in Commonwealth countries canceled their orders, and multiple British firms opted to enhance their old 1900 arrays instead of taking a chance on the new line.

ICL management worsened this anticipatory dread by deciding to release the most powerful and expensive models in the line first. In thrall to the demands of their biggest users, they misread the market, losing contracts with companies that needed small and mid-range machines, many of which had been waiting for the new product line to upgrade from 1900 mainframes. For instance, ICL lost a contract to replace the National Freight Corporation's 1900 in 1975, the year after the 2900 series came out. The company took its business to Honeywell as a result of the delayed release of the lower-end 2900 models.[126] As Martin Campbell-Kelly notes in his history of ICL, the "vacuum between ICL's small 2904 and the medium-sized 2960 left the existing 1900-series customer base vulnerable to the competition," and IBM began to aggressively market its 1900 series emulator for its System/370 in order to catch unhappy ICL users. Although ICL had a 1900 emulator for its 2900 range, it did not initially market the emulator, because the company was determined to sell the 2900s on their own merits.[127]

At the government's behest, ICL had put far too much money into the research and design of the high-end 2900 range at the expense of smaller systems, even though mainframe sales were falling precipitously and the sales of smaller systems were dramatically rising.[128] ICL's product line continued to lose touch with the market in the late 1970s, eventually forcing the company to license American technology to replace their aging small-business machine lines and to enter into a partnership with Fujitsu in the early 1980s for access to semiconductor technology.[129] As the 1980s began, mainframes formed the "unprofitable core" of ICL's business, and the high-end 2900 series computers soaked up the vast majority of the company's resources despite their growing unprofitability. In an era when more and more customers were turning to decentralized systems and using smaller computers and microcomputers, ICL had effectively been set up for failure.[130]

Those in charge of computer oversight in the Civil Service did not renege on any orders or allow departments to renege, however.[131] The Stationery Office held firm, though in a resigned fashion: "The size of HMSO's computer commitment and its tradition of use of ICL machinery would oblige it to continue with that company." HMSO had spent years anticipating the new ICL mainframe line, gearing its work organization toward those machines, and demanding their specific features and capabilities.[132] The CSD consoled itself and multiple other departments with the claim that migration from ICL 1900s would be easiest when upgrading to another ICL machine. The Post Office placed one of the "biggest and least surprising" contracts for three of ICL's high-end 2970 mainframes, but the Post Office's use for the machines—centralized telephone billing for the nation's entire customer base—was not, to say the least, a common usage model.[133] The large purchase was an exception that proved the rule that ICL's offerings were out of touch with most customers' needs. Sales forecasts for the 2900 series "were unrealistically ambitious for the market size," and ICL had neglected its other products in the meantime. ICL had become "essentially a one-product company," and its one product was not in tune with the current computing landscape.[134]

Remaining government support for ICL evaporated quickly after the release of the 2900 line, though ICL received a farewell £26 million in loans. Redundancies and labor problems at ICL's Northern Ireland factory signaled the beginning of the end for Britain's home-grown computing industry, even as the government pursued alliances for it with European computer manufacturers, like France's state-controlled CII. The days when "Britain, through ICL," might have "achieved strategic independence in the area of computer supply, an essential attribute to sovereign power and leadership in Europe," were long gone.[135] Instead, the late seventies marked an era of increasingly desperate attempts to find a way to keep ICL profitable and operational while reducing the burden on the state to support it. Technological supremacy and realigning the balance of trade through computer exports were no longer at stake; simply saving the thirty-three thousand jobs ICL provided in the United Kingdom now became the goal.[136] The Ministry of Commerce related that the new engineering subgroup IEL "has some 1700 employees of whom 1340 are men." The destruction of this highly skilled, majority male workforce could not easily be ignored: "There is an urgent need to find new work if this level of employment is to be maintained," the Ministry implored.[137]

The men of the British computer industry, however, were subject to the same technological and economic forces that had for decades hurt women. Their jobs were also now imperiled by the government's computer centralization policies. The focus on technocratic control that had begun by reshaping the government's computer labor force had percolated up to shape the British computing industry as well.

In 1981, when ICL closed a deal with the electronics giant Fujitsu, it was in a state of transition technologically. The deal with Fujitsu gave ICL access to cutting-edge semiconductor technology that ICL was incapable of designing and producing itself. This move helped the company look forward as the era of mainframes waned. With the benefits of decentralized computing becoming apparent, giving power and flexibility to lower-order managers by using smaller machines could allow government departments to more effectively control workflow and set their own agendas. Ultimately, ICL canceled almost half of the planned 2900 mainframes in its somewhat paradoxically named "New Range."[138] The most successful machine in the line ultimately turned out to be a lower-end one.

Those in charge of the vast, unified government computing system for which the 2900 range had been designed now began to change the system's organization.[139] The advent of terminals connected by data links brought new work patterns—and new problems for workers. Civil Service leaders refused to accept that these new technologies required any higher level of skill or that workers performing these jobs might be trained for more complex work. Microelectronics helped to widen the rift between more desirable and less desirable computer work. As mid-level operation and programming jobs were largely recategorized out of existence, jobs at the top end continued to become more male dominated while women became firmly mired in data entry.

In fact, because the facilities for timing and measuring work output increased with the use of linked terminals, many data-input staff found themselves pushed to do more work, faster, for the same amount of pay.[140] The Taylorization of clerical work that computing had long enabled began to intensify. Clerical unions' resistance proved mostly futile, particularly because the government hoped to eliminate an estimated quarter of a million jobs through the increased use of microelectronics.[141] Microcomputing, like the mainframe before, was now the technology on which government leaders pinned their hopes for an efficiency revolution.[142]

Because of these changes, computer operators from the machine class who still worked in relatively desirable roles in mainframe installations had reached a dead end. Computer operation in the Civil Service had never been a university graduate's job, instead requiring passes in four O-level subjects. As the seventies ended, supervisory computer posts and many programmer jobs now all but required a degree. As a result, day release for further training was rarely offered to operators. Civil Service managers felt that "most operators [were] unsuitable for such progression."[143] As computer work professionalized and educational qualifications in computer science and programming became available, the "rigid barrier" between lower-level operation and programming jobs and higher-level programming, systems analysis, and management jobs became fully impenetrable for most women.[144] Although salaries within the Civil Service went as high as £7,000–£10,000 per year by 1980, computer operators could only hope to attain 50–65 percent of that amount. Prospects in industry were better, by anywhere from 3 to 20 percent, and so the government continued to hemorrhage workers—over 60 percent annually in some computing centers.[145]

For years, the Civil Service had tried to professionalize computing work by drawing executives into both operating and programming, but a review of the executive class grading structure in the 1970s began to reverse this trend. Soon, all operating work was removed from executive-level jobs, and instead a new assistant programmer grade was created at the level of clerical officer. These workers would perform the sort of operation and programming tasks that old machine class operators had done. Because this job category was in the clerical class, however, it was inaccessible to machine grade computer operators and drew its hires from the pool of clerical staff.[146] The status of computer operation in the offices of the nation's largest employer had come nearly full circle, once again sinking in status and relying on a rapidly feminizing clerical labor force.

On the other hand, the intense drive to find programmers with management ability had not lessened throughout the 1970s, and so managerial jobs that involved even simple programming—simpler than the programming that machine class operators often performed—continued to rise in status. The Civil Service began exchanges with industry for men from the age of twenty-eight to thirty-eight, the age range for executive officers, to further develop their computing skills. A typical candidate had several years of experience operating ICL or IBM machines, knew machine code and at least one programming language, and, most importantly, had staff reporting to him and was "clearly fitted for increased responsibility."[147] In all but the last respect, the members of these computing skills exchanges had the same capabilities as most government machine operators.[148] Despite current stereotypes about technical skill being a masculine trait, in the 1970s the technical side of the computer work was still not where women were expected to fall short. It was for other reasons that women increasingly left the field.

The Economic Toll of Technocracy

In the early 1970s, ICL had warned the government that "computers, to date, have not been applied in any great depth to the improvement of jobs, careers and personnel development of the employed population."[149] Half a decade and hundreds of millions of pounds after the inauguration of Labour's technological revolution, this admission did not bode well for ICL's relationship with the ever more automated Civil Service and nationalized industries. ICL was being asked to provide highly complex, cutting-edge computers for a poorly trained and labor-starved administrative system.

In the Civil Service, over seven hundred thousand workers required more than £800 million in wages, all tracked and paid by computerized payroll.[150] The cost of the computers that ran the government only amounted to about one-twentieth of wages for civil servants. Staff, not computers, were the overwhelming expense. Yet most staff had been perpetually neglected. One leader of the Society of Civil Servants went so far as to tell her superiors that "peasant work" was all that was left to the majority of civil servants working in computing. Her attempts to lobby the government for changes in how programmer training was doled out and how higher-level computing work was outsourced went nowhere.[151] Even as the Society of Civil Servants struggled to keep the black box of government computing open, the diminution of the civil servant's role in computing had already begun. Government computing would soon change from a sprawling in-house project to a largely outsourced one as the CCA began to realize not only the costliness but the incredible unwieldiness of trying to design its own giant, integrated data-processing system.

By the time Margaret Thatcher came to power in 1979, ICL could not rely on much further government aid. However, Thatcher's decision to turn away from investing in the computing industry did not mean less government intervention. In the 1980s, the government continued to exercise its rights to change ICL's upper management and continued to encourage mergers in the industry.[152] Thatcher's push for the government to have less direct influence over industry by adopting a laissez-faire economic model focused on privatization seemed like a change of course, but in many ways it was similar to computer policies that had come before. Her plans deployed conservative social goals to support an economic sea change, in much the same way that Wilson's pseudosocialist technology rhetoric had strengthened traditional hierarchies even as he talked about a computer-led social revolution.

Machines were only one part of the system, however, and ICL's limited horizons were in large part an outcome of the government's prior failures to effectively engineer a labor force that would have enabled a more diverse range of computing options to be envisioned and used. The Treasury, HMSO, and Civil Service Department deliberately neglected available computer workers and refused to invest in training and grooming them for the positions that needed to be filled in government and industry, instead designing policies aimed at centralizing technological control out of their hands. Enacted over the course of decades under successive administrations, these policies reverberated throughout Britain's economy as it struggled to modernize and grow. The attempts to reengineer society in line with technocratic goals too often focuses on extending entrenched inequalities inimical to the functioning of a modern economy. Despite its many cutting-edge technological achievements, Britain effectively failed to modernize in the late twentieth century because true economic and social modernization required changing the ingrained power structures that the state still actively supported.

Technological change alone could not modernize Britain because technology is constituted from economic and social patterns. The deeply conservative, class-bound, and gender-stratified nature of the British economy meant that its technological institutions followed and strengthened particular forms of hierarchy. In the end, this made computer technology a highly conservative, rather than revolutionary, force. Technological change cannot be revolutionary if it fails to change the social and political structures of a society and instead heightens inequalities and divisions that are already present. Strictly speaking, there never was a computer revolution—despite the many advances that British computer pioneers made. Instead, there was a gradual technological evolution that was built around the project of maintaining and strengthening deeply rooted class and gender hierarchies.

The changes wrought by computerization were designed to allow existing forms of power to flourish. Even in the face of clear failure, the government pursued computing policies for its own massive bureaucracy that lashed computerization to centralization, because such moves enhanced authority for those at the top, preserving the hierarchies intrinsic to the operation of the Civil Service and the state itself. The nation's economy similarly functioned on a substrate of class and gender differentiation that meant certain workers were valued less than others, often in arbitrary ways. Perceiving computing primarily as a management tool worked to the disadvantage of women technologists and potential technologists, creating a powerful set of structural constraints rather than a system of direct discrimination targeted at individuals. However, it also meant that these forms of hierarchy powerfully influenced the progress of computerization itself, through impacting the state's computerization projects, the shape of computer technology, and the computer industry. The highly gendered technocratic ideals that prompted the government to reengineer its data-processing labor force became ground zero for changes that affected the entire British economy.[153] As the EEC censure pointed out, savings gained through gendered labor discrimination were a key part of how Britain attempted to modernize. Unexpectedly and unintentionally, however, these measures became a severe liability: Undervaluing and discarding women's computer labor did not just help destroy the computer industry, it also ensured skilled labor shortages in a growing field.

The specific neglect of women's competencies and skills in the computer labor market injured the nation's economic growth by holding back a new field, causing enormous waste and expense during the public sector's attempts to computerize. More nebulous effects, like costs arising from the loss of potential innovations, were also a consequence of the state's specific brand of gendered technocracy. In addition, because almost all women were underpaid (or not paid) for their work, the overall gross national product suffered. Pigou's quip that a man who marries his housekeeper lowers the GNP encapsulates the problem with discriminatory gendered labor practices: Structures that require or encourage huge pools of skilled labor to leave the paid workforce or take lower-paid work are not a sign of healthy, growing economies.[154]

The EEC recognized this and sought member states with economies that had sufficiently modernized to bring them past this point, or nations that agreed on the need to do so in the near term. Britain's decades-long struggle with the EEC was perhaps the clearest signal that the country had "modernized" on an outdated economic model. Aware that feminized labor was formative to the British economy but unable to see the ways in which this was problematic, Civil Service leaders and successive prime ministers enacted policies that constructed and organized high technology around a gender-stratified labor force, a style of change that was not beneficial in the long term. Believing in a fiction of progress through technology alone and the importance of centralized technopolitical control, the state's course of action through decades of computerization had a panoply of unintended effects. It hurt the British economy, hindered the functioning of the state, undercut the health of national high technology labor markets through deskilling women technologists, and destroyed the British computer industry. The state increased gender stratification using computers; it used new technological tools to strengthen the position of those at the top of social and political hierarchies at the expense of economic and social progress.

In this sense, the failure of British computing points to the problem with seeking a "technological fix." Technologies often cement or widen existing social and economic divisions rather than break them down. Often, this is an intentional part of a technology's implementation. For the nation that invented the computer and pioneered many other advances in computing, the continual reconsolidation of gendered labor divisions had grave effects on the quickly growing information technology sector that was shaping its economy. In the end, ignoring women as a ready source of skilled labor not only resulted in a failure to meet the challenges of governance facing the nation, but ultimately defined British computing as a whole.

Conclusion: Reassembling the History of Computing around Gender's Formative Influence

When the Conservatives regained power in 1979 with the election of Margaret Thatcher, the image of a technologically advanced Britain based on public sector patronage and guidance had evaporated. Thatcher focused on cutting public sector costs, from the Civil Service and nationalized industries to the welfare state built up in the decades following World War II. Now believing that private industry and modified free market policies could succeed where the socialist and protectionist policies of the past had failed, the Conservatives discarded the British computer industry as an instrument of the nation's international economic and political objectives.[1] The government's attempts to mold the industry's output to the British state's specific organizational needs were largely over.

While ICL struggled in the 1970s, the government increasingly turned to the cheaper solutions offered by IBM. Seeing his company's business sliding away, the managing director of ICL, Arthur Humphreys, quipped: "There is no problem in the computer business which could not be solved by the demise of IBM."[2] ICL could no longer compete with IBM's prices or service when it came to mainframes, and as minicomputer technology increased in use and importance, computer experts in government and industry began to criticize ICL for its mainframe-centric product line and research agenda. The Select Committee on Science and Technology, convened to study the prospects of the British computing industry, took ICL to task, even though it was government technology specialists who had strongly encouraged the computer giant to focus on advanced mainframe systems. ICL had spent the seventies planning ever-larger mainframes rather than smaller computers that lent themselves to decentralized control. Despite this, ICL's most successful lines in fact were comprised of smaller, less technologically robust systems.[3] By the early 1980s, ICL's mainframe division soaked up two-thirds of the company's R & D budget but constituted less than a third of its profits.

Throughout the 1970s, computerization and labor shortages remained hopelessly intertwined, with ICL dragged along for the ride. As it continued to flounder, critics of ICL ignored the very real labor problems upon which British computing was built. The mismatch between the small available pool of technical expertise and the tools ICL provided worsened. IBM's products and service model helped ameliorate this skills gap, but ICL did not have the "manpower" to follow suit.

The "continuing shortage of capable people who [could] develop and implement computer systems" meant that the massive social services of the state were hobbled by inefficiency. In 1971, the overall cost of the National Health Service was more than £1,700 million per year and it employed over six hundred thousand workers whose jobs depended on the workings of computer installations, even if they did not directly interact with them.[4] Computing—first electromechanical and then electronic—had been critical to the success of the NHS from its inception. One of its highest priorities in the 1970s was better use of data and of "highly skilled" computer people.

In a report prepared by ICL for the parliamentary Select Committee on Science and Technology to "identify advanced applications of computers that the Government might beneficially undertake," the priorities of the NHS held pride of place, because "by improving the service to patients, there would be a reduction in time lost due to sickness," which would be "beneficial to the national economy and well-being."[5] Although both ICL management and government ministers could discern the connections between well-functioning technological systems and well-functioning social systems in this instance, few seemed to see the connections between the disregard of women's skilled labor and the repercussions it had on the computer industry. The connecting thread between labor, government organization, and British computing remained obscured by decades of gender discrimination. Only the most radical feminist Labour reformers explicitly drew a connection between the waste of human capital that women's unequal position in the workforce engendered and the nation's economic and political fortunes as a whole.

Soon, ICL publicly conceded its inability to provide Britain with the computing solutions it needed. ICL's chairman told IBM that, as the heir apparent to the global computing market, IBM now had a moral duty to perform its technological role responsibly and not attempt to create an American empire through computing technology. An American technological empire might well "end up a political system," ICL's chairman warned presciently, citing the importance of technology in consolidating Britain's global empire in centuries past. The irony of asking IBM to operate without the same imperialistic ideals that had shaped and motivated ICL from its inception seemed lost on ICL's chairman.[6]

Below the fold in the same issue of *ICL News* that printed the chairman's comments, a different article announced yet another round of layoffs at ICL, along with the grim promise of more "vigorous streamlining" to come.[7] The passing of the torch to IBM was more than mere symbolism. The contracts the government and British industry once placed with ICL quickly melted away. As Fujitsu gradually bought a majority of ICL, taking on the responsibility for the upkeep of ICL's workers and relieving the British government of the burden of keeping it afloat, the government was finally off the hook for the computer giant it had created in 1968.[8] ICL's disappearance, however, did not mean that the government's problems with computerization had also disappeared.

In *The Government Machine*, Jon Agar discusses how organizational goals dictated technological changes in the machinery of data processing within the Civil Service. Electronic computers were the crux of this change, and yet no group within the Civil Service could competently "claim authority on the dual aspects of administration and technology" even by the 1970s, notes Agar. The workforce that the government had been trying to create in order to smoothly integrate electronic computing had failed to materialize. As a result, the "skills were not in the right place" to allow the state to take advantage of, or even recognize, "the potentiality of small computers and networks" as they became available.[9] Technological decentralization was thwarted because it ran counter to a mainframe-era understanding of bureaucratic best practices that demanded as much centralization as possible.[10]

A Labor-Starved Technological System

Although the British government realized the major benefits that could accrue by leveraging women's labor in times of military conflict, for the most part it ignored the power of this labor force to remake the British economy in peacetime. By encouraging the majority of its clerical workforce to cluster in low-level and often temporary jobs, Britain neglected the lessons of labor rationalization learned during two world wars.

While the government's project to transform itself and the nation through electronic computerization continued to falter, high turnover and rampant job dissatisfaction plagued the new nonexecutive ADP class. The successor to the machine operator grades, this ADP class represented the legacy of feminization within government computing. Although it was supposed to be geared to the particular job and career needs of computer programmers and operators, it unhelpfully isolated workers in a subclass of jobs just like the earlier machine grades had, implicitly positioning computer work as less flexible and desirable. As a result, it failed to make the staffing and maintenance of the government's huge, centralized computing installations any less troublesome. Trained ADP workers—computer operators and programmers—could find better pay and prospects in the private sector. Often, these workers simply took advantage of Civil Service job training before fleeing to industry.[11]

But the hiring and training practices of the Civil Service only worsened the shortage of computer workers in the private sector. Rather than training all workers who might have aptitude, the government diminished the potential computer labor pool throughout the country by hiring and training only a small minority of available applicants. Because private sector companies could usually offer better salaries and more flexible terms of employment for workers who were in high demand, it was the government itself that was hardest hit by its own discriminatory training practices. The desirable and scarce computer workers it trained continually flowed out of government jobs.

To ease the situation, many Civil Service managers reconsidered allowing lower clerical officers to perform some of the "simpler" programming tasks. Department heads also consistently made use of temporarily promoted workers, who would be demoted again once more suitable, management-level ADP workers could be recruited. And, more time and money was wasted training many ambivalent, would-be ADP workers from the executive grades who never put their training to use, lowering productivity and holding back computerization projects. High-tech labor shortages continued to cause significant waste through the early 1980s, to the alarm of managers throughout government and industry.

As a result, the Civil Service once again began to turn toward—rather than away from—women computer workers, hiring them into positions that had formerly been earmarked for male executives. In the late seventies and early eighties, the Treasury considered actively recruiting former women employees who had left to have families. This was the first time such a policy had been explicitly formulated since World War II. "We are mindful that an untapped source of trained staff may be women who have left us to start families, but who still live locally," noted one report on the worsening staff shortages at the main Civil Service computer center. It added, "We are actively investigating ways of facilitating their continued or renewed employment (for example, by increasing part-time working) as part of a wider study of these issues in the Treasury as a whole."[12] In a time of crisis, the government once again tried to utilize a feminized computing labor force that was partly of its own creation. Yet these moves came only in response to labor shortages that precluded the hiring and retention of the government's first-choice workers. In the sixties and seventies, software entrepreneurs like Stephanie "Steve" Shirley cleverly benefited from this gendered labor discrimination. By offering flexible hours and the option to work from home, Shirley's software startup was able to tap into a deep pool of skilled women programmers who had left the labor force to raise children.[13] It took policymakers decades to come to the same conclusion.

As labor shortages continued to spill over from the public sector to the private sector, government commissions studying computer manpower presented evidence that did not bode well for the country's progress as a whole.[14] A major Institute of Manpower study, begun in 1978, declared that the availability of "skilled computer manpower" remained inadequate at every level of industry and government. From computer hardware and software companies to organizations that simply used computers, Britain lacked the proper labor in the proper quantities. The report stated in no uncertain terms that "the rapid expansion in the demand for computers and related products has resulted in a serious shortage of skilled manpower," not just in government, but nationally.[15]

Tackling the question of why this change in the technological landscape had resulted in *recurring* labor shortages, rather than just an initial period of shortage, the Institute of Manpower researchers focused on the "enormous" number of people in "the potentially eligible population who could be trained in DP [data processing] skills" and yet were not. They did this without paying any attention to gender, however, instead focusing exclusively on divisions of class in what they assumed to be an exclusively male workforce. Gender discrimination barely rated a mention; its role was not yet recognized or accepted. Even when looking directly at the problem of computer labor, government studies could not understand the impact of women workers. This was ironic, because the fact that computing had been dominated by women before it was dominated by men formed the entire background of the problem. Even without realizing this, however, the Institute of Manpower recognized that there was no way of coming up with a plan to solve the nation's computer labor troubles by 1985 as the government had asked.

Computer work's organization reified these long-standing divisions between technical and general aptitude, manual and professional work, and feminine and masculine skill sets. Even during the labor shortages of the late 1970s and early 1980s, civil servants with all the requisite technical qualifications and with adequate work performance still were regarded as unsuitable for promotion to vacant, higher ADP positions as the government struggled to upskill computer work in image—though not in fact. Some candidates for promotion at the government's Chessington computer center, for instance, had not been allowed to advance "because the [promotions] board considered that they did not match up to the general criteria for promotion to Higher Executive Officer as distinct from their specific expertise in ADP."[16] Yet the department used these same workers, who were judged inadequate for promotion, to indefinitely cover vacant higher executive officer posts. General aptitude was a highly gendered construct. In everything but name, these women were in fact the computer experts that the government was desperately seeking to hire. Gender and class, much more than skill, determined workers' roles in the computing hierarchy.

At a time "when industry [was] short of skilled labor and unemployment high," utilizing workers like these for more than data input and low-level computer operation was critical to economic growth, the Institute of Manpower report stated, but again it failed to mention gender.[17] The Treasury was slowly coming to realize the importance of leveraging women workers more effectively, evidenced by its beginning to offer more flexible schedules and family benefits for married women workers.[18] Yet these course corrections were limited and had little effect on firmly ingrained day-to-day hiring practices. Women's inequality in the workforce was still seen as ancillary rather than as a major causal factor shaping high-tech labor problems.

Demographic trends promised to worsen the problem. Rising numbers of women in offices and white-collar work meant that women were now the fastest-growing group of clerical labor. Women's overall workforce participation had steadily risen since 1951, with married women making the highest gains, whereas men's workforce participation declined slightly.[19] In 1980, 41 percent of all women worked in clerical occupations, and women made up nearly 78 percent of the total clerical workforce.[20] This explosive growth put women into direct contact with computerization far more often than men and made their labor integral to the electronic data handling on which the British economy increasingly relied.[21]

Gender, Not Women, as a Category of Historical Analysis

In 1992 Teresa Rees, a University of Wales researcher, produced a report for the Commission of the European Communities on the domestic "brain drain" in high technology. The subject was women's underrepresentation in jobs created by new digital information technologies, especially in positions of power and responsibility. In the report, she attempted to explain and offer solutions for the problem of skill shortages in information technology by investigating the underutilization of women. She reported that culturally constructed roles for women and men in Britain, and European society more broadly, fed a cycle of perpetual skill shortage and led to a lack of acknowledgment of women's technical skills and achievements.[22]

By the late 1980s, working with computers had acquired a distinctly masculine image within British society. So much so that, as influential labor researcher Cynthia Cockburn noted, "for a woman to aspire to technical competence is, in a very real sense, to transgress the rules of gender."[23] Today, despite decades of equal pay legislation and significant investment in educational strategies designed to change this situation on both sides of the Atlantic, patterns of underachievement and perceptions of women as less technically competent persist within Anglo-American culture, business, and higher education. Yet this image of incompetence is a recent historical construction. It is not rooted in some sort of natural evolution of the field, nor is it a reflection of women's demonstrated skills, aptitudes, and interests.

In 1958, British Tabulating Machines—the same company that built the codebreaking Bombes for the government during World War II—sent a computer operator named Andrina Wood (see figure 6.1) around the world to "demonstrate" BTM's new general-purpose electronic computers. "During her stay in Australia she is demonstrating the [electronic] Hec machine in operation at two exhibitions and is supervising training of local staff," reported BTM's employee magazine. This assignment made Wood a vector of international technological transfer and an early electronic computer expert, yet she would not have been described as such.

Perhaps most important to modern eyes is the note added almost as an afterthought to the article on Wood: "The programmes for the

Figure 6.1
Andrina Wood at the console of a BTM computer. *Tabacus: The Magazine of the British Tabulating Company*, August 1958.

work being demonstrated were written entirely by Miss Wood before her departure."[24] Women computer operators, though not given the title, were usually programmers as well. Kept from assuming the title of programmer or the mantle of expert by a variety of cultural and professional constraints, these operators nonetheless did more than simply operate. That they remain unknown is an effect of how the field was intentionally professionalized out of their reach, rather than an indictment of their expertise or potential.

In recent years, historical studies of women in computing have begun to proliferate. Many of these focus on the important task of uncovering women's contributions and adding them back into the historical record. Most of them focus on computer programmers, because programming has become seen as important, lucrative, and foundational. Understandably, many of these studies focus on women who have a claim to greatness or whose activities put them at the center of major historical events—like Grace Hopper, the ENIAC women, or Dame Stephanie Shirley. Yet the experiences of these exceptional women only begin to hint at the story of most women in computing. They are as much exceptions to the rule as the handful of great men whose achievements have come to define the contours of computer lore. Even the focus on more ordinary women who could lay claim to the identity of programmer risks obscuring the much larger group of women who worked with computers, many of whom programmed, without it defining their job or personal identity. Career-based identities historically privilege a male subject, rarely taking into account the often circuitous and discontinuous nature of women's working lives or the social pressures placed upon women to privilege nonprofessional categories in constructing their identities.

Wood's importance therefore lies not in being exceptional, but in being representative of the vast, largely hidden store of women's labor and expertise in early computing. The fact that there were many women performing jobs like hers—operating early electronic computers, teaching others how to use them, and convincing companies to buy them—literally defined the progress of computerization. Despite the perennial emphasis in the history of computing on machines and the men who designed and later programmed them, these women computer operators filled many of the early computer industry's most important roles, functioning as technical experts, technological emissaries, and forming the critical mass of computer labor. Before they disappeared they defined the shape of computing, and after they disappeared their absence continued to shape the field.

As a result, the women operators who form the core of this study exist as much on a discursive level as they do on the level of an embodied labor force. Their work identities were formed by job classifications and management language that was carefully deployed to protect a status quo of structural inequality. They were submerged by a kind of technological fetishism that insisted on focusing on machines at the expense of labor. The process of trying to reclaim these women's voices from the dustbin of history is also, paradoxically, an exercise in further privileging those with the most access to power. A focus on individual voices tends to reproduce the narrative structures and historiographical methods that erased the impact of gender from the history of computing in the first place, positioning most women as too low level, peripheral, or anonymous to be a valid, formative part of computer history. The majority of these workers cannot speak through the archives as individuals, only as a group, and the explanatory power of their experiences lies in this realization. Discussing women as a class of labor in computing, rather than searching for exceptional women, fundamentally changes the narrative of computerization and postindustrial progress previously taken for granted. Instead of a progressively modernizing economy and a narrative of steadily increasing labor equality, computerization investigated through the lens of gendered class structures highlights how modernizing nations preserved, rather than dispensed with, regressive social ideals. Using gender as a category of historical analysis shows how the absence of women has defined technological change and shaped key technologies.

These women's experiences also elucidate the power dynamics behind how technology often heightens existing power differences.[25] From manufacturing processes dating back to the early days of industrialization, technological progress has, in the words of Langdon Winner, meant that some technologies are "heralded as wonderful breakthroughs by some social interests and crushing setbacks by others," in ways that often break down along the intersecting lines of class, race, and gender.[26] As Eden Medina puts it, in her study of Chile's Cybersyn Project, "The state and its priorities shape how technology is designed and used."[27] Technology can support marginalized groups in the best cases, or it can participate in furthering their marginalization.

All History of Computing Is Gendered History

Queer theorists like Judith Butler have shown that, as a category of social difference that structures society, gender is not static but performative, imitative, and dynamic. By its very nature, it needs to change and be constantly reinterpreted in order to retain its cultural utility and power. Gendered mores have the ability to construct and order social relations as historical circumstances change, but they are repeatedly reformulated in conjunction with those circumstances.

As a category made real by social performance, gender can be understood neither as something natural and unconflicted nor as something consciously assumed by individuals choosing freely between identities. Instead, gendered categories represent the aggregate of a series of actions, social negotiations, institutional practices, and constantly changing cultural understandings that, far from being purely descriptive, strongly tend to produce the phenomena they set out to describe or accommodate.[28] Furthermore, gender as a category of analysis is critically reliant on sexuality and the presumption, proscription, or prescription of particular styles of sexual behavior. The assumed or "cultural" heterosexuality of women workers—the firm expectation that they would be wives and mothers rather than have careers—determined their experiences and treatment as "women." Heteronormativity, as much as sexism, shaped their lives and work, making any analysis of gender in this case also an implicit analysis of the impact of sexuality on computing history.

The expectation of women's dependence and their failure to achieve career-long employment, paired with the opposite expectation for men, became a self-fulfilling prophecy for much of the twentieth century. In the case of careers in computing, this situation was especially disappointing, because there was an initial period in which computing work was seen as well-suited to women, and this era overlapped with more than a decade during which the field had not yet rigidly professionalized. Although some women—and some working-class men—benefited from this situation, lasting career gains were usually only possible for those who had uninterrupted careers and who were judged suitable for supervisory roles.

Professional identities are the result of complex webs of social and economic privileges. They are defined by contemporaneous institutional practices, but also by cultural and technical change. The fiction that they are freely chosen is belied by the fact that they exist specifically to limit choice and erect barriers to entry. The perception of a masculine ideal for computer workers is, in and of itself, an issue that has been recognized by researchers, educators, and even businesses as a critical stumbling block for industries struggling to find and retain talented, highly skilled workers.[29] Even today, the US Census Bureau reports, for instance, that men with science, technology, engineering, and mathematics (STEM) degrees are twice as likely to be hired into STEM jobs as women with the same qualifications—ensuring that no matter how many women fill STEM pipelines problems with women's underrepresentation and undervaluation will continue.[30] Contemporary situations like this become less surprising when one sees how the professional identity of computer workers is tied to a history of structural discrimination that has nothing to do with skill.

The historical patterns described in this book are all the more relevant to current experience in the United States because of the British government's long-standing commitment to equality of pay and opportunity in the Civil Service. The "fair field with no favor" of the Civil Service and nationalized industries mirrors contemporary discourses in Western nations that assert the existence of meritocracy in the face of clear evidence to the contrary. Even today, women cluster at the lower levels of the computing industry, not for lack of technical talent but because they are seen as less able leaders. The low proportion of women CEOs in high-technology fields and elsewhere is not a new issue, or a coincidence: It is the legacy of structural discrimination and the persistent devaluation of women's abilities.

Although discrimination animates this history, this story is about more than unequal treatment of women. It explains how gendered relationships shape technology, affect the workings of the state, and ultimately impact the fortunes of nations. To all appearances, these women computer workers formed an ideal group to excel in the new, high-tech economy evolving in modern Britain. That they did not sheds light on the ways that conservative social norms attach to power-enhancing technologies. The example of the sprawling British public sector shows why computing was first institutionalized as a feminized sphere of work and then self-consciously reengineered as a field of masculine endeavor as a result of new ideas about how to wield power within the apparatus of the state. Deployed as a centralizing technology designed to concentrate power, computing was necessarily antithetical to equal opportunity. This is why, despite women's long experience working with and within the machinery of government, the field masculinized as the power of electronic computing became clear. Power and masculinity went hand in hand; Stephanie Shirley's company only succeeded once she began signing her letters "Steve," and though she did receive government contracts once she was known to be a woman, she was repeatedly put in her place. One minister "pinched her bottom" as she was making a successful bid for a government job.[31]

High-level civil servants made technological decisions that determined how the government would function under successive administrations, but they often chose poorly, neglecting available labor to groom a male-identified technocrat class that was supposed to transform the entire nation by melding electronics with executive decision-making. When this transformation did not come to pass, the effects of these staffing decisions rippled upward, changing the organization of computing in government and the types of technologies the government encouraged industry to produce.

The Legacy of Feminization

Although historically specific, the reasons for this gendered labor flip in British computing nonetheless shed light on many of the institutional processes that have resulted in the gendering of postindustrial workforces elsewhere. When a specific technology becomes aligned with those in power, rather than being seen as merely technical, it enters the realm of technocracy. Those who are already in power—usually white men of upper or upper middle class backgrounds—are slotted into jobs associated with the technology, despite often having little or no technical skill. The larger socio-technical system becomes reengineered from the top down in order to accommodate and extend existing patterns of privilege and power.

In their research on feminized labor markets and male-dominated fields of work, Barbara Reskin and Patricia Roos have discussed this phenomenon in order to show why women often lose out in the labor market. Particularly in well-remunerated or traditionally male fields, they argue that we must redirect our inquiry away from the "characteristics of female workers, to the structural properties of labor markets." Labor markets are, for the most part, "shaped by the preferences of employers and male workers" who have the most power in establishing the shape of the workforce in desirable fields.[32] Reskin and Roos have shown how a boom-and-bust cycle of feminization and masculinization in most labor markets relies on employers' gendered preferences for certain workers over others.

The British case holds applicable lessons for other high-technology workforces within institutions constructed in the varied, but often broadly similar, cultural molds of Anglo-American tradition, particularly ones that continue to evolve today. Skills are not enough to undo gendered labor discrimination, because historically such discrimination has not been about finding the people with the most skills. Indeed, technocratic control is far less about technical skill than about power. Recently, much has been made of attempts in both Britain and the United States to get girls and women into computing and other science, technology, and engineering jobs, with the expectation that these initiatives can fix the gender imbalances in STEM fields along with the socioeconomic power imbalances that come along with them. However, history shows that initiatives like these mean little if the participants being targeted for empowerment in a field are still disempowered in the wider world. In this context, training increasing numbers of women and girls to program may simply succeed in creating a flooded labor market and a newly feminized sphere of computer labor rather than boosting women's social and economic power in the long term.

Certain highly skilled fields within computing are already feminizing again, with an attendant loss of status and pay. Software engineering jobs can also now be easily moved to other countries with lower labor costs and higher labor availability, further depressing wages. Meanwhile, Silicon Valley emits a rhetoric of labor scarcity and corporations there lobby the government intensely to bring more H1B visa holders from countries like India and China into US computing work. This much-reported but fictitious labor scarcity obscures the reality of how large numbers of STEM workers are treated. Most H1B workers earn less and have less control over their career choices than American workers doing the exact same jobs. The changing landscape of computing today offers possibilities for deskilling by gender, race, class, and nationality, but historically this is nothing new. The persistent "leaky pipeline" effect of women leaving the STEM fields for which they trained masks a deeper historical problem. Initiatives to get girls, women, and people of color to train for STEM jobs cannot undo the underlying structures of power that have been designed into technological systems over the course of decades. Despite the rhetoric of meritocracy, patterns like these will not be undone by the individual career choices of workers, especially if they belong to groups that lack the power to participate in the structures of dominance and control that created institutionalized discrimination in a given organization or industry in the first place.

The process of rendering invisible certain categories of workers—and the importance of their work—was critical to the success of early large-scale computing projects aligned with the informational needs of governments. Similar practices of labor submersion continue in computing, broadly defined, today—such as the hundreds of thousands of invisible content-management workers who decide what information is safe for the web, shaping our understanding of culture and protecting the economic interests of major corporations.[33] In this way, histories of hidden or devalued computing labor connect powerfully with current trends in information technology and prompt questions about the categories of privilege that silently structure our computing systems today.

For decades, the British government saw undoing the long-standing feminization of their data-processing workforce as critical to the success of British computing and to the governance of the nation itself. Meanwhile, the actual solution to British computerization problems got lost in the divide that the government constructed between the technical and the technocratic. In order to leverage computing technology most effectively, the British would have had to adopt management and governance philosophies that did not encourage a systematic squandering of the vast majority of its own technically minded labor force. The government's failure to do so was not actually a technical problem, and the larger political and economic effects of that failure could not be solved by a technological fix. At its root, gender inequality shaped and enabled one of the most important technological changes in Britain's history. In this way, a social problem became a technological one that hastened British decline in the twentieth century.

Appendix: Timeline of Key Events

September 1939	Bletchley Park is set up to provide a hub for intelligence and codebreaking work for the war effort.
1940	The first complement of WRNS members arrive at Bletchley.
March 1940	The first of the electromechanical Bombes is installed at Bletchley.
July–October 1940	The Battle of Britain, the most intense period of German aerial bombing of major British cities during the Blitz, contributes to more lives being lost on the home front than at the actual front.
December 1941	Britain begins conscripting women workers for the war effort. Initially all women between the ages of twenty and thirty-one are called up for service in wartime industries, except for mothers of children under age fourteen.
Summer 1941	WRNS operate over 200 electromechanical Bombes to help speed codebreaking.
June 1943	The faster but unreliable Heath Robinson machine starts to be used for codebreaking the more complex Lorenz cypher.
December 1943	Colossus becomes operational at Post Office Research Station owing to the efforts of Tommy Flowers and his team.
January 1944	Colossus is shipped to Bletchley Park. It is operated and programmed by the WRNS, using William Tutte's "statistical method" for codebreaking.
Early 1944	Joan Clarke becomes deputy head of Hut 8, the area of Bletchley involved in hand-codebreaking.

June 1, 1944	Colossus II is assembled and tested at Bletchley and becomes operational, providing crucial intelligence information for the success of the D-Day landings.
September 1945	Members of the WRNS destroy all but two Colossus computers on Churchill's orders. The remaining two are moved to GCHQ for intelligence and research. The last of the two remains operational until 1960.
1946	The marriage bar is repealed in government, technically allowing women to keep their jobs after marriage. In practice, however, it changes little.
1948	The Machine Grades are created in the Civil Service.
May 1949	The EDSAC, which formed the basis for the LEO I of 1951, becomes operational at the University of Cambridge.
Summer 1949	The Manchester Mark I runs the first stored program. It is commercialized as the Ferranti Mark I, the first of which is delivered in February 1951.
1950	The National Physical Laboratory Pilot ACE becomes operational. Led by Alan Turing, this project would become the basis for English Electric's commercial line of DEUCE computers.
1952	The Great Smog kills several thousand Londoners owing to the fact that only low-quality, dirty-burning coal is available off ration to citizens for home heating.
1954	Wartime rationing ends.
1955	Equal Pay for government employees is introduced. Unequal pay remains legal in private industry.
1957	The Windscale nuclear weapons plant catches on fire, leading to Britain's worst nuclear disaster.
1959	Powers-Samas and British Tabulating Machines merge to form ICT.
1963	Wilson declares a "white hot technological revolution" is necessary to save Britain's global standing. Wilson is elected prime minister the following year.
1963	Ferranti merges with ICT.

1963	Britain attempts to join the EEC and is rejected.
1963	English Electric and LEO Computers merge to form English Electric–LEO.
1964	The Ministry of Technology is created by Prime Minister Harold Wilson.
1967	Britain attempts to join the EEC and is rejected for the second time.
1968	International Computers LTD (ICL) is created through a government-backed merger of English Electric LTD and ICT LTD; the government promises the company preferential treatment in government contracts in return for influence over their product line.
1971	The Heath government begins to distance itself from ICL, removing price protections and allowing departments the option of buying IBM computers.
1973	Britain joins the EEC.
1974	A series of strikes in industry and government, including strikes by computer workers, prompt Prime Minister Edward Heath to implement the "three-day week" and declare more states of emergency than any previous prime minister.
1975	The existence of the Colossus computers is revealed to the public, despite government reluctance, after decades of being kept secret under the Official Secrets Act.
1975	A National Equal Pay Act, passed in 1970, comes into force, and a National Sex Discrimination Act is passed as a requirement of Britain's entry into the EEC. The measures do little to equalize women's position and the EEC brings infringement proceedings against the United Kingdom in 1975 as a result.
1978–1979	Labor union strikes during the "Winter of Discontent" wrack government and industry.
1983	The EEC censures Britain for not enacting the gender equality standards required of EEC member states.
1990	Fujitsu acquires an 80 percent stake in ICL.

1998	ICL becomes a fully owned subsidiary of Fujitsu.
2002	The ICL name is dropped.
2008	A working replica of Colossus II is completed at the National Museum for the History of Computing in Block H of Bletchley Park—the original site of the Colossus computers. In the years following, many women whose stories were nearly lost come forward to talk about their secret wartime computer work.

Notes

Epigraph

1. For more information, see Economic Development Committee for the Electronics Industry, Computer Sector Working Party, Manpower Sub-Committee, Discussion Papers on Education and Training; Final Report and Government Response, 1979–1980, ED 212/216, the National Archives of the United Kingdom (TNA).

Introduction

1. Minutes, April 20, 1959, STAT 14/2320, TNA.

2. *Tabacus: The Company Magazine of the British Tabulating Company*, May 1957, 4.

3. *ICL News*, November 1970, 8.

4. In particular: Janet Abbate, *Recoding Gender: Women's Changing Participation in Computing* (Cambridge, MA: MIT Press, 2012); Nathan Ensmenger, *The Computer Boys Take Over: Computers, Programmers, and the Politics of Technical Expertise* (Cambridge, MA: MIT Press, 2010); and Jennifer Light, "When Computers Were Women," *Technology and Culture* 40, no. 3 (1999): 455–483.

5. Langdon Winner discusses several classic examples of this in "Do Artifacts Have Politics?," *Daedalus* 109, no. 1 (1980): 121–136.

6. Martin Campbell-Kelly and John Hendry have written histories that focus on the problems of the British computing industry. Campbell-Kelly's definitive history of ICL explores British computing through the lens of business history to show how the story of the corporation is inseparable from the nation's computing aspirations, and Hendry has written about how the government funded and tried to encourage computing research. See Martin Campbell-Kelly, *I.C.L.: A Business and Technical History* (Oxford: Oxford University Press, 1989); and John Hendry, *Innovating for Failure: Government Policy and the Early British Computer Industry* (Cambridge, MA: MIT Press, 1989).

7. David Edgerton, *The Shock of the Old: Technology and Global History since 1900* (Oxford: Oxford University Press, 2007).

8. Often, the history of computing in the twentieth century is seen as a masculine story of invention and entrepreneurship, focusing particularly on the United States and its global economic and technological hegemony after World War II. When women do appear in this "great man" style of history, they often do so as the exceptions that prove the rule or as lower-level workers to whom little attention is paid. Janet Abbate has argued that an early emphasis on the creation and design of hardware in the history of computing has had the unintended consequence of obscuring women's work in computing, because men were primarily the inventors and designers of computer hardware. See Abbate, "Women and Gender in the History of Computing," *IEEE Annals of the History of Computing* 25, no. 4 (2003): 4–8.

9. IBM's approach of heterogeneously engineering the contexts into which its systems would be placed and its success in doing so is one strong supporting example. The idea of the social construction of technology (SCOT) also shows how systems are interdependent with their social contexts and succeed or fail through adoption and use. See, for example, Wiebe E. Bijker, *Of Bicycles, Bakelites, and Bulbs: Toward a Theory of Sociotechnical Change* (Cambridge, MA: MIT Press 1995); Ronald Kline and Trevor Pinch, "Users as Agents of Technological Change: The Social Construction of the Automobile in the Rural United States," *Technology and Culture* 37, no. 4 (October 1996): 763–795; or Brian Woods and Nick Watson, "In Pursuit of Standardization: The British Ministry of Health's Model 8F Wheelchair, 1948–1962," *Technology and Culture* 45, no. 3 (July 2004): 540–568.

10. For instance, Ruth Schwartz Cowan reverses the narrative of technological progress by taking gendered labor into account when analyzing the changes wrought by automating housework with appliances. See Cowan, *More Work for Mother: The Ironies of Household Technology from the Open Hearth to the Microwave* (New York: Basic Books, 1983).

11. Light, "When Computers Were Women"; and Jean Jennings Bartik, *Pioneer Programmer: Jean Jennings Bartik and the Computer that Changed the World*, ed. Jon T. Rickman, and Kim D. Todd (Kirksville, MO: Truman State University Press, 2013).

12. Nathan Ensmenger, "Power to the People: Toward a Social History of Computing," *IEEE Annals of the History of Computing* 26, no. 1 (2004): 94–96. Ensmenger expands on the relationships among society, computing, and technocracy in *The Computer Boys Take Over*.

13. Thomas Misa, ed., *Gender Codes: Why Women Are Leaving Computing* (Hoboken, NJ: Wiley, 2010); J. McGrath Cohoon and William Aspray, eds., *Women and Information Technology: Research on Underrepresentation* (Cambridge, MA: MIT Press, 2006); and Jane Margolis and Allan Fisher, *Unlocking the Clubhouse: Women in Computing* (Cambridge, MA: MIT Press, 2001).

14. Abbate, *Recoding Gender*.

15. See Anna Clark, *The Struggle for the Breeches: Gender and the Making of the British Working Class* (Berkeley: University of California Press, 1995); Ivy Pinchbeck, *Women Workers and the Industrial Revolution 1750–1850* (London:

Virago, 1981); and Jane Rendall, *Women in an Industrializing Society: England, 1750–1880* (Oxford: Blackwell, 1991).

16. Maxine Berg, "What Difference Did Women's Work Make to the Industrial Revolution?," *History Workshop* 35 (Spring 1993): 22–44.

17. David Noble's study of automatically controlled machine tools, for instance, shows management's attempts to remove skilled workers' control over the process of production through automation. Noble provides compelling evidence to suggest that the transfer of power from labor to management was not a side effect of automation but a prime motivating factor in management's decision to automate, even though the machinery was expensive and failure prone. Technology often is not used to effect higher efficiency and productivity, but is used instead as a tool of social control influenced by factors that extend beyond the workplace. Noble, *Forces of Production: A Social History of Industrial Automation* (New York: Knopf, 1984).

18. For background, see David Alan Grier, *When Computers Were Human* (Princeton, NJ: Princeton University Press, 2006); and Corinna Schlombs, "A Gendered Job Carousel," in Thomas Misa, ed., *Gender Codes: Why Women Are Leaving Computing* (Hoboken, NJ: Wiley, 2010), 75–94.

19. Catherine Hall, *White, Male and Middle-Class: Explorations in Feminism and History* (New York: Routledge, 1992), 75. In large part, Catherine Hall argues, this was a result of the Anglican Evangelical movement, which embarked on several campaigns to reorder Britons' morality in response to the reorganization of people's lives by the rise of industrial capitalism. See also Kathleen Canning, *Languages of Labor and Gender: Female Factory Work in Germany, 1850–1914* (Ithaca: Cornell University Press, 1996). Canning's study shows how working class politics created gendered work within and outside the factory that was remarkably similar to British ideals. Instead of focusing on moral cleanliness through behavioral attributes, however, German concerns turned instead to the potentially unhealthy nature of factory work, an issue for state regulation throughout Western Europe and in Great Britain in the nineteenth and twentieth centuries that took on a different resonance in Germany due to the influence of the eugenics movement.

20. Hall, *White, Male and Middle-Class*, 95–96.

21. Meta Zimmeck, "The 'New Woman' in the Machinery of Government: A Spanner in the Works?," in *Government and Expertise: Specialists, Administrators, and Professionals, 1860–1919*, ed. Roy MacLeod (Cambridge: Cambridge University Press, 1988), 185–202.

22. Meta Zimmeck, "Jobs for the Girls: The Expansion of Clerical Work for Women, 1850–1914," in *Unequal Opportunities: Women's Employment in England 1800–1918*, ed. Angela V. John (New York: Blackwell, 1986), 153.

23. Ibid., 160.

24. Laura Lee Downs, "Industrial Decline, Rationalization and Equal Pay: The Bedaux Strike at Rover Automobile Company," *Social History* 15, no. 1 (1990): 45–73.

25. Jane E. Lewis, "Women Clerical Workers in the Late Nineteenth and Early Twentieth Centuries," in *The White-Blouse Revolution: Female Office Workers since 1870*, ed. Gregory Anderson (Manchester, UK: Manchester University Press, 1988), 34.

26. Jon Agar has discussed the computerization of the British Civil Service and argued that that computers represented an apotheosis of the civil servant. Agar discusses women only briefly, however, and does not discuss the impact feminized labor had on those making decisions about computerization. Agar, *The Government Machine: A Revolutionary History of the Computer* (Cambridge, MA: MIT Press, 2003).

27. "To Train or Not to Train?," *Office Methods and Machines*, September 1967, 17. On the flip side, women's representation in manufacturing work for new technologies also continued to grow: through the 1960s, IBM UK measured its production times for computer internals in "girl hours" rather than "man hours" to highlight the composition of their high-skill but low-cost hardware assembly and testing workforce. See Interdepartmental Study Group on Application of Computer Techniques to Clerical Work: 1956–1957, T 222/1314, TNA.

28. As Katie Hindmarch-Watson has pointed out in discussing another type of government labor (telegraph boys), a focus on the massive technological infrastructure of the state has threatened to submerge the individuals whose lives and labor define these systems. Hindmarch-Watson, "Male Prostitution and the London GPO: Telegraph Boys' 'Immorality' from Nationalization to the Cleveland Street Scandal," *Journal of British Studies* 51, no. 3 (2012): 594–617.

29. Both James Cortada and Alistair Black et al. discuss this process in pre-electronic offices. See Cortada, *Before the Computer: IBM, NCR, Burroughs, and Remington Rand and the Industry They Created, 1865–1956* (Princeton, NJ: Princeton University Press, 1993); and Alistair Black, Dave Muddiman, and Helen Plant, *The Early Information Society: Information Management in Britain before the Computer* (Aldershot, UK: Ashgate, 2007).

30. Susan Pedersen has investigated how this widespread expectation of economic dependence for women, even in the face of employment data to the contrary, powerfully informed Britain's economy and political goals in the twentieth century. Through her detailed comparison of British and French family allowances, Pedersen shows that British welfare policies created an idealized nuclear family and protected the concept of a male breadwinner wage. If women were not supported by gainfully employed husbands, then their wages were nevertheless supposed to be rendered unnecessary by the state's welfare measures for families. In a political sense, women could not exist without the family. Welfare benefits were repeatedly used to support the government's arguments against equal pay for women. Pedersen, *Family, Dependence, and the Origins of the Welfare State: Britain and France, 1914–1945* (New York: Cambridge University Press, 1993), 413.

31. See the recommendations of the 1942 Beveridge Report on social insurance that created the welfare state and the NHS institutionalized women's position

in the economy along the lines of domesticity and dependence, assuming that most women were housewives and tailoring their benefits to match that assumption, even in a period of skyrocketing women's employment. For decades, these welfare measures were used by the government to argue against equal pay for women on the basis that the state was already adequately seeing to their economic concerns through provisioning welfare designed for housewives. William Beveridge, *Social Insurance and Allied Services* (London: HMSO, 1943), 15.

32. As Arthur C. Pigou quipped in the *The Economics of Welfare* (1932), "If a man marries his housekeeper or his cook, the national dividend is diminished" (33). In other words, the man who marries his housekeeper lowers the gross national product. When earners are taken out of the labor force and their work is no longer remunerated, this lowers the total economic output of a nation, as measured by metrics like GNP and GDP that gauge the health of a nation's economy. Constraints like these continue to structure economies in the present; one need only consider debates about work–life balance and the second shift to see this process continuing to play out today.

33. Eden Medina, *Cybernetic Revolutionaries: Technology and Politics in Allende's Chile* (Cambridge, MA: MIT Press, 2014).

34. For a US perspective, see Andrew Meade McGee, "Stating the Field: Institutions and Outcomes in Computer History," *IEEE Annals of the History of Computing* 34, no. 1 (January–March 2012): 104, 102–103; for an example of international attempts to control other nations through computing, see Honghong Tinn, "Cold War Politics: Taiwanese Computing in the 1950s and 1960s," *IEEE Annals* 32, no. 1 (2010): 92–95.

35. For studies of computing from the perspectives of industry and engineering, see Martin Campbell-Kelly and William Aspray, *Computer: A History of the Information Machine* (New York: Basic Books, 1996); Campbell-Kelly, *I.C.L.*; Peter J. Bird, *LEO: The First Business Computer* (Wokingham, UK: Hasler Publishing Ltd., 1994); Cortada, *Before the Computer*; and, Bruno Latour, *Science in Action: How to Follow Scientists and Engineers through Society* (Cambridge, MA: Harvard University Press, 1987).

36. Taking on a professional identity was, and still is, an act of privilege defined by gender, class background, and many other categories of social power, particularly if the professional identity in question is high in status. See, for instance, the struggles of women engineers today to lay claim to the identity of "engineer" and present themselves as legitimate incarnations of that professional identity. In 2015, a twitter campaign started by Isis Wenger using the #ILookLikeAnEngineer hashtag invited women engineers to publicly claim their professional identity by posting pictures of themselves and thereby acculturating the public to a more racially and gender-diverse image of professional engineers. Isis Anchalee, "You May Have Seen My Face on the BART," The Coffeelicious, August 1, 2014, https://medium.com/the-coffeelicious/you-may-have-seen-my-face-on-bart-8b9561003e0f#.8znagygsb. Different activists extended this effort to other prestigious professions, notably via the following hashtags: #ILookLikeAPhysi-

cist, #ILookLikeASurgeon, and #ILookLikeAProfessor. For the last, see Sara B. Pritchard, Adeline Koh, and Michelle Moravec, "We Look like Professors, Too," *Inside Higher Ed*, August 10, 2015, https://www.insidehighered.com/views/2015/08/10/essay-explains-new-hashtag-campaign-draw-attention-diversity-professors-and-their.

37. Joan Woollcombe, "Women at Work: Computers Need People," *Times* (London), October 20, 1970, 19.

1 War Machines

1. See B. Jack Copeland, ed., *Colossus: The Secrets of Bletchley Park's Codebreaking Computers* (Oxford: Oxford University Press, 2006).

2. In *The Imitation Game* (2014, directed by Morten Tyldum), Alan Turing is turned into a lone hero, to the extent that the work of other codebreakers and of machines other than the Bombes—which he was instrumental in designing—are removed from the story.

3. Michael Smith, *Station X: The Codebreakers of Bletchley Park* (London: Channel Four Books, 1998), 175.

4. See Janet Abbate, *Recoding Gender: Women's Changing Participation in Computing* (Cambridge, MA: MIT Press, 2012) for a further discussion of women's roles in computing in the United States and the United Kingdom from World War II to the present.

5. This resonates with labor history in other arenas of paid work. See Laura Lee Downs, *Manufacturing Inequality: Gender Division in the French and British Metalworking Industries, 1914–1939* (Ithaca: Cornell University Press, 1995) for an example of how historical understandings of industrial labor have been changed by gender analysis, or Julia Kirk Blackwelder, *Now Hiring: The Feminization of Work in the United States, 1900–1995* (College Station: Texas A&M University Press, 1997), which argues that twentieth-century labor history is in fact defined by the changes wrought by labor feminization.

6. Janet Abbate has argued that an early emphasis on hardware design in computing history has had the unintended consequence of obscuring women's computing work, because men were primarily hardware inventors and designers. Abbate, "Women and Gender in the History of Computing," *IEEE Annals of the History of Computing* 25, no. 4 (2003): 4–8.

7. See Abbate, *Recoding Gender*; Nathan Ensmenger, *The Computer Boys Take Over: Computers, Programmers, and the Politics of Technical Expertise* (Cambridge, MA: MIT Press, 2010); David Alan Grier, *When Computers Were Human* (Princeton, NJ: Princeton University Press, 2005); Thomas Misa, ed., *Gender Codes: Why Women Are Leaving Computing* (Hoboken, NJ: Wiley, 2010); J. McGrath Cohoon and William Aspray, *Women and Information Technology: Research on Underrepresentation* (Cambridge, MA: MIT Press, 2006); Jennifer Light, "When Computers Were Women," *Technology and Culture* 40, no. 3 (1999): 455–483; and Carla Freeman, *High Tech and High Heels in the*

Global Economy: Women, Work, and Pink-Collar Identities in the Caribbean (Durham, NC: Duke University Press, 2000).

8. For other industries, see Downs, *Manufacturing Inequality*; Blackwelder, *Now Hiring*; and Joan Wallach Scott, *The Glassworkers of Carmaux: French Craftsmen and Political Action in a Nineteenth-Century City* (Cambridge, MA: Harvard University Press, 1974).

9. Interdepartmental Study Group on Application of Computer Techniques to Clerical Work: 1956–1957, T 222/1314, the National Archives of the UK (TNA).

10. L. J. Comrie, "The Application of Commercial Calculating Machines to Scientific Computing, *Mathematical Tables and Other Aids to Computation (MTAC)* 2, no. 16 (1946): 149–159; Martin Campbell-Kelly, William Aspray, Nathan Ensmenger, and Jeff Yost, *Computer: A History of the Information Machine*, 3rd ed. (Boulder, CO: Westview Press, 2014), chapter 3; M. J. Croarken, "L. J. Comrie and the Origins of the Scientific Computing Service," *IEEE Annals of the History of Computing* 21, no. 4 (1999): 70–71; and Mary Croarken, *Early Scientific Computing in Britain* (Oxford: Clarendon Press, 1990).

11. L. J. Comrie, "Careers for Girls," *The Mathematical Gazette* 28, no. 280 (1944): 90–95

12. Equivalent to £1.50 to £2.00. L. J. Comrie, *The Hollerith and Powers Tabulating Machines, Based on a Lecture Delivered to the Office Machinery User's Association of the London School of Economics and Lectures Delivered at University College London* (London: British Library[BL], 1933), 5–15.

13. Comrie, "Careers for Girls," 94.

14. Treasury, Letter to Mr. Pike Lees, "Teleprinter Operators," December 31, 1941, T 162/942, TNA.

15. Jane E. Lewis, "Women Clerical Workers in the Late Nineteenth and Early Twentieth Centuries," in *The White Blouse Revolution: Female Office Workers since 1870*, ed. Gregory Anderson (New York: St. Martin's Press, 1988), 34.

16. Ronald Whelan, "The Use of Hollerith Equipment in Bletchley Park," undated report c. 1995, HW 25/22, TNA, 1.

17. *Times* (London), "How the 'Call-Up' Affects Women of Britain," February 24, 1942.

18. Women between the ages of twenty and thirty-one.

19. Copeland, *Colossus*, 161.

20. Memorandum, "Training of Women," February 1942, LAB 79/32, Womanpower Debate, TNA.

21. Ruth Milkman has discussed the "idiom of sex-typing" during World War II in American manufacturing. In *Gender at Work: The Dynamics of Job Segregation by Sex during World War II* (Urbana: University of Illinois Press, 1987), Milkman argues that although the work women did during the war expanded enormously, employers maintained gendered job categories in order to validate

prewar job segregation and to maintain traditional ideas about the suitability of types of work based on to gender.

22. Memorandum, "Training of Women," February 1942, LAB 79/32, TNA.

23. *Times* (London), "Factory Accidents to Women Big Rise during the War, Sir W. Garrett's Report," October 8, 1942.

24. Cover letter and Report, "Womanpower Debate," March 3, 1942, LAB 79/32, TNA.

25. John Costello, *Virtue under Fire: How World War II Changed Our Social and Sexual Attitudes* (Boston: Little, Brown and Co., 1986), 156.

26. Women's Bureau, *Womanpower Committees*, 49.

27. The British Bombes were in part adapted from the Polish *Bomba* machines.

28. Smith, *Station X*, 175.

29. Recently, commemorative news articles and volumes of reminiscences have increasingly tried to revise the historical importance of these workers, but in order to remain legible to the larger reading public they must do so within the same general framework of existing wartime narratives that implicitly or explicitly position women's work as secondary and supplemental.

30. Copeland, *Colossus*, 161.

31. Workers at the Bletchley Park Historical site continue to research the shape of wartime intelligence operations there through soliciting personal accounts of various parts of the highly atomized organization.

32. According to the Bletchley Park Historical Trust exhibits at Bletchley Park.

33. Michael Smith, *The Secrets of Station X: How Bletchley Park Codebreakers Helped Win the War* (London: Biteback Publishing, 2011), 49.

34. Ibid.

35. "Bird" was—and is—a condescending term, similar in connotation to the American slang usage of "chick." As a result, "wrens" retains a familiar, slightly disrespectful connotation, analogous to the twentieth-century practice of referring to women as "girls." For that reason, I have referred to WRNS members by their formal appellation for the most part in the text, with the exception of direct quotations.

36. I. J. Good, D. Michie, and G. Timms, *General Report on Tunny with Emphasis on Statistical Methods*, 1945, 278, HW 25/5, General Report on Tunny, TNA.

37. Eleanor Ireland, interview by Janet Abbate for the IEEE History Center, April 23, 2001, The Institute of Electrical and Electronics Engineers, http://ethw.org/Oral-History:Eleanor_Ireland.

38. Good et al., *General Report on Tunny*, 276.

39. It was important for WRNS members to have "good social recommendations." Good et al., *General Report on Tunny*, 278.

40. Poland had earlier designed a type of codebreaking Bombe known as the *Bomba Kryptologiczna*, but changes to heighten the security of the German

Enigma code required the later British design to take a different approach. Only in late 1942 did the British share the design of the Bombe with the US Navy, allowing the Navy to design its own Bombes for decoding Enigma.

41. "Report on Enigma Decipherment," signed by A.D. Knox, P. F. G. Twinn, W. G. Welchman, A. M. Turing, and J. R. Jeffreys, November 1, 1939, HW 14/2, TNA.

42. For video and audio of a rebuilt Bombe in operation at Bletchley, see http://www.youtube.com/watch?v=ukOPgaAokoA#t=73.

43. German Lorenz SZ-40 and SZ-42 versions of encryption were in use for higher-level communications later in the war and were all broken with the aid of Colossus. B. Jack Copeland, "Colossus: Breaking the German 'Tunny' Code at Bletchley Park: An Illustrated History," *The Rutherford Journal* 3 (2010), http://www.rutherfordjournal.org/article030109.html.

44. Copeland, "Colossus."

45. For a discussion of Turing that takes into account the importance of his role in the history of technology via a queer analytical lens, see Jacob Gaboury's "A Queer History of Computing," February 19, 2013, http://rhizome.org/editorial/2013/feb/19/queer-computing-1.

46. The contraptions of American cartoonist Rube Goldberg are analogous. See, for example, Maynard Frank Wolfe, *Rube Goldberg: Inventions!* (New York: Simon and Schuster, 2011) compared with William Heath Robinson and Geoffrey Beare, *Heath Robinson Contraptions* (London: Duckworth Overlook, 2007).

47. The British named the codes they were trying to break after fish—hence Tunny, Sturgeon, and so on. The Tunny machine took its name from the code it was designed to break.

48. Copeland, *Colossus*, 162.

49. Eleanor Ireland, interview by Janet Abbate.

50. See, for example, Will Lissner, "Mechanical Brain Has Its Troubles" (December 14, 1947, *New York Times*, 49), which reports the ENIAC's useful uptime as only two hours per week, with the majority of the system's working time instead being spent on testing, troubleshooting, or other support activities.

51. British Telecom, "BT remembers Tommy Flowers' Achievements," http://home.bt.com/news/btlife/bt-remembers-tommy-flowers-achievements-11363857904783.

52. Estimates of the number of tubes in the original Colossus vary from 1,800 to 1,900, though Flowers himself recalls that it had 1,500 tubes. The machines that followed, like the Mark II Colossus, had closer to 2,400 tubes. T. H. Flowers, "The Design of Colossus," *Annals of the History of Computing* 5 (1983): 239–252.

53. Copeland, "Colossus." Copeland notes that Colossus was functioning successfully in Flowers's lab at the Dollis Hill Post Office Research Station in early December 1943, though it was not installed at Bletchley until January 1944.

54. One can get some sense of the noisiness of Colossus from the rebuilt replica at the National Museum of Computing at Bletchley Park. See http://marhicks.net/blog/?p=4 for video of the rebuilt Colossus in action.

55. Good et al., *General Report on Tunny*, 276.

56. Copeland, "Colossus."

57. Memo from N. W. Meyers to Colonel Gambier-Parry, May 1, 1942, HW 14/36, TNA.

58. Copeland, *Colossus*, 160, 163.

59. Ibid., 166.

60. Herbert, Memo from November 10, 1942, HW 14/57, TNA.

61. Mark Ward, "Museum Reunion for Colossus Computer Veterans" BBC News, September 22, 2014, http://www.bbc.com/news/technology-29311068; National Museum of the History of Computing, "Celebrating Colossus at 70," Milton Keynes, UK, February 10, 2014, http://www.tnmoc.org/news/notes-museum/picture-colossus-70.

62. "Bletchley Veteran Recalls Work on Colossus," BBC News Video, February 6, 2014, http://www.bbc.com/news/technology-26076085.

63. Good et al., *General Report on Tunny*, 30.

64. Copeland, *Colossus*, 163. Less flattering portraits of the WRNS recruits were often related in the memoirs of the lower-level cryptanalysts who sometimes worked alongside them. One recalled how he fell asleep while checking punched sheets. When he made a breakthrough shortly thereafter, he noted, "The young ladies were jealous"; see F. H. Hinsley and Alan Stripp, *Codebreakers: The Inside Story of Bletchley Park* (Oxford: Oxford University Press, 1993). His implication that even while napping he outclassed the WRNS recruits intellectually was not uncharacteristic of lower-level male cryptanalysts, who sought to separate themselves from the women workers. Another Bletchley story blames a Colossus operator, supposedly distracted while applying lipstick, for a machine room fire.

65. Churchill's statement is emblazoned on the pedestal of a bronze goose statue at the Bletchley Park historical site.

66. Copeland, *Colossus*, 267. One WRNS member, Helen Currie, recalls typing up this official history of Bletchley Park while still on site after VE Day, yet she did not write her own account until sixty years later. Her job had been to operate the Tunny decoders.

67. One biographer of the Bletchley Park cryptographers simply attributes this to what he described as the normal mode of operation in "those deeply sexist times." Copeland, *Colossus*, 159.

68. Good et al., *General Report on Tunny*, 278.

69. "STAFF: Hut 6" progress report, May 5, 1942, HW 14/36, TNA.

70. *Times* (London), "To Fathers of Boys," November 4, 1942.

71. RAF Section C.C. & C.S., "A.C.A.S.(I)," May 4, 1942, HW 14/36, TNA.

72. Good et al., *General Report on Tunny*, 279.

73. Copeland, *Colossus*, 162–163.

74. Good et al., *General Report on Tunny*, 278.

75. Interview with Rozanne Colchester by Robert McCrum, "Women Spies in the Second World War," *The Guardian*, November 6, 2010, http://www.guardian.co.uk/world/2010/nov/07/women-spies-second-world-war.

76. Good et al., *General Report on Tunny*, 278.

77. Ibid., 279.

78. Ibid.

79. Ibid., 278.

80. Copeland, *Colossus*, 160, 163.

81. "MOST SECRET: Non-Morse (Teleprinter) Transmissions" report, May 3, 1942, HW 14/36, TNA.

82. "ISK Section" memo to Cmdr. Travis, February 12, 1942, HW 14/28, TNA.

83. Until the declassification of the *General Report on Tunny* in the year 2000 by the British Government, much of the information about the work of the WRNS was lost, limited to scattered personal accounts.

84. Lorna Cockayne, interview by British Computer Society, http://www.bcs.org/upload/mp3/lorna-cockayne-enigma.mp3.

85. Copeland, *Colossus*, 161.

86. Eleanor Ireland, interview by Janet Abbate.

87. Copeland, *Colossus*, 161.

88. Ibid., 171–172.

89. Doreen Luke, *My Road to Bletchley Park* (Cleobury Mortimer, UK: M. & M. Baldwin, 2003).

90. Ibid.

91. Ibid.

92. Eleanor Ireland, interview by Janet Abbate.

93. Anne B. Godwin, "Chairman's Address, TUC Women's Congress," *Report of the Annual Conference of Representatives of Trade Unions Catering for Women Workers*, 1955, 20, GB0152 MSS.292/4/12/1–17, The Modern Records Center, University of Warwick (MRC).

94. For more on computing as a nexus connecting the British state and society, see Jon Agar's *The Government Machine: A Revolutionary History of the Computer* (Cambridge, MA: MIT Press, 2003).

95. Annie Burman, "Gendering Decryption—Decrypting Gender: The Gender Discourse of Labour at Bletchley Park 1939–1945," MA thesis, Uppsala University, 2013, http://uu.diva-portal.org/smash/get/diva2:625771/FULLTEXT01.pdf.

96. See, for example, a letter to the *Times* (London), "War Output: Use of Skilled Labor," January 6, 1942, for a representative view.

97. "Codebreaker," London Science Museum exhibit, London, UK, July 2012.

98. Visit by author to Bletchley Park Historical Site and National Computing Museum, Milton Keynes, UK, July 1, 2012.

99. Michael Clodfelter, *Warfare and Armed Conflicts: A Statistical Reference to Casualty and Other Figures, 1500–2000* (Jefferson, NC: McFarland, 2002), 583; and Central Statistical Office, *Statistical Digest of the War* (London: HMSO, 1951), 11, 37, 40.

100. *Times* (London), "Compensation for War Injury," January 8, 1943, 2.

101. This was not unusual, as trade unions had not suspended pay claim negotiations during the war either. Women's Bureau, *Womanpower Committees*, 49.

102. F. Bath, Memo to Mrs. Arnott, T 162/942, TNA.

103. Memo from Department Head to Mrs. Johnstone, March 11, 1947, T 162/942, TNA; Treasury, "National Whitley Council Committee on Structure of the Post-War Civil Service: Future Establishment of Temporary Staff," May 29, 1946, T 162/942, TNA.

104. Anne B. Godwin, "Chairman's Address, TUC Women's Congress."

105. Interview with Mary Coombs by Thomas Lean, British Library "Voices of Science" Oral History Collection, 2010, Part 1 of 9, http://sounds.bl.uk/Oral-history/Science/021M-C1379X0016XX-0001V0.

106. Ronald Whelan, "The Use of Hollerith Equipment in Bletchley Park," undated report c. 1995, HW 25/22, TNA, 31.

107. Ibid.

108. Sex Disqualification (Removal) Act, 9 & 10 Geo. 5, c. 71.

109. The government argued that although the act said that marriage did not preclude employment, it did not guarantee that married women would be allowed to keep their jobs. See Harold L. Smith, ed., *British Feminism in the Twentieth Century* (Amherst: University of Massachusetts Press, 1990), 52–53.

110. United Kingdom, *Parliamentary Debates*, Lords, 5th ser., vol. 152 (1922), cols. 1012–1036.

111. Civil Service National Whitley Council Committee, *The Marriage Bar in the Civil Service* (London: HMSO, 1946), 4.

112. Baroness Beatrice Nancy Seear, interview by Betty Scharf, February 1991, 8/NLS/4, WL. Seear also moved the first successful national equal pay bill in the House of Lords in 1972.

113. Civil Service National Whitley Council Committee, *The Marriage Bar*, 13.

114. Baroness Beatrice Nancy Seear, interview by Betty Scharf, February 1991, 8/NLS/4, WL.

115. Royal Commission on Equal Pay, *Report of the Royal Commission on Equal Pay, 1944–46* (London: HMSO, 1946), 119, quoting the Atkin Report, *Women in Industry* (London: War Cabinet Committee, 1919).

116. Royal Commission on Equal Pay, *Report of the Royal Commission on Equal Pay, 1944–46*, 118.

117. Enid Hutchison, interview by Betty Scharf, February 1991, 8/NLS/4, GB 0106 7/DME, Papers of Dorothy Elizabeth Evans, WL.

118. Marriage bars in the private sector continued, both formally and informally, for decades afterward. Barclay's Bank, a major employer in London, did not repeal its official marriage bar until 1963.

119. Enid Hutchison, interview by Betty Scharf.

120. Ibid.

121. Enid Hutchison, interview by Betty Scharf.

122. Civil Service National Whitley Council Committee, *The Marriage Bar*, 15.

123. Ibid., 4.

124. Ibid., 14.

125. Royal Commission on Equal Pay, *Report of the Royal Commission on Equal Pay, 1944–46*, quoting the *1929–1931 Commission on the Civil Service Report*, 9.

126. Civil Service National Whitley Council Committee, *The Marriage Bar*, 13.

127. Ibid.

128. Mavis Tate, MP, Equal Pay Campaign Pamphlet, "Equal Work Deserves Equal Pay," 1954.

129. TUC Women's Congress, *Report of the Annual Conference of Representatives of Trade Unions Catering for Women Workers*, 1953, 25, GB0152 MSS.292/4/12/1–17, Women Workers (Report of the Annual Conference of Representatives of Trade Unions Catering for Women Workers), 1953–1970, MRC.

130. Civil Service National Whitley Council Committee, *The Marriage Bar*, 14.

131. Alan Turing, *A.M. Turing's Original 1945 Proposal for the Development of an Electronic Computer, Reprinted with a Foreword by D.W. Davies, Superintendent of the Computer Science Division* (London: National Physical Laboratory, Division of Computer Science, 1972), 2.

132. David Mindell has discussed the historical construction of human–machine interaction and the legacy of earlier kinds of control and feedback mechanisms on modern machine operators in *Between Human and Machine: Feedback, Control, and Computing before Cybernetics* (Baltimore: Johns Hopkins University Press, 2002). Mindell argues that this history strongly influenced the current shape of control and feedback in computing; even where the technologies may seem discontinuous, similar mechanisms of control and abstractions of the problem of control remain and build upon one another.

133. Perhaps the clearest example of this is described by Fred Brooks in *The Mythical Man Month* (New York: Addison-Wesley, 1975) when he quips that the addition of more programmers to a late project will make it even later. Brooks's example shows both the impossibility of getting rid of the human brake (as long as technologies are user-centric) as well as the diminishing returns human intervention can create in complex systems.

134. Simon Lavington's study of Elliott-Automation argues that the company's fortunes and power in the marketplace, and in fact those of all British computing companies, were intertwined with the needs and hegemonic discourses of

the state. Lavington, *Moving Targets: Elliott-Automation and the Dawn of the Computer Age in Britain, 1947–67* (London: Springer, 2011).

135. For more on British computing as a nexus interconnecting state, society, and technology, see Agar, *The Government Machine.*

2 Peacetime Data Processing

1. Susan Pedersen's *Family, Dependence, and the Origins of the Welfare State: Britain and France, 1914–1945* (Cambridge: Cambridge University Press, 1993) discusses how these attitudes became institutionalized in state policy.

2. Civil Service Clerical Association, circular, "Statement of Case for the Revision of the Pay of the Clerical Class," 1950, GB0152 MSS.415/CPSA, Box 76, CSCA Circulars, 1961–1969, MRC. Major government committees and reports on productivity in industry and government from roughly 1946 to 1953 are too numerous to consider individually, but include the reports of the Anglo-American Council on Productivity (1947–52), the Committee on Industrial Productivity (1948–1950), the British Productivity Council (1952–1956), Committee on Industrial Productivity: Panel on Technology and Operational Research (1948–1950, T 222/409), and the European Productivity Committee (1953–1960).

3. Arbitration Awards of the Industrial Court, "Arbitration Tribunal Ruling on Clerical Assistants, Grade I, Established Typists and Shorthand Typists and Clerical Officers in the General Clerical Class: Extra Remuneration when performing duties of a higher post—Qualifying period," January 27, 1937, 4, 6/NCS, Box 279, Civil Service Cases, 1937–1940, WL.

4. Civil Service National Whitley Council Committee, *The Marriage Bar in the Civil Service* (London: HMSO, 1946), 15.

5. Ibid.

6. Ibid.

7. Foreign Office, Departmental Whitley Council Staff Side, *Annual Report 1953*, 1954, 1, Folder A7/1, 6/NCS, Box 279, NAWCS, General Reports for the years 1933–1958, WL.

8. Kelly BéruBé et al., "London Smogs: Why Did They Kill?," *Proceedings of the Royal Microscopical Society* 40, no. 3 (2005): 171–183.

9. Foreign Office, Departmental Whitley Council Staff Side, *Annual Report 1953*. Cheaper than ordinary house coal, "nutty slack" was available unrationed from the National Coal Board starting December 1, 1952. The Great Smog occurred less than a week later, from December 5 to December 9. *Times* (London), "National Coal Board: Nutty Slack Off the Ration (Advertisement)," November 25, 1952; *Times* (London), "Nutty Slack an Abomination," October 2, 1953; and *Times* (London), "Clean Air Act Urged by Beaver Committee," November 26, 1954.

10. Whitley Council, *Annual Report 1953*.

11. NAWCS, *Annual Report 1950*, 7, 6/NCS, Box 279, WL.

12. Foreign Office, Departmental Whitley Council Staff Side, *Annual Report 1954*, March 1955, 1, Folder A7/1, 6/NCS, Box 279, WL.

13. Royal Commission on Equal Pay, *Report of the Royal Commission on Equal Pay, 1944–46* (London: HMSO, 1946), 8. Before the rise caused by the war, women made up about a quarter of the Civil Service, and after the war surge their proportion stabilized at about a third of the workforce.

14. United Kingdom, *Parliamentary Debates*, Commons, 5th ser., vol. 524 (1954), cols. 1906–1907.

15. See Harold Smith, "The Problem of 'Equal Pay for Equal Work' in Great Britain during World War II," *Journal of Modern History* 53, no. 4 (1981): 652–672.

16. Financial Secretary to the Treasury, Great Britain, *Estimates for Civil Service for the Year Ending 31st March, 1948, Annual Report, 1946–47* (London: HMSO, 1946), iii.

17. United Kingdom, *Parliamentary Debates*, Commons, 5th ser., vol. 438 (1947), col. 1069–1075.

18. William Beveridge, *Social Insurance and Allied Services* (London: HMSO, 1942), Cmd. 6404, 122–125.

19. Council of Women Civil Servants, "Gradual Scheme for Equal Pay," August 14, 1947, 6/CCS, Box 258 Council of Women Civil Servants, WL; United Kingdom, *Parliamentary Debates*, Commons, 5th ser., vol. 524 (1954), col. 1916; and Letter from Conservative Candidates, 1951, 6/NCS, Box 258 Parliamentary Elections, WL. For more on the groundnut scheme, see Alan Wood, *The Groundnut Affair* (London: The Bodley Head, 1950); Minister of Food and Secretary of State for the Colonies, *The Future of the Overseas Food Corporation* (London: HMSO, 1951), Cmnd. 8125; and Minister of Food, *Report on a Plan for the Mechanized Production of Groundnuts in East and Central Africa (Groundnuts Scheme)* (London: HMSO, 1946–1947), Cmd. 7030.

20. *Office Machinery*, July 1958, 555.

21. For the earlier history of this change, see Meta Zimmeck, "Jobs for the Girls: The Expansion of Clerical Work for Women, 1850–1914," in *Unequal Opportunities: Women's Employment in England, 1850–1914*, ed. Angela V. John (New York: Blackwell, 1986).

22. C. Morgan, "The Powers Girl," *Vickers News*, January 1951, 2.

23. "For Programming Plugboards," *Office Magazine*, April 1960, 363.

24. Punched cards were divided into forty-five to eighty columns of twelve rows, each column representing one character. Eighty column cards were based on the IBM standard introduced in 1928, which continued to be used in the age of electronic computing. Famously, IBM's business selling cards accounted for roughly a fifth of its revenue and 30 percent of its bottom line in the 1950s. IBM100 Corporate History, "The IBM Punched Card," http://www-03.ibm.com/ibm/history/ibm100/us/en/icons/punchcard.

25. L. J. Comrie, Superintendent of HM Nautical Almanac Office, *The Hollerith and Powers Tabulating Machines, Based on a Lecture Delivered to the Office*

Machinery User's Association of the London School of Economics and Lectures Delivered at University College London (Edinburgh: Neill and Company, 1933). Printed for private circulation, BL, 12.

26. *Office Machinery*, July 1958, 555.

27. Personnel Dept. General Post Office, Letter Savings Department, "Enquiry from Headquarters about Experience with Open Competition Clerical Assistants as Machine Operators," March 15, 1945, NSC 22/68, TNA.

28. Letter from Mr. Ramsey to Miss Hudson, March 22, 1945, NSC 22/68, TNA.

29. Personnel Dept. General Post Office, Letter Savings Department, "Enquiry from Headquarters."

30. Letter from Mr. Ramsey to Miss Hudson.

31. For more on the skills required for machine-aided calculation work in the pre-electronic era, see David Alan Grier, *When Computers Were Human* (Princeton, NJ: Princeton University Press, 2006).

32. Letter from Miss Hudson to Mr. Shaw, March 26, 1945, NSC 22/68, TNA.

33. Ibid.

34. Letter from Mr. Ramsey to Miss Hudson.

35. Post Office Savings Dept., Memo, April 17, 1945, NSC 22/68, TNA.

36. Treasury, "Establishments Circular No. 19/54: Establishment of Machine Operators," April 21, 1954, STAT 14/632, TNA.

37. Statistical Office Minutes, "Establishment of Machine Operators," October 19, 1950, STAT 14/632, Machine Operating Class in Stationery Office, Establishment of Machine Operators, TNA.

38. TUC Women's Congress, *Report of the Annual Conference of Representatives of Trade Unions Catering for Women Workers*, 1953, 10, GB0152 MSS.292/4/12/1–17, MRC.

39. So prevalent was domestic service work in women's range of career options that the Women's Congress of the TUC believed that "raising the status of the domestic worker meant raising women's status in general." Attempts to raise the status of machine work were similarly attempts to raise the status of women in general. TUC Women's Congress, *Report of the Annual Conference*, 1953, 10–16, GB0152 MSS.292/4/12/1–17, MRC.

40. TUC Women's Congress, *Report of the Annual Conference*, 24.

41. Royal Commission on the Civil Service, *Report of the Royal Commission on the Civil Service, 1953–55* (London: HMSO, 1955), 3, 10. For population numbers in 1951, see the UK Office for National Statistics, http://www.ons.gov.uk/ons/interactive/historic-uk-population-pyramid/index.html.

42. Civil Service National Whitley Council Committee, *The Marriage Bar*, 4.

43. L. H. H. Thompson, Treasury, "Establishment Officers Circular No. 1/48: Introduction of a Machine Operator Class," January 2, 1948, OS 1/656, Duplicator Operators and Machine Operators (Clerical), 1943–1956, TNA.

44. Civil Service National Whitley Council Committee, *The Marriage Bar*, 15.

45. F. Bath, Memo to Mrs. Arnott, "Future Establishment of Temporary Staff," January 29, 1947, T 162/942, Establishment of Temporary Staff in Professional Scientific and Technical Classes, TNA.

46. Clerical staff switched onto machine operation work gained extra pay for attaining proficiency on certain machines but lost promotion prospects, making the benefit of changing job categories short term. Post Office, "Machines and Machine Operators in the PTO," 1917–1954, PT 1/102 Machines and Machine Operators including Mechanisation in PTO, TNA.

47. Typing was perhaps the most iconic women's job during this period. In 1951, roughly thirty thousand women worked in this expanding job class. The typing grades did not hire men and held no opportunity for promotion or pay increase after the age of twenty-eight; it was still assumed that women would voluntarily leave the workforce around that age and that if she returned to work later she would not need a good wage since she would be dependent on a husband. Equal Pay Clippings Folder, 3, 10, 6/CCS, Box 258, WL.

48. Treasury, Circular to All Civil Service Departments, "Establishment Officers Circular No. 1/48, Special Measures for Establishment of Machine Operators," January 2, 1948, OS 1/656, Duplicator Operators, and Machine Operators (Clerical), TNA.

49. Ibid.

50. The CSCA formed in 1921 and was affiliated with the national Trades Union Congress (TUC) until the government forced state employees to disaffiliate from the TUC in 1927. It once again affiliated with the TUC in 1946. In 1969, the CSCA changed its name to the Civil and Public Services Association (commonly known as the CPSA).

51. *NAWCS Annual Report*, 1948, 3; Meeting Minutes, December 16, 1935, 6/NCS, Box 279, Folder A6/1, WL.

52. The CSCA went so far as to reprint a letter from Treasury executives stating that the Treasury was prepared to negotiate with the CSCA as well as the NAWCS, yet the CSCA somehow drew the opposite conclusion from the text, using it to confirm its claim to closed-shop negotiations. Civil Service Clerical Associations (CSCA), "Who Did the Job?," 6/NCS NAWCS, Box 282, WL.

53. Royal Commission on Equal Pay, *Report of the Royal Commission on Equal Pay, 1944–46*, paragraphs 142, 224–228; United Kingdom, *Parliamentary Debates*, Commons, 5th ser., vol. 438 (1947), cols. 1069–1075; Council of Women Civil Servants, "Notes on 'The Rate for the Job'," 6/CCS, Box 258, Folder: Correspondence between Equal Pay Campaign Committee and Council of Women Civil Servants, 1948–1956, WL.

54. Anne B. Godwin, "Chairman's Address, TUC Women's Congress," *Report of the Annual Conference of Representatives of Trade Unions Catering for Women Workers*, 1955, 20, GB0152 MSS.292/4/12/1–17, MRC.

55. P. D. Proctor, Staff Memo, April 6, 1939, T 162/942, TNA.

56. Ministry of Information, "Comparison between the Work of Teleprinter Operators and Typists," c. 1940, T 162/942, TNA. Men were also seen as more

useful if overnight shifts were required. P. D. Proctor, Staff Memo, April 6, 1939, T 162/942, TNA.

57. Treasury, Memorandum to Mr. Pike-Lees, December 31, 1941, T 162/942, TNA.

58. Department Head, Spheroidal Trigonometry Division Minutes, May 29, 1951, OS 1/656, TNA.

59. Ibid.

60. See, for example, Barbara Reskin and Patricia Roos, eds., *Job Queues, Gender Queues: Explaining Women's Inroads into Male Occupations* (Philadelphia: Temple University Press, 1990).

61. Ordnance Survey Departmental Minutes, July 10, 1951, OS 1/656, TNA.

62. Ordnance Survey Departmental Minutes, May 25, 1951, OS 1/656, TNA.

63. F. G. C. Bentley in the Ordnance Survey, Letter to Treasury, February 16, 1948, OS 1/656, TNA.

64. Response to F. G. C. Bentley, from Rhodes in Treasury, March 8, 1948, OS 1/656, TNA.

65. Department Head, Spheroidal Trigonometry Division Minutes, OS 1/656, TNA.

66. The government files supporting this point are too numerous to mention. Emblematic files containing language on the makeup of the grade throughout the 1950s and 1960s include T 215/1595–1599; NSC 22/68, Clerical Assistant Grade; BA 22/319, Pay and Costing Implications of Machine Operator Grading 1970; AIR 77/384, Recruitment and Retention of Machine Operators; and AN 171/398–399, Equal Pay, Equal Work: Shorthand Typists and Machine Operators, TNA.

67. Ordnance Survey Departmental Minutes, September 9, 1949, OS 1/656, TNA.

68. Ordnance Survey Departmental Minutes, August 21, 1952, OS 1/656, TNA.

69. TUC Women's Congress, *Report of the Annual Conference*, 1953, 1, 10–13, GB0152 MSS.292/4/12/1–17, MRC.

70. Royal Commission on Equal Pay, *Report of the Royal Commission on Equal Pay, 1944–46*, paragraphs 142, 224–228; United Kingdom, *Parliamentary Debates*, Commons, 5th ser., vol. 438 (1947), cols. 1069–1075; Council of Women Civil Servants, "Notes on 'The Rate for the Job,'" 6/CCS, Box 258, Folder: Correspondence Between Equal Pay Campaign Committee and Council of Women Civil Servants, 1948–1956, WL.

71. Staff Side National Whitley Council Representative, Question in Circular C.R. 14589, and letter from CSCA to Ordnance Survey "Senior Machine Operators—Female Supervisor," March 6, 1953, OS 1/656, TNA.

72. Ordnance Survey, "Circular EOC 69/48," October 1948, OS 1/656, TNA.

73. Treasury, "Establishments Circular 21/58 Revised Salary Scales," August 28, 1953, OS 1/656, TNA.

74. OS 1/656, TNA.

75. Ibid.

76. Ibid.

77. *National Association of Women Civil Servants (NAWCS) Annual Report*, 1948, 11–12, 6/NCS, Boxes 279–282: NAWCS General Reports for the years 1933–1958, WL.

78. "Pay Scales for Machine Operators (Calculators, Accounting, and Punched Card Machines) 1951," OS 1/656, TNA.

79. Ibid.

80. NAWCS, "Pamphlet for Machine Operators," 1950, 6/NCS, Box 282 Pamphlets Folder, WL.

81. CSCA, "Who Did the Job?"

82. CSCA, "Senior Machine Operators-Female Supervisor," March 6, 1953, OS 1/656, TNA.

83. *NAWCS Annual Report*, 1957, 11, 6/NCS, Boxes 279–282, WL.

84. Ibid.

85. M. E. Drummond, "The Computer at Play," *Office Magazine*, June 1958, 546.

86. *Tabacus: The Company Magazine of the British Tabulating Company*, January 1957, 13.

87. Women's Trades Union Congress, *Women Workers, Proceedings of 1960 meeting at Hastings*, 21–22, GB0152 MSS.292/4/12/pieces 1–17, Women Workers (Report of the Annual Conference of Representatives of Trade Unions Catering for Women Workers), 1953–1970, MRC.

88. TUC, "Confidential Memo: Technological Developments Including Automation," July 19, 1962, GB0152 MSS.292B/571.82/1, Automation: Trade Unions' Attitudes 1961–1970, MRC.

89. Select Committee on Science and Technology, *Report on Session 1969–1970*, Vol. 1 (London, HMSO, 1971), 451.

90. The government recorded its first dedicated administrative computer as being installed in the London Post Office in September 1958. Of the administrative computers that followed in the next five years, 64 percent were ICTs, 12 percent were LEOs, and 24 percent were IBMs, according to an internal 1968 government report. This report seems to have left out some computers, however; their numbers were implied by later reports. Central Computing Agency, "Schedule 1A: Computers for Administrative Purposes, Installed in Departments up to 30 December 1968," October 22, 1968, HN 1/67, Consultations with Civil Service Staff Associations about ADP, TNA.

91. Select Committee on Science and Technology, Session 1969–1970, *UK Computer Industry, Vol. 1, Minutes of Evidence* (London: HMSO, 1970), 457.

92. Ibid., 451.

93. "Data Processing—with or without Computers," *Office Magazine*, December 1958, 1010.

94. Royal Commission on Equal Pay, *Report of the Royal Commission on Equal Pay, 1944–46*, 117.

95. United Kingdom, *Parliamentary Debates*, Commons, 5th ser., vol. 489 (1951), cols. 527–528.

96. United Kingdom, *Parliamentary Debates*, Commons, 5th ser., vol. 438 (1947), col. 1070.

97. Treasury, "Minutes of Evidence, 20th April 1945," reprinted in the pamphlet "Equal Pay" by Elaine Burton, 10, 6/EPC, Box 261, Evidence Given Before the Royal Commission on Equal Pay by the NAWCS, WL.

98. Communist Party of Great Britain, "Equal Pay for Equal Work: The Price of This Pamphlet Is the Same for Men or Women!" 1944, 6/EPC, Box 262, Equal Pay Campaign and Evidence to the Equal Pay Commission, WL.

99. Royal Commission on Equal Pay, *Report of the Royal Commission on Equal Pay, 1944–46*, 122, 125.

100. Ibid.

101. Ibid., 216.

102. Interview with Mary Coombs by Thomas Lean, British Library "Voices of Science" Oral History Collection, 2010, Part 1 of 9, http://sounds.bl.uk/Oral-history/Science/021M-C1379X0016XX-0001V0.

103. For an extended discussion of this issue, see Pedersen, *Family, Dependence, and the Origins of the Welfare State*.

104. Beveridge, *Social Insurance*, 122–125. The chart on page 123 refers to "housewives" as including married women who are gainfully employed, yet does not include these 1.4 million women in either the "gainfully employed" or the "otherwise employed" categories of analysis, highlighting that married women had always previously received benefits through their husbands. In the new system of social services, they were covered under the "Housewives Policy" and were not considered to be "persons depending for their maintenance upon remuneration received under a contract of service."

105. Equal Pay Clippings Folder, 6/CCS, Box 258, Council of Women Civil Servants, WL.

106. Royal Commission on the Civil Service, *Report of the Royal Commission on the Civil Service, 1953–55*, 93, 115, 123–124.

107. Ibid., Appendix IV, 209, 208, 210, 207–220.

108. Civil Service National Whitley Council Committee, *The Marriage Bar*, 14–15.

109. Department of Scientific and Industrial Research, *Money for Effort: Report on Problems of Progress in Industry* (London: HMSO, 1961), 21.

110. Cathy Gillespie and Ann Sayce (government computer operators), interview by the author, January 5, 2006, London.

111. Treasury, "National Whitley Council Committee on Structure of the Post-War Civil Service: Future Establishment of Temporary Staff" and "Comparison

between the Work of Teleprinter Operators and Typists," May 29, 1946, T 162/942, TNA.

112. Royal Commission on the Civil Service, *Report of the Royal Commission on the Civil Service, 1953–55*, 152.

113. See Jon Agar, *The Government Machine: A Revolutionary History of the Computer* (Cambridge, MA: MIT Press, 2003) for an extended discussion of this metaphor.

114. Stephanie Shirley, with Richard Askwith, *Let IT Go: The Story of the Entrepreneur Turned Ardent Philanthropist* (Luton, UK: AUK Limited, 2012).

115. NAWCS, *Annual Report*, 1950, 4, 6/NCS, Boxes 279–282, WL.

116. *To Be a Woman*, directed by Jill Craigie (n.p.: Outlook Films, 1951). Joan Wallach Scott's work on the glassmaking industry in nineteenth-century France discusses an earlier instance of deskilling in this field. Scott, *The Glassworkers of Carmaux: French Craftsmen and Political Action in a Nineteenth-Century City* (Cambridge, MA: Harvard University Press, 1974).

117. The Universal Declaration of Human Rights adopted by the UN General Assembly on December 10, 1948, stated in Article 23 that "everyone, without any discrimination, has the right to equal pay for equal work."

118. United Kingdom, *Parliamentary Debates*, Commons, 5th ser., vol. 438 (1947), cols. 1069–1070.

119. The Sex Disqualification (Removal) Act of 1919 was intended to remove the bar against women from holding certain government jobs, but it was rendered toothless through narrow interpretation. Federation of Women Civil Servants, "Statement of Case presented to the Royal Commission on the Civil Service," June 1930, 6/JCS/C4, Joint Committee on Women in the Civil Service, 1919–1954, WL.

120. Royal Commission on the Civil Service, *Report of the Royal Commission on the Civil Service, 1953–55*, 11.

121. Ibid., vol. 489 (1951), cols. 527–528.

122. Ibid., vol. 524 (1954), col. 1913.

123. Ibid., cols. 1903–1904.

124. Labour MPs moved a bill for equal pay in March 1954. This lit a fire under the Conservative government to act on the issue. Rather than debate and potentially pass Labour's bill, the Conservative government entered into talks with the staff via the National Whitley Council to negotiate (limited) implementation of equal wages. See Harold Smith, "The Politics of Conservative Reform: The *Equal Pay* for Equal Work Issue, 1945–1955," *The Historical Journal* 35, no. 2 (June 1992): 401–415.

125. NAWCS, *Annual Report*, 1956, 1, 6/NCS, Boxes 279–282, WL.

126. Royal Commission on Equal Pay, *Report of the Royal Commission on Equal Pay, 1944–46*, 9.

127. Letter from J. J. S. Shaw to G. F. Green, November 17, 1958, T 215/1595, CSA: Typists and Machine Operators' Survey 1956–1958, TNA.

128. British Transport Commission, Memorandum of Meetings of Railways Staff Conference, December 5, 1957, and February 14, 1958, 4, RAIL 1172/2467, Rates of Pay—Machine Operators, TNA.

129. This file shows women's machine operator pay scales as roughly 10 percent lower than men's machine operator pay scales in 1957. Twentieth Supplement to Establishments Circular No 27/56, May 13, 1957, CAOG 16/213, Pay, Machine Operator Grades, TNA.

130. Treasury, Memorandum "Equal Pay: Excluded Grade Posts," August 17, 1960, AN 171/398, TNA.

131. British Transport Commission, Memorandum, RAIL 1172/2467, TNA.

132. Aeronautical Research Council, *Training and Careers for Computers*, 1955, 2, DSIR 23/23112, TNA.

133. Select Committee on Science and Technology, Session 1969–1970, *UK Computer Industry, Vol. 1, Minutes of Evidence,* 451.

134. By way of comparison, it might be said that the cultural impact and reach of Lyons Teashops in this period was akin to that of Starbucks coffee shops in contemporary America. Lyons shops were not only ubiquitous but also an important part of city culture where people went to sit and linger.

135. See David Caminer, John Aris, Peter Hermon, and Frank William Land, *LEO: The Incredible Story of the World's First Business Computer* (New York: McGraw Hill, 1998); and Georgina Ferry, *A Computer Called LEO: Lyons Teashops and the World's First Office Computer* (London: Fourth Estate, 2003).

136. See David T. Caminer, "... And How to Avoid Them," *The Computer Journal* 1, no. 1 (1958); and J. R. M. Simmons, *LEO and the Managers: A Theory of Management Organization* (London: MacDonald, 1962).

137. M. A. Wright, "Study of Use of Computers for Clerical Work: A Report on Visit to US," 1956, T 222/773, National Physical Laboratory, TNA.

138. Electrodatia, "Computer at Play," *Office Magazine*, June 1958, 467.

139. Agar, *The Government Machine*. Agar, however, does not see gender as a critical component of this machine.

140. Treasury, Internal Letter, February 17, 1954, T 222/964, Possible Use of Computers for Electronic Payroll Work 1954–1958, TNA.

141. Ibid.

142. Anne B. Godwin, "Chairman's Address," 1955, 21–22, GB0152 MSS.292/4/12/1–17, MRC.

3 Luck and Labor Shortage

1. *Times* (London), "Britain Must Lead the Computer Race: Mr. Wilson's Warning," July 17, 1965, 4.

2. Ibid.

3. Tudor Jones, *Remaking the Labour Party: From Gaitskell to Blair* (New York: Routledge, 1996), 77–80.

4. J. Cowie, J. W. Hermann, and P. D. Maycock, "The British Computer Scene, Part I: The Government Impact on the Computer Scene" (London: Office of Naval Research, 1967), 13.

5. During the Conservative Party's control of the country from 1951 to 1964, the government outlined, but mostly failed to institute, modernization agendas focused on greater government direction and control of high technology. Once returned to power, the Labour Party quipped that these were "thirteen wasted years," but in fact both parties believed there was a need to support science and technology for much-needed modernization—and both backed the idea that direct state intervention was a critical tool in this endeavor.

6. Philip Ziegler, *Wilson: The Authorized Life of Lord Wilson of Rievaulx* (London: Weidenfeld and Nicolson, 1993), 143.

7. Initially, Frank Cousins (general secretary of the Transport and General Workers' Union) was appointed minister of technology, but his views did not match Wilson's vision, and he resigned in 1966. Tony Benn succeeded him and built MinTech into an important force in the national conversation on technology and economic revival.

8. *Times* (London), "Computer Production and Installation in U.K.," October 4, 1960.

9. Select Committee on Science and Technology, Session 1969–1970, *UK Computer Industry, Vol. 1, Minutes of Evidence* (London: HMSO, 1970), 457.

10. As Jon Agar has argued, this process ultimately led to a replacement of many levels of civil servants by machine, but the process was slow and uneven. Agar, *The Government Machine: A Revolutionary History of the Computer* (Cambridge, MA: MIT Press, 2003).

11. For a full-length study of the Lyons computing project that became LEO Computers, see Georgina Ferry, *A Computer Called LEO: Lyons Teashops and the World's First Office Computer* (London: Fourth Estate, 2003).

12. Lyons made a handshake agreement with the Cambridge team under Maurice Wilkes. In exchange for a payment of a mere £3,000 to the Cambridge team, the agreement would allow Lyons to build its own copy of the EDSAC if it worked. The EDSAC ran its first successful program in 1949, and Lyons began reenvisioning the machine and adapting it to business use soon after. Wilkes was an intellectual successor of the ENIAC and EDVAC projects, to which he had been exposed through brief study in the United States.

13. LEO Computers, "The Scope for Electronic Computers in the Office: Reprint of a Paper Submitted to the Office Management Association," May 1955, 3, NAHC/LEO/D1–7, LEO Press Clippings, NAHCM.

14. Interview with Lucy Slater by Janet Abbate, "Anecdotes: How Did You First Get into Computing?," ed. Anne Fitzpatrick, *IEEE Annals of the History of Computing* 25, no. 4 (2003): 78.

15. Interview with Mary Coombs by Thomas Lean, British Library "Voices of Science" Oral History Collection, 2010, Part 1 of 9, http://sounds.bl.uk/Oral-history/Science/021M-C1379X0016XX-0001V0.

16. Colin Hobson (employee of LEO Computers), e-mail interview by the author, December 18, 2005, London.

17. *Times* (London), "Electronic Computer Demonstrated Drum Capable of Storing 250,000 Digits," February 18, 1955; *Times* (London), "Computer Process for Insurance Work (Business and Finance)," March 2, 1959; *Times* (London), "EMIDEC Computer for Sainsburys," May 12, 1959; *Times* (London), "190,000 Computer for Air Ministry Pay," August 6, 1959; *Times* (London), "It's Quicker By Computer: 'Leo' Works Out Rail Distances," June 24, 1957; *Times* (London), "Assurance Companies Share Computer," April 18, 1960; *Times* (London), "'Eric' Joins L.C.C. Computer Will Cost £30,000 to Install," April 13, 1960 (the organization rented the computer for £60,000 per year, but claimed it only cost £30,000 per year because of the money it would save); *Times* (London), "Computer Production and Installation in U.K.," October 4, 1960.

18. The government recorded its first dedicated administrative computer as the ICT 1201, installed in the London Post Office in September 1958, though ICT wasn't officially created from the merger of BTM and Powers-Samas until 1959. Of the administrative computers that followed in the next five years, 64 percent were ICT, 12 percent were LEO, and 24 percent were IBM. Central Computing Agency, "Schedule 1A: Computers for Administrative Purposes, Installed in Departments up to 30 December 1968," October 22, 1968, HN 1/67, TNA.

19. *Times* (London), "The Computer that Failed: Workers Go Home Without Wages," April 11, 1959.

20. *Times* (London), "Boots New Computor at Nottingham," October 7, 1960.

21. Hobson, interview by the author.

22. Ibid.

23. "Installation Problem," *Tabacus: The Magazine of the British Tabulating Company*, March 1957, 5.

24. *Report by a Committee of Enquiry on Health, Welfare, and Safety in Non-Industrial Employment and Hours of Employment for Juveniles (Health, Welfare and Safety)*, Cmnd. 7664 (1948–1949).

25. For example, Bill to make further and better provisions for health, welfare and safety in offices and for purposes connected therewith, 1959–1960 (80) iii.35; and Bill to provide for securing the safety, health and welfare of persons employed in offices and for purposes connected therewith (Offices Regulation), 1957–1958 (29) iii.83.

26. *Office Magazine*, February 1960, 161. For a snapshot of the pollution crisis in London during this period, see Peter Thorsheim, "Interpreting the London Fog Disaster of 1952," in *Smoke and Mirrors: The Politics and Culture of Air Pollution*, ed. E. Melanie Dupuis (New York University Press, 2004). Between

two thousand and four thousand people are estimated to have died from respiratory ailments as a result of the week-long smog.

27. *Times* (London), "Electronic Computer Exhibition," October 14, 1958.

28. *Times* (London), "Electronic Computer Demonstrated Drum."

29. *Times* (London), "£190,000 Computer for Air Ministry Pay"; *Times* (London), "£350,000 Computer System for Lloyds Bank," July 27, 1960.

30. Treasury, Memorandum from Lees to Donaldson, October 26, 1965, STAT 14/3093, Treasury Investigations: Combined Tabulating Installation; Automatic Data Processing (ADP) Bureau Service 1964–1967, TNA.

31. *Times* (London), "Hollerith Computer Centre," October 1, 1958.

32. Treasury, "Provision of Computer Facilities for Treasury, 1965–1968," T 199/1090, Provision of Computer Facilities for Treasury 1965–1968, TNA.

33. *Report of the Ministry of Pensions and National Insurance for the Year 1960*, Cmnd. 1458 (1960–1961), 75.

34. Ibid., 118; *Times* (London), "Largest Computer for Pensions," August 18, 1961.

35. *Report of the Ministry of Pensions and National Insurance for the Year 1960*, Cmnd. 1458 (1960–1961), 75, 41.

36. Ibid., 118.

37. Select Committee on Science and Technology, Session 1969–1970, *UK Computer Industry, Vol. 1, Minutes of Evidence,* 446.

38. *Times* (London), "Computer Growth in Western Europe," June 2, 1965.

39. Ibid.

40. *Times* (London), "Computors May Fill Nine Percent of All Office Posts by 1975," December 16, 1965.

41. "The Neuter Computer," *Office Magazine*, January 1960, 47.

42. Office of Population Censuses and Surveys, *Census 1961, Great Britain, Summary Tables* (London: HMSO, 1966), 64, 67. The exact figures are 7,781,850 for total female workforce and 2,694,800 for women whose primary census designation was clerical work. The latter figure does not include all office machine operators or clerks, whose numbers were partially recorded within different census job groups. Only those not subsumed in other census categories have been included. This leaves out up to 750,000 female clerical workers.

43. "Practical Economics of the EMP," *Powers Magazine*, May 1955, 7.

44. "To Train or Not to Train?," *Office Methods and Machines*, September 1967, 15–17, T 222/1314, TNA.

45. Ministry of Labour, *Statistics on Incomes, Prices, Employment, and Production*, no. 19 (London: HMSO, December 1966), 4–5.

46. J. B. Archer, "The Office Manager's Guide to Greater Efficiency at Lower Cost, Part 6: Staff Problems, Interviews, Wages," *Office Magazine*, December 1965, 1020.

47. The one exception was Ferranti Computers, which showed men operators in their advertising as often as women. Ferranti aimed at a slightly different, niche market—the scientific and engineering market, rather than the broader business or administrative computing market. Most companies' ads featured workers, or worker stand-ins, who resembled ones the target business audience would feel most comfortable hiring. For more general calculation and data-processing applications, like payroll, billing, and administrative programs, these were women.

48. "EE-LEO brochure for LECTOR System," NAHC/LEO/D2, NAHCM; *ICT Data Processing Journal*, February 1963, 15.

49. ICT, "Progress in the North," advertising brochure, 1962, NAHC/ICT/C96, ICL Advertisements, NAHCM.

50. "To Train or Not to Train?," *Office Methods and Machines*, September 1967, 15–17, T 222/1314, TNA.

51. "Powers-Samas Service Bureau in Delhi," *Powers Magazine*, July 1955, 4.

52. For more on the influence of foreign companies on India and India's influence on American and British computing, see Ross Bassett, *The Technological Indian* (Cambridge, MA: Harvard University Press 2016).

53. "Powers-Samas Service Bureau in Delhi," *Powers Magazine*, July 1955, 6. For more on the export of British social mores into high-technology sectors in previously colonized nations, see Carla Freeman, *High Tech and High Heels in the Global Economy: Women, Work and Pink-Collar Identities in the Caribbean* (Durham, NC: Duke University Press, 1999).

54. "Powers-Samas in the Sudan and India," *The Powers Magazine*, March 1954, 11.

55. *ICT Data Processing Journal*, no. 12, 21 (1962) and no. 11, 23 (1961).

56. "ICT in India," *ICT Magazine*, no. 9 (1961): 28–29.

57. Ibid.

58. Ross Bassett, "Aligning India in the Cold War Era: Indian Technical Elites, the Indian Institute of Technology at Kanpur, and Computing in India and the United States," *Technology and Culture* 50, no. 4 (October 2009): 783–810. See also Ramesh Subramanian's work on culturally specific design in early Indian computing. Subramanian, "Technology Policy and National Identity: The Microcomputer Comes to India," *IEEE Annals of the History of Computing* 36, no. 3 (July–September 2014): 19–29.

59. Joseph M. Grieco, *Between Dependency and Autonomy: India's Experience with the International Computer Industry* (Berkeley: University of California Press, 1984), 25–27.

60. Edward Said's landmark work, *Orientalism* (New York: Pantheon Books, 1978), describes the dynamics by which cultural (mis)representations become part and parcel of imperial dominance.

61. "HOT Stuff in GOSO," *ICL Marketing*, February 6, 1970, front page. Statistics compiled by Joseph Grieco in *Between Dependence and Autonomy* (table, page 26) suggest this figure may have been much lower.

62. For instance, see the Queen inspecting an automatic punch at the opening of ICT's new factory in Castlereagh. *ICT Magazine*, no. 9 (1961): 9.

63. Advertisement for ICL Baric Remote Computing Service, *ICL News*, September 1970, 3.

64. Advertisement for SUSIE computer, *Office Methods and Machines*, September 1967, 33.

65. *Office Methods and Machines Magazine*, September 1967, 33; *ICL Computers International*, September 1970, 3.

66. Centre for Computing History (Cambridge, UK) online collection, http://www.computinghistory.org.uk/det/22364/BCL-Susie-V-Programming-Manual.

67. Interview with Dame Stephanie Shirley by Janet Abbate, "Anecdotes: How Did You First Get into Computing?," ed. Anne Fitzpatrick, *IEEE Annals of the History of Computing* 25, no. 4 (2003): 79–80.

68. *ICT House Magazine*, September 1964, 8.

69. *ICL News*, November 1970, front page.

70. Hobson, interview by the author.

71. Hobson, interview by the author. Hobson genuinely recalled seeing bicycle chains on ICT products; it is possible he saw chains that looked similar to bike chains on peripherals such as printers. Other people working in that era recall "bike chains" on the IBM 1403 line printer, which used a chain to move the typefaces. John Smith, "Reminiscences of the IBM 1401," *Resurrection: The Bulletin of the Computer Conservation Society*, no. 51 (Summer 2010), http://www.cs.man.ac.uk/CCS/res/res51.htm.

72. LEO III was transistor based.

73. As opposed to low-level programming languages; see note 82. Intercode was a subset of Autocode, a language designed to program the Ferranti-Manchester Mark I.

74. Hobson, interview by the author.

75. Ann Sayce (government computer operator), interview by the author, January 5, 2006, London.

76. LEO bureau operators like Hobson, often regarded as elite among operators, were given formal training in programming in addition to operator training. The innate skill of bureau operators before such training, however, was no different from any other group of operators. Hobson recalled that in the close-knit, all-male operator environment of the bureau, "it was like a big adventure in which we were all, down to the guys that made the tea, involved. Indeed, a man who was employed to do fetching and carrying (there was a lot of paper to move!) started to show interest in what we were doing so the operators trained him up, pushed him into the next selection test and he ended up working on my shift." Hobson, interview by the author.

77. David Forward, "My Recollections of LEO at Shell-Mex and BP," collected by Peter Bird, NAHC/LEO III/6, NAHCM.

78. Hobson, interview by the author. Hobson also recalled one female punch operator with a similar promotion story: She was able to make the leap from punching to becoming a data assembly clerk, which entailed controlling work going to the operators, scheduling work with commercial customers and Lyons's own departments, and ensuring that the correct new data was associated with the data that had been carried forward. She was also responsible for scheduling nonregular work. Although women were shut out of operation work at LEO, the relatively important and responsible position that this punch operator was able to attain showed that gendered promotion structures at LEO were more fluid than the makeup of their operator workforce might lead one to assume.

79. Hobson, interview by the author.

80. Interview with Mary Lee Berners-Lee by Janet Abbate, "Anecdotes: How Did You First Get into Computing?," ed. Anne Fitzpatrick, *IEEE Annals of the History of Computing* 25, no. 4 (2003): 78–79. Mary Lee Berners-Lee is also the mother of Tim Berners-Lee, inventor of the World Wide Web.

81. *Evening Standard*, "Know Nothing about Computers?," staff wanted ad, July 21 and 23, 1965.

82. *Low-level programming* refers to programs written directly in the machine code of the system they are intended to run on or in an assembler language. As such, low-level programs are close in symbolic representation to the structure of the machine. In addition, operators sometimes had to correct programs by directly editing their binary representation on punch cards. High-level programming languages abstract away many of the hardware details of the machine, allowing for more portable and reusable programs.

83. Under the General Certificate of Education rubric—the main method of grading secondary-level student educational achievement in the United Kingdom at the time—students who did not achieve A levels could be awarded the lower O-level qualification instead.

84. Cathy Gillespie and Ann Sayce (government computer operators), interview by the author, January 5. 2006, London.

85. Pension plans, when mentioned in an advertisement seeking young employees, were almost exclusively targeted toward young men. Young women generally still lost pension rights upon marriage, and therefore, if they opted or were allowed to contribute to a pension plan at all, they would take a lump-sum payout of their contributions in the form of a "marriage bonus" upon marriage. The money was intended to help them set up a married household.

86. Gillespie and Sayce, interview by the author.

87. Sayce, interview by the author.

88. Gillespie and Sayce, interview by the author.

89. Gillespie, interview by the author.

90. Gillespie and Sayce, interview by the author.

91. Sayce, interview by the author.

92. Audrey Hunt and Irene Rauta, *Fifth Form Girls: Their Hopes for the Future*, ed. Social Survey Division of the Office of Population Censuses and Surveys on behalf of the Department of Education and Science (London: HMSO 1975), 9.

93. Gillespie, interview by the author.

94. Ann Sayce recalled that by tweaking the scheduling of jobs, she was able to hold the speed record for processing jobs using ASP.

95. HN 1/38, Industrial Relations in the Civil Service: Government Computing 1973–1979, TNA.

96. Cathy Gillespie, personal collection, 1970.

97. *ICT House Magazine*, July 1964.

98. *ICL News*, August 1970, 2.

99. Louise Morley Cochrane, *Anne in Electronics* (London: Chatto & Windus, 1960).

100. Ibid., 137.

101. Bixby, "Recruitment and Retention," 48–49, AIR 77/384, TNA.

102. Ibid.

103. Letters from Transport Salaried Staffs Association to the Secretary of the British Transport Commission, July 18, 1961, and July 15, 1963, AN 171/398, Equal Pay, Equal Work: Shorthand Typists and Machine Operators, TNA.

104. In 1971, punchers and other support staff made up 49.1 percent of all computer staff in the central government; they made up 5,200.5 workers out of 10,590 total. (The half worker was one of many part-time workers.) These figures underestimate the number of computer staff as they did not include over 1,000 other government computer workers in scientific and military computing installations. In addition, they did not account for workers who used computers but did not have a title designating them as primarily ADP staff. "ADP Staff 1970/1971," Section A(1), HN1/62, TNA.

4 The Rise of the Technocrat

1. From 1965 to 1969, the government spent an average of nearly £5.5 million on new computers annually, and the amount spent on new computers more than doubled between 1967 and 1969. By the end of the decade, there were more than two hundred mainframes in the central government, totaling over £36 million. See Select Committee on Science and Technology, Session 1969–1970, *UK Computer Industry, Vol. 1, Minutes of Evidence* (London: HMSO, 1970), 457.

Before a department could purchase a computer, the government required studies to establish the need for the computing system. Ideally, such studies would show a cost benefit, although the actual savings often fell short of what was projected. In addition, projected cost savings were not explicitly necessary:

"Cost is not the only criterion on which ADP projects are judged and projects which do not show a positive present value ... may be given Treasury approval if it can be shown that additional indirect savings will accrue, or that some operating advantage will be given." Treasury, "ADP Projects: Notes for Guidance of Departments," June 1966 and November 1967, HN 1/60 Civil Service Dept., Policy and Planning, Ministry of Technology, Use of Data Processing in Government, TNA.

2. T 224/900 Economic Situation 1965: Deferment of Expenditure On Capital Projects, Application to Computers, TNA.

3. Dockyard strikes in 1966 and again in 1970 frustrated Britain's already-flagging export position.

4. Fulton Committee, *The Civil Service Vol. 1. Report of the Committee 1966–1968* (London: HMSO, 1968), Cmnd. 3638.

5. See, for example, the 1968 strike of women workers at the Ford UK plant in Dagenham for equal pay, and the Grunwick film processing plant strike in Willesden, London in 1976. In the latter strike the workers were primarily Indian immigrants and the strike was largely led by women workers.

6. *Times* (London), "Computer Strikes to be Escalated," June 18, 1965.

7. STAT 14/3239 Strikes, Effects on HMSO and Emergency Arrangements to Alleviate Disruption, Computer Maintenance ICL/Asset Dispute, TNA.

8. "Introduction of Computers as a Cause for Redundancy," 1961–1962, T 216/710, Redundancy Owing to the Introduction of Computers, TNA.

9. David Noble describes a similar situation in *Forces of Production*, in which management uses a technological change in order to break existing unions' control over the shop floor. Noble, *Forces of Production: A Social History of Industrial Automation* (New York: Knopf, 1984).

10. C. R. Currie, Ministry of Agriculture, letter to W. R. Atkinson, Management Services Computers Division, CSD, July 9, 1970, HN 1/22, Report on Development of Computers in Government: Forecast for next ten years 1969–1971, TNA.

11. The Home Civil Service alone employed close to seven hundred thousand workers through the mid-1960s and the early 1970s. Rodney Lowe, *The Official History of the British Civil Service: Reforming the Civil Service, Volume I: The Fulton Years, 1966–81* (London: Routledge, 2011), 5–6.

12. C. R. Currie, letter to W. R. Atkinson.

13. W. S. Ryrie, "Computers," May 9, 1974, T 316/308, Investment Appraisal for Government Computer Projects 1971–1974, TNA.

14. Four and a half million pounds out of the total was earmarked for British computers. Her Majesty's Stationery Office (HMSO), "List of Government ADP Projects," January 1, 1965, STAT 14/3093, ADP installations in Government in 1965 and Staffing, TNA.

15. "ADP Staffing and Projects," HN 1/67, Consultation with Civil Service Staff Association about Automated Data Processing (ADP) 1968–1971, TNA.

16. Civil Service Department Memo, "Computer Planning in Central Government—Note by the CSD," January 1971, HN 1/62, TNA, 2.

17. United Kingdom, *Hansard Parliamentary Debates*, 5th ser., vol. 787 (1969), col. 361W.

18. "Down among the Datacrats," *Civil Service Opinion* 48, no. 557 (February 1970): 54, HN 1/67, TNA.

19. Cathy Gillespie and Ann Sayce (government computer operators), interview by the author, January 5, 2006, London.

20. C. W. Blundell, letter to F.G. Burrett, Civil Service Department (CSD), February 25, 1969, STAT 14/2765 Review of Machine Operator Grades 1961–1970, TNA.

21. Treasury, "Machine Grades: Notes of an Interdepartmental Meeting," May 8, 1964, STAT 14/2765, TNA.

22. J. Cowie, J. W. Hermann, and P. D. Maycock, "The British Computer Scene, Part II: The British Computer Industry" (London: Office of Naval Research, 1967), 13.

23. "ADP Staffing and Projects," July 1968, HN 1/67, TNA.

24. D. W. G. Wass, Treasury, confidential letter to P. W. Buckerfield, HMSO, June 14, 1963, STAT 14/2765, TNA.

25. Treasury, "Government Statistical Services Advisory Committee on Computers," August 31, 1967, Appendix E, HN 1/16, TNA, 5.

26. "Notes of a Meeting between the Official and Staff Sides," December 21, 1959, HN 1/16 ADP Staffing Problems Other than Shift Working 1956–1967, TNA.

27. *Times* (London), "The World of Management, Computers: For the Want of a Man," January 29, 1968, clipping, STAT 14/3484 Central Computer Bureau Organization and Staffing; J. D. W. Janes, *Observer Weekend Review*, "The Computer as Bureaucrat," February 18, 1962, clipping, T 216/710, Redundancy Owing to Introduction of Computers 1961–1962.

28. A. J. Long, HMSO, letter to N. E. A. Moore, Treasury, December 11, 1959, T 222/1323, Demonstration of Electronic Computers to and Consultation with Civil Service National Whitley Council and Staff Associations about Introduction in Government Offices 1959–1960, TNA.

29. Ibid.

30. Treasury, "Government Statistical Services Advisory Committee on Computers," August 31, 1967, Appendix E, HN 1/16, TNA. Executive class workers were a step above the two hundred thousand clerical class members and two steps above the twenty-five thousand or so workers in the machine operator class. Although machine operators often took umbrage at the notion that they were on the same level as clerical class workers, who had no particular technical expertise, the Treasury report associated machine operators with feminized labor and therefore saw their position as an "ancillary technical class" at the same level as the very lowest class of clerical workers.

31. Treasury, "Government Statistical Services Advisory Committee on Computers."

32. UK Atomic Energy Authority (AEA), "Computer Operations Staffing: Note by the London Office," September 28, 1966, AB 46/16, Authority-Wide Computer Operations Staffing, 1965–1969, TNA.

33. J. D. W. Janes, Treasury Organization and Methods Division, "Electronic Computers 'Oil' the Wheels of Government," June 1962, 11, T 216/710, TNA.

34. *Financial Times*, "Grading Staff for Computer Operations," November 29, 1966.

35. Minutes, April 20, 1959, STAT 14/2320, Accounts Division: Combined Tabulating Installation Staff Inspection Report 1958–1959, TNA.

36. Minutes, April 20, 1959, and May 20, 1959, STAT 14/2320, TNA.

37. Ibid.

38. Combined tabulating installation (CTI), "Report: Staff Inspection," STAT 14/2320, TNA.

39. STAT 14/3604, Central Computer Bureau 1968–1972, TNA; STAT 14/3303, TNA.

40. Treasury, "Notes of Confidential Interdepartmental Meeting," May 28, 1962, T 216/710, TNA.

41. D. W. G. Wass, Treasury, letter to W. Donaldson, HMSO, April 25, 1962, STAT 14/2765, Review of Machine Operator Grades 1961–1970, TNA.

42. Wass, letter to Donaldson; Treasury, "Notes of Confidential Interdepartmental Meeting."

43. Interview with Mary Coombs by Thomas Lean, British Library "Voices of Science" Oral History Collection, 2010, Part 1 of 9, http://sounds.bl.uk/Oral-history/Science/021M-C1379X0016XX-0001V0.

44. Treasury, "Notes of Confidential Interdepartmental Meeting."

45. Ibid.

46. Treasury, "Machine Grades," notes of an interdepartmental meeting, May 8, 1964, STAT 14/2765, TNA.

47. Ibid.

48. *Times* (London), "Civil Service Rebuff Treasury on Pay Offer," May 5, 1964.

49. Ibid.

50. Dolly Smith Wilson, "A New Look at the Affluent Worker: The Good Working Mother in Post-War Britain," *Twentieth Century British History* 17, no. 2 (2006): 206–229. Sheila Rowbotham, in *Hidden from History* (London: Pluto Press, 1973), discusses the links between gender inequality and the inequalities of class fought by labor activists. Her work speaks to a moment in the sixties and seventies when British feminism was reviving in large part by using labor agitation as a way to gain greater rights and status for women.

51. Minutes, April 19, 1966, STAT 14/2727, 1961–1969, TNA.

52. Central Computer Bureau (CCB), "Steering Committee Meeting Report," June 8, 1967, and June 5, 1968, STAT 14/3303, Shift Working of Computer Operators: Applications for Vacancies and Other Papers 1966–1969, TNA.

53. Sixteen senior machine operators (SMOs), thirty-seven machine operators (MOs), and forty-five machine assistants (MAs) carried over from the CTI to the CCB. Minutes, April 19, 1966; Rex Affolter, "Authorized Complement of Central Computer Bureau," April 14, 1966; and Establishments and Organization Division, "Development of Central Computer Bureau, Complement of Machine Grades," October 1966, STAT 14/2727 Progress Reports on CCB, 1961–1969, TNA.

54. Thirty-one SMOs, forty-eight MOs, and 103 MAs worked at the CCB by October of 1966. Establishments and Organization Division, "Development of Central Computer Bureau," October 1966, STAT 14/2727, TNA.

55. STAT 24/2727, TNA; STAT 14/3093, TNA.

56. ICT Ltd., "1900 Series" brochure, September 1964, copy available at https://archive.org/stream/bitsavers_icticl1900lProcessorSep64_1402011/1904_Central_Processor_Sep64#page/n1/mode/2up (accessed June 9, 2015).

57. HMSO, "Estimates 1972/1973 Computers" and "ADP Common Services, Organization and Articulation," February 11, 1972, 1, HN 1/15, TNA.

58. F. G. Burrett, CSD, letter to C. W. Blundell, HMSO Norwich Computing Installation, March 21, 1969, STAT 14/2765, TNA.

59. "Established SMOs," report, February 1, 1969, STAT 14/2765, TNA.

60. C. W. Blundell, HMSO Norwich Computing Installation, letter to F. G. Burrett, CSD, February 25, 1969, STAT 14/2765, TNA.

61. Ibid.

62. Roger Mortensen, "Economic Nightmare," Letter to ed., *Civil Service Opinion* 48, no. 557 (February 1970): 54, HN 1/67, TNA.

63. Blundell, letter to Burrett, February 25, 1969, STAT 14/2765, TNA.

64. Select Committee on Science and Technology, *Report on Session 1969–1970*, Vol. 1 (London: HMSO, 1971), 364.

65. T 224/900, TNA.

66. AEA, AB 46/16, Authority-Wide Computer Operations Staffing 1965–1969, TNA.

67. V. Griffin, "Computer Operations Staffing"; A. H. Armstrong, memorandum to S. J. Sharman, November 16, 1966; R. N. Simeone, memorandum to A. L. Scott, January 9, 1967, AB 46/16, TNA.

68. Roommate rentals could go as low as £200 per year. Data collected from survey of London *Times* classified ads from 1963 to 1967.

69. P. Dawson, and W. L. M. French, "AEA Computer Operations Staffing Covering Developments to Mid 1966," October 1966, AB 46/16, TNA.

70. Ibid.

71. Culham's commercial operators were all women.

72. P. Dawson, and W. L. M. French, "AEA Computer Operations Staffing Covering Developments to Mid 1966."

73. Windscale Accident Inquiry: Report of the Inquiry, with papers and correspondence belonging to Sir William Penney, 1957, AB 86/25, TNA.

74. CSD, Memorandum, April 26, 1977, AB 46/16, TNA.

75. *Times* (London), "Ministry of Technology in Computer Business," October 20, 1965.

76. Minutes, June 30, 1965, LAB 12/1471, TNA.

77. P.R. Bixby, Chief Scientist of the Royal Air Force, "Recruitment and Retention of Machine Operators," November 1967, 5, AIR 77/384, Recruitment and Retention of Machine Operators, TNA.

78. In this round of calls for programmers, recruits were accepted from clerical grades 3, 4, and 5. By decade's end, only pensioned recruits from grade 6 were accepted. LAB 12/1553, Shift Working of Computer Operators: Applications for Vacancies and Other Papers 1966–1969, TNA.

79. The computer labor shortage was often reported in the press, not just discussed within government; for instance, *Times* (London), "Urgent Need for Computer Training: Burden Must be Taken from Manufacturers," June 30, 1965.

80. Memorandum from Drake to Shipton, May 20, 1965, LAB 12/1471, Policy Considerations on Recruitment of Programmers and Computer Operators, TNA.

81. T. H. Caulcott, Treasury circular, March 12, 1965, LAB 12/1471, TNA.

82. J. Bruce, note, May 25, 1965, LAB 12/1471, TNA.

83. "Career Prospects for Women Civil Servants," *Civil Service Opinion* 48, no. 557 (February 1970): 52, HN 1/67, TNA.

84. T. H. Caulcott, Treasury circular, March 12, 1965, LAB 12/1471, TNA.

85. Bixby, "Recruitment and Retention," November 1967, 49, AIR 77/384, TNA.

86. Fulton Committee, *The Civil Service Vol. 1. Report of the Committee 1966–1968*.

87. Shipton, minutes, June 8, 1966, LAB 12/1471, TNA.

88. HN 1/62 Central Computing Agency, Papers of Origin, TNA.

89. July 1968, HN 1/67, TNA.

90. Civil Service Department, "MS(C) 46/288/05 ADP Staff 1970-71," HN 1/62, Central Computing Agency, Papers of Origin, TNA, 5.

91. Ibid.

92. "Losses of ADP Staff," 1971, HN 1/62, TNA.

93. "Down among the Datacrats."

94. Ibid.

95. "Losses of ADP Staff," 1971, HN 1/62, TNA.

96. Ibid.

97. Select Committee on Science and Technology, *Report on Session 1969–1970*, Vol. 1, 446.

98. Ibid.

99. "Computers in Government Ten Years Ahead: Notes of an Informal Meeting with the National Staff Side," September 21, 1970, HN 1/22, TNA.

100. CSD, memorandum, August 6, 1969, HN 1/67, TNA.

101. HN 1/72, Interdepartmental Working Party on Computer Personnel: Implementation of Recommendations 1972–1973, TNA.

102. HN 1/72, Interdepartmental Working Party on Computer Personnel: Implementation of Recommendations 1972–1973, TNA.

103. "ADP Staff 1970/71, MS(C) 46/288/05," HN1/62, TNA, 2.

104. "ADP Staff as at 31 March 1971, Administrative/Machine Grades," chart, HN 1/62.

105. Janes, "Electronic Computers 'Oil' the Wheels of Government," T 216/710, TNA.

106. J. T. Whittaker, CSD, memorandum, April 30, 1969, HN 1/60, TNA.

107. By 1969, when the responsibilities for computer advising and installation had reached a state of permanent flux and yet another agency—the National Computing Center—had been created to advise on computing, many departments had simply accepted the problem. "It is freely acknowledged that the procedures are more cumbersome than they would have to be if fewer departments were involved," wrote one CSD official. "Nevertheless, business-type computer schemes are complex and government ones more so than most; cutting down the interplay between departments would help, but it would be absurd to suppose that extremely radical changes are possible in a government environment." Civil Service Department, "Brief on Memorandum by the Minister of Technology on Data Processing in Government," April 1969, HN 1/60, TNA.

108. In 1949, the government set up the National Research Development Corporation—a self-supporting public body established under the auspices of the Department of Scientific and Industrial Research—to ensure that British technology was supported and developed in the public interest. Through the NRDC, the government strongly influenced the shape and potential of the computer industry for decades, culminating in the Ministry of Technology's backing of the merger that created ICL. See John Hendry, *Innovating for Failure: Government Policy and the Early British Computer Industry* (Cambridge, MA: MIT Press. 1989), 155.

109. Select Committee on Science and Technology, *Report on Session 1969–1970*, Vol. 1, 456–457.

110. Ibid., 364.

111. Ibid., 455.

112. Martin Campbell-Kelly, *I.C.L.: A Business and Technical History* (Oxford: Oxford University Press, 1990), 204. See this history for a full discussion of the business history of ICT and the merger that led to ICL.

113. Select Committee on Science and Technology, *Report on Session 1969–1970*, Vol. 1, 364.

114. "Computer Merger: Note by the Ministry of Technology," in Confidential Ministry of Technology report, "A Brief History of the Computer Mergers Scheme," June 9, 1969, Annex C, T 325/161, TNA.

115. Select Committee on Science and Technology, *Report on Session 1969–1970*, Vol. 1, 352.

116. Letter from S. W. Spain in CSD to J. W. Nichols in Department of Trade and Industry (formerly of MinTech), April 5, 1971, HN 1/62, TNA.

117. W. R. Atkinson, memorandum on "Computers in Government—Reorganization of the MS(C) Division," September 7, 1970, HN 1/62, TNA, 4.

118. Simon Lavington's study of Elliott-Automation argues that the company's fortunes and power in the marketplace, and in fact those of all British computing companies, were intertwined with the needs and hegemonic discourses of the state. Lavington, *Moving Targets: Elliott-Automation and the Dawn of the Computer Age in Britain, 1947–67* (London: Springer, 2011).

119. Harold Wilson as quoted in Ben Pimlott, *Harold Wilson* (New York: Harper Collins, 1992), 348.

120. David Edgerton has shown how the narrative of British decline in the twentieth century does not necessarily reflect the actuality of Britain's position. As Edgerton has argued, Britain remained a powerful, imperial, war-faring state and an "empire of machines" throughout the twentieth century. He shows persuasively that technology and technocracy were far stronger powers within the supposedly declining welfare state of Britain after World War II than previous histories acknowledge and that the divisions between humanists and technocrats have been overstated, as in the near-parody of British culture presented in C. P. Snow's description of the two cultures of the humanities and the sciences. Indeed, the shift toward technocracy, technocratic management, and the alignment of cultural goals with technological ones was a hallmark of British society throughout the twentieth century and was well underway even before Wilson's pronouncement of the era of White Heat. Nonetheless, the idea of decline had an important influence on government leaders and a major effect on public discourse. Edgerton, *The Warfare State: Britain, 1920–1970* (Cambridge: Cambridge University Press, 2006).

121. *Times* (London), "Buying Policy Aids ICL, Says MinTech," April 30, 1970.

122. See White Paper Cmnd. 3660, June 1968.

123. Anthony Wedgewood Benn, letter to Chancellor of the Exchequer, March 7, 1968, reproduced in the appendix of the confidential Ministry of Technology report, "A Brief History of the Computer Mergers Scheme," June 9, 1969, T 325/161, TNA.

124. Campbell-Kelly, *I.C.L.*, 257.

125. The merger that created ICL was under discussion from 1964 until 1968, when it was completed. The government supported ICL with grants and preferential purchasing into the 1970s. Annex C/6, T325/161, MinTech: History of the Computer Merger 1964–1968, TNA.

126. Select Committee on Science and Technology, *Report on Session 1969–1970*, Vol. 1, 456–457.

127. As Campbell-Kelly discusses in his history of ICL, referencing Anthony Sampson's *The New Anatomy of Britain* (New York: Stein and Day, 1971), the trend of high-level government workers moving into positions of authority in industry in this period resulted in conservative and often counterproductive corporate strategies.

128. "Computer Planning in Central Government—Note by the CSD," January 1971, HN 1/62, TNA, 2.

129. J. T. Whittaker, CSD, memorandum, April 30, 1969, HN 1/60, TNA.

130. CSD, "Comments on a Brief Memorandum on Data Processing in Government by the Ministry of Technology," April 1969, HN 1/60, TNA.

131. Whittaker, memorandum, April 30, 1969, HN 1/60, TNA.

132. Civil Service Department, "Brief on Memorandum by the Minister of Technology on Data Processing in Government," April 1969, HN 1/60, TNA.

133. P. T. F. Kelly, letter in response to memorandum on data processing in government by the Minister of Technology, March 20, 1969, HN 1/60, TNA.

134. Stanley Gill, memorandum to ADP Planning Committee, January 30, 1968, HN 1/60, TNA.

135. Ibid.

136. Sir Richard Clarke, "Note on the ICL Merger: 1964–1968," in the confidential Ministry of Technology report, "A Brief History of the Computer Mergers Scheme," June 9, 1969, T 325/161, TNA.

137. For a detailed discussion of this dynamic, see Hendry, *Innovating for Failure*, chapter 13.

138. Jon Agar, *The Government Machine: A Revolutionary History of the Computer* (Cambridge, MA: MIT Press, 2003), 341.

139. J. A. Annand, "Computers in Government Ten Years Ahead," November 7, 1969, HN 1/22, TNA.

140. CSD, "Computer Planning in Central Government, Note by the CSD," January 1971, HN 1/62, TNA.

141. Ryrie, "Computers," T 316/308, TNA.

142. There were still roughly two to three times as many machine operator class computer operators in 1975 as there were executive class operators. The statistics are inexact due to the inclusion of clerical officers in the pool. "ADP Staff Return," 1970–1971, Section E and F, HN 1/62, TNA.

143. "Appendix D.1: Vacancies at 31 March 1971 for Admin/Exec/Clerical/Machine Grades," HN 1/62, TNA lists the number of unfilled higher-level

computing jobs as 395.5. This report shows the extent of labor starvation of government computing systems; the openings recorded only cover staff from SMO positions up through clerical and executive class computing jobs. The openings for machine operators, machine assistants, and punch operators are not included; if they were, this number would have been much higher, potentially as large as eight hundred to one thousand.

144. Select Committee on Science and Technology, Session 1969–1970, *UK Computer Industry, Vol. 1, Minutes of Evidence*, 452.

145. Internal Government Job Advertisements, 1968, LAB 12/1553, Shift Working of Computer Operators: Applications for Vacancies and Other Papers 1966–1969, TNA.

146. Department of Employment and Productivity, letter to Treasury, September 27, 1968, LAB 12/1516, General Application of ADP 1965–1968, TNA.

147. T 216/710, Redundancy Owing to Computers 1961–1962, TNA.

148. "Novices to Experts in Three Easy Months," *ICL Computer International*, no. 13 (1970): 1, BL.

149. *Civil Service Opinion* 48, no. 557 (February 1970): 52, HN 1/67, TNA.

150. Letter from the Society of Technical Civil Servants, November 16, 1962, GB0152 MSS.292B/134/8, Women in Industry, Industrial Charter for Women Workers: 1968, MRC.

151. Civil Service Department, "Brief on Memorandum by the Minister of Technology on Data Processing in Government," April 1969, HN 1/60, TNA.

5 The End of White Heat and the Failure of British Technocracy

1. CSD, memorandum, April 26, 1977, AB 46/16, TNA.

2. J. A. Annand, "Computers in Government Ten Years Ahead," November 7, 1969, HN 1/22, TNA.

3. In his history of the National Research Development Corporation, John Hendry shows that the research support for the British computing industry paled in comparison with the money the US government gave to US computing research. Hendry, *Innovating for Failure: Government Policy and the Early British Computer Industry* (Cambridge, MA: MIT Press, 1989).

4. As Hendry notes in *Innovating for Failure*, though Britain did not have the same culture of entrepreneurship in computing, "what entrepreneurship there was could perhaps have been better exploited by government agencies" (165).

5. ICT machines were also included in this 71 percent, as they were considered retroactively to be ICL products. CSD, "Computer Planning in Central Government, Note by the CSD," January 1971, HN 1/62, TNA.

6. The Civil Service Department, which now had the most power in the computer-provisioning process, estimated that 85 percent or more of government computers would be ICL machines by 1975. CSD, "Computer Planning in Central Government."

7. As Amartya Sen and others have shown, women's economic weakness constructs, rather than merely results from, the organization of an economy. As such, sexism often plays a major role in weakening an economy and lowering a nation's productive output overall. In discussing the economic impacts of sexism, Sen goes so far as to argue that women's mortality in developing nations functions not simply as an economic indicator but as a factor that actually determines the health and future growth of a nation's economy. Amartya Sen, "Women's Survival as a Development Problem," *Bulletin of the American Academy of Arts and Sciences* 43, no. 2 (November 1989): 14–29.

8. See Sheila Rowbotham, *Beyond The Fragments: Feminism and the Making of Socialism* (London: Merlin, 1980).

9. ICL, "ICL's Relations with the Government," 1975, NAHC/ICL/Aq1, National Archive for the History of Computing, Manchester, UK (NAHCM).

10. CSD, "Computer Planning in Central Government, Note by the CSD," January 1971; and Central Computer and Telecommunication Agency, "ADP Staff 1970/1971," Section A(1), HN 1/62, TNA.

11. Martin Campbell-Kelly, *I.C.L.: A Business and Technical History* (Oxford: Oxford University Press, 1989).

12. Head of Management of Computers Division, "Restricted, Staff in Confidence: Memorandum on Computers in Central Government," July 20, 1970, HN 1/22, Computers in Central Government: Ten Years Ahead, TNA.

13. G. Bowen, memorandum, July 23, 1965, HN 1/40, TNA.

14. Ministry of Technology, "Confidential: History of the Computer Merger Scheme, 1964–68," Annex C/6, 1968, T 325/161, History of the Computer Merger, TNA.

15. HN 1/40, TNA.

16. United Kingdom, *Hansard Parliamentary Debates*, 5th ser., vol. 787 (1969), col. 361W.

17. Ibid., vol. 721 (1965), col. 32–3W.

18. Ibid., vol. 724 (1966), col. 7–8.

19. CCA, "Procurement of Computers for Government Departments," Annex I, 1965, HN 1/40, Purchase and Supply of ADP Equipment, 1964–1970, TNA.

20. CCA, "Computers to be Regarded as British," appendix, February 1966, HN 1/26 Procurement Policy, Use of British Computers 1965–1972, TNA.

21. J. S. Whyte, letter from Treasury to Ministry of Technology, September 24, 1965, HN 1/26, Procurement Policy, Use of British Computers 1965–1972, TNA.

22. R. J. Berger, Letter from Honeywell to the CCA, August 4, 1972, HN 1/26, TNA.

23. Maurice Dean, Ministry of Technology, letter to P. Allen, January 6, 1965, HN 1/26, Procurement Policy, Use of British Computers 1965–1972, TNA.

24. CAB 163/230, Release of Information on Wartime Computers, 1970–1974, TNA.

25. Kenneth Owen, "Anglo–US talks on Soviet Sales Bid by ICL," *Times* (London), December 21, 1970.

26. Anthony Benn, "ICL Computers for USSR, Memorandum by the Minister of Technology," May 17, 1968, CAB 148/37, Cabinet Papers, TNA.

27. Chair of the Board of Trade, "Computers and Export to China," October 19, 1966, PREM 13/1967, Office of the Prime Minister, TNA; Special Correspondent, "Russia Grants ICL Special Trading Status," *Times* (London), July 10, 1970.

28. T316/308, Investment Appraisal for Government Computer Projects 1971–1974, TNA.

29. CCA, "Investment Appraisal for Computer Projects," 1972, T 316/308, TNA.

30. Mrs. J. Percy-Davis, "CCA Central Planning Document on Computers: CGO(73)3," December 20, 1973, T 316/308, TNA.

31. T 316/308, TNA.

32. Ministerial Committee on Economic Policy, "Secret: Brief on CPRS Report on the UK Computer Industry," January 1972, 1, HN 1/15, Arrangements for the Setting up of the Central Computer Agency (CCA) 1972, TNA.

33. Ibid.

34. Ibid.

35. Ibid.

36. Anonymous, "Down among the Datacrats," *Civil Service Opinion* 48, no. 557 (February 1970): 1, HN 1/67, TNA.

37. PREM 15/412, Government Machinery: Computers 1970–1971, TNA.

38. HN series, TNA. Less than a decade later, responsibility for computing would again revert to the Treasury. In 1970, the Ministry of Technology was absorbed into the Department of Trade and Industry on Heath's ascension to the office of prime minister. Because MinTech was a special ministry set up by Wilson, Heath was not obliged to maintain it.

39. HN 1/15, Arrangements for the Setting up of the Central Computer Agency (CCA) 1972, TNA.

40. CCA, "Notes of a Tuesday Meeting Held in Sir William Armstrong's Room, Management in Confidence," January 18, 1972, HN 1/15, TNA.

41. HMSO, "ADP Common Services: Organization and Articulation," February 11, 1972, 3, HN 1/15, TNA.

42. CCA Study Group, "Industrial Action: Effects on Computing in Government (Secret)," June 1973, para. 32, HN 1/38 Industrial relations in the Civil Service: Government Computing 1973–1979, TNA.

43. Barbara Castle, *In Place of Strife: A Policy for Industrial Relations, 1968–1969* (London: HMSO, 1969), Cmnd. 3888.

44. Heath's four declared states of emergency were the most declared by any British prime minister. Although Heath declared states of emergency in response to the dockworkers' and miners' strikes, a multiplicity of comparatively lesser but still extremely serious strikes plagued his time in office. These included a major Post Office strike, transport workers' strikes, and industrial action by several civil service groups.

45. Interdepartmental Study Group, "Confidential: Report of Industrial Action in Government Computing Installations," October 1973, HN 1/38, TNA.

46. United Kingdom, *Parliamentary Debates*, Commons, 5th ser., vol. 833 (1972), col. 363–364.

47. Aylward, "Computers in National Administration," 9, HN 1/72, TNA.

48. CCA, "Staffing of Computer Projects," 7, 13, HN 1/72. TNA.

49. R. D. Aylward, CCA, "Computers in National Administration," October 31, 1972, 5, HN 1/72, TNA.

50. Working Party on Computer Personnel, "Brief for Meeting with Mr. Cooper on 15 November 1972 on Senior Staff for Computers," 2, HN 1/72, Working Party on Computer Personnel 1970–1972, Implementation of Recommendations, TNA.

51. United Kingdom, *Hansard Parliamentary Debates*, 5th ser., vol. 833 (1972), col. 363–364.

52. CCA, "Industrial Action," HN 1/38, TNA.

53. Ibid.

54. Ibid., para. 9.

55. Ibid., para. 22.

56. T.R. Anderson,"Letters: IBM Employee Replies to Clive Jenkins," Greenock Telegraph, June 13, 1977; CW 2/30–34, Employment Protection Act 1975: IBM UK Ltd. London and Greenock, 1975–1977, TNA.

57. Ibid.

58. S. W. Spain, "High Quality Staff for ADP Work, Table I: Forecast of Numbers of Staff Required, 1972–1977," December 21, 1972, 7, HN 1/72, TNA.

59. This report projects the numbers of ADP staff rising from about 9,000 to 16,600, with data preparation making up about half, operations making up about 20 percent, and systems and programming making up about 30 to 40 percent of the total. Spain, "High Quality Staff," 7, HN 1/72, TNA.

60. R. Gapp, "Staffing," November 3, 1972, 3, HN 1/72, TNA.

61. Department of National Savings to CCA, letter, January 11, 1973, HN 1/38, TNA. The National Savings Bank was known as the Post Office Savings Bank before 1969.

62. Department of National Savings to CCA, letter, January 11, 1973, HN 1/38, TNA.

63. See, for instance, *Times* (London), "2,000 Civil Servants Start Strike Today," March 21, 1973; *Times* (London), "Whitehall Union Plans to Join TUC," March

10, 1973; *Times* (London), "More Civil Service Strikes Planned," March 8, 1973.

64. *Times* (London), "2,000 Civil Servants Start Strike Today."

65. CCA, "Industrial Action," para. 21, HN 1/38, TNA.

66. Ibid., para. 18 and app. II.

67. Laura Lee Downs gives an example not only of the existence of gendered classes of workers in British industry but also of British companies' explicit interventions to perpetuate such classes of female workers in her article on Rover's abortive attempt to concede equal pay in order to institute a Fordist model. Downs, "Industrial Decline, Rationalization and Equal Pay: The Bedaux Strike at Rover Automobile Company," *Social History* 15, no. 1 (1990): 45–73.

68. CAOG 16/213, Pay: Machine Operator Grades, 1957–1970, TNA.

69. Central Computer and Telecommunication Agency, "ADP Staff 1970/1971," 6, HN 1/62, TNA.

70. HN 1/68, TNA.

71. Treasury, "Notes of Confidential Interdepartmental Meeting held on 28 May 1962," T 216/710, Redundancy Owing to the Introduction of Computers, TNA.

72. Indeed, ADP staff had been growing at a rate of at least 25 percent per year for 12 years. CCA, "Management in Confidence: Report of the Interdepartmental Working Party on Staffing of Computer Projects," September 1972, HN 1/72, TNA.

73. "ADP Staff 1970/1971, MS(C) 46/288/05" HN1/62, TNA, 2.

74. HN 1/22, Report on Development of Computers in Government: Forecast for Next Ten Years 1969–1971, TNA.

75. Aylward, "Computers in National Administration," 9, HN 1/72, TNA.

76. See chapter 4 in Janet Abbate, *Recoding Gender: Women's Changing Participation in Computing* (Cambridge, MA: MIT Press, 2012).

77. "Down among the Datacrats," 40, HN 1/67.

78. Doris Lancaster, Assistant General Secretary of the Society of Civil Servants, "Software: A Time for Hard Thinking," April 19, 1971, HN 1/68, Consultation with Civil Service Staff Association about ADP, 1971–1972, TNA.

79. ICL, "Some Practical Steps," 3, PREM 15/412, TNA.

80. One exception to the feminization of punching occurred shortly after World War II, when severely disabled war veterans were trained as punchers. Otherwise, women dominated punching work.

81. Prolonged exposure to noise at or above 85 decibels is currently understood to cause gradual hearing loss, according to the US National Institute on Deafness and Other Communication Disorders.

82. D. O. Hagger, "Management of Data Preparation Staff," December 20, 1971, para. 8, HN 1/25, Management Issues Arising from Introduction of Data Preparation Work 1970–1979, TNA.

83. Charlotte Robinson and Colin Cave, Offices Group, Directorate of Building Development, Dept. of the Environment, "Report on Noise and Some Other Environmental Aspects in Data Preparation Rooms for the Inland Revenue," April 1970, 5, HN 1/25, TNA.

84. Ibid., 5–11.

85. Hagger, "Management of Data Preparation Staff," para. 24, 42–44, HN 1/25, TNA.

86. HN 1/25, TNA.

87. House of Commons, Secretary of State for the Home Department, *Equality for Women* (London: HMSO), Cmnd. 5724, 2.

88. Office of Population Censuses and Survey, *Census 1961, Great Britain, Summary Tables* (London: HMSO, 1966), 64, 67, 4–5; Office of Population Censuses and Survey, *Census 1971, Great Britain, Economic Activity: Part I* (London: HMSO, 1973), 1.

89. Office of Population Censuses and Surveys, *Census 1961, Great Britain, Summary Tables* (London: HMSO, 1966), 67; Office of Population Censuses and Surveys, *Census 1971, Great Britain, Part II, 10% Sample* (London: HMSO, 1974), 54.

90. "To Train or Not to Train?," *Office Methods and Machines*, September 1967, 15–17, T 222/1314, TNA.

91. Ibid.

92. David Gowland and Arthur Turner, *Britain and European Integration, 1945–1998: A Documentary History* (London: Routledge, 2000), 127–135.

93. Office of Population Censuses and Surveys, *Census 1971, Great Britain, Economic Activity: Part I* (London: HMSO, 1973), 1.

94. Audrey Hunt, *A Survey of Women's Employment: A 1965 Government Social Survey*, ed. Social Survey Division Office of Population Censuses and Surveys (London: HMSO, 1968), 22–23.

95. Hunt, *Women's Employment*, 22–23.

96. Women's salaries in these areas lagged by only 1.4 to 1.6 percent in 1967. These figures covered roughly equal numbers of men and women (approximately one million each). They did not, however, account for part-time workers or for employees paid hourly wages instead of salary. Ministry of Labour, *Statistics on Incomes, Prices, Employment, and Production*, no. 23 (London: HMSO, December 1967), 49.

97. House of Commons, Secretary of State for the Home Department, *Equality for Women*, 2.

98. CCA, "Industrial Action," para. 18 and app. II, HN 1/38, TNA.

99. Downs, "Industrial Decline," 45–73.

100. Barbara Castle, *The Castle Diaries, 1964–1970* (London: Weidenfeld and Nicolson, 1984); and Castle, *Fighting All the Way* (London: Macmillan, 1993).

101. Baroness Beatrice Nancy Seear, interview by Betty Scharf, February 1991, 8/NLS/4, WL.

102. Jean Martin and Ceridwen Roberts, *Women and Employment: A Lifetime Perspective* (London: Office of Population Censuses and Surveys, 1984), 25.

103. *Equal Pay Act 1970*, c. 41, para. 4, 5.

104. Margherita Rendel, "Legislating for Equal Pay and Opportunity for Women in Britain," *Signs* 3, no. 4 (1978).

105. Z. Tzannatos, "Narrowing the Gap: Equal Pay in Britain 1970–1986," *Long Range Planning* 20, no. 2 (1987): 74.

106. Bill [passed, cap. 41] to Prevent Discrimination, as Regards Terms and Conditions of Employment, between Men and Women [as Amended by Standing Committee H] (Equal Pay (No. 2)), 130, 1969–1970, I.1173.

107. Z. Tzannatos, "Narrowing the Gap," 74.

108. Audrey Hunt, *Women and Paid Work: Issues of Equality* (New York: St. Martin's Press, 1988), 106.

109. Seear, interview by Scharf.

110. Orley Ashenfelter and Richard Layard, "Incomes Policy and Wage Differentials," *Economica* 50, no. 198 (May 1983): 127–133.

111. LAB 112/95, TNA.

112. Censuses and Surveys, *1961, Summary Tables*, 4–5; Office of Population Censuses and Surveys, *Census 1971, Great Britain, Age, Marital Condition and General Tables* (London: HMSO, 1974), 26–27; and Office of Population Censuses and Surveys, *Census 1981, National Report Great Britain*, Part 1 (London: HMSO, 1983), 15.

113. Sue Puddefoot, "A Tender Missive to Mr Wilson," *Times* (London), February 14, 1968, 9.

114. Central Office of Information for Department of Employment, *Jobs for Young Girls* (1969), 49 sec.; TNA, *Public Information Films, 1964–1979*, http://www.nationalarchives.gov.uk/films/1964to1979/filmpage_jobs.htm.

115. "EEC Rules against UK Sex Discrimination Laws," *Accountancy* 95, no. 1085 (January 1984): 19.

116. This resulted in Britain passing the 1983 addendum to the Equal Pay Act, which came into force in January 1984.

117. Hunt, *Women and Paid Work*, 198.

118. Ibid., 200–201.

119. Ibid., 199.

120. Office of Population Censuses and Surveys, *Census 1971, Great Britain, Economic Activity, Part IV, 10% Sample* (London: HMSO, 1974), 52, 54, 64.

121. STAT 14/2765, Review of Machine Operator Grades 1961–1970, TNA.

122. HN 1/72, TNA.

123. Martin and Roberts, *Women and Employment*, 21–25.

124. House of Commons, Secretary of State for the Home Department, *Equality for Women*, 4.

125. STAT 14/4457, Computer Systems-Liaison with CCB-Conversion to ICL 2900 1976–1977, TNA.

126. "ICL's Top-Down Policy Backfires," *Computer Weekly* 449 (1975): 1.

127. Campbell-Kelly, *I.C.L.*, 326.

128. Ibid., 323.

129. Ibid., 327, 340.

130. Ibid., 339–340.

131. STAT 14/4457, Computer Systems-Liaison with CCB-Conversion to ICL 2900 1976–1977, TNA.

132. Ibid.

133. "Post Office Order for Three 2970 Machines," *Computer Weekly* 456 (1975): 48.

134. Campbell-Kelly, *I.C.L.*, 346, 340.

135. ICL, "ICL's Relations with the Government."

136. Treasury, "Confidential Report: Computers and Electronics," January 2, 1973, 3, T 316/308, TNA.

137. Stevens to Lewin, brief from Ministry of Commerce in memorandum, "IEL Castlereagh," September 28, 1972, CJ 4/630, ICL Ltd. Castlereagh, Belfast, TNA.

138. Campbell-Kelly, *I.C.L.*, 311.

139. HN 1/25, Management Issues Arising from Introduction of Data Preparation Work 1970–1979, TNA.

140. HN 1/1, Effects on Staff of Technical Developments in Computing, 1979, TNA.

141. C. J. Hancock and Working Group, "Personnel Implications of New Microelectronics Technology," August 22, 1979, para. 4, HN 1/1, Effects on Staff of Technical Developments in Computing, 1979, TNA.

142. STAT 14/2972, TNA.

143. P. J. Walsh, "Notes of Visit to University of London Computer Center," November 3, 1980, para. 5, CSPR 5/52, University Computer Operators: Background Papers 1980, TNA.

144. Society of Civil Servants, *Annual Report*, 1972, 30, HN 1/72, TNA.

145. CSPR 5/52, TNA.

146. Society of Civil Servants, *Annual Report*, 1972, 30, HN 1/72, TNA.

147. HN 1/30, Exchange of Computer Staff between the Civil Service and the Private Sector, 1968–1980, TNA.

148. House of Commons, Secretary of State for the Home Department, *Equality for Women*, 2.

149. ICL, "Some Practical Steps in Advanced Management in Government: ICL Report to the Select Committee on Science and Technology," 1970, 30, PREM 15/412, TNA.

150. United Kingdom, *Hansard Parliamentary Debates*, 5th ser., vol. 793 (1969), col. 427–428.

151. CCA, "Staff in Confidence," October 25, 1972, HN 1/72, TNA.

152. For instance, the government allowed Standard Telephones and Cables (STC) to take over ICL without having to fear being looked at for monopolistic practices. Campbell-Kelly, *I.C.L.*, 348–349.

153. Not to be confused with technocratic feminism, the application of technocratic ideals to feminist objectives or the adoption of technocratic values by feminist scientists and engineers. See Laura Micheletti Puaca, *Searching for Scientific Womanpower: Technocratic Feminism and the Politics of National Security, 1940–1980* (Chapel Hill: University of North Carolina Press, 2014).

154. "Thus, if a man marries his housekeeper or his cook, the national dividend is diminished." Arthur C. Pigou, "The National Dividend," in *The Economics of Welfare*, 4th ed. (London: Macmillan and Co., 1932), 33.

Conclusion

1. Upon taking power, Thatcher sold off the government's interest in ICL. Martin Campbell-Kelly, *I.C.L.: A Business and Technical History* (Oxford: Oxford University Press, 1989), 333.

2. *Times* (London), "Government Ordering Criticized by ICL," March 10, 1970.

3. Campbell-Kelly, *I.C.L.*, 316, 339.

4. ICL, "Some Practical Steps in Advanced Management in Government: ICL Report to the Select Committee on Science and Technology," 1970, 14, PREM 15/412, TNA. The budget for the NHS was projected to grow by at least 8 percent each year.

5. ICL, "Some Practical Steps," 16.

6. "US Told to Face Your Responsibilities," *ICL News*, June 1971, front page.

7. "Why We Are Matching Resources with Needs," *ICL News*, June 1971, front page.

8. After taking over the international portion of Singer Business Machines in 1976 in an attempt to expand its presence in the world minicomputer market, ICL merged with Standard Telephones and Cables in 1984 in an effort to better incorporate telecommunication into its computing product line. Throughout the 1980s, Fujitsu Corporation steadily gained a greater share of ICL, initially partnering with ICL to provide lower-cost hardware for minicomputer ranges. By the late 1980s, Fujitsu owned a majority of ICL, rising to 84 percent in 1993, and in 2002 the ICL name was dropped. Government officials discussed how to get off the hook for ICL as early as 1972 in the Ministerial Committee on

Economic Policy, "Secret: Brief on CPRS Report on the UK Computer Industry," January 1972, 1, HN 1/15, Arrangements for the Setting up of the Central Computer Agency (CCA) 1972, TNA.

9. Jon Agar, *The Government Machine: A Revolutionary History of the Computer* (Cambridge, MA: MIT Press, 2003), 367.

10. In *The Control Revolution: Technological and Economic Origins of the Information Society* (Cambridge MA: Harvard University Press, 1986), James R. Beniger investigates the history of the control of work processes to argue for its importance in the eventual construction of the modern concept of the information society. Beniger believed that data processing within bureaucracies represented a revolution in generalized control. *Control revolution* is the term Beniger gives to the vast, co-constitutive changes in business and technology that occurred in the late nineteenth to early twentieth centuries, which, he argues, led to the synthesis of the structures required for modern systems of information processing and the top-down control allowed by these systems.

11. F. E. R. Butler, "Chessington Computer Center: Staffing Situation," June 1982, HN 1/85, Wastage of Automated Data Processing (ADP) Staff from Government Computer Installations, 1978–1983, TNA.

12. Butler, "Staffing Situation," para. vi, HN 1/85, TNA.

13. See Janet Abbate, *Recoding Gender: Women's Changing Participation in Computing* (Cambridge, MA: MIT Press, 2012) for a detailed discussion of Shirley's business.

14. Institute of Manpower Studies, *Computer Manpower in the 80s: The Supply and Demand for Computer Related Manpower to 1985* (London: National Economic Development Office, 1980), FG 4/968, TNA; Select Committee, *Computer Industry in the 1970s*.

15. Institute of Manpower Studies, *Computer Manpower in the 80s*, iii.

16. Butler, "Staffing Situation," para. i. Such distinctions seemed pointless and confusing even to some managers within the Civil Service by this point; the report section in question was flagged with a big question mark by one of its management-level readers.

17. Electronic Computers SWP, *Manpower Sub-Committee, Second Interim Report* (London: HMSO, 1979).

18. HN 1/85, TNA.

19. Rosemary Crompton, *Women and Work in Modern Britain* (Oxford: Oxford University Press, 1997), 26.

20. Jean Martin and Ceridwen Roberts, *Women and Employment: A Lifetime Perspective* (London: Office of Population Censuses and Surveys, 1984), 23; Jane E. Lewis, "Women Clerical Workers in the Late Nineteenth and Early Twentieth Centuries," in *The White Blouse Revolution: Female Office Workers since 1870*, ed. Gregory Anderson (Manchester, UK: Manchester University Press, 1988), 34.

21. Institute of Manpower Studies, *Computer Manpower in the 80s*, xvii, FG 4/968, TNA. Only in exceptional cases, as in the case of Dame Stephanie Shirley's software services company, were women sought out as ideal employees. Shirley specifically hired women programmers who had been shut out of other jobs because, as mothers, they needed the option to work at home. Even so, Shirley's business model was the exception that proved the rule: In general, neither industry nor government knew how to accommodate women in order to maximize their productivity. See Stephanie Shirley, with Richard Askwith, *Let IT Go: The Story of the Entrepreneur Turned Ardent Philanthropist* (London: Andrews UK, 2012); and Janet Abbate's discussion of Shirley in *Recoding Gender*.

22. Teresa Rees, *Skill Shortages, Women and the New Information Technologies* (Luxembourg: Office for Official Publications of the European Communities, 1992), 26–27. Far from being confined to the European context, similar processes have constructed technical skills in other large, industrialized, Western nations. Ruth Oldenziel makes a similar argument for the American engineering context in *Making Technology Masculine: Men, Women and Modern Machines in America, 1870–1945* (Amsterdam: Amsterdam University Press, 1999), whereas J. McGrath Cohoon and William Aspray investigate the issue transnationally in the collection *Women and Information Technology: Research on Underrepresentation* (Cambridge, MA: MIT Press, 2006).

23. Cynthia Cockburn, "Women and Technology: Opportunity Is Not Enough," in *The Changing Experience of Employment*, ed. Kate Purcell et al. (London: Macmillan, 1986), 185.

24. *Tabacus: The Magazine of the British Tabulating Company*, August 1958, 8.

25. Other categories of privilege, like race, still remain to be integrated into narratives of early computing. Early efforts to do so, such as Lisa Nakamura's work, have shown remarkable similarities to and intersections with the history of gendered labor. Nakamura's work on Fairchild Semiconductor's employment of Native American women as hardware manufacturers shows how the use of Native American women's labor presaged the trend toward offshoring and outsourcing that has come to define the postindustrial, high-tech economy. Nakamura also struggles with recovering the stories of women who exist primarily as a group represented in visual materials—publicity images that "document their participation through visual and discursive means," but "never in their own voices." Lisa Nakamura, "Indigenous Circuits: Navajo Women and the Racialization of Early Electronics Manufacture," *American Quarterly* 64, no. 4 (December 2013): 919–941.

26. Langdon Winner, *The Whale and the Reactor: A Search for Limits in an Age of High Technology* (Chicago: University of Chicago Press, 1986), 26.

27. See Eden Medina's *Cybernetic Revolutionaries: Technology and Politics in Allende's Chile* (Cambridge, MA: MIT Press, 2014). Quotes are from Eden Medina, "The Cybersyn Revolution: Five Lessons from a Socialist Computing Project in Salvador Allende's Chile," *Jacobin Magazine*, no. 17, https://www.jacobinmag.com/2015/04/allende-chile-beer-medina-cybersyn.

28. Judith Butler, *Bodies That Matter: On the Discursive Limits of "Sex"* (New York: Routledge, 1993), 22.

29. See, for example, the business study by Sylvia Ann Hewlett et al., *The Athena Factor: Reversing the Brain Drain in Science, Engineering, and Technology* (Cambridge, MA: Harvard Business Review Press, 2008).

30. Liana Christin Landivar, "Disparities in STEM Employment by Sex, Race, and Hispanic Origin," American Community Survey Reports, ACS-24 (Washington, DC: US Census Bureau, 2013).

31. Angela Levin, "Philanthropist Stephanie Shirley: You Can Only Spend So Much," *The Telegraph*, November 5, 2012, http://www.telegraph.co.uk/women/womens-business/9655905/Philanthropist-Stephanie-Shirley-You-can-only-spend-so-much.html.

32. Barbara Reskin and Patricia Roos, eds., *Job Queues, Gender Queues: Explaining Women's Inroads into Male Occupations* (Philadelphia: Temple University Press, 1990), 108–109.

33. Sarah Roberts, "Commercial Content Moderation: Digital Laborers' Dirty Work," in *The Intersectional Internet: Race, Sex, Class and Culture Online*, ed. Safiya Umoja Noble and Brendesha M. Tynes (New York: Peter Lang, 2016).

Bibliography

Archival Sources

The following is a list of the archival sources used, separated by archive.

The British Library, London
The British Library holds an assortment of literature published by British computer companies, ranging from programming manuals to in-house magazines published for and by employees of each company.

Ferranti Journal, 1954–1970.

ICT Data Processing Journal, 1961–1967.

ICT House Magazine, 1959–1964.

ICL Computer International, 1968–1970.

ICL News, 1970–1971.

ICL Computer International, 1972.

Office Magazine, 1954–1965.

Office Methods and Machines, 1950–1967.

Powers-Samas Magazine (also called *The Powers Magazine*, *Powers-Samas Gazette*), 1946–1958.

Tabacus: The Magazine of the British Tabulating Company, 1957–1959.

London Metropolitan Archives
The London Metropolitan Archives hold the Lyons Teashops Newsletter, which contained information collected for and by employees.

ACC/3527/290, Lyons Mail Newsletter.

The Modern Records Center, University of Warwick

The Modern Records Center holds a variety of trade union related records, including documents and publications from the Women's Trade Union Congress.

GB0152 MSS.192/CA, Clerical and Administrative Workers' Union, 1940–1972, Association of Professional, Executive, Clerical and Computer Staff, 1972–1989.

GB0152 MSS.292/4/12/pieces 1–17, Women Workers (Report of the Annual Conference of Representatives of Trade Unions Catering for Women Workers), 1953–1970.

GB0152 MSS.292/4/14/1–8, TUC Non-Manual Workers Conference Reports, 1961, 1964–1966.

GB0152 MSS.292/60.2/2a-2b, Organization of women, Publicity, 1936–1956.

GB0152 MSS292/60.2/3, Organization of women, Publicity, 1958–1960.

GB0152 MSS 292/60.21/1, The Industrial News for Women Newsletters.

GB0152 MSS.292B/118/3, Wages, Equal Pay.

GB0152 MSS.292B/119/1–6, Wages, Equal Pay, 1963–1970.

GB0152 MSS.292B/128.7/1–2, Factory Acts, Working Hours of Women and Young People.

GB0152 MSS.292B/128.9/1–3, Hours, Shift System.

GB0152 MSS.292B/134/6, Women, Information conferences, 1962–1964.

GB0152 MSS.292B/134/7, Women in industry, Industrial charter for women workers, 1962–1964.

GB0152 MSS.292B/134/8, Women in industry, Industrial charter for women workers, 1968.

GB0152 MSS.292B/134/1–10, Women in industry, International Labour Office, 1961–1970.

GB0152 MSS.292B/135/1–3, Unemployment, 1960–1970.

GB0152 MSS.292B/136/1–2, Full employment, 1961–1970.

GB0152 MSS.292B/787.7/5, Central Office of Information, 1960–1970.

GB0152 MSS.296/REG/280.12/A–G, Automation, 1955–1970.

GB0152 MSS.296/REG/280.28, Productivity Agreements, 1969.

GB0152 MSS.296/REG, Council of Civil Service Unions, 1918–1994.

GB0152 MSS.415/CPSA Box 76, CSCA Circulars, 1961–1969.

GB0152 MSS.415/CPSA Box 165, CSCA Annual Reports, 1955–1967.

GB0152 MSS.292B/572.13/1, Science and Technology, Committee on Manpower Resources, 1966.

GB0152 MSS.292B/571.143/4, "Work Study and Computers: 1970 ICL Seminar," Feb. 1970.

GB0152 MSS.292B/571.2/2, DSIR Correspondence with TUC, 1962–1965.

GB0152 MSS.292B/571.811/1, Automation, Foundation of Automation and Employment Ltd., 1962–1970.

GB0152 MSS.292B/571.811/3, National Electronic Council, 1967–1968.

GB0152 MSS.292B/571.82/1–3, Automation, Trade Unions' Attitude, 1961–1970.

GB0152 MSS.292B/571.822, Automation and Women Workers TUC questionnaire and report, 1960–1962.

GB0152 File MSS.292B/571.822/1, Automation, OECD European Conference, 1966.

GB0152 MSS.292B/571.87/3, Industrial and Economic Research on Automation and European Productivity, Meeting in Rome, 1967.

The National Archives, London

The National Archives of the UK provided the lion's share of material for this history, including internal government documents, records pertaining to ICL, and employment records. Individual files consulted at the National Archives are too numerous to list. The following is a list of the file series used, followed by a list of specific files referenced in the notes.

Series

AB Series: Records of the United Kingdom Atomic Energy Authority and its predecessors.

AIR Series: Records created or inherited by the Air Ministry, the Royal Air Force, and related bodies.

AN Series: Records created or inherited by the British Transport Commission, the British Railways Board, and related bodies.

BA Series: Records of the Civil Service Department.

BT Series: Records of the Board of Trade and of successor and related bodies.

CAB Series: Records of the Cabinet Office.

CAOG Series: Records created or inherited by the Crown Agents for Overseas Governments and Administrations.

CJ Series: Records created or inherited by the Northern Ireland Office.

CSC Series: Records of the Civil Service Commission.

CSPR Series: Records of the Civil Service Pay Research Unit.

CW Series: Records of the Advisory, Conciliation, and Arbitration Service.

DSIR Series: Records created or inherited by the Department of Scientific and Industrial Research and those of related bodies.

ED Series: Records created or inherited by the Department of Education and Science and those of related bodies.

FG Series: Records of the National Economic Development Council and National Economic Development Office.

HN Series: Records of the Central Computer and Telecommunications Agency and predecessors.

HO Series: Records created or inherited by the Home Office, Ministry of Home Security, and related bodies.

HW Series: Records created and inherited by Government Communications Headquarters (GCHQ).

LAB Series: Records of departments responsible for labor and employment matters and related bodies.

MH Series: Records created or inherited by the Ministry of Health and successors, local government boards, and related bodies.

NSC Series: Records created and inherited by the National Savings Committee, the Post Office Savings Department, and the Department for National Savings.

OS Series: Records of the Ordnance Survey of Great Britain.

PREM Series: Records of the Prime Minister's Office.

PT Series: Records of the Public Trustee Office.

RAIL Series: Records of the prenationalization railway companies, the prenationalization canal and related companies, the London Passenger Transport Board, and successors.

STAT Series: Records of the Stationery Office.

T Series: Records created and inherited by HM Treasury.

Selected Files

AIR 77/384, Recruitment and Retention of Machine Operators.

AN 171/398, Equal Pay, Equal Work: Shorthand Typists and Machine Operators.

AN 171/398–399, Equal Pay, Equal Work: Shorthand Typists and Machine Operators.

BA 22/319, Pay and Costing Implications of Machine Operator Grading, 1970.

CAB 148/37, Cabinet Papers.

CAB 163/230, Release of Information on Wartime Computers, 1970–1974.

CAOG 16/213, Pay: Machine Operator Grades, 1957–1970.

CJ 4/630, ICL Ltd., Castlereagh, Belfast.

CSPR 5/52, University Computer Operators: Background Papers, 1980.

CW 2/30–34, Employment Protection Act 1975: IBM UK Ltd. London and Greenock, 1975–1977.

DSIR 23/23112, Aeronautical Research Council, Training and Careers for Computers.

ED 212/216, Economic Development Committee for the Electronics Industry, Computer Sector Working Party, Manpower Sub-Committee, Discussion Papers on Education and Training; Final Report and Government Response, 1979–1980.

FG 4/968, Select Committee, Computer Industry in the 1970s.

HN 1/1, Effects on Staff of Technical Developments in Computing, 1979.

HN 1/15, Arrangements for the Setting Up of the Central Computer Agency (CCA), 1972.

HN 1/16, ADP Staffing Problems Other than Shift Working, 1956–1967.

HN 1/22, Report on Development of Computers in Government: Forecast for Next Ten Years, 1969–1971.

HN 1/25, Management Issues Arising from Introduction of Data Preparation Work, 1970–1979.

HN 1/26, Procurement Policy, Use of British Computers, 1965–1972.

HN 1/30, Exchange of Computer Staff Between the Civil Service and the Private Sector, 1968–1980.

HN 1/38, Industrial Relations in the Civil Service: Government Computing, 1973–1979.

HN 1/40, Purchase and Supply of ADP Equipment, 1964–1970.

HN 1/60, Civil Service Department, Policy and Planning, Ministry of Technology, Use of Data Processing in Government.

HN 1/62, Central Computing Agency, Papers of Origin.

HN 1/67, Consultation with Civil Service Staff Association about Automated Data Processing (ADP), 1968–1971.

HN 1/68, Consultation with Civil Service Staff Association about ADP, 1971–1972.

HN 1/72, Interdepartmental Working Party on Computer Personnel: Implementation of recommendations, 1972–1973.

HN 1/85, Wastage of Automated Data Processing (ADP) staff from Government computer installations, 1978–1983.

HW 25/5, General Report on Tunny with Emphasis on Statistical Methods, 1945.

LAB 112/95, Incomes Policy Attack on Inflation, Equal Pay.

LAB 12/1471, Policy Considerations on Recruitment of Programmers and Computer Operators.

LAB 12/1516, General Application of ADP, 1965–1968.

LAB 12/1553, Shift Working of Computer Operators: Applications for Vacancies and Other Papers, 1966–1969.

LAB 79/32, Womanpower Debate.

LAB 8/1795, U.S. Department of Labor Women's Bureau, Womanpower Committees During World War II, United States and British Experience.

MH 108/564, Application of the Regulations, Interpretation of the terms Administrative, Professional, and Clerical, Subclerical Grades: Punch Card Operators, etc.

NSC 22/68, Clerical Assistant Grade.

OS 1/656, Duplicator Operators and Machine Operators (Clerical), 1943–1956.

PREM 13/1967, Office of the Prime Minister.

PREM 15/412, Government Machinery: Computers, 1970–1971.

PT 1/102, Machines and Machine Operators including Mechanisation in P.T.O.

RAIL 1172/2467, Rates of Pay, Machine Operators.

STAT 14/2320, Accounts Division: Combined Tabulating Installation Staff Inspection Report, 1958–1959.

STAT 14/2727, Progress Reports on CCB, 1961–1969.

STAT 14/2765, Review of Machine Operator Grades, 1961–1970.

STAT 14/2972, Central Computing Agency.

STAT 14/3093, ADP installations in Government in 1965 and Staffing.

STAT 14/3093, Treasury Investigations: Combined Tabulating Installation; Automatic Data Processing (ADP) Bureau Service, 1964–1967.

STAT 14/3239, Strikes, Effects on HMSO and Emergency Arrangements to Alleviate Disruption, Computer Maintenance ICL/Asset Dispute.

STAT 14/3303, Shift working of computer operators: Applications for vacancies and other papers, 1966–1969.

STAT 14/3484, Central Computer Bureau Organization and Staffing.

STAT 14/4457, Computer Systems-Liaison with CCB-Conversion to ICL 2900, 1976–1977.

STAT 14/632, Machine Operating Class in Stationery Office, Establishment of Machine Operators.

T 162/942, Establishment of Temporary Staff in Professional Scientific and Technical Classes.

T 199/1090, Provision of Computer Facilities for Treasury, 1965–1968.

T 215/1595, CSA: Typists and Machine Operators' Survey, 1956–1958.

T 216/710, Redundancy Owing to Computers, 1961–1962.

T 222/1314, Interdepartmental Study Group on Application of Computer Techniques to Clerical Work, 1956–1957.

T 222/1323, Demonstration of Electronic Computers to and Consultation with Civil Service National Whitley Council and Staff Associations about Introduction in Government Offices, 1959–1960.

T 222/409, Committee on Industrial Productivity: Panel on Technology and Operational Research, 1948–1950.

T 222/773, National Physical Laboratory.

T 222/964, Possible Use of Computers for Electronic Payroll Work, 1954–1958.

T 224/900, Economic Situation 1965: Deferment of expenditure on capital projects, application to computers.

T 316/308, Investment Appraisal for Government Computer Projects, 1971–1974.

T 325/161, History of the Computer Merger.

The National Archive for the History of Computing, University of Manchester

The UK National Archive for the history of computing contains reports, brochures, and ephemera from several major British computer companies.

NAHC/FER, Box 1 of 6, Folder FER/A1, Press clippings.

NAHC/FER, Box 3, Ferranti Computer Programming Documentation.

NAHC/FER, Box 4, Reports.

NAHC/FER, Box 5, Ferranti Documentation and Reports.

NAHC/FER/81–5, Talks between Ferranti and Prof. Williams at Manchester University to Build a Computer to Be Installed There, 1948.

NAHC/FER/C136, Research and Development.

NAHC/FER/C15c, Ferranti Computer Programming Documentation.

NAHC/FER/C18–C19, Ferranti Reports and Brochures.

NAHC/FER/C20b, Ferranti Atlas Schematics.

NAHC/FER/C2–C4, Technical Reports.

NAHC/FER/C30, Box 6, History of the Ferranti Computer Department.

NAHC/FER/C7–C13, Box 2, Technical Reports.

NAHC/LEO/A1–A9, News Clippings, LEO Employee Recollections

NAHC/LEO/D1–7, LEO Press Clippings.

NAHC/ICT/C96, ICL Advertisements.

NAHC/LEO/D7, Press Clippings.

The Vickers Archive, University of Cambridge

The Vickers Archive contains files on the Powers-Samas company, which was a subsidiary of the major British defense contractor Vickers Ltd.

Files on Powers-Samas: Vickers 133, 651, 771, 906, 1461.

The Women's Library, London

The Women's Library, located at London Metropolitan University when this research was carried out (and now located at the London School of Economics), provided records of the equal pay campaign as well as records of women civil servants and women's clerical unions.

331.420941, TOB Equal Pay Campaign Committee Film. *To Be a Woman*. Dir. Jill Craigie. National Union of Women Teachers, 1950.

6/CCS, Box 258, Council of Women Civil Servants.

6/EPC, Boxes 261, 262, Equal Pay Campaign and Evidence to the Equal Pay Commission.

6/JCS, Boxes 339–341, Folders A1–3, C1, C4, C5, and E9, Joint Committee on Women in the Civil Service, 1919–1954.

6/NCS, Boxes 279–282, NAWCS general reports for the years 1933–1958, NAWCS pamphlets, misc.

6/NCS/E2/1–3, National Association of Women Civil Servants.

6/WES/2, items 1–32, Records of the Women's Engineering Society. Booklets, 1945, 1958–1980.

6/WES/3/1/4, Records of the Women's Engineering Society. General, 1947–1964.

6/WES/311/4, UN Reports on Women's Equality.

8/NLS/4, Baroness Beatrice Nancy Seear, b. August 7, 1913. Interview by Betty Scharf, February 1991.

8/NLS/4, Enid Hutchison, b. July 15, 1909. Interview by Betty Scharf, February 1991.

GB 0106 7/DME, Papers of Dorothy Elizabeth Evans.

Interviews

These include interviews conducted by the author as well as interviews conducted by other historians.

Lorna Cockayne, interview conducted by British Computer Society. "Lorna Cockayne: Enigma," date unknown. Accessed July 20, 2016. http://www.bcs.org/upload/mp3/lorna-cockayne-enigma.mp3.

Rozanne Colchester, interview conducted by Robert McCrum. "Women Spies in the Second World War," *The Guardian*, November 6, 2010. Accessed June 9, 2016. http://www.guardian.co.uk/world/2010/nov/07/women-spies-second-world-war.

Mary Coombs, interview conducted by Thomas Lean. British Library "Voices of Science" Oral History Collection, 2010. Accessed June 9, 2016. http://sounds.bl.uk/Oral-history/Science/021M-C1379X0016XX-0001V0.

Cathy Gillespie and Ann Sayce (former computer operators), transcript of oral interview conducted by author. British Library, January 5, 2006.

Cathy Gillespie (former computer operator), email interview conducted by author. January 8–9, 2006, July 7, 2006.

Colin Hobson (former computer operator), email interview conducted by author. December 18–21, 2005.

Eleanor Ireland, interview conducted by Janet Abbate for the IEEE History Center, April 23, 2001 (the Institute of Electrical and Electronics Engineers, 2001). http://ethw.org/Oral-History:Eleanor_Ireland.

Peter Stern (former programmer trainee), transcript of interview conducted by author. British Library, August 15, 2005.

Censuses, Selected Government Reports, and Parliamentary Debates

Beveridge, William. *Social Insurance and Allied Services*. London: HMSO, 1942. Cmd. 6404.

Biddle, Eric H. *Manpower, a Summary of the British Experience*. Chicago: Public Administration Service, 1942.

Castle, Barbara. *In Place of Strife: A Policy for Industrial Relations*. London: HMSO, 1969. Cmnd. 3888.

Central Office of Information for Department of Employment. *Jobs for Young Girls*. 1969. 49 sec. National Archives (UK), *Public Information Films 1964–1979*. Accessed May 27, 2016. http://www.nationalarchives.gov.uk/films/1964to1979/filmpage_jobs.htm.

Central Statistical Office. *Statistical Digest of the War*. London: HMSO, 1951.

Chapman, R. A. *Teaching Public Administration*. London: Joint University Council for Social and Public Administration, Hamilton House, 1973.

Civil Service National Whitley Council Committee. *Marriage Bar in the Civil Service*. London: HMSO, 1946. Cmnd. 6886.

Council for Scientific Policy, and the University Grants Committee. *Report of a Joint Working Group on Computers for Research*. London: HMSO, 1966. Cmnd. 2883.

Cowie, J., J. W. Hermann, and P. D. Maycock, "The British Computer Scene, Part I: The Government Impact on the Computer Scene." London: Office of Naval Research, 1967.

Cowie, J., J. W. Hermann, and P. D. Maycock, "The British Computer Scene, Part II: The British Computer Industry." London: Office of Naval Research, 1967.

Department of Scientific and Industrial Research, Great Britain. *Problems of Progress in Industry*. London: HMSO, 1957–1964.

Directorate-General for Employment Commission of the European Communities, Industrial Relations and Social Affairs. *Office Automation and Social*

Change in Europe. Luxembourg: Office for Official Publications of the European Communities, 1992.

Electronic Computers SWP. *Manpower Sub-Committee, Final Report: Follow Up of Recommendations*. London: HMSO, 1981.

Electronic Computers SWP. *Manpower Sub-Committee, More Information: Economic Development Committee for the Electronics Industry, Computer Sector Working Party, Manpower Sub-Committee.* Discussion papers on education and training; final report and government response. 1979–1980. London: HMSO, 1980.

Electronic Computers SWP. *Manpower Sub-Committee, Second Interim Report.* London: HMSO, 1979.

Financial Secretary to the Treasury, Great Britain. *Estimates for Civil Service for the Year Ending 31st March, 1947, Annual Report, 1945–46*. London: HMSO, 1945.

Financial Secretary to the Treasury, Great Britain. *Estimates for Civil Service for the Year Ending 31st March, 1948, Annual Report, 1946–47*. London: HMSO, 1946.

Fulton Committee. *The Civil Service Vol. 1. Report of the Committee 1966–1968*. London: HMSO, 1968. Cmnd. 3638.

Hartmann, Heidi I., Robert E. Kraut, and Louise A. Tilly, eds. *Computer Chips and Paper Clips: Technology and Women's Employment. Vol. 1*. Washington, DC: National Academy Press, 1986.

House of Commons. *Equal Pay Act 1954*. Edited by Douglas Houghton, Alice Bacon, Wedgwood Benn, Barbara Castle, and Charles Pannell. London: HMSO, 1954.

House of Commons, Secretary of State for the Home Department. *Equality for Women*. London: HMSO, 1974. Cmd. 5724.

House of Commons, Secretary of State for Education and Science. *Attainments of the School Leaver: Government Observations on the Tenth Report of the Expenditure Committee*. London: HMSO, 1978. Cmd. 7124.

Hunt, Audrey. *Management Attitudes and Practices Towards Women at Work*. Edited by Social Survey Division Office of Population Censuses and Surveys. London: HMSO, 1975.

Hunt, Audrey. *A Survey of Women's Employment: A 1965 Government Social Survey*. Edited by Ministry of Labour Government Social Survey. London: HMSO, 1968.

Hunt, Audrey, Judith Fox, and Michael Bradley. *Post-Training Careers of Government Training Center Trainees*. Edited by Social Survey Division Office of Population Censuses and Surveys. London: HMSO, 1972.

Hunt, Audrey, and Irene Rauta. *Fifth Form Girls: Their Hopes for the Future.* Edited by Social Survey Division of the Office of Population Censuses and Surveys on behalf of the Department of Education and Science. London: HMSO, 1975.

Institute of Manpower Studies. *Computer Manpower in the 80s: The Supply and Demand for Computer-Related Manpower to 1985*. London: National Economic Development Office, 1980.

Labour Party. *Labour's Programme for Britain*. London: The Labour Party, 1976.

Martin, Jean, and Ceridwen Roberts. *Women and Employment: A Lifetime Perspective*. London: Office of Population Censuses and Surveys, 1984.

Minister of Food. *Report on a Plan for the Mechanized Production of Groundnuts in East and Central Africa (Groundnuts Scheme)*. London: HMSO, 1946–1947. Cmd. 7030.

Minister of Food and Secretary of State for the Colonies. *The Future of the Overseas Food Corporation*. London: HMSO, 1951. Cmnd. 8125.

Ministry of Labour. *Statistics on Incomes, Prices, Employment, and Production*, no. 19. London: HMSO, December 1966.

Ministry of Labour. *Statistics on Incomes, Prices, Employment, and Production*, no. 23. London: HMSO, December 1967.

National Economic Development Council. *NEDC Industrial Strategy: Electronic Computers*. London: HMSO, 1976.

Office of Population Censuses and Survey. *Census 1951, England and Wales, General Report*. London: HMSO, 1958.

Office of Population Censuses and Survey. *Census 1951, England and Wales, Industry Tables*. London: HMSO, 1957.

Office of Population Censuses and Survey. *Census 1961, Great Britain, Summary Tables*. London: HMSO, 1966.

Office of Population Censuses and Survey. *Census 1971, Great Britain, Age Marital Condition and General Tables*. London: HMSO, 1974.

Office of Population Censuses and Survey. *Census 1971, Great Britain, Part II, 10% Sample*. London: HMSO, 1974.

Office of Population Censuses and Survey. *Census 1971, Great Britain, Economic Activity: Part I*. London: HMSO, 1973.

Office of Population Censuses and Survey. *Census 1971, Great Britain, Economic Activity, Part IV, 10% Sample*. London: HMSO, 1974.

Office of Population Censuses and Survey. *Census 1971, National Report Great Britain, Part 1*. London: HMSO, 1974.

Office of Population Censuses and Survey. *Census 1981, National Report Great Britain, Part 1*. London: HMSO, 1983.

Rees, Teresa. *Skill Shortages, Women and the New Information Technologies*. Luxembourg: Office for Official Publications of the European Communities, 1992.

Royal Commission on the Civil Service. *Report of the Royal Commission on the Civil Service, 1953–55*. London: HMSO, 1955. Cmd. 9613.

Royal Commission on Equal Pay. *Report of the Royal Commission on Equal Pay, 1944–46*. London: HMSO, 1946. Cmd. 6937.

Select Committee on Science and Technology. *Report on Session 1969–1970*, Vol. 1. London: HMSO, 1971.

Select Committee on Science and Technology, Session 1969–1970. *UK Computer Industry, Vol. 1, Minutes of Evidence*. London: HMSO, 1970.

Select Committee on Science and Technology (Sub-Committee A), Session 1970–1971. *Prospects for the United Kingdom Computer Industry in the 1970s. Vol. I, Report*. London: HMSO, 1971. (HC621-I.)

Select Committee on Science and Technology (Sub-Committee A), Session 1970–1971. *Prospects for the United Kingdom Computer Industry in the 1970s. Vol. II, Minutes of Evidence*. London: HMSO, 1971. (HC621-II.)

Select Committee on Science and Technology (Sub-Committee A), Session 1970–1971. *Prospects for the United Kingdom Computer Industry in the 1970s. Vol. III, Appendices*. London: HMSO, 1971. (HC621-III.)

Select Committee on Science and Technology (Sub-Committee A), Session 1970–1971. *Prospects for the United Kingdom Computer Industry in the 1970s, Reply by the Department of Trade and Industry, with Evidence Taken Before Subcommittee D, 3 August 1972*. London: HMSO, 1972. (HC473.)

Select Committee on Science and Technology (Sub-Committee A), Session 1972–1973. *Second Report on the UK Computer Industry (First Part)*. London: HMSO, 1973. (HC309.)

Select Committee on Science and Technology (Sub-Committee A). *Second Report on the UK Computer Industry (First Part), Minutes of Evidence*. London: HMSO, 1973. (HC97-1.)

Select Committee on Science and Technology (U.K. Computer Industry Sub-Committee), Session 1974. *Minutes of Evidence*. London: HMSO, 1974. (HC199.)

Turing, Alan. *A. M. Turing's Original Proposal for the Development of an Electronic Computer, Reprinted with a Foreword by D.W. Davies, Superintendent of the Computer Science Division*. London: National Physical Laboratory, Division of Computer Science, 1972.

United Kingdom. *Hansard Parliamentary Debates*, 5th ser., vol. 721. 1965.

United Kingdom. *Hansard Parliamentary Debates*, 5th ser., vol. 724. 1966.

United Kingdom. *Hansard Parliamentary Debates*, 5th ser., vol. 787. 1969.

United Kingdom. *Hansard Parliamentary Debates*, 5th ser., vol. 793. 1969.

United Kingdom. *Hansard Parliamentary Debates*, 5th ser., vol. 833. 1972.

United Kingdom. *Hansard Parliamentary Debates*, Lords, 5th ser., vol. 152. 1972.

United Kingdom. *Parliamentary Debates*, Commons, 5th ser., vol. 438 (1947), cols. 1069–1075.

Industry Reports, Management Literature, and Computing Manuals

Banking, Insurance, and the Finance Union (BIFU). *Jobs for the Girls? The Impact of Automation on Women's Jobs in the Finance Industry*. London: BIFU, 1988.

British Conference on Automation and Computation. "Discussion Meetings on the Reliability and Maintenance of Digital Computer Systems. Managerial and Engineering Aspects. January 20th and 21st 1960." London: The Institution of Electrical Engineers and the British Computer Society Ltd., 1960.

Cochrane, Louise. *Anne in Electronics*. London: Chatto & Windus, 1960.

Comrie, L. J. *The Hollerith and Powers Tabulating Machines: Based on a Lecture Delivered under the Auspices of the Office Machinery Users' Association of LSE on 20 November 1929 and Two of the Newmach Lectures delivered at UCL March 2 and 9, 1933*. Edinburgh: Neill and Company, 1933. Printed for private circulation. British Library.

Ferranti Ltd. "A Program for Power System Load Studies (CS252)." January 1960.

Ferranti Ltd. "Classified Index of Computer Literature (CS268)." June 1960.

Ferranti Ltd. "Classified Index of Computer Literature, Library Services, and Films (CS382)." June 1963.

Ferranti Ltd. "Data Preparation and Operating Instructions for the Solutions of Simultaneous Linear Equations (CS306)." August 1961.

Ferranti Ltd. "Ferranti Data Links (CS310)." October 1961.

Ferranti Ltd. "Ferranti Mercury Computer Programming Manual, Issue 1 (CS158)." July 1957.

Ferranti Ltd. "Ferranti Mercury Computer: Multiple Input/Output Facilities (CS246)." September 1959.

Ferranti Ltd. "Ferranti Mercury Computer: Programs Available in the Interchange Scheme (CS281 A)." March 1960.

Ferranti Ltd. "Ferranti Orion: 2 Sample Complete Programs (CS296)." May 1951.

Ferranti Ltd. "Ferranti Orion: Sorting Time Graphs (CS297)." June 1961.

Ferranti Ltd. "Ferranti Pegasus Computer: Programs Available in the Interchange Scheme (CS206 A)." August 1959.

Ferranti Ltd. "Ferranti Pegasus Computer: Tape Code Conversion (CS267)." June 1960.

Ferranti Ltd. "Ferranti Pegasus, Perseus and Mercury Computers: Interchangeability and Compatibility of Magnetic Tapes (CS234)." July 1959.

Ferranti Ltd. "Ferranti Punched Tape Data Links (CS343)." September 1962.

Ferranti Ltd. "Introduction to NEBULA (the Natural Electronic Business Language) (CS275)." October 1960.

Ferranti Ltd. "Mercury: Punched Card Input/Output and Line Printer (CS251)." January 1960.

Ferranti Ltd. "Operating Instructions for Using Electrodata Magnetic Tape Mechanisms (CS233)." May 1959.

Ferranti Ltd. "Pegasus Program MK 1B for Multiple Regression Analysis by S. A. Robinson, B.Sc., A. R. C. S. & R. J. Taylor, B.Sc., F.S.S. of The British Iron and Steel Research Association (CS273)." October 1960.

Ferranti Ltd. "Process Control Equipment (CS295)." April 1961.

Ferranti Ltd. "Programming with the 7168 Word Store (CS265)." April 1960.

Ferranti Ltd. "Table of Contents of Orion Programming Manual (Provisional) (CS374)." August 1963.

Ferranti Ltd. "The Computer Library Service (CS223 D)." April 1961.

Ferranti Ltd. "The Field of Application of the Ferranti Sirius Computers (CS239)." June 1959.

Ferranti Ltd. "The Teletype Punch (CS271)." September 1960.

Ferranti Ltd. "The Transactor Data Transmission Equipment (CS238)." June 1959.

Ferranti Ltd. "User's Specification of Pegasus 2." January 1960.

Howell, D. A. "Public Administration and Educational Administration: Some Thoughts on the Chapman Report, 'Teaching Public Administration.'" *Educational Management Administration & Leadership* 32, no. 2 (1974): 32–37.

ICL. *1900 Series Software*. London: ICL, 1971.

ICL. *2903 Range, Direct Data Entry: Extended System*. 2nd ed. London: ICL, 1978.

ICL. *An Introduction to Electronic Data Processing*. 2nd ed. London: ICL, 1971.

ICL. *Glossary of Basic Computer Terms*. London: ICL, 1970.

ICL/CES. *Computer Education in Schools: Computer Studies, Book 1*. London: ICL, 1978.

Institute of Directors. *What Every Director Should Know About Automation: Report of a One-Day Conference on Automation, London, 12 December 1963*. London: Institute of Directors, 1964.

Linton, Andrew. *Introduction to Mechanized Accounts and Computers*. London: Sir Isaac Pitman and Sons Ltd., 1966.

Lockspeiser, Ben. *Man and His Machines: Automation and Computerization—Their Origins and Effects*. London: Lawrence Bros. Ltd., 1960.

Manual of Modern Business Equipment. *Adding and Calculating Machines*. 2nd ed. London: Macdonald and Evans, 1961.

Manual of Modern Business Equipment. *Punched Card Systems*. 2nd ed. London: Macdonald and Evans, 1964.

Office Magazine. *Methods at Work: Procedures, Ideas and Data Gathered from the Pages of Office Magazine*. London: Office Magazine, 1962.

Trades Union Congress. "Automation and Technological Change." London: Trades Union Congress, 1965.

Nonarchival Sources

Abbate, Janet. "The Pleasure Paradox: Bridging the Gap between Popular Images of Computing and Women's Historical Experiences." In *Gender Codes: Why Women Are Leaving Computing*, edited by Thomas Misa, 213–227. Hoboken, NJ: Wiley, 2010.

Abbate, Janet. *Recoding Gender: Women's Changing Participation in Computing*. Cambridge, MA: MIT Press, 2012.

Abbate, Janet. "Women and Gender in the History of Computing." *IEEE Annals of the History of Computing* 25, no. 4 (2003): 4–8.

Agar, Jon. *The Government Machine: A Revolutionary History of the Computer*. Cambridge, MA: MIT Press, 2003.

Akera, Atsushi. "Engineers or Managers? The Systems Analysis of Electronic Data Processing in the Federal Bureaucracy." In *Systems, Experts, and Computers: The Systems Approach in Management and Engineering, World War II and After*, edited by Agatha C. Hughes and Thomas P. Hughes, 191–220. Cambridge, MA: MIT Press, 2000.

Alford, B. W. E. *Britain in the World Economy since 1880, Social and Economic History of England*. London: Longman, 1996.

Allen, Ann Taylor. "Feminism, Social Science, and the Meanings of Modernity: The Debate on the Origin of the Family in Europe and the United States, 1860–1914." *American Historical Review* 104, no. 4 (1999): 1085–1113.

Ambrosius, Gerold, and William H. Hubbard. *A Social and Economic History of Twentieth-Century Europe*. Cambridge, MA: Harvard University Press, 1989.

Amsden, A. H., ed. *The Economics of Women and Work*. New York: St. Martin's Press, 1980.

Anchalee, Isis. "You May Have Seen My Face on the BART." The Coffeelicious, August 1, 2014. Accessed DATE. https://medium.com/the-coffeelicious/you-may-have-seen-my-face-on-bart-8b9561003e0f#.8znagygsb.

Anderson, Benedict R. O'G. *Imagined Communities: Reflections on the Origin and Spread of Nationalism*. London: Verso, 1983.

Anderson, Gregory. *The White-Blouse Revolution: Female Office Workers since 1870*. New York: St. Martin's Press, 1988.

Anderson, T. R. "Letters: IBM Employee Replies to Clive Jenkins." *Greenock Telegraph*, June 13, 1977.

Archer, J. B. "The Office Manager's Guide to Greater Efficiency at Lower Cost, Part 6: Staff Problems, Interviews, Wages." *Office Magazine*, December 1965, 1020.

Armitage, David. "Greater Britain: A Useful Category of Historical Analysis?" *American Historical Review* 104, no. 2 (1999): 427–445.

Aron, Cindy Sondik. *Ladies and Gentlemen of the Civil Service: Middle-Class Workers in Victorian America*. New York: Oxford University Press, 1987.

Ashenfelter, Orley, and Richard Layard. "Incomes Policy and Wage Differentials." *Economica* 50, no. 198 (1983): 127–143.

Aspray, W., F. Mayadas, and M. Vardi, eds. *Globalization and the Offshoring of Software*. New York: ACM, 2006.

Aspray, William. *Chasing Moore's Law: Information Technology Policy in the United States*. Raleigh, NC: SciTech Publishers, 2004.

Aspray, William. *John von Neumann and the Origins of Modern Computing*. Cambridge, MA: MIT Press, 1990.

Baker, R. J. S. *Administrative Theory and Public Administration*. London: Hutchison, 1972.

Banks, Olive. *The Politics of British Feminism, 1918–1970*. Aldershot, UK: E. Elgar Pub, 1993.

Baron, A., ed. *Work Engendered: Toward a New History of American Labor*. Ithaca: Cornell University Press, 1991.

Barrow, Logie, and Ian Bullock. *Democratic Ideas and the British Labour Movement, 1880–1914*. Cambridge: Cambridge University Press, 1996.

Bartik, Jean Jennings. *Pioneer Programmer: Jean Jennings Bartik and the Computer that Changed the World*. Edited by Jon T. Rickman and Kim D. Todd. Kirksville, MO: Truman State University Press, 2013.

Basalla, George. *The Evolution of Technology, Cambridge History of Science*. Cambridge: Cambridge University Press, 1988.

Bassett, Ross. "Aligning India in the Cold War Era: Indian Technical Elites, the Indian Institute of Technology at Kanpur, and Computing in India and the United States." *Technology and Culture* 50, no. 4 (October 2009): 783–810.

Bassett, Ross. *The Technological Indian*. Cambridge, MA: Harvard University Press, 2016.

BBC News Video. "Bletchley Veteran Recalls Work on Colossus." February 6, 2014. Accessed June 3, 2016. http://www.bbc.com/news/technology-26076085.

Beniger, James R. *The Control Revolution: Technological and Economic Origins of the Information Society*. Cambridge, MA: Harvard University Press, 1986.

Berg, Maxine. "What Difference Did Women's Work Make to the Industrial Revolution?" *History Workshop* 35 (Spring 1993): 22–44.

Berg, Maxine. "Women's Work, Mechanisation and the Early Phases of Industrialization in England." In *Historical Meanings of Work*, edited by P. Joyce. Cambridge: Cambridge University Press, 1987.

Berners-Lee, Mary Lee. Interview with Janet Abbate. "Anecdotes: How Did You First Get into Computing?" Edited by Anne Fitzpatrick. *IEEE Annals of the History of Computing* 25, no. 4 (2003): 78–79.

BéruBé, Kelly, A. Whittaker, T. Jones, T. Moreno, and L. Merolla. "London Smogs: Why Did They Kill?" *Proceedings of the Royal Microscopical Society* 40, no. 3 (2005): 171–183.

Biersack, Aletta, Lynn Avery Hunt, and NetLibrary Inc. *The New Cultural History Essays*. Berkeley: University of California Press, 1989.

Bijker, Wiebe E. *Of Bicycles, Bakelites, and Bulbs: Toward a Theory of Sociotechnical Change*. Cambridge, MA: MIT Press, 1995.

Bijker, Wiebe E., Thomas Parke Hughes, and T. J. Pinch. *The Social Construction of Technological Systems: New Directions in the Sociology and History of Technology*. Cambridge, MA: MIT Press, 1987.

Bijker, Wiebe E., and John Law. *Shaping Technology/Building Society: Studies in Sociotechnical Change*. Cambridge, MA: MIT Press, 1992.

Bird, Peter J. *LEO: The First Business Computer*. Wokingham, UK: Hasler Publishing Ltd., 1994.

Bix, Amy. *Girls Coming to Tech! A History of American Engineering Education for Women*. Cambridge, MA: MIT Press, 2014.

Black, Alistair, Dave Muddiman, and Helen Plant. *The Early Information Society: Information Management in Britain before the Computer*. Aldershot, UK: Ashgate, 2007.

Blackwelder, Julia Kirk. *Now Hiring: The Feminization of Work in the United States, 1900–1995*. College Station: Texas A&M University Press, 1997.

Blom, Ida, Karen Hagemann, and Catherine Hall. *Gendered Nations: Nationalisms and Gender Order in the Long Nineteenth Century*. Oxford: Berg, 2000.

Bolter, J. *David. Turing's Man: Western Culture in the Computer Age*. Chapel Hill: University of North Carolina Press, 1984.

Briggs, Asa, and John Saville. *Essays in Labour History, 1918–1939*. Hamden, CT: Archon Books, 1977.

British Telecom. "BT Remembers Tommy Flowers' Achievements." May 23, 2014. Accessed June 3, 2016. http://home.bt.com/news/btlife/bt-remembers-tommy-flowers-achievements-11363857904783.

Brooks, Fred. *The Mythical Man Month*. New York: Addison-Wesley, 1975.

Brown, R. G. S. *The Administrative Process in Britain*. London: Methuen, 1971.

Burchell, G., C. Gordon, and P. Miller, eds. *The Foucault Effect: Studies in Governmentality*. Chicago: University of Chicago Press, 1991.

Burgess, Keith. *The Challenge of Labour: Shaping British Society, 1850–1930*. New York: St. Martin's Press, 1980.

Burman, Annie. "Gendering Decryption—Decrypting Gender: The Gender Discourse of Labour at Bletchley Park, 1939–1945." MA thesis, Uppsala University, 2013. Accessed June 5, 2016. http://uu.diva-portal.org/smash/get/diva2:625771/FULLTEXT01.pdf.

Burton, Antoinette M. *After the Imperial Turn: Thinking with and through the Nation*. Durham, NC: Duke University Press, 2003.

Burton, Antoinette M. *Burdens of History: British Feminists, Indian Women, and Imperial Culture, 1865–1915*. Chapel Hill: University of North Carolina Press, 1994.

Burton, Antoinette M. *Gender, Sexuality and Colonial Modernities*. New York: Routledge, 1999.

Butler, Judith. *Bodies That Matter: On the Discursive Limits of "Sex."* New York: Routledge, 1993.

Butler, Judith. *Gender Trouble: Feminism and the Subversion of Identity*. New York: Routledge, 1990.

Caine, Barbara. *English Feminism, 1780–1980*. Oxford: Oxford University Press, 1997.

Caminer, David. "... And How to Avoid Them." *Computer Journal* 1, no. 1 (1958): 11–14.

Caminer, David. "Behind the Curtain at LEO: A Personal Reminiscence." *IEEE Annals of the History of Computing* 25, no. 2 (2003): 3–13.

Caminer, David. "LEO and its Applications: The Beginning of Business Computing." *Computer Journal* 40, no. 10 (1997): 585–597.

Caminer, David, John Aris, Peter Hermon, and Frank William Land. *LEO: The Incredible Story of the World's First Business Computer*. New York: McGraw Hill, 1998.

Campbell, Alan, Nina Fishman, and John McIlroy. *British Trade Unions and Industrial Politics*. Aldershot, UK: Ashgate, 1999.

Campbell-Kelly, Martin. *I.C.L.: A Business and Technical History*. Oxford: Oxford University Press, 1990.

Campbell-Kelly, Martin, William Aspray, Nathan Ensmenger, and Jeff Yost. *Computer: A History of the Information Machine*. 3rd ed. Boulder, CO: Westview Press, 2014.

Canaday, Margot. *The Straight State: Sexuality and Citizenship in Twentieth-Century America*. Princeton, NJ: Princeton University Press, 2009.

Canning, Kathleen. *Gender History in Practice: Historical Perspectives on Bodies, Class, and Citizenship*. Ithaca: Cornell University Press, 2006.

Canning, Kathleen. *Languages of Labor and Gender: Female Factory Work in Germany, 1850–1914*. Ithaca: Cornell University Press, 1996.

Carew, Anthony. "The Anglo-American Council on Productivity (1948–52): The Ideological Roots of the Post-War Debate on Productivity in Britain." *Journal of Contemporary History* 26, no. 1 (1991): 49–69.

Carmichael, Hamish. *Another ICL Anthology*. Surbiton, UK: Laidlaw Hicks Publishers, 1998.

Carroll, Paul. *Big Blues: The Unmaking of IBM*. New York: Crown Publishers, 1993.

Castle, Barbara. *The Castle Diaries, 1964–1970*. London: Weidenfeld and Nicolson, 1984.

Castle, Barbara. *The Castle Diaries, 1974–1976*. London: Weidenfeld and Nicolson, 1980.

Castle, Barbara. *Fighting All the Way*. London: Macmillan, 1993.

Ceruzzi, Paul E. *A History of Modern Computing*. Cambridge, MA: MIT Press, 2003.

Chandler, Alfred Dupont, Jr. *The Visible Hand: The Managerial Revolution in American Business*. Cambridge, MA: Belknap Press, 1977.

Chapman, R. A. *Teaching Public Administration*. London: Joint University Council for Social and Public Administration, Hamilton House, 1973.

Chaudhuri, N., and M. Strobel, eds. *Western Women and Imperialism: Complicity and Resistance*. Bloomington: Indiana University Press, 1992.

Chick, Martin. *Industrial Policy in Britain, 1945–1951: Economic Planning, Nationalisation, and the Labour Governments*. Cambridge: Cambridge University Press, 1998.

Childs, David. *Britain since 1939: Progress and Decline*. New York: St. Martin's Press, 1995.

Clark, Anna. *The Struggle for the Breeches: Gender and the Making of the British Working Class*. Berkeley: University of California Press, 1995.

Clodfelter, Michael. *Warfare and Armed Conflicts: A Statistical Reference to Casualty and Other Figures, 1500–2000*. Jefferson, NC: McFarland, 2002.

Coates, David. *Industrial Policy in Britain*. New York: St. Martin's Press, 1996.

Coates, David. *The Question of UK Decline: State, Society and Economy*. New York: Harvester Wheatsheaf, 1994.

Cochrane, Louise Morley. *Anne in Electronics*. London: Chatto & Windus, 1960.

Cockburn, Cynthia. *Brothers: Male Dominance and Technological Change*. London: Pluto Press, 1983.

Cockburn, Cynthia. *Machinery of Dominance: Women, Men, and Technical Know-How*. London: Pluto Press, 1985.

Cockburn, Cynthia. "Women and Technology: Opportunity Is Not Enough." In *The Changing Experience of Employment: Restructuring and Recession*, edited by K. Purcell, S. Wood, A. Waton, and S. Allen, 173–187. London: Macmillan, 1986.

Cohoon, J. McGrath, and William Aspray, eds. *Women and Information Technology: Research on Underrepresentation*. Cambridge, MA: MIT Press, 2006.

Colley, Linda. *Captives: Britain, Empire and the World, 1600–1850*. London: Jonathan Cape, 2002.

Colley, Linda. "Whose Nation? Class and National Consciousness in Britain 1750–1830." *Past & Present*, no. 113 (1986): 97–117.

Colman, Jonathan. *A 'Special Relationship?' Harold Wilson, Lyndon B. Johnson and Anglo-American Relations 'at the Summit', 1964–68*. Manchester: Manchester University Press, 2004.

Comrie, L. J. "The Application of Commercial Calculating Machines to Scientific Computing." *Mathematical Tables and Other Aids to Computation (MTAC)* 2, no. 16 (1946): 149–159.

Comrie, L. J. "Careers for Girls." *The Mathematical Gazette* 28, no. 280 (1944): 90–95.

Conekin, Becky, Frank Mort, and Chris Waters. *Moments of Modernity: Reconstructing Britain, 1945–1964*. London: Rivers Oram Press, 1999.

Coopey, R., ed. *Information Technology Policy: An International History*. Oxford: Oxford University Press, 2004.

Copeland, B. Jack. "Colossus: Breaking the German 'Tunny' Code at Bletchley Park: An Illustrated History." *The Rutherford Journal* 3 (2010). Accessed DATE. http://www.rutherfordjournal.org/article030109.html.

Copeland, B. J., ed. *Colossus: The Secrets of Bletchley Park's Codebreaking Computers*. Oxford: Oxford University Press, 2006.

Cortada, James W. *Before the Computer: IBM, NCR, Burroughs, and Remington Rand and the Industry They Created, 1865–1956*. Princeton, NJ: Princeton University Press, 1993.

Cortada, James W. *The Digital Hand*. Vol. 3, *How Computers Changed the Work of American Public Sector Industries*. New York: Oxford University Press, 2007.

Costello, John. *Virtue under Fire: How World War II Changed our Social and Sexual Attitudes*. Boston: Little, Brown and Co., 1986.

Cowan, Ruth Schwartz. "The Consumption Junction: A Proposal for Research Strategies in the Sociology of Technology." In *The Social Construction of Technological Systems: New Directions in the Sociology and History of Technology*, edited by W. E. Bijker, T. P. Hughes, and T. Pinch, 253–272. Cambridge, MA: MIT Press, 1987.

Cowan, Ruth Schwartz. *More Work for Mother: The Ironies of Household Technology from the Open Hearth to the Microwave*. New York: Basic Books, 1983.

Cowan, Ruth Schwartz. *A Social History of American Technology*. New York: Oxford University Press, 1997.

Croarken, Mary. *Early Scientific Computing in Britain*. Oxford: Clarendon Press, 1990.

Croarken, M. J. "L. J. Comrie and the Origins of the Scientific Computing Service." *IEEE Annals of the History of Computing* 21, no. 4 (1999): 70–71.

Crompton, Rosemary. *Women and Work in Modern Britain*. Oxford: Oxford University Press, 1997.

Crompton, Rosemary. "Class Theory and Gender." *British Journal of Sociology* 40, no. 4 (1989): 565–587.

Crowther, M. A. "Family Responsibility and State Responsibility in Britain before the Welfare State." *Historical Journal* 25, no. 1 (1982): 131–145.

Daunton, Martin J. "Payment and Participation: Welfare and State-Formation in Britain, 1900–1951." *Past & Present*, no. 150 (1996): 169–216.

Daunton, Martin J. *Royal Mail: The Post Office since 1840*. London: Athlone Press, 1985.

Davidoff, Leonore, and Catherine Hall. *Family Fortunes: Men and Women of the English Middle Class, 1780–1850*. Chicago: University of Chicago Press, 1987.

Davies, Andrew, and Steven Fielding. *Workers' Worlds: Cultures and Communities in Manchester and Salford, 1880–1939*. Manchester: Manchester University Press, 1992.

Dean, Carolyn J. *The Frail Social Body: Pornography, Homosexuality, and Other Fantasies in Interwar France*. Berkeley: University of California Press, 2000.

de Haan, Francisca. *Gender and the Politics of Office Work, the Netherlands, 1860–1940*. Amsterdam: Amsterdam University Press, 1998.

Dintenfass, Michael. *The Decline of Industrial Britain, 1870–1980*. London: Routledge, 1992.

Dorey, Peter. *British Politics since 1945*. Oxford: Blackwell, 1995.

Dorey, Peter. *The Labour Governments, 1964–1970*. London: Routledge, 2006.

Downs, Laura Lee. *Manufacturing Inequality: Gender Division in the French and British Metalworking Industries, 1914–1939*. Ithaca: Cornell University Press, 1995.

Downs, Laura Lee. "Industrial Decline, Rationalization and Equal Pay: The Bedaux Strike at Rover Automobile Company." *Social History* 15, no. 1 (1990): 45–73.

Edgerton, David. *The Shock of the Old: Technology and Global History since 1900*. Oxford: Oxford University Press, 2007.

Edgerton, David. *The Warfare State: Britain, 1920–1970*. Cambridge: Cambridge University Press, 2006.

Electrodatia. "Computer at Play." *Office Magazine*, June 1958.

English, Richard, and Michael Kenny. *Rethinking British Decline*. New York: St. Martin's Press, 2000.

Ensmenger, Nathan. *The Computer Boys Take Over: Computers, Programmers, and the Politics of Technical Expertise. History of Computing*. Cambridge, MA: MIT Press, 2012.

Ensmenger, Nathan. "From 'Black Art' to Industrial Discipline: The Software Crisis and the Management of Programmers." PhD diss., University of Pennsylvania, 2001.

Ensmenger, Nathan. "Letting the 'Computer Boys' Take Over: Technology and the Politics of Organizational Transformation.", *International Review of Social History* 48, no. S11 (2003): 153–180.

Ensmenger, Nathan. "Making Programming Masculine." In *Gender Codes: Why Women are Leaving Computing*, edited by Thomas Misa, 115–142. Hoboken, NJ: Wiley, 2010.

Ensmenger, Nathan. "Power to the People: Toward a Social History of Computing." *IEEE Annals of the History of Computing* 26, no. 1 (2004): 94–96.

Ensmenger, Nathan. "The Question of Professionalism in the Computer Fields." *IEEE Annals of the History of Computing* 23, no. 4 (2001): 1–19.

Ferry, Georgina. *A Computer Called LEO: Lyons Teashops and the World's First Office Computer*. London: Fourth Estate, 2003.

Fischer, Claude S. *America Calling: A Social History of the Telephone to 1940*. Berkeley: University of California Press, 1992.

Fisher, Kate. *Birth Control, Sex, and Marriage in Britain, 1918–1960*. Oxford: Oxford University Press, 2006.

Fletcher, Ian Christopher, Laura E. Nym Mayhall, and Philippa Levine. *Women's Suffrage in the British Empire: Citizenship, Nation, and Race*. London: Routledge, 2000.

Floud, Roderick, and Deirdre N. McCloskey. *The Economic History of Britain since 1700*. 2nd ed. Cambridge: Cambridge University Press, 1994.

Flowers, T. H. "The Design of Colossus." *Annals of the History of Computing* 5 (1983): 239–252.

Foucault, Michel. *The History of Sexuality, Vol. 1: An Introduction*. New York: Vintage Books, 1990.

Fraser, Nancy. *Unruly Practices: Power, Discourse, and Gender in Contemporary Social Theory*. Minneapolis: University of Minnesota Press, 1989.

Freeman, Carla. *High Tech and High Heels in the Global Economy: Women, Work, and Pink-Collar Identities in the Caribbean*. Durham, NC: Duke University Press, 2000.

Freeman, Peter, and William Aspray. *The Supply of Information Technology Workers in the United States*. Washington, DC: Computing Research Association, 1999.

Frevert, Ute. *Women in German History: From Bourgeois Emancipation to Sexual Liberation*. Oxford: Berg, 1989.

Fritzsche, Peter. "Machine Dreams: Airmindedness and the Reinvention of Germany." *American Historical Review* 98 (1993): 685–709.

Fyrth, Jim. *Labour's Promised Land? Culture and Society in Labour Britain, 1945–51*. London: Lawrence & Wishart, 1995.

Gaboury, Jacob. "A Queer History of Computing." *Rhizome*, February 19, 2013. Accessed DATE. http://rhizome.org/editorial/2013/feb/19/queer-computing-1.

Gamble, Andrew. *The Free Economy and the Strong State: The Politics of Thatcherism*. 2nd ed. Basingstoke, UK: Macmillan, 1994.

Glucksmann, Miriam. *Women Assemble: Women Workers and the New Industries in Inter-War Britain*. London: Routledge, 1990.

Glynn, Sean, and Alan Booth. *Modern Britain: An Economic and Social History*. New York: Routledge, 1996.

Goodyear, Sara Suleri. *The Rhetoric of English India*. Chicago: University of Chicago Press, 1992.

Gowland, David, and Arthur Turner. *Britain and European Integration, 1945–1998: A Documentary History*. London: Routledge, 2000.

Graves, Robert, and Alan Hodge. *The Long Week End: A Social History of Great Britain, 1918–1939*. New York: W. W. Norton, 1963.

Gray, Robert. "Factory Legislation and the Gendering of Jobs in the North of England, 1830–1860." *Gender & History* 5, no. 1 (1993): 56–80.

Greer, Germaine. *The Female Eunuch*. New York: Bantam, 1972.

Grieco, Joseph. *Between Dependence and Autonomy: India's Experience with the International Computer Industry*. Berkeley: University of California Press, 1984.

Grier, David Alan. "The ENIAC, the Verb 'to Program' and the Emergence of Digital Computers." *Annals of the History of Computing* 18, no. 1 (1996): 51–55.

Grier, David Alan. "The Math Tables Project of the Work Projects Administration: The Reluctant Start of the Computing Era." *Annals of the History of Computing* 20, no. 3 (1998): 33–50.

Grier, David Alan. *When Computers Were Human*. Princeton, NJ: Princeton University Press, 2006.

Gullace, Nicoletta. *"The Blood of Our Sons": Men, Women, and the Renegotiation of British Citizenship During the Great War*. New York: Palgrave Macmillan, 2002.

Gupta, Parthasarathi. *Imperialism and the British Labour Movement, 1914–1964*. London: Macmillan, 1975.

Haigh, Thomas. "Inventing Information Systems: The Systems Men and the Computer, 1950–1968." Special issue, "Computers and Communications Networks," *Business History Review* 75, no. 1, (2001): 15–61.

Halbwachs, Maurice. *Collective Memory*. Edited and translated by Lewis A. Coser. Chicago: University of Chicago Press, 1992.

Hall, Catherine. *White, Male and Middle-Class: Explorations in Feminism and History*. New York: Routledge, 1992.

Haraway, Donna Jeanne. *Modest_Witness@Second_Millennium.FemaleMan© Meets_ Oncomouse™: Feminism and Technoscience*. New York: Routledge, 1997.

Harrison, Brian. "Class and Gender in Modern British Labour History." *Past & Present*, no. 124 (1989): 121–158.

Headrick, Daniel R. *The Tools of Empire: Technology and European Imperialism in the Nineteenth Century*. New York: Oxford University Press, 1981.

Hecht, Gabrielle. *The Radiance of France: Nuclear Power and National Identity after World War II*. Cambridge, MA: MIT Press, 1998.

Hendry, John. *Innovating for Failure: Government Policy and the Early British Computer Industry*. Cambridge, MA: MIT Press, 1989.

Hendry, John. "The Teashop Computer Manufacturer: J. Lyons, LEO and the Potential and Limits of High-Tech Diversification." *Business History* 29 (1987): 73–102.

Hewlett, Sylvia Ann, Carolyn Buck Luce, Lisa J. Servon, Laura Sherbin, Peggy Shiller, Eytan Sosnovich, and Karen Sumberg. *The Athena Factor: Reversing the Brain Drain in Science, Engineering, and Technology*. Cambridge, MA: Harvard Business Review Press, 2008.

Hicks, Marie. "De-Brogramming the History of Computing." *IEEE Annals of the History of Computing* 35, no. 1 (January–March 2013): 88.

Hicks, Marie. "Meritocracy and Feminization in Conflict: Computerization in the British Government." In *Gender Codes: Why Women are Leaving Computing*, edited by Thomas Misa, 95–114. Hoboken, NJ: Wiley, 2010.

Hicks, Marie. "Only the Clothes Changed: Women Operators in British Computing and Advertising, 1950–1970." *IEEE Annals of the History of Computing* 32, no. 4 (October–December 2010): 5–17.

Hindmarch-Watson, Katie. "Male Prostitution and the London GPO: Telegraph Boys' 'Immorality' from Nationalization to the Cleveland Street Scandal." *Journal of British Studies* 51, no. 3 (2012): 594–617.

Hinsley, F. H., and Alan Stripp. *Codebreakers: The Inside Story of Bletchley Park*. Oxford: Oxford University Press, 1993.

Hobsbawm, E. J. *Nations and Nationalism since 1780: Programme, Myth, Reality*. 2nd ed. Cambridge: Cambridge University Press, 1992.

Hoggart, Richard. *The Uses of Literacy*. New Brunswick, NJ: Transaction Publishers, 1998.

Hoover, Kenneth R. "The Rise of Conservative Capitalism: Ideological Tensions within the Reagan and Thatcher Governments." *Comparative Studies in Society and History* 29, no. 2 (1987): 245–268.

Hopkins, Eric. *The Rise and Decline of the English Working Classes 1918–1990: A Social History*. New York: St. Martin's Press, 1991.

Horowitz, Roger, and Arwen Mohun. *His and Hers: Gender, Consumption, and Technology*. Charlottesville: University Press of Virginia, 1998.

Hounshell, David A. *From the American System to Mass Production, 1800–1932: The Development of Manufacturing Technology in the United States*. Baltimore: Johns Hopkins University Press, 1984.

Howell, D. A. "Public Administration and Educational Administration: Some Thoughts on the Chapman Report, 'Teaching Public Administration.'" *Educational Management Administration & Leadership* 32, no. 2 (1974): 32–37.

Hughes, Thomas P. *Rescuing Prometheus*. New York: Pantheon Books, 1998.

Hughes, Thomas P. "Technology as Systems, Controls, and Information." In *Human-Built World: How to Think about Technology and Culture*, 77–110. Chicago: University of Chicago Press, 2004.

Hunt, Audrey. *Women and Paid Work: Issues of Equality*. New York: St. Martin's Press, 1988.

Jacob, Margaret C. *Scientific Culture and the Making of the Industrial West*. New York: Oxford University Press, 1997.

John, Angela V., ed. *Unequal Opportunities: Women's Employment in England, 1800–1918*. New York: Blackwell, 1986.

Johnson, Paul. *Twentieth-Century Britain: Economic, Social, and Cultural Change*. London: Longman, 1994.

Jones, Tudor. *Remaking the Labour Party: From Gaitskell to Blair*. New York: Routledge, 1996.

Joyce, Patrick. *The Historical Meanings of Work*. Cambridge: Cambridge University Press, 1987.

Kasson, John F. *Civilizing the Machine: Technology and Republican Values in America, 1776–1900*. New York: Penguin Books, 1977.

Keeling, C. D. *Management in Government*. London: Allen and Unwin, 1972.

Keep, Christopher. "The Cultural Work of the Type-Writer Girl." *Victorian Studies* 40, no. 3 (1997): 401–426.

Kent, Susan Kingsley. *Gender and Power in Britain, 1640–1990*. London: Routledge, 1999.

Kirk, Neville. *Change, Continuity and Class: Labour in British Society, 1850–1920*. Manchester: Manchester University Press, 1998.

Klawe, Maria, and Nancy Leveson. "Women in Computing: Where Are We Now?" *Communications of the ACM* 38, no. 1 (1995): 29–35.

Kline, Ronald, and Trevor Pinch. "Users as Agents of Technological Change: The Social Construction of the Automobile in the Rural United States." *Technology and Culture* 37, no. 4 (October 1996): 763–795.

Koven, Seth, and Sonya Michel. "Womanly Duties: Maternalist Politics and the Origins of Welfare States in France, Germany, Great Britain, and the United States, 1880–1920." *American Historical Review* 95, no. 4 (1990): 1076–1108.

Kuhn, T. *The Structure of Scientific Revolutions*. 2nd ed. Chicago: University of Chicago Press, 1962.

Kuisel, Richard F. *Seducing the French: The Dilemma of Americanization*. Berkeley: University of California Press, 1993.

Land, F. F. "The First Business Computer: A Case Study in User-Driven Automation." *IEEE Annals of the History of Computing* 22, no. 3 (2000): 16–26.

Landauer, Thomas K. *The Trouble with Computers: Usefulness, Usability, and Productivity*. Cambridge, MA: MIT Press, 1995.

Landivar, Liana Christin. "Disparities in STEM Employment by Sex, Race, and Hispanic Origin." American Community Survey Reports, ACS-24. Washington, DC: US Census Bureau, 2013.

Latour, Bruno. *Science in Action: How to Follow Scientists and Engineers through Society*. Cambridge, MA: Harvard University Press, 1987.

Latour, Bruno. "Where Are the Missing Masses? The Sociology of a Few Mundane Artifacts." In *Shaping Technology/Building Society*, edited by Wiebe E. Bijker and John Law, 225–258. Cambridge, MA: MIT Press, 1992.

Lavington, Simon. *Moving Targets: Elliott-Automation and the Dawn of the Computer Age in Britain, 1947–67*. London: Springer, 2011.

Layton, Edwin T. *The Revolt of the Engineers: Social Responsibility and the American Engineering Profession*. Cleveland, OH: Case Western Reserve University Press, 1971.

Lerman, Nina, Ruth Oldenziel, and Arwen Mohun. *Gender and Technology: A Reader*. Baltimore: Johns Hopkins University Press, 2003.

Leslie, Stuart W. *The Cold War and American Science: The Military-Industrial-Academic Complex at MIT and Stanford*. New York: Columbia University Press, 1993.

Levin, Angela. "Philanthropist Stephanie Shirley: You Can Only Spend So Much." *The Telegraph*, November 5, 2012. Accessed June 10, 2015. http://www.telegraph.co.uk/women/womens-business/9655905/Philanthropist-Stephanie-Shirley-You-can-only-spend-so-much.html.

Lewis, Jane E. "Women Clerical Workers in the Late Nineteenth and Early Twentieth Centuries." In *The White-Blouse Revolution: Female Office Workers since 1870*, edited by Gregory Anderson, 27–47. Manchester, UK: Manchester University Press, 1988.

Lewis, Jane. *Women in England, 1870–1950: Sexual Divisions and Social Change*. Sussex: Wheatsheaf Books, 1984.

Light, Jennifer. "When Computers Were Women." *Technology and Culture* 40, no. 3 (1999): 455–483.

Lissner, Will. "Mechanical Brain Has Its Troubles." *New York Times*, December 14, 1947, 49.

Lovell, Terry. *British Feminist Thought: A Reader*. Oxford: Blackwell, 1990.

Lowe, Rodney. *The Official History of the British Civil Service: Reforming the Civil Service, Volume I: The Fulton Years, 1966–81*. London: Routledge, 2011.

Luke, Doreen. *My Road to Bletchley Park*. Cleobury Mortimer, UK: M. & M. Baldwin, 2003.

MacKenzie, Donald A., and Judy Wajcman. *The Social Shaping of Technology: How the Refrigerator Got Its Hum*. Milton Keynes, UK: Open University Press, 1985.

MacKenzie, John M. *Imperialism and Popular Culture*. Manchester: Manchester University Press, 1986.

MacLeod, R., ed. *Government and Expertise: Specialists, Administrators, and Professionals, 1860–1919*. Cambridge: Cambridge University Press, 1988.

Mahoney, Michael S. "The Histories of Computing(s)." *Interdisciplinary Science Reviews* 30, no. 2 (2005): 119–135.

Malone, Carolyn. "Gendered Discourses and the Making of Protective Labor Legislation in England, 1830–1914." *Journal of British Studies* 37, no. 2 (1998): 166–191.

Margolis, Jane, and Allan Fisher. *Unlocking the Clubhouse: Women in Computing*. Cambridge, MA: MIT Press, 2001.

Marks, Gary. *Unions in Politics: Britain, Germany, and the United States in the Nineteenth and Early Twentieth Centuries*. Princeton, NJ: Princeton University Press, 1989.

Marriott, John. *The Culture of Labourism: The East End between the Wars*. Edinburgh: Edinburgh University Press, 1991.

Marsh, David, Jim Buller, Colin Hay, Jim Johnston, Peter Kerr, Stuart McAnulla, and Matthew Watson. *Postwar British Politics in Perspective*. Malden, MA: Polity Press, 1999.

Martindale, Hilda. *Women Servants of the State, 1870–1938: A History of Women in the Civil Service*. London: Allen & Unwin, 1938.

Marwick, Arthur. *British Society since 1945*. London: Penguin, 2003.

Marwick, Arthur. *The Home Front: The British and the Second World War*. London: Thames and Hudson, 1976.

Marwick, Arthur. *The Sixties: Cultural Revolution in Britain, France, Italy, and the United States, 1958–1974*. Oxford: Oxford University Press, 1998.

Mayntz, R., and T. P. Hughes, eds. *The Development of Large Technical Systems*. Frankfurt: Campus Verlag, 1988.

McAlpine, Margaret. *So You Want to Work with Computers?* London: Hodder Wayland, 2004.

McGee, Andrew Meade. "Stating the Field: Institutions and Outcomes in Computer History." *IEEE Annals of the History of Computing* 34, no. 1 (2012): 104, 102–103.

Medina, Eden. *Cybernetic Revolutionaries: Technology and Politics in Allende's Chile*. Cambridge, MA: MIT Press, 2014.

Medina, Eden. "The Cybersyn Revolution: Five Lessons from a Socialist Computing Project in Salvador Allende's Chile." *Jacobin Magazine*, no. 17 (Spring 2015). Accessed June 3, 2016. https://www.jacobinmag.com/2015/04/allende-chile-beer-medina-cybersyn.

Medina, Eden. "Designing Freedom, Regulating a Nation: Socialist Cybernetics in Allende's Chile." *Journal of Latin American Studies* 38, no. 3 (2006): 571–606.

Milkman, Ruth. *Gender at Work: The Dynamics of Job Segregation by Sex during World War II*. Urbana: University of Illinois Press, 1987.

Mindell, David A. *Between Human and Machine: Feedback, Control, and Computing before Cybernetics*. Baltimore: Johns Hopkins University Press, 2002.

Misa, Thomas J. *Gender Codes: Why Women Are Leaving Computing*. Hoboken, NJ: Wiley, 2010.

Misa, Thomas J. "How Machines Make History, and How Historians (and Others) Help Them to Do So." *Science, Technology & Human Values* 13, nos. 3–4 (1988): 308–331.

Misa, Thomas J., Philip Brey, and Andrew Feenberg. *Modernity and Technology*. Cambridge, MA: MIT Press, 2003.

Mohun, Arwen. *Steam Laundries: Gender, Technology, and Work in the United States and Great Britain, 1880–1940*. Baltimore: Johns Hopkins University Press, 1999.

Mokyr, Joel. *The Lever of Riches: Technological Creativity and Economic Progress*. New York: Oxford University Press, 1990.

Mort, Frank. "Social and Symbolic Fathers and Sons in Postwar Britain." *Journal of British Studies* 38, no. 3, Masculinity and the Lower Middle Class (1999): 353–384.

Mumford, Lewis. *Technics and Civilization*. New York: Harcourt Brace and Company, 1934.

Nakamura, Lisa. "Indigenous Circuits: Navajo Women and the Racialization of Early Electronics Manufacture." *American Quarterly* 64, no. 4 (December 2013): 919–941.

National Museum of the History of Computing. "Celebrating Colossus at 70." Milton Keynes, UK, February 10, 2014. Accessed June 3, 2016. http://www.tnmoc.org/news/notes-museum/picture-colossus-70.

Noble, David F. *America by Design: Science, Technology, and the Rise of Corporate Capitalism*. New York: Knopf, 1977.

Noble, David F. *Forces of Production: A Social History of Industrial Automation*. New York: Knopf, 1984.

Nye, David E. *Narratives and Spaces: Technology and the Construction of American Culture*. New York: Columbia University Press, 1997.

O'Brien, Patrick K. "Britain's Economy between the Wars: A Survey of a Counter-Revolution in Economic History." *Past & Present*, no. 115 (1987): 107–130.

O'Connor, Julia S. "Gender, Class and Citizenship in the Comparative Analysis of Welfare State Regimes: Theoretical and Methodological Issues." *British Journal of Sociology* 44, no. 3 (1993): 501–518.

Oldenziel, Ruth. *Making Technology Masculine: Men, Women and Modern Machines in America, 1870–1945*. Amsterdam: Amsterdam University Press, 1999.

Owen, Geoffrey. *From Empire to Europe: The Decline and Revival of British Industry since the Second World War*. London: HarperCollins, 1999.

Panel on Technology and Women's Employment, Committee on Women's Employment and Related Social Issues, Commission on Behavioral and Social Sciences and Education, and National Research Council. *Computer Chips and*

Paper Clips: Technology and Women's Employment. Volume 2, Case Studies and Policy Perspectives. Washington, DC: National Academy of Sciences, 1987.

Pedersen, Susan. *Family, Dependence, and the Origins of the Welfare State: Britain and France, 1914–1945*. Cambridge: Cambridge University Press, 1993.

Pedersen, Susan. "Gender, Welfare, and Citizenship in Britain during the Great War." *American Historical Review* 95, no. 4 (1990): 983–1006.

Perkin, Harold James. *The Rise of Professional Society: England since 1880*. London: Routledge, 1989.

Pigou, Arthur C. "The National Dividend." In *The Economics of Welfare*, 4th ed., 31–42. London: Macmillan and Co., 1932.

Pimlott, Ben. *Harold Wilson*. New York: Harper Collins, 1992.

Pinchbeck, Ivy. *Women Workers and the Industrial Revolution, 1750–1850*. 3rd ed. London: Virago, 1981.

Pollard, Sidney. *The Development of the British Economy, 1914–1990*. 4th ed. New York: E. Arnold, 1992.

Pritchard, Sara B., Adeline Koh, and Michelle Moravec. "I Look like a Professor, Too." *Inside Higher Ed*, August 10, 2015. Accessed June 3, 2016. https://www.insidehighered.com/views/2015/08/10/essay-explains-new-hashtag-campaign-draw-attention-diversity-professors-and-their.

Puaca, Laura Micheletti. *Searching for Scientific Womanpower: Technocratic Feminism and the Politics of National Security, 1940–1980*. Chapel Hill: University of North Carolina Press, 2014.

Poovey, Mary. *Uneven Developments: The Ideological Work of Gender in Mid-Victorian England*. Chicago: University of Chicago Press, 1988.

Pugh, Martin. *Women and the Women's Movement in Britain, 1914–1999*. New York: St. Martin's Press, 2000.

Purcell, Kate, Stephen Wood, Alan Waton, and Sheila Allen. *The Changing Experience of Employment*. Edited by British Sociological Association. London: Macmillan, 1986.

Rau, Erik P. "Technological Systems, Expertise, and Policy Making: The British Origins of Operational Research." In *Technologies of Power: Essays in Honor of Thomas Parke Hughes and Agatha Chipley Hughes*, edited by Michael Thad Allen and Gabrielle Hecht. Cambridge, MA: MIT Press, 2001.

Rendall, Jane. *Women in an Industrializing Society: England, 1750–1880*. Oxford: Blackwell, 1991.

Rendel, Margherita. "Legislating for Equal Pay and Opportunity for Women in Britain." *Signs* 3, no. 4 (1978): 897–908.

Reskin, Barbara F., and Patricia Roos, eds. *Job Queues, Gender Queues: Explaining Women's Inroads into Male Occupations*. Philadelphia: Temple University Press, 1990.

Rhodes, Richard. *Visions of Technology: A Century of Vital Debate about Machines, Systems, and the Human World*. New York: Simon & Schuster, 1999.

Ridley, F. F. "Public Administration: Cause for Discontent." *Public Administration* 50 (Spring 1972): 65–77.

Ritschel, Daniel. "A Corporatist Economy in Britain? Capitalist Planning for Industrial Self-Government in the 1930s." *English Historical Review* 106, no. 418 (1991): 41–65.

Roberts, M. J. D. "Feminism and the State in Later Victorian England." *Historical Journal* 38, no. 1 (1995): 85–110.

Roberts, Mary Louise. *Civilization without Sexes: Reconstructing Gender in Postwar France, 1917–1927*. Chicago: University of Chicago Press, 1994.

Roberts, Sarah. "Commercial Content Moderation: Digital Laborers' Dirty Work." In *The Intersectional Internet: Race, Sex, Class and Culture Online*, edited by Safiya Umoja Noble and Brendesha M. Tynes. New York: Peter Lang, 2016.

Robinson, William Heath, and K. R. G. Browne. *How to Make a Garden Grow*. London: Hutchison, 1938.

Robinson, William Heath, and Geoffrey Beare. *Heath Robinson Contraptions*. London: Duckworth Overlook, 2007.

Rollins, Judith. *Between Women: Domestics and Their Employers*. Philadelphia: Temple University Press, 1985.

Roper, Michael, and John Tosh. *Manful Assertions: Masculinities in Britain since 1800*. New York: Routledge, 1991.

Rose, Sonya O. *Limited Livelihoods: Gender and Class in Nineteenth-Century England*. Berkeley: University of California Press, 1992.

Rose, Sonya O. "Sex, Citizenship, and the Nation in World War II Britain." *American Historical Review* 103, no. 4 (1998): 1147–1176.

Ross, Kristin. *Fast Cars, Clean Bodies: Decolonization and the Reordering of French Culture*. Cambridge, MA: MIT Press, 1995.

Rowbotham, Sheila. *Beyond The Fragments: Feminism and the Making of Socialism*. London: Merlin, 1980.

Rowbotham, Sheila. *A Century of Women: The History of Women in Britain and the United States*. London: Viking, 1997.

Rowbotham, Sheila. *Hidden from History*. London: Pluto Press, 1973.

Rowbotham, Sheila. *The Past Is before Us: Feminism in Action since the 1960s*. London: Pandora, 1989.

Rowbotham, Sheila, and Huw Beynon. *Looking at Class: Film, Television and the Working Class in Britain*. London: Rivers Oram Press, 2001.

Rubinstein, W. D. *Capitalism, Culture, and Decline in Britain, 1750–1990*. London: Routledge, 1993.

Said, Edward. *Orientalism*. New York: Pantheon Books, 1978.

Sampson, Anthony. *The New Anatomy of Britain*. New York: Stein and Day, 1971.

Sanderson, Michael, and the Economic History Society. *Education and Economic Decline in Britain, 1870 to the 1990s*. Cambridge: Cambridge University Press, 1999.

Schafer, Valérie, and Benjamin G. Thierry. *Connecting Women: Women, Gender and ICT in Europe in the Nineteenth and Twentieth Century*. Cham, Switzerland: Springer, 2015.

Schlombs, Corinna. "A Gendered Job Carousel." In *Gender Codes: Why Women Are Leaving Computing*, edited by Thomas Misa, 75–94. Hoboken, NJ: Wiley, 2010.

Scott, Joan Wallach. "Feminism's History." *Journal of Women's History* 16, no. 2 (2004): 10–29.

Scott, Joan Wallach. *Gender and the Politics of History*. Rev. ed. New York: Columbia University Press, 1999.

Scott, Joan Wallach. *The Glassworkers of Carmaux: French Craftsmen and Political Action in a Nineteenth-Century City*. Cambridge, MA: Harvard University Press, 1974.

Seccombe, Wally. "Patriarchy Stabilized; the Construction of the Male-Breadwinner Wagenorm in Nineteenth Century Britain." *Social History* 11, no. 1 (1986): 53–76.

Seleski, Patty. "Women, Work and Cultural Change in Eighteenth and Early Nineteenth Century London." In *Popular Culture in England 1500–1850*, edited by Tim Harris. New York: St. Martin's Press, 1995.

Sen, Amartya. "Women's Survival as a Development Problem." *Bulletin of the American Academy of Arts and Sciences* 43, no. 2 (November 1989): 14–29.

Shannon, Richard. *The Crisis of Imperialism, 1865–1915*. London: Hart-Davis MacGibbon, 1974.

Sharpe, Jenny. *Allegories of Empire: The Figure of Woman in the Colonial Text*. Minneapolis: University of Minnesota Press, 1993.

Shirley, Stephanie, with Richard Askwith. *Let IT Go: The Story of the Entrepreneur Turned Ardent Philanthropist*. London: Andrews UK, 2012.

Shirley, Stephanie. Interview with Janet Abbate. "Anecdotes: How Did You First Get into Computing?" Edited by Anne Fitzpatrick. *IEEE Annals of the History of Computing* 25, no. 4 (2003): 79–80.

Simmons, J. R. M. *Leo and the Managers: A Theory of Management Organization*. London: MacDonald, 1962.

Sked, Alan, and Chris Cook. *Post-War Britain: A Political History*. New York: Penguin, 1984.

Slater, Lucy. Interview with Janet Abbate. "Anecdotes: How Did You First Get into Computing?" Edited by Anne Fitzpatrick. *IEEE Annals of the History of Computing* 25, no. 4 (2003): 78.

Slaton, Amy E. *Race, Rigor and Selectivity in U.S. Engineering: The History of an Occupational Color Line*. Cambridge, MA: Harvard University Press, 2010.

Slayton, Rebecca. *Arguments that Count: Physics, Computing, and Missile Defense, 1949–2012*. Cambridge, MA: MIT Press, 2013.

Smith, Bonnie G. "The Contribution of Women to Modern Historiography in Great Britain, France, and the United States, 1750–1940." *American Historical Review* 89, no. 3 (1984): 709–732.

Smith, Harold L., ed. *British Feminism in the Twentieth Century*. Amherst: University of Massachusetts Press, 1990.

Smith, Harold L. "The Politics of Conservative Reform: The *Equal Pay* for Equal Work Issue, 1945–1955." *The Historical Journal* 35, no. 2 (June 1992): 401–415.

Smith, Harold L. "The Problem of 'Equal Pay for Equal Work' in Great Britain during World War II." *Journal of Modern History* 53, no. 4 (1981): 652–672.

Smith, Harold L. "The Womanpower Problem in Britain during the Second World War." *Historical Journal* 27, no. 4 (1984): 925–945.

Smith, John. "Reminiscences of the IBM 1401." *Resurrection: The Bulletin of the Computer Conservation Society*, no. 51 (Summer 2010). http://www.cs.man.ac.uk/CCS/res/res51.htm.

Smith, M. R., and L. Marx, eds. *Does Technology Drive History? The Dilemma of Technological Determinism*. Cambridge, MA: MIT Press, 1994.

Smith, Michael. *The Secrets of Station X: How Bletchley Park Codebreakers Helped Win the War*. London: Biteback Publishing, 2011.

Smith, Michael. *Station X: The Codebreakers of Bletchley Park*. London: Channel Four Books, 1998.

Stebenne, David L. "IBM's 'New Deal': Employment Policies of the International Business Machines Corporation, 1933–1956." *Journal of the Historical Society* 5, no. 1 (2005): 47–77.

Stern, Nancy B. *From ENIAC to UNIVAC: Appraisal of the Eckert-Mauchly Computers*. Bedford, MA: Digital Press, 1981.

Stoler, Laura Ann. "Making Empire Respectable: The Politics of Race and Sexual Morality." *American Ethnologist* 16, no. 4 (1989): 634–660.

Strasser, Susan, Charles McGovern, and Matthias Judt. *Getting and Spending: European and American Consumer Societies in the Twentieth Century*. Cambridge: Cambridge University Press, 1998.

Strobel, Margaret. *European Women and the Second British Empire*. Bloomington: Indiana University Press, 1991.

Subramanian, Ramesh. "Technology Policy and National Identity: The Microcomputer Comes to India." *IEEE Annals of the History of Computing* 36, no. 3 (2014): 19–29.

Summerfield, Penny. *Reconstructing Women's Wartime Lives: Discourse and Subjectivity in Oral Histories of the Second World War*. Manchester: Manchester University Press, 1998.

Symeonidis, George. *The Effects of Competition: Cartel Policy and the Evolution of Strategy and Structure in British Industry*. Cambridge, MA: MIT Press, 2002.

Tabili, Laura. "The Construction of Racial Difference in Twentieth-Century Britain: The Special Restriction (Coloured Alien Seamen) Order, 1925." *Journal of British Studies* 33, no. 1 (1994): 54–98.

Taylor, Miles. "Patriotism, History and the Left in Twentieth-Century Britain." *Historical Journal* 33, no. 4 (1990): 971–987.

Thane, Pat. "The Working Class and State 'Welfare' in Britain, 1880–1914." *Historical Journal* 27, no. 4 (1984): 877–900.

Thompson, E. P. "Time, Work-Discipline, and Industrial Capitalism." *Past & Present*, no. 38 (1967): 56–97.

Thorpe, Andrew. *A History of the British Labour Party*. 2nd ed. New York: Palgrave, 2001.

Thorsheim, Peter. "Interpreting the London Fog Disaster of 1952." In *Smoke and Mirrors: The Politics and Culture of Air Pollution*, edited by E. Melanie Dupuis. New York: New York University Press, 2004.

Tinn, Honghong. "Cold War Politics: Taiwanese Computing in the 1950s and 1960s," *IEEE Annals* 32, no. 1 (2010): 92–95.

Tiratsoo, Nick, and Jim Tomlinson. *The Conservatives and Industrial Efficiency, 1951–64: Thirteen Wasted Years?* New York: LSE/Routledge, 1998.

Tiratsoo, Nick, and Jim Tomlinson. *Industrial Efficiency and State Intervention: Labour, 1939–51*. New York: Routledge, 1993.

"To Train or Not to Train?" *Office Methods and Machines*, September 1967, 15–17.

Tomlinson, Jim. "Conservative Modernization: Too Little Too Late." *Contemporary British History* 33, no. 3 (1997): 18–38.

Tomlinson, Jim. *Government and the Enterprise since 1900: The Changing Problem of Efficiency*. Oxford: Oxford University Press, 1994.

Tosh, John. *A Man's Place: Masculinity and the Middle-Class Home in Victorian England*. New Haven, CT: Yale University Press, 1999.

Tranter, N. L. *British Population in the Twentieth Century*. New York: St. Martin's Press, 1996.

Trentmann, Frank. "The Transformation of Fiscal Reform: Reciprocity, Modernization, and the Fiscal Debate within the Business Community in Early Twentieth-Century Britain." *Historical Journal* 39, no. 4 (1996): 1005–1048.

Turing, Alan. *A.M. Turing's Original Proposal for the Development of an Electronic Computer, Reprinted with a Foreword by D.W. Davies, Superintendent of the Computer Science Division*. London: National Physical Laboratory, Division of Computer Science, 1972.

Tzannatos, Zafiris. "Narrowing the Gap: Equal Pay in Britain, 1970–1986." *Long Range Planning* 20, no. 2 (1987): 69–75.

Usselman, Steven. "IBM and Its Imitators: Organizational Capabilities and the Emergence of the International Computer Industry." *Business and Economic History* 18, no. 2 (1993): 30–39.

Usselman, Steven. "Determining the Middle Landscape: Competing Narratives in the History of Technology." *Reviews in American History* 23, no. 2 (1995): 370–377.

Vickery, Amanda. *Women, Privilege, and Power: British Politics, 1750 to the Present*. Stanford, CA: Stanford University Press, 2001.

Wajcman, Judy. *Feminism Confronts Technology*. Cambridge, MA: Polity Press, 1991.

Walkowitz, Judith R. *Prostitution and Victorian Society: Women, Class, and the State*. Cambridge: Cambridge University Press, 1980.

Ward, Mark. "Museum Reunion for Colossus Computer Veterans." BBC News, September 22, 2014. http://www.bbc.com/news/technology-29311068.

Warner, Michael. *The Trouble with Normal: Sex, Politics and the Ethics of Queer Life*. New York: Free Press, 1999.

Warwick, Paul. "Did Britain Change? An Inquiry into the Causes of National Decline." *Journal of Contemporary History* 20, no. 1 (1985): 99–133.

Webster, Juliet. *Office Automation: The Labour Process and Women's Work in Britain*. Hemel Hempstead, UK: Harvester Wheatsheaf, 1990.

Welchman, Gordon. *The Hut Six Story: Breaking the Enigma Codes*. London: M & M Baldwin, 1997.

Westwood, Sallie. *All Day, Every Day: Factory and Family in the Making of Women's Lives*. Urbana: University of Illinois Press, 1985.

Whiteside, Noel, and Robert Salais. *Governance, Industry, and Labour Markets in Britain and France: The Modernising State in the Mid-Twentieth Century*. New York: Routledge, 1998.

Wiener, Martin J. *English Culture and the Decline of the Industrial Spirit, 1850–1980*. Harmondsworth, UK: Penguin, 1985.

Wiesner, Merry E. *Gender in History*. Malden, MA: Blackwell, 2001.

Wilson, Dolly Smith. "A New Look at the Affluent Worker: The Good Working Mother in Post-War Britain." *Twentieth Century British History* 17, no. 2 (2006): 206–229.

Wilson, Harold. *The Labour Government, 1964–1970: A Personal Record*. London: Weidenfeld and Nicolson, 1971.

Wilson, Harold. *Memoirs: The Making of a Prime Minister, 1916–1964*. London: Weidenfeld and Nicolson, 1986.

Wilson, Harold. *The New Britain: Labour's Plan Outlined by Harold Wilson*. London: Penguin, 1964.

Wilson, Harold. *Purpose in Politics: Selected Speeches by Harold Wilson*. London: Wiedenfeld and Nicolson, 1964.

Winner, Langdon. *Autonomous Technology: Technics-Out-of-Control as a Theme in Political Thought*. Cambridge, MA: MIT Press, 1977.

Winner, Langdon. "Do Artifacts Have Politics?" *Daedalus* 109, no. 1 (1980): 121–136.

Winner, Langdon. *The Whale and the Reactor: A Search for Limits in an Age of High Technology*. Chicago: University of Chicago Press, 1986.

Winterbotham, Frederick W. *The Ultra Secret: The Inside Story of Operation Ultra, Bletchley Park and Enigma*. London: Purnell Book Services, 1974.

Wolfe, Maynard Frank. *Rube Goldberg: Inventions!* New York: Simon and Schuster, 2011.

Wood, Alan. *The Groundnut Affair*. London: The Bodley Head, 1950.

Woods, Brian, and Nick Watson. "In Pursuit of Standardization: The British Ministry of Health's Model 8F Wheelchair, 1948–1962." *Technology and Culture* 45, no. 3 (July 2004): 540–568.

Woodward, Donald. "Wage Rates and Living Standards in Pre-industrial England." *Past & Present*, no. 91 (1981): 28–46.

Woollcombe, Joan. "Women at Work: Computers Need People." *Times* (London), October 20, 1970, 19.

Wright, Rosemary, and Jerry A. Jacobs. "Male Flight from Computer Work: A New Look at Occupational Resegregation and Ghettoization." *American Sociological Review* 59, no. 4 (1994): 511–536.

Ziegler, Philip. *Wilson: The Authorized Life of Lord Wilson of Rievaulx*. London: Weidenfeld and Nicolson, 1993.

Zimmeck, Meta. "Jobs for the Girls: The Expansion of Clerical Work for Women, 1850–1914." In *Unequal Opportunities: Women's Employment in England 1800–1918*, edited by Angela V. John, 153–178. New York: Blackwell, 1986.

Zimmeck, Meta. "The 'New Woman' in the Machinery of Government: A Spanner in the Works?" In *Government and Expertise: Specialists, Administrators, and Professionals, 1860–1919*, edited by Roy MacLeod, 185–202. Cambridge: Cambridge University Press, 1988.

Zimmeck, Meta. "Strategies and Stratagems for the Employment of Women in the British Civil Service." *Historical Journal* 27, no. 4 (1984): 901–924.

Zweiniger-Bargielowska, Ina. *Women in Twentieth-Century Britain*. Harlow: Longman, 2001.

Index

Printed in the United States
by Baker & Taylor Publisher Services

Printed in the United States
by Baker & Taylor Publisher Services